C++

By

EXAMPLE

que

Greg Perry

C++ By Example

© 1992 by Que

Library of Congress Catalog Card Number: 92-64353

ISBN: 1-56529-038-0

96   95   94   93   92   8   7   6   5   4   3   2   1

Interpretation of the printing code: the rightmost double-digit number is the year of the book's printing; the rightmost single-digit number, the number of the book's printing. For example, a printing code of 92-1 shows that the first printing of the book occurred in 1992.

Publisher
Lloyd Short

Publishing Manager
Joseph Wikert

Development Editor
Stacy Hiquet

Production Editor
Kezia Endsley

Copy Editor
Bryan Gambrel

Technical Editor
Tim Moore

Editorial Assistants
Rosemarie Graham
Melissa Keegan

Book Design
Scott Cook
Michele Laseau

Production Analyst
Mary Beth Wakefield

Cover Design
Jean Bisesi

Indexer
Johnna VanHoose

Production
Caroline Roop (Book Shepherd)
Jeff Baker, Paula Carroll,
Michelle Cleary, Brook Farling,
Kate Godfrey, Bob LaRoche,
Laurie Lee, Jay Lesandrini,
Cindy L. Phipps, Linda Seifert,
Phil Worthington

Composed in Palatino and MCPdigital typefaces by Prentice Hall Computer Publishing.
Screen reproductions in this book were created by means of the program Collage Plus
from Inner Media, Inc., Hollis, NH.

Dedication

Dr. Rick Burgess, you shaped my life. Good or bad, I'm what I am thanks to your help. I appreciate the many hours we've shared together.

G.M.P.

About the Author

Greg Perry has been a programmer and trainer for the past 14 years. He received his first degree in computer science, then he received a Masters degree in corporate finance. He currently is a professor of computer science at Tulsa Junior College, as well as a computer consultant and a lecturer. Greg Perry is the author of 11 other computer books, including *QBASIC By Example* and *C By Example*. In addition, he has published articles in several publications, including *PC World, Data Training,* and *Inside First Publisher*. He has attended computer conferences and trade shows in several countries, and is fluent in nine computer languages.

Acknowledgments

Much thanks to Stacy Hiquet and Joseph Wikert at Prentice Hall (Que) for trusting me completely with the direction and style of this book. The rest of my editors: Kezia Endsley, Bryan Gambrel, and the Technical Editor, Tim Moore, kept me on track so the readers can have an accurate and readable text.

The Tulsa Junior College administration continues to be supportive of my writing. More importantly, Diane Moore, head of our Business Services Division, Tony Hirad, and Elaine Harris, are friends who make teaching a joy and not a job.

As always, my beautiful bride Jayne, and my parents Glen and Bettye Perry, are my closest daily companions. It is for them I work.

Trademark Acknowledgments

Que Corporation has made every attempt to supply trademark information about company names, products, and services mentioned in this book. Trademarks indicated below were derived from various sources. Que Corporation cannot attest to the accuracy of this information.

AT&T is a registered trademark of American Telephone & Telegraph Company

FORTRAN and COBOL are trademarks of International Business Machines Corporation (IBM).

Turbo BASIC is a registered trademark of Borland International, Inc.

Turbo C is a registered trademark of Borland International, Inc.

Microsoft QuickC and MS-DOS are registered trademarks of Microsoft Corporation.

ANSI is a registered trademark of American National Standards Institute.

Overview

Contents

Introduction

Every day, more and more people learn and use the C++ programming language. I have taught C to thousands of students in my life. I see many of those students now moving to C++ in their school work or career. The C++ language is becoming an industry-accepted standard programming language, using the solid foundation of C to gain a foothold. C++ is simply a better C than C.

C++ By Example is one of several books in Que's new line of *By Example* series. The philosophy of these books is simple: The best way to teach computer programming concepts is with multiple examples. Command descriptions, format syntax, and language references are not enough to teach a newcomer a programming language. Only by looking at numerous examples and by running sample programs can programming students get more than just a "feel" for the language.

Who Should Use This Book

This book teaches at three levels: beginning, intermediate, and advanced. Text and numerous examples are aimed at each level. If you are new to C++, and even if you are new to computers, this book attempts to put you at ease and gradually build your C++ programming skills. If you are an expert at C++, this book provides a few extras for you along the way.

The Book's Philosophy

This book focuses on programming *correctly* in C++ by teaching structured programming techniques and proper program design. Emphasis is always placed on a program's readability rather than "tricks of the trade" code examples. In this changing world, programs should be clear, properly structured, and well-documented, and this book does not waver from the importance of this philosophy.

This book teaches you C++ using a holistic approach. In addition to learning the mechanics of the language, you learn tips and warnings, how to use C++ for different types of applications, and a little of the history and interesting asides about the computing industry.

Many other books build single applications, adding to them a little at a time with each chapter. The chapters of this book are stand-alone chapters, and show you complete programs that fully demonstrate the commands discussed in the chapter. There is a program for every level of reader, from beginning to advanced.

This book contains almost 200 sample program listings. These programs show ways that you can use C++ for personal finance, school and business record keeping, math and science, and general-purpose applications that almost everybody with a computer can use. This wide variety of programs show you that C++ is a very powerful language that is easy to learn and use.

Appendix F, "The Mailing List Application," is a complete application—much longer than any of the other programs in the book—that brings together your entire working knowledge of C++. The application is a computerized mailing-list manager. Throughout the chapters that come before the program, you learn how each command in the program works. You can modify the program to better suit your own needs. (The comments in the program suggest changes you can make.)

Overview of This Book

This book is divided into eight parts. Part I introduces you to the C++ environment, as well as introductory programming concepts. Starting with Part II, the book presents the C++ programming language commands and built-in functions. After mastering the language, you can use the book as a handy reference. When you need help with a specific C++ programming problem, turn to the appropriate area that describes that part of the language to see numerous examples of code.

To get an idea of the book's layout, read the following description of each section of the book:

Part I: Introduction to C++

This section explains what C++ is by describing a brief history of the C++ programming language and presenting an overview of C++'s advantages over other languages. This part describes your computer's hardware, how you develop your C++ programs, and the steps you follow to enter and run programs. You begin to write C++ programs in Chapter 3.

Part II: Using C++ Operators

This section teaches the entire set of C++ operators. The rich assortment of operators (more than any other programming language except APL) makes up for the fact that the C++ programming language is very small. The operators and their order of precedence are more important to C++ than most programming languages.

Part III: C++ Constructs

C++ data processing is most powerful due to the looping, comparison, and selection constructs that C++ offers. This part shows you how to write programs flowing with control computations that produce accurate and readable code.

Part IV: Variable Scope and Modular Programming

To support true structured programming techniques, C++ must allow for local and global variables, as well as offer several ways to pass and return variables between functions. C++ is a very strong structured language that attempts, if the programmer is willing to "listen to the language," to protect local variables by making them visible only to the parts of the program that need them.

Part V: Character Input/Output and String Functions

C++ contains no commands that perform input or output. To make up for this apparent oversight, C++ compiler writers supply several useful input and output functions. By separating input and output functions from the language, C++ achieves better portability between computers; if your program runs on one computer, it will work on any other.

This part also describes several of the other built-in math, character, and string functions available with C++. These functions keep you from having to write your own routines to perform common tasks.

Part VI: Arrays and Pointers

C++ offers single and multidimensional arrays that hold multiple occurrences of repeating data, but that do not require much effort on your part to process.

Unlike many other programming languages, C++ also uses pointer variables a great deal. Pointer variables and arrays work together to give you flexible data storage that allow for easy sorting and searching of data.

Part VII: Structures and File Input/Output

Variables, arrays, and pointers are not enough to hold the types of data that your programs require. Structures allow for more powerful grouping of many different kinds of data into manageable units.

Your computer would be too limiting if you could not store data to the disk and retrieve that data back in your programs. Disk files are required by most "real world" applications. This section describes how C++ processes sequential and random-access files and teaches the fundamental principles needed to effectively save data to the disk. The last chapter in this section introduces object-oriented programming and its use of *classes*.

Part VIII: References

This final section of the book includes a reference guide to the ASCII table, the C++ precedence table, and to keywords and functions in C++. Also in this section are the mailing list application and the answers to the review questions.

Conventions Used in This Book

The following typographic conventions are used in this book:

♦ Code lines, variables, and any text you see on-screen are in monospace.

♦ Placeholders on format lines are in *italic monospace*.

♦ Filenames are in regular text, all uppercase (CCDOUB.CPP).

♦ Optional parameters on format lines are enclosed in flat brackets ([ ]). You do **not** type the brackets when you include these parameters.

♦ New terms, which are also found in the glossary, are in *italic*.

Index to the Icons

The following icons appear throughout this book:

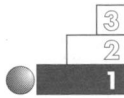

Level 1 difficulty

 Level 2 difficulty

 Level 3 difficulty

 Tip

 Note

 Caution

 Pseudocode

The pseudocode icon appears beside pseudocode, which is typeset in *italic* immediately before the program. The pseudocode consists of one or more sentences indicating what the program instructions are doing, in English. Pseudocode appears before selected programs.

Margin Graphics (Book Diagrams)

To help your understanding of C++ further, this book includes numerous *margin graphics*. These margin graphics are similar to *flowcharts* you have seen before. Both use standard symbols to represent program logic. If you have heard of the adage "A picture is worth a thousand words," you will understand why it is easier to look at the margin graphics and grasp the overall logic before dissecting programs line-by-line.

Throughout this book, these margin graphics are used in two places. Some graphics appear when a new command is introduced, to explain how the command operates. Others appear when new commands appear in sample programs for the first time.

The margin graphics do not provide complete, detailed explanations of every statement in each program. They are simple instructions and provide an overview of the new statements in question. The symbols used in the margin graphics, along with descriptions of them, follow:

Terminal symbol
(`{`,`}`,`Return...`)

Assignment staement (`total = total + newvalue; ctr = ctr = 1;...`)

Input/output
(`scanf`, `print f...`)

Calling a function

Small circle; loop begin

Large dot; begining and end of `IF-THEN`, `IF-THEN-ELSE`, and `Switch`

Input/output of arrays; assumes implied `FOR` loop(s) needed to deal with array I/O

Comment bracket; used for added info, such as name of a function

7

The margin graphics, the program listings, the program comments, and the program descriptions in the book provide many vehicles for learning the C++ language!

Companion Disk Offer

If you'd like to save yourself hours of tedious typing, use the order form in the back of this book to order the companion disk for *C++ By Example*. This disk contains the source code for all complete programs and sample code in this book, as well as the mailing-list application that appears in Appendix F. Additionally, the answers to many of the review exercises are included on the disk.

Part I

Introduction to C++

Welcome to C++

C++ is a recent addition to the long list of programming languages now available. Experts predict that C++ will become one of the most widely used programming languages within two to three years. Scan your local computer bookstore's shelves and you will see that C++ is taking the programming world by storm. More and more companies are offering C++ compilers. In the world of PCs, both Borland and Microsoft, two of the leading names of PC software, offer full-featured C++ compilers.

Although the C++ language is fairly new, having become popular within the last three years, the designers of C++ compilers are perfecting this efficient, standardized language that should soon be compatible with almost every computer in the world. Whether you are a beginning, an intermediate, or an expert programmer, C++ has the programming tools you need to make your computer do just what *you* want it to do. This chapter introduces you to C++, briefly describes its history, compares C++ to its predecessor C, shows you the advantages of C++, and concludes by introducing you to hardware and software concepts.

What C++ Can Do for You

C++ is currently defined by American Telephone & Telegraph, Incorporated, to achieve conformity between versions of C++.

Imagine a language that makes your computer perform to your personal specifications! Maybe you have looked for a program that keeps track of your household budget—exactly as you prefer—but haven't found one. Perhaps you want to track the records of a small (or large) business with your computer, but you haven't found a program that prints reports exactly as you'd like them. Possibly you have thought of a new and innovative use for a computer and you would like to implement your idea. C++ gives you the power to develop all these uses for your computer.

If your computer could understand English, you would not have to learn a programming language. But because it does not understand English, you must learn to write instructions in a language your computer recognizes. C++ is a powerful programming language. Several companies have written different versions of C++, but almost all C++ languages available today conform to the AT&T standard. *AT&T-compatible* means the C++ language in question conforms to the standard defined by the company that invented the language, namely, American Telephone & Telegraph, Incorporated. AT&T realizes that C++ is still new and has not fully matured. The good people there just completed the AT&T C++ 3.0 standard to which software companies can conform. By developing a uniform C++ language, AT&T helps ensure that programs you write today will most likely be compatible with the C++ compilers of tomorrow.

> **NOTE:** The AT&T C++ standard is only a suggestion. Software companies do not have to follow the AT&T standard, although most choose to do so. No typical computer standards committee has yet adopted a C++ standard language. The committees are currently working on the issue, but they are probably waiting for C++ to entrench the programming community before settling on a standard.

C++ is called a "better C than C."

Companies do not have to follow the AT&T C++ 3.0 standard. Many do, but add their own extensions and create their own version to do more work than the AT&T standard includes. If you are using the AT&T C++ standard, your program should successfully run on any other computer that also uses AT&T C++.

AT&T developed C++ as an improved version of the C programming language. C has been around since the 1970s and has matured into a solid, extremely popular programming language. *ANSI,* the American National Standards Institute, established a standard C programming specification called ANSI C. If your C compiler conforms to ANSI C, your program will work on any other computer that also has ANSI C. This compatibility between computers is so important that AT&T's C++ 3.0 standard includes almost every element of the ANSI C, plus more. In fact, the ANSI C committee often requires that a C++ feature be included in subsequent versions of C. For instance, function prototypes, a feature not found in older versions of ANSI C, is now a requirement for approval by the ANSI committee. Function prototypes did not exist until AT&T required them in their early C++ specification.

C++ By Example teaches you to program in C++. All programs conform to the AT&T C++ 2.1 standard. The differences between AT&T 2.1 and 3.0 are relatively minor for beginning programmers. As you progress in your programming skills, you will want to tackle the more advanced aspects of C++ and Version 3.0 will come more into play later. Whether you use a PC, a minicomputer, a mainframe, or a supercomputer, the C++ language you learn here should work on any that conform to AT&T C++ 2.1 and later.

There is a debate in the programming community as to whether a person should learn C before C++ or learn only C++. Because C++ is termed a "better C," many feel that C++ is an important language in its own right and can be learned just as easily as C. Actually, C++ pundits state that C++ teaches better programming habits than the plain, "vanilla" C. This book is aimed at the beginner programmer, and the author feels that C++ is a great language with which to begin. If you were to first learn C, you would have to "unlearn" a few things when you moved to C++. This book attempts to use the C++ language elements that are better than C. If you are new to programming, you learn C++ from the start. If you have a C background, you learn that C++ overcomes many of C's limitations.

When some people attempt to learn C++ (and C), even if they are programmers in other computer languages, they find that C++ can be cryptic and difficult to understand. This does not have to be the case. When taught to write clear and concise C++ code in an order that builds on fundamental programming concepts, programmers find that C++ is no more difficult to learn or use than any other programming language. Actually, after you start using it, C++'s modularity makes it even easier to use than most other languages. Once you master the programming elements this book teaches you, you will be ready for the advanced power for which C++ was designed—*object-oriented programming* (OOP). The last chapter of this book, "Introduction to Object-Oriented Programming," offers you the springboard to move to this exciting way of writing programs.

Even if you've never programmed a computer before, you will soon understand that programming in C++ is rewarding. Becoming an expert programmer in C++—or in any other computer language—takes time and dedication. Nevertheless, you can start writing simple programs with little effort. After you learn the fundamentals of C++ programming, you can build on what you learn and hone your skills as you write more powerful programs. You also might see new uses for your computer and develop programs others can use.

The importance of C++ cannot be overemphasized. Over the years, several programming languages were designed to be "the only programming language you would ever need." PL/I was heralded as such in the early 1960s. It turned out to be so large and took so many system resources that it simply became another language programmers used, along with COBOL, FORTRAN, and many others. In the mid-1970s, Pascal was developed for smaller computers. Microcomputers had just been invented, and the Pascal language was small enough to fit in their limited memory space while still offering advantages over many other languages. Pascal became popular and is still used often today, but it never became *the* answer for all programming tasks, and it failed at being "the only programming language you would ever need."

When the mass computer markets became familiar with C in the late 1970s, C also was promoted as "the only programming language you would ever need." What has surprised so many skeptics (including this author) is that C has practically fulfilled this promise! An incredible number of programming shops have converted to C. The appeal of C's efficiency, combined with its portability among computers, makes it the language of choice. Most of today's familiar spreadsheets, databases, and word processors are written in C. Now that C++ has improved on C, programmers are retooling their minds to think in C++ as well.

The programmer help-wanted ads seek more and more C++ programmers every day. By learning this popular language, you will be learning the latest direction of programming and keeping your skills current with the market. You have taken the first step: with this book, you learn the C++ language particulars as well as many programming tips to use and pitfalls to avoid. This book attempts to teach you to be not just a C++ programmer, but a better programmer by applying the structured, long-term programming habits that professionals require in today's business and industry.

The Background of C++

The UNIX operating system was written almost entirely in C.

Before you jump into C++, you might find it helpful to know a little about the evolution of the C++ programming language. C++ is so deeply rooted in C that you should first see where C began. Bell Labs first developed the C programming language in the early 1970s, primarily so Bell programmers could write their UNIX operating system for a new DEC (Digital Equipment Corporation) computer. Until that time, operating systems were written in assembly language, which is tedious, time-consuming, and difficult to maintain. The Bell Labs people knew they needed a higher-level programming language to implement their project quicker and create code that was easier to maintain.

Because other high-level languages at the time (COBOL, FORTRAN, PL/I, and Algol) were too slow for an operating system's code, the Bell Labs programmers decided to write their own language. They based their new language on Algol and BCPL. Algol is still used in the European markets, but is not used much in America. BCPL strongly influenced C, although it did not offer the various data types that the makers of C required. After a few versions, these Bell programmers developed a language that met their goals well. C is efficient (it is sometimes called a high, low-level language due to its speed of execution), flexible, and contains the proper language elements that enable it to be maintained over time.

15

In the 1980s, Bjourn Stroustrup, working for AT&T, took the C language to its next progression. Mr. Stroustrup added features to compensate for some of the pitfalls C allowed and changed the way programmers view programs by adding object-orientation to the language. The object-orientation aspect of programming started in other languages, such as Smalltalk. Mr. Stroustrup realized that C++ programmers needed the flexibility and modularity offered by a true OOP programming language.

C++ Compared with Other Languages

C++ requires more stringent data-type checking than does C.

If you have programmed before, you should understand a little about how C++ differs from other programming languages on the market. C++ is efficient and has much stronger typing than its C predecessor. C is known as a *weakly typed* language; variable data types do not necessarily have to hold the same type of data. (Function prototyping and type casting help to alleviate this problem.)

For example, if you declare an integer variable and decide to put a character value in it, C enables you to do so. The data might not be in the format you expect, but C does its best. This is much different from stronger-typed languages such as COBOL and Pascal.

If this discussion seems a little over your head at this point, relax. The upcoming chapters will elaborate on these topics and provide many examples.

C++ is a small, block-structured programming language. It has fewer than 46 keywords. To compensate for its small vocabulary, C++ has one of the largest assortment of *operators* such as +, -, and && (second only to APL). The large number of operators in C++ might tempt programmers to write cryptic programs that have only a small amount of code. As you learn throughout this book, however, you will find that making the program more readable is more important than saving some bytes. This book teaches you how to use the C++ operators to their fullest extent, while maintaining readable programs.

C++'s large number of operators (almost equal to the number of keywords) requires a more judicious use of an *operator precedence* table. Appendix D, "C++ Precedence Table," includes the C++ operator precedence table. Unlike most other languages that have only four or five levels of precedence, C++ has 15. As you learn C++, you have to master each of these 15 levels. This is not as difficult as it sounds, but its importance cannot be overstated.

C++ also has no input or output statements. You might want to read that sentence again! C++ has no commands that perform input or output. This is one of the most important reasons why C++ is available on so many different computers. The I/O (input/output) statements of most languages tie those languages to specific hardware. BASIC, for instance, has almost twenty I/O commands— some of which write to the screen, to the printer, to a modem, and so forth. If you write a BASIC program for a microcomputer, chances are good that it cannot run on a mainframe without considerable modification.

C++'s input and output are performed through the abundant use of operators and function calls. With every C++ compiler comes a library of standard I/O functions. I/O functions are *hardware independent*, because they work on any device and on any computer that conform to the AT&T C++ standard.

To master C++ completely, you have to be more aware of your computer's hardware than most other languages would require you to be. You certainly do not have to be a hardware expert, but understanding the internal data representation makes C++ much more usable and meaningful.

It also helps if you can become familiar with binary and hexadecimal numbers. You might want to read Appendix A, "Memory Addressing, Binary, and Hexadecimal Review," for a tutorial on these topics before you start to learn the C++ language. If you do not want to learn these topics, you can still become a good C++ programmer, but knowing what goes on "under the hood" makes C++ more meaningful to you as you learn it.

C++ and Microcomputers

C was a relatively unknown language until it was placed on the microcomputer. With the invention and growth of the microcomputer, C blossomed into a worldwide computer language. C++

extends that use on smaller computers. Most of readers of *C++ By Example* are probably working on a microcomputer-based C++ system. If you are new to computers, this section will help you learn how microcomputers were developed.

In the 1970s, NASA created the *microchip,* a tiny wafer of silicon that occupies a space smaller than a postage stamp. Computer components were placed on these microchips, hence computers required much less space than before. NASA produced these smaller computers in response to their need to send rocket ships to the moon with on-board computers. The computers on Earth could not provide split-second accuracy for rockets because radio waves took several seconds to travel between the Earth and the moon. Through development, these microchips became small enough so the computers could travel with a rocket and safely compute the rocket's trajectory.

The space program was not the only beneficiary of computer miniaturization. Because microchips became the heart of the *micro*computer, computers could now fit on desktops. These microcomputers cost much less than their larger counterparts, so many people started buying them. Thus, the home and small-business computer market was born.

Today, microcomputers are typically called *PCs* from the widespread use of the original IBM PC. The early PCs did not have the memory capacity of the large computers used by government and big business. Nevertheless, PC owners still needed a way to program these machines. BASIC was the first programming language used on PCs. Over the years, many other languages were ported from larger computers to the PC. However, no language was as successful as C in becoming the worldwide standard programming language. C++ seems to be the next standard.

Before diving into C++, you might take a few moments to familiarize yourself with some of the hardware and software components of your PC. The next section, "An Overview of Your Computer," introduces you to computer components that C++ interacts with, such as the operating system, memory, disks, and I/O devices. If you are already familiar with your computer's hardware and software, you might want to skip to Chapter 2, "What Is a Program?," and begin using C++.

An Overview of Your Computer

Your computer system consists of two parts: *hardware* and *software*. The hardware consists of all the physical parts of the machine. Hardware has been defined as "anything you can kick." Although this definition is coarse, it illustrates that your computer's hardware consists of the physical components of your PC. The software is everything else. Software comprises the programs and data that interact with your hardware. The C++ language is an example of software. You can use C++ to create even more software programs and data.

Hardware

Figure 1.1 shows you a typical PC system. Before using C++, you should have a general understanding of what hardware is and how your hardware components work together.

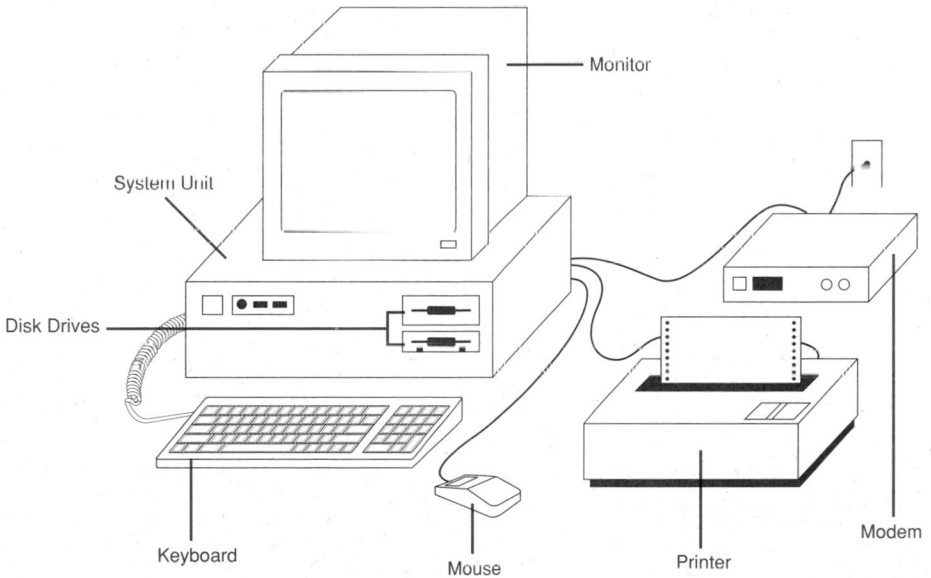

Figure 1.1. A typical PC system.

The System Unit and Memory

The *system unit* is the large, box-shaped component of the computer. This unit houses the PC's microprocessor. You might hear the microprocessor called the *CPU*, or *central processing unit.* The CPU acts like a traffic cop, directing the flow of information throughout your computer system. The CPU is analogous also to the human brain. When you use a computer, you are actually interacting with its CPU. All the other hardware exists so the CPU can send information to you (through the monitor or the printer), and you can give instructions to the CPU (through the keyboard or the mouse).

The CPU also houses the computer's internal *memory.* Although the memory has several names, it is commonly referred to as *RAM* (random-access memory). RAM is where the CPU looks for software and data. When you run a C++ program, for example, you are instructing your computer's CPU to look in RAM for that program and carry out its instructions. C++ uses RAM space when it is loaded.

A byte is a single character of memory.

RAM is used for many things and is one of the most important components of your computer's hardware. Without RAM, your computer would have no place for its instructions and data. The amount of RAM can also affect the computer's speed. In general, the more RAM your computer has, the more work it can do and the faster it can process data.

The amount of RAM is measured by the number of characters it can hold. PCs generally hold approximately 640,000 characters of RAM. A character in computer terminology is called a *byte,* and a byte can be a letter, a number, or a special character such as an exclamation point or a question mark. If your computer has 640,000 bytes of RAM, it can hold a total of 640,000 characters.

All the zeros following RAM measurements can become cumbersome. You often see the shortcut notation *K* (which comes from the metric system's *kilo,* meaning *1000*) in place of the last three zeros. In computer terms, K means exactly 1024 bytes; but this number is usually rounded to 1000 to make it easier to remember. Therefore, 640K represents approximately 640,000 bytes of RAM. For more information, see the sidebar titled "The Power of Two."

The limitations of RAM are similar to the limitations of audio cassette tapes. If a cassette is manufactured to hold 60 minutes of music, it cannot hold 75 minutes of music. Likewise, the total number of characters that compose your program, the C++ data, and your computer's system programs cannot exceed the RAM's limit (unless you save some of the characters to disk).

You want as much RAM as possible to hold C++, data, and the system programs. Generally, 640K is ample room for anything you might want to do in C++. Computer RAM is relatively inexpensive, so if your computer has less than 640K bytes of memory, you should consider purchasing additional memory to increase the total RAM to 640K. You can put more than 640K in most PCs. There are two types of additional RAM: *extended* memory and *expanded* memory (they both offer memory capacity greater than 640K). You can access this extra RAM with some C++ systems, but most beginning C++ programmers have no need to worry about RAM beyond 640K.

The Power of Two

Although K means approximately 1000 bytes of memory, K equates to 1024. Computers function using *on* and *off* states of electricity. These are called *binary* states. At the computer's lowest level, it does nothing more than turn electricity on and off with many millions of switches called *transistors*. Because these switches have two possibilities, the total number of states of these switches—and thus the total number of states of electricity—equals a number that is a power of 2.

The closest power of 2 to 1000 is 1024 (2 to the 10th power). The inventors of computers designed memory so that it is always added in kilobytes, or multiples of 1024 bytes at a time. Therefore, if you add 128K of RAM to a computer, you are actually adding a total of 131,072 bytes of RAM (128 times 1024 equals 131,072).

Because K actually means *more* than 1000, you always have a little more memory than you bargained for! Even though your computer might be rated at 640K, it actually holds more than 640,000 bytes (655,360 to be exact). See Appendix A, "Memory Addressing, Binary, and Hexadecimal Review," for a more detailed discussion of memory.

The computer stores C++ programs to RAM as you write them. If you have used a word processor before, you have used RAM. As you type words in your word-processed documents, your words appear on the video screen and also go to RAM for storage.

Despite its importance, RAM is only one type of memory in your computer. RAM is *volatile;* when you turn the computer off, all RAM is erased. Therefore, you must store the contents of RAM to a nonvolatile, more permanent memory device (such as a disk) before you turn off your computer. Otherwise, you lose your work.

Disk Storage

A *disk* is another type of computer memory, sometimes called *external memory.* Disk storage is nonvolatile. When you turn off your computer, the disk's contents do not go away. This is important. After typing a long C++ program in RAM, you do not want to retype the same program every time you turn your computer back on. Therefore, after creating a C++ program, you save the program to disk, where it remains until you're ready to retrieve it again.

Disk storage differs from RAM in ways other than volatility. Disk storage cannot be processed by the CPU. If you have a program or data on disk that you want to use, you must transfer it from the disk to RAM. This is the only way the CPU can work with the program or data. Luckily, most disks hold many times more data than the RAM's 640K. Therefore, if you fill up RAM, you can store its contents on disk and continue working. As RAM continues to fill up, you or your C++ program can keep storing the contents of RAM to the disk.

This process might sound complicated, but you have only to understand that data must be transferred to RAM before your computer can process it, and saved to disk before you shut your computer off. Most the time, a C++ program runs in RAM and retrieves data from the disk as it needs it. In Chapter 30, "Sequential Files," you learn that working with disk files is not difficult.

There are two types of disks: *hard disks* and *floppy disks.* Hard disks (sometimes called *fixed disks*) hold much more data and are many times faster to work with than floppy disks. Most of your C++ programs and data should be stored on your hard disk. Floppy disks are good for backing up hard disks, and for transferring data and programs from one computer to another. (These removable floppy disks are often called *diskettes*.) Figure 1.2 shows two common sizes, the 5 1/4-inch disk and the 3 1/2-inch disk. These disks can hold from 360K to 1.4 million bytes of data.

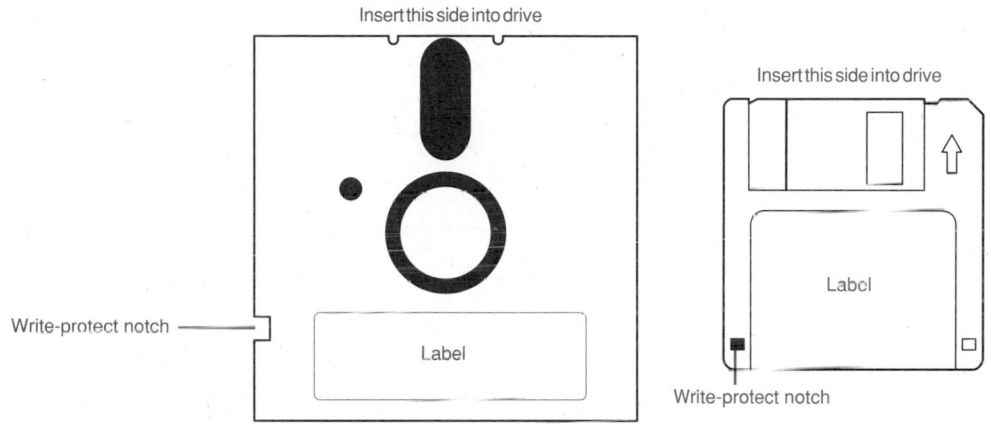

Figure 1.2. 5 1/4-inch disk and 3 1/2-inch disk.

Before using a new box of disks, you have to format them (unless you buy disks that are already formatted). Formatting prepares the disks for use on your computer by writing a pattern of paths, called *tracks*, where your data and programs are stored. Refer to the operating system instruction manual for the correct formatting procedure.

Disk drives house the disks in your computer. Usually, the disk drives are stored in your system unit. The hard disk is sealed inside the hard disk drive, and you never remove it (except for repairs). In general, the floppy disk drives also are contained in the system unit, but you insert and remove these disks manually.

Disk drives have names. The computer's first floppy disk drive is called drive A. The second floppy disk drive, if you have one, is called drive B. The first hard disk (many computers have only one) is called drive C. If you have more than one hard disk, or if your hard disk is logically divided into more than one, the others are named drive D, drive E, and so on.

Disk size is measured in bytes, just as RAM is. Disks can hold many millions of bytes of data. A 60-million-byte hard disk is common. In computer terminology, a million bytes is called a *megabyte,* or *M.* Therefore, if you have a 60-megabyte hard disk, it can hold approximately 60 million characters of data before it runs out of space.

The Monitor

The television-like screen is called the *monitor.* Sometimes the monitor is called the *CRT* (which stands for the primary component of the monitor, the *cathode-ray tube*). The monitor is one place where the output of the computer can be sent. When you want to look at a list of names and addresses, you could write a C++ program to list the information on the monitor.

The advantage of screen output over printing is that screen output is faster and does not waste paper. Screen output, however, is not permanent. When text is *scrolled* off-screen (displaced by additional text coming on-screen), it is gone and you might not always be able to see it again.

All monitors have a *cursor,* which is a character such as a blinking underline or a rectangle. The cursor moves when you type letters on-screen, and always indicates the location of the next character to be typed.

Monitors that can display pictures are called *graphics monitors.* Most PC monitors are capable of displaying graphics and text, but some can display only text. If your monitor cannot display colors, it is called a *monochrome* monitor.

Your monitor plugs into a *display adapter* located in your system unit. The display adapter determines the amount of resolution and number of possible on-screen colors. *Resolution* refers to the number of row and column intersections. The higher the resolution, the more rows and columns are present on your screen and the sharper your text and graphics appear. Some common display adapters are MCGA, CGA, EGA, and VGA.

The Printer

The printer provides a more permanent way of recording your computer's results. It is the "typewriter" of the computer. Your printer can print C++ program output to paper. Generally, you can print anything that appears on your screen. You can use your printer to print checks and envelopes too, because most types of paper work with computer printers.

The two most common PC printers are the *dot-matrix* printer and the *laser* printer. A dot-matrix printer is inexpensive, fast, and uses a series of small dots to represent printed text and graphics. A laser printer is faster than a dot-matrix, and its output is much sharper because a laser beam burns toner ink into the paper. For many people, a dot-matrix printer provides all the speed and quality they need for most applications. C++ can send output to either type of printer.

The Keyboard

Figure 1.3 shows a typical PC keyboard. Most the keys are the same as those on a standard typewriter. The letter and number keys in the center of the keyboard produce their indicated characters on-screen. If you want to type an uppercase letter, be sure to press one of the Shift keys before typing the letter. Pressing the CapsLock key shifts the keyboard to an uppercase mode. If you want to type one of the special characters above a number, however, you must do so with the Shift key. For instance, to type the percent sign (%), you would press Shift-5.

Like the Shift keys, the Alt and Ctrl keys can be used with some other keys. Some C++ programs require that you press Alt or Ctrl before pressing another key. For instance, if your C++ program prompts you to press Alt-F, you should press the Alt key, then press F while still holding down Alt, then release both keys. Do not hold them both down for long, however, or the computer keeps repeating your keystrokes as if you typed them more than once.

The key marked Esc is called the *escape* key. In many C++ programs, you can press Esc to "escape," or exit from, something you started and then wanted to stop. For example, if you prompt your C++ compiler for help and you no longer need the help message, you can press Esc to remove the help message from the screen.

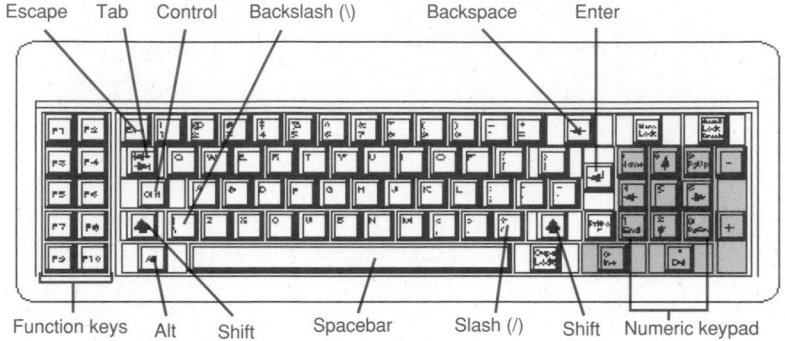

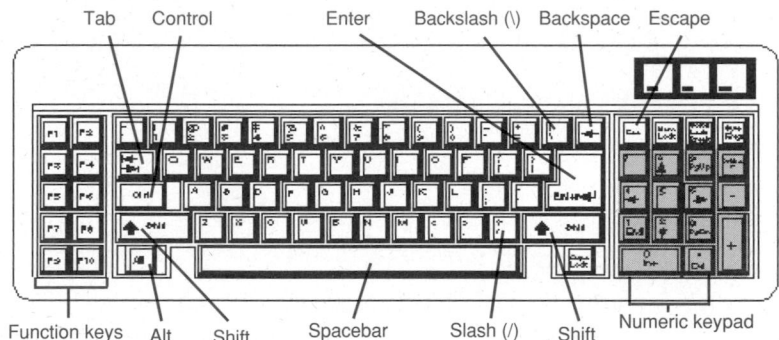

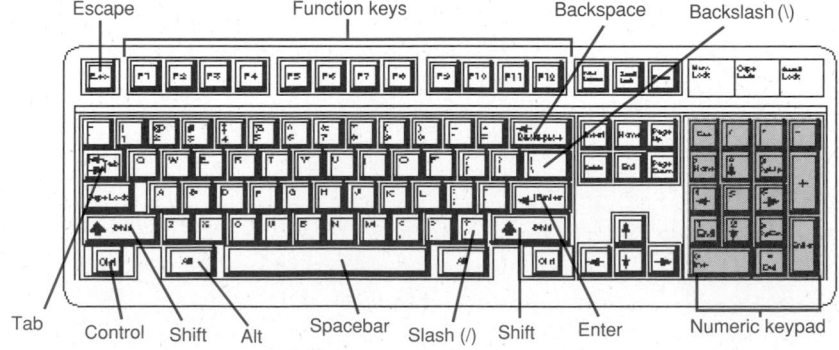

Figure 1.3. The various PC keyboards.

The group of numbers and arrows on the far right of the keyboard is called the *numeric keypad.* People familiar with a 10-key adding machine usually prefer to type numbers from the keypad rather than from the top row of the alphabetic key section. The numbers on the keypad work only when you press the NumLock key. If you press NumLock a second time, you disable these number keys and make the arrow keys work again. To prevent confusion, many keyboards have separate arrow keys and a keypad used solely for numbers.

The arrows help you move the cursor from one area of the screen to another. To move the cursor toward the top of the screen, you have to press the up arrow continuously. To move the cursor to the right, you press the right-arrow, and so on. Do not confuse the Backspace key with the left-arrow. Pressing Backspace moves the cursor backward one character at a time—erasing everything as it moves. The left-arrow simply moves the cursor backward, without erasing.

The keys marked Insert and Delete (Ins and Del on some keyboards) are useful for editing. Your C++ program editor probably takes advantage of these two keys. Insert and Delete work on C++ programs in the same way they work on a word processor's text. If you do not have separate keys labeled Insert and Delete, you probably have to press NumLock and use the keypad key 0 (for Insert) and period (for Delete).

PgUp and PgDn are the keys to press when you want to scroll the screen (that is, move your on-screen text either up or down). Your screen acts like a camera that pans up and down your C++ programs. You can move the screen down your text by pressing PgDn, and up by pressing PgUp. (Like Insert and Delete, you might have to use the keypad for these operations.)

The keys labeled F1 through F12 (some keyboards go only to F10) are called *function keys.* The function keys are located either across the top of the alphabetic section or to the left of it. These keys perform an advanced function, and when you press one of them, you usually want to issue a complex command, such as searching for a specific word in a program. The function keys in your C++ program, however, do not necessarily produce the same results as they might in another program, such as a word processor. In other words, function keys are *application-specific.*

> **CAUTION:** Computer keyboards have a key for number 1, so do not substitute the lowercase *l* to represent the number 1, as you might on a typewriter. To C++, a *1* is different from the letter *l*. You should be careful also to use *0* when you mean zero, and *O* when you want the uppercase letter *O*.

The Mouse

The mouse is a relatively new input device. The mouse moves the cursor to any on-screen location. If you have never used a mouse before, you should take a little time to become skillful in moving the cursor with it. Your C++ editor (described in Chapter 2, "What is a Program?") might use the mouse for selecting commands from its menus.

Mouse devices have two or three buttons. Most of the time, pressing the third button produces the same results as simultaneously pressing both keys on a two-button mouse.

The Modem

A modem can be used to communicate between two distant computers.

A PC *modem* enables your PC to communicate with other computers over telephone lines. Some modems, called *external modems*, sit in a box outside your computer. *Internal modems* reside inside the system unit. It does not matter which one you have, because they operate identically.

Some people have modems so they can share data between their computer and that of a long-distance friend or off-site co-worker. You can write programs in C++ that communicate with your modem.

A Modem by Any Other Name...

The term *digital computer* comes from the fact that your computer operates on binary (on and off) digital impulses of electricity. These digital states of electricity are perfect for your computer's equipment, but they cannot be sent over normal telephone lines. Telephone signals are called *analog* signals, which are much different from the binary digital signals in your PC.

Therefore, before your computer can transmit data over a telephone line, the information must be *modulated* (converted) to analog signals. The receiving computer must have a way to *demodulate* (convert back) those signals to digital.

The modem is the means by which computer signals are modulated and demodulated from digital to analog and vice versa. Thus, the name of the device that *modulates* and *demodulates* these signals is *modem.*

Software

No matter how fast, large, and powerful your computer's hardware is, its software determines what work is done and how the computer does it. Software is to a computer what music is to a stereo system. You store software on the computer's disk and load it in your computer's memory when you are ready to process the software, just as you store music on a tape and play it when you want to hear music.

Programs and Data

No doubt you have heard the phrase, *data processing.* This is what computers actually do: they take data and manipulate it into meaningful output. The meaningful output is called *information.* Figure 1.4 shows the *input-process-output* model, which is the foundation of everything that happens in your computer.

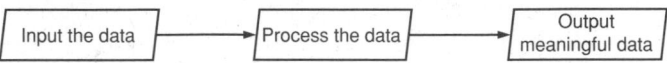

Figure 1.4. Data processing at its most elementary level.

In Chapter 2, "What Is a Program?," you learn the mechanics of programs. For now, you should know that the programs you write in C++ process the data that you input in the programs. Both data and programs compose the software. The hardware acts as a vehicle to gather the input and produce the output. Without software, computers would be worthless, just as an expensive stereo would be useless without some way of playing music so you can hear it.

The input comes from input devices, such as keyboards, modems, and disk drives. The CPU processes the input and sends the results to the output devices, such as the printer and the monitor. A C++ payroll program might receive its input (the hours worked) from the keyboard. It would instruct the CPU to calculate the payroll amounts for each employee in the disk files. After processing the payroll, the program could print the checks.

MS-DOS

MS-DOS (Microsoft disk operating system) is a system that lets your C++ programs interact with hardware. MS-DOS (commonly called DOS) is always loaded into RAM when you turn on your computer. DOS controls more than just the disks; DOS is there so your programs can communicate with all the computer's hardware, including the monitor, keyboard, and printer.

Figure 1.5 illustrates the concept of DOS as the "go-between" with your computer's hardware and software. Because DOS understands how to control every device hooked to your computer, it stays in RAM and waits for a hardware request. For instance, printing the words `"C++ is fun!"` on your printer takes many computer instructions. However, you do not have to worry about all those instructions. When your C++ program wants to print something, it tells DOS to print it. DOS always knows how to send information to your printer, so it takes your C++ program requests and does the work of routing that data to the printer.

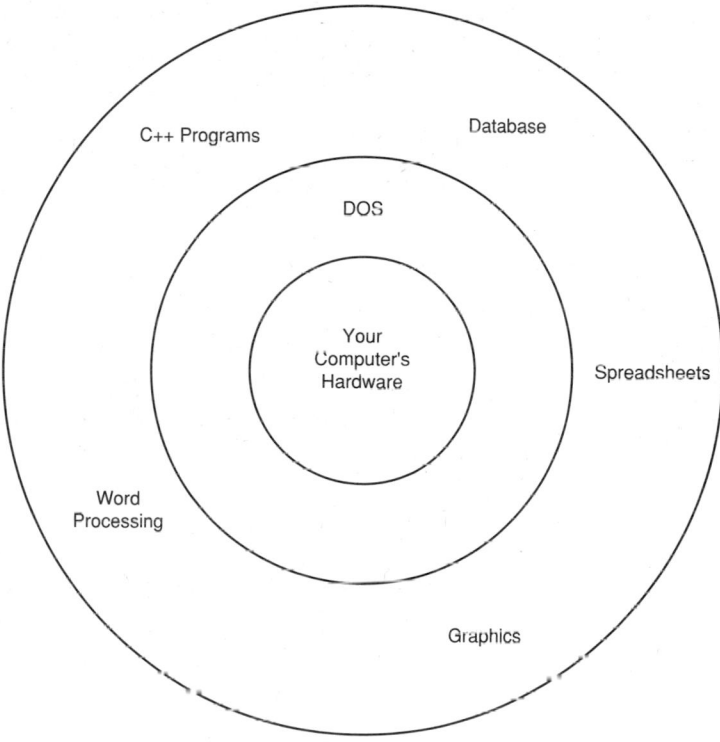

Figure 1.5. DOS interfaces between hardware and software.

Many people program computers for years and never take the time to learn why DOS is there. You do not have to be an expert in DOS, or even know more than a few simple DOS commands, to be proficient with your PC. Nevertheless, DOS does some things that C++ cannot do, such as formatting disks and copying files to your disks. As you learn more about the computer, you might see the need to better understand DOS. For a good introduction to using DOS, refer to the book *MS-DOS 5 QuickStart* (Que).

> **NOTE:** As mentioned, DOS always resides in RAM and is loaded when you start the computer. This is done automatically, so you can use your computer and program in C++ without worrying about how to transfer DOS to RAM. It is important to remember that DOS always uses some of your total RAM.

Figure 1.6 shows you the placement of DOS, C++, and your C++ data area in RAM. This formation is a typical way to represent RAM—several boxes stacked on top of each other. Each memory location (each byte) has a unique *address*, just as everybody's residence has a unique address. The first address in memory begins at 0, the second RAM address is 1, and so on until the last RAM location, many thousands of bytes later.

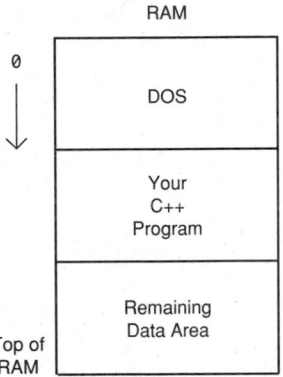

Figure 1.6. **After MS-DOS and a C++ program, there is less RAM for data.**

Your operating system (whether you use MS-DOS, PC DOS, DR DOS, or UNIX) takes part of the first few thousand bytes of memory. The amount of RAM that DOS takes varies with each computer's configuration. When working in C++, the C++ system sits on top of DOS, leaving you with the remainder of RAM for your program and data. This explains why you might have a total of 512K of RAM and still not have enough memory to run some programs—DOS is using some of the RAM for itself.

Review Questions

The answers to each chapter's review questions are in Appendix B, aptly named "Answers to Review Questions."

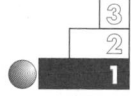

1. What is the name of one of the programming languages from which C was developed?

2. True or false: C++ is known as a "better C."

3. In what decade was C++ developed?

4. True or false: C++ is too large to fit on many microcomputers.

5. Which usually holds more data: RAM or the hard disk?

6. What device is needed for your PC to communicate over telephone lines?

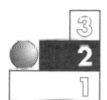

7. Which of the following device types best describes the mouse?

   a. Storage

   b. Input

   c. Output

   d. Processing

8. What key would you press to turn off the numbers on the numeric keypad?

9. What operating system is written almost entirely in C?

10. Why is RAM considered volatile?

11. True or false: The greater the resolution, the better the appearance of graphics on-screen.

12. How many bytes is 512K?

13. What does *modem* stand for?

Summary

C++ is an efficient, powerful, and popular programming language. Whether you are new to C++ or an experienced programmer, C++ is all you need to program the computer to work the way you want it to.

This chapter presented the background of C++ by walking you through the history of its predecessor, the C programming language. C++ adds to C and offers some of the most advanced programming language commands that exist today.

The rest of this book is devoted to teaching you C++. Chapter 2, "What Is a Program?," explains program concepts so you can begin to write C++ programs.

What Is a Program?

This chapter introduces you to fundamental programming concepts. The task of programming computers has been described as rewarding, challenging, easy, difficult, fast, and slow. Actually, it is a combination of all these descriptions. Writing complex programs to solve advanced problems can be frustrating and time-consuming, but you can have fun along the way, especially with the rich assortment of features that C++ has to offer.

This chapter also describes the concept of programming, from a program's inception to its execution on your computer. The most difficult part of programming is breaking the problem into logical steps that the computer can execute. Before you finish this chapter, you will type and execute your first C++ program.

This chapter introduces you to

♦ The concept of programming

♦ The program's output

♦ Program design

♦ Using an editor

♦ Using a compiler

◆ Typing and running a C++ program

◆ Handling errors

After you complete this chapter, you should be ready to learn the C++ programming language elements in greater detail.

Computer Programs

Before you can make C++ work for you, you must write a C++ program. You have seen the word *program* used several times in this book. The following note defines a program more formally.

> **NOTE:** A *program* is a list of instructions that tells the computer to do things.

Keep in mind that computers are only machines. They're not smart; in fact, they're quite the opposite! They don't do anything until they are given detailed instructions. A word processor, for example, is a program somebody wrote—in a language such as C++—that tells your computer exactly how to behave when you type words into it.

You are familiar with the concept of programming if you have ever followed a recipe, which is a "program," or a list of instructions, telling you how to prepare a certain dish. A good recipe lists these instructions in their proper order and with enough description so you can carry out the directions successfully, without assuming anything.

If you want your computer to help with your budget, keep track of names and addresses, or compute your gas mileage, it needs a program to tell it how to do those things. You can supply that program in two ways: buy a program somebody else wrote, or write the program yourself.

Writing the program yourself has a big advantage for many applications: The program does exactly what *you* want it to do. If you buy one that is already written, you have to adapt your needs to those of the author of the program. This is where C++ comes into play. With the C++ programming language (and a little studying), you can make your computer carry out your own tasks precisely.

To give C++ programming instructions to your computer, you need an *editor* and a *C++ compiler.* An editor is similar to a word processor; it is a program that enables you to type a C++ program into memory, make changes (such as moving, copying, inserting, and deleting text), and save the program more permanently in a disk file. After you use the editor to type the program, you must compile it before you can run it.

The C++ programming language is called a *compiled* language. You cannot write a C++ program and run it on your computer unless you have a C++ compiler. This compiler takes your C++ language instructions and translates them into a form that your computer can read. A C++ compiler is the tool your computer uses to understand the C++ language instructions in your programs. Many compilers come with their own built-in editor. If yours does, you probably feel that your C++ programming is more integrated.

To some beginning programmers, the process of compiling a program before running it might seem like an added and meaningless step. If you know the BASIC programming language, you might not have heard of a compiler or understand the need for one. That's because BASIC (also APL and some versions of other computer languages) is not a compiled language, but an *interpreted* language. Instead of translating the entire program into machine-readable form (as a compiler does in one step), an interpreter translates each program instruction—then executes it—before translating the next one. The difference between the two is subtle, but the bottom line is not: Compilers produce *much* more efficient and faster-running programs than interpreters do. This seemingly extra step of compiling is worth the effort (and with today's compilers, there is not much extra effort needed).

Because computers are machines that do not think, the instructions you write in C++ must be detailed. You cannot assume your computer understands what to do if some instruction is not in your program, or if you write an instruction that does not conform to C++ language requirements.

After you write and compile a C++ program, you have to *run*, or *execute*, it. Otherwise, your computer would not know that you

To program in C++

↓

Write program using editor

↓

Compile with C++ compiler

↓

Test program

↓

want it to follow the instructions in the program. Just as a cook must follow a recipe's instructions before making the dish, so too your computer must execute a program's instructions before it can accomplish what you want it to do. When you run a program, you are telling the computer to carry out your instructions.

The Program and Its Output

While you are programming, remember the difference between a program and its output. Your program contains only the C++ instructions that you write, but the computer follows your instructions only *after* you run the program.

Throughout this book, you often see a *program listing* (that is, the C++ instructions in the program) followed by the results that occur when you run the program. The results are the output of the program, and they go to an output device such as the screen, the printer, or a disk file.

Program Design

Design your programs before you type them.

You must plan your programs before typing them into your C++ editor. When builders construct houses, for example, they don't immediately grab their lumber and tools and start building! They first find out what the owner of the house wants, then they draw up the plans, order the materials, gather the workers, and finally start building the house.

The hardest part of writing a program is breaking it into logical steps that the computer can follow. Learning the C++ language is a requirement, but it is not the only thing to consider. There is a method of writing programs, a formal procedure you should learn, that makes your programming job easier. To write a program you should:

1. Define the problem to be solved with the computer.

2. Design the program's output (what the user should see).

3. Break the problem into logical steps to achieve this output.

4. Write the program (using the editor).

5. Compile the program.

6. Test the program to assure it performs as you expect.

As you can see from this procedure, the typing of your program occurs toward the end of your programming. This is important, because you first have to plan *how* to tell the computer how to perform each task.

Your computer can perform instructions only step-by-step. You must assume that your computer has no previous knowledge of the problem, so it is up to you to provide that knowledge, which, after all, is what a good recipe does. It would be a useless recipe for a cake if all it said was: "Bake the cake." Why? Because this *assumes* too much on the part of the baker. Even if you write the recipe in step-by-step fashion, proper care must be taken (through planning) to be sure the steps are in sequence. Wouldn't it be foolish also to instruct a baker to put the ingredients into the oven before stirring them?

This book adheres to the preceding programming procedure throughout the book, as each program appears. Before you see the actual program, the thought process required to write the program appears. The goals of the program are presented first, then these goals are broken into logical steps, and finally the program is written.

Designing the program in advance guarantees that the entire program structure is more accurate and keeps you from having to make changes later. A builder, for example, knows that a room is much harder to add after the house is built. If you do not properly plan every step, it is going to take you longer to create the final, working program. It is always more difficult to make major changes after you write your program.

Planning and developing according to these six steps becomes much more important as you write longer and more complicated programs. Throughout this book, you learn helpful tips for program design. Now it's time to launch into C++, so you can experience the satisfaction of typing your own program and seeing it run.

Using a Program Editor

The instructions in your C++ program are called the *source code*. You type source code into your computer's memory by using your program editor. After you type your C++ source code (your program), you should save it to a disk file before compiling and running the program. Most C++ compilers expect C++ source programs to be stored in files with names ending in .CPP. For example, the following are valid filenames for most C++ compilers:

MYPROG.CPP

SALESACT.CPP

EMPLYEE.CPP

ACCREC.CPP

Many C++ compilers include a built-in editor. Two of the most popular C++ compilers (both conform to the AT&T C++ 2.1 standard and include their own extended language elements) are Borland's C++ and Microsoft's C/C++ 7.0 compilers. These two programs run in fully integrated environments that relieve the programmer from having to worry about finding a separate program editor or learning many compiler-specific commands.

Figure 2.1 shows a Borland C++ screen. Across the top of the screen (as with Microsoft C/C++ 7.0) is a menu that offers pull-down editing, compiling, and running options. The middle of the screen contains the body of the program editor, and this is the area where the program goes. From this screen, you type, edit, compile, and run your C++ source programs. Without an *integrated environment*, you would have to start an editor, type your program, save the program to disk, exit the editor, run the compiler, and only *then* run the compiled program from the operating system. With Borland's C++ and Microsoft C/C++ 7.0, you simply type the program into the editor, then—in one step—you select the proper menu option that compiles and runs the program.

```
≡   File  Edit  Search  Run  Compile  Debug  Project  Options    Window  Help
                            \CPP\C12CNT1.CPP                                1
// Filename: C12CNT1.CPP
// Program to print a message 10 times
#include <iostream.h>
main()
{
    int ctr = 0;    // Holds the number of times printed

    do
      { cout << "Computers are fun!\n";
        ctr++;                      // Add one to the count,
                                    // after each printf()
      } while (ctr < 10);           // Print again if fewer
                                    // than 10 times

    return 0;
        1:1
[■]                              Message                        2=[↑]
 Compiling ..\..\CPP\C12CNT1.CPP:
•Linking C12CNT1.EXE:

F1 Help  F10 Menu
```

Figure 2.1. Borland Turbo C++'s integrated environment.

If you do not own an integrated environment such as Borland C++ or Microsoft C/C++, you have to find a program editor. Word processors can act as editors, but you have to learn how to save and load files in a true ASCII text format. It is often easier to use an editor than it is to make a word processor work like one.

On PCs, DOS Version 5 comes with a nice, full-screen editor called EDIT. It offers menu-driven commands and full cursor-control capabilities. EDIT is a simple program to use, and is a good beginner's program editor. Refer to your DOS manual or a good book on DOS, such as *MS-DOS 5 QuickStart* (Que), for more information on this program editor.

Another editor, called EDLIN, is available for earlier versions of DOS. EDLIN is a line editor that does not allow full-screen cursor control, and it requires you to learn some cryptic commands. The advantage to learning EDLIN is that it is always included with all PCs that use a release of DOS prior to Version 5.

If you use a computer other than a PC, such as a UNIX-based minicomputer or a mainframe, you have to determine which editors are available. Most UNIX systems include the vi editor. If you program on a UNIX operating system, it would be worth your time to learn vi. It is to UNIX what EDLIN is to PC operating systems, and is available on almost every UNIX computer in the world.

Mainframe users have other editors available, such as the ISPF editor. You might have to check with your systems department to find an editor accessible from your account.

> **NOTE:** Because this book teaches the generic AT&T C++ standard programming language, no attempt is made to tie in editor or compiler commands—there are too many on the market to cover them all in one book. As long as you write programs specific to the AT&T C++, the tools you use to edit, compile, and run those programs are secondary; your goal of good programming is the result of whatever applications you produce.

Using a C++ Compiler

After you type and edit your C++ program's source code, you have to compile the program. The process you use to compile your program depends on the version of C++ and the computer you are using. Borland C++ and Microsoft C/C++ users need only press Alt-R to compile and run their programs. When you compile programs on most PCs, your compiler eventually produces an *executable* file with a name beginning with the same name as the source code, but ends with an .EXE file extension. For example, if your source program is named GRADEAVG.CPP, the PC would produce a compiled file called GRADEAVG.EXE, which you could execute at the DOS prompt by typing the name gradeavg.

> **NOTE:** Each program in this book contains a comment that specifies a recommended filename for the source program. You do not have to follow the file-naming conventions used in this book; the filenames are only suggestions. If you use a mainframe, you have to follow the dataset-naming conventions set up by your system administrator. Each program name in the sample disk (see the order form at the back of the book) matches the filenames of the program listings.

UNIX users might have to use the cfront compiler. Most cfront compilers actually convert C++ code into regular C code. The C code is then compiled by the system's C compiler. This produces an executable file whose name (by default) is A.OUT. You can then run the A.OUT file from the UNIX prompt. Mainframe users generally have company-standard procedures for compiling C++ source programs and storing their results in a test account.

Unlike many other programming languages, your C++ program must be routed through a *preprocessor* before it is compiled. The preprocessor reads preprocessor directives that you enter in the program to control the program's compilation. Your C++ compiler automatically performs the preprocessor step, so it requires no additional effort or commands to learn on your part.

You might have to refer to your compiler's reference manuals or to your company's system personnel to learn how to compile programs for your programming environment. Again, learning the programming environment is not as critical as learning the C++ language. The compiler is just a way to transform your program from a source code file to an executable file.

Your program must go through one additional stage after compiling and before running. It is called the *linking,* or the *link editing* stage. When your program is linked, a program called the linker supplies needed runtime information to the compiled program. You can also combine several compiled programs into one executable program by linking them. Most of the time, however, your compiler initiates the link editing stage (this is especially true with integrated compilers such as Borland C++ and Microsoft C/ C++) and you do not have to worry about the process.

Figure 2.2 shows the steps that your C++ compiler and link editor perform to produce an executable program.

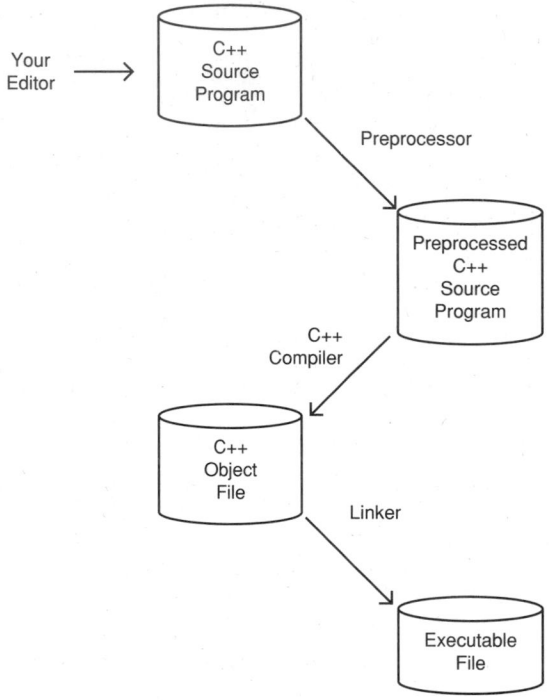

Figure 2.2. Compiling C++ source code into an executable program.

Running a Sample Program

Before delving into the specifics of the C++ language, you should take a few moments to become familiar with your editor and C++ compiler. Starting with the next chapter, "Your First C++ Program," you should put all your concentration into the C++ programming language and not worry about using a specific editor or compiling environment.

Therefore, start your editor of choice and type Listing 2.1, which follows, into your computer. Be as accurate as possible—a single typing mistake could cause the C++ compiler to generate a series of errors. You do not have to understand the program's content at this point; the goal is to give you practice in using your editor and compiler.

Listing 2.1. **Practicing with the editor.**

Comment the program with the program name.
Include the header file iostream.h so the output properly works.
Start of the main() *function.*
 Define the BELL *constant, which is the computer's beep.*
 Initialize the integer variable ctr *to 0.*
 Define the character array fname *to hold 20 elements.*
 Print to the screen What is your first name?.
 Accept a string from the keyboard.
 Process a loop while the variable ctr *is less than five.*
  Print the string accepted from the keyboard.
  Increment the variable ctr *by 1.*
 Print to the screen the character code that sounds the beep.
 Return to the operating system.

```
// Filename: C2FIRST.CPP
// Requests a name, prints the name five times, and rings a bell.

#include <iostream.h>


main()
{
   const char BELL='\a';      // Constant that rings the bell
   int ctr=0;        // Integer variable to count through loop
   char fname[20];      // Define character array to hold name

   cout << "What is your first name? ";    // Prompt the user
   cin >> fname;              // Get the name from the keyboard
   while (ctr < 5)                  // Loop to print the name
```

```
{                                          // exactly five times.
  cout << fname << "\n";
  ctr++;
}
cout << BELL;                    // Ring the terminal's bell
return 0;
}
```

Be as accurate as possible. In most programming languages—and especially in C++—the characters you type into a program must be very accurate. In this sample C++ program, for instance, you see parentheses, (), brackets, [], and braces, {}, but you cannot use them interchangeably.

The *comments* (words following the two slashes, //) to the right of some lines do not have to end in the same place that you see in the listing. They can be as long or short as you need them to be. However, you should familiarize yourself with your editor and learn to space characters accurately so you can type this program exactly as shown.

Compile the program and execute it. Granted, the first time you do this you might have to check your reference manuals or contact someone who already knows your C++ compiler. Do not worry about damaging your computer: Nothing you do from the keyboard can harm the physical computer. The worst thing you can do at this point is erase portions of your compiler software or change the compiler's options—all of which can be easily corrected by reloading the compiler from its original source. (It is only remotely likely that you would do anything like this, even if you are a beginner.)

Handling Errors

Because you are typing instructions for a machine, you must be very accurate. If you misspell a word, leave out a quotation mark, or make another mistake, your C++ compiler informs you with an error message. In Borland C++ and Microsoft C/C++, the error probably appears in a separate window, as shown in Figure 2.3. The most common error is a *syntax error,* and this usually implies a misspelled word.

```
 ≡  File  Edit  Search  Run  Compile  Debug  Project  Options    Window  Help
───────────────────────── \CPP\C12CNT1.CPP ───────────────────────1──
// Filename: C12CNT1.CPP
// Program to print a message 10 times
#include <istream.h>
main()
{
   int ctr = 0;    // Holds the number of times printed

   do
     { cout << "Computers are fun!\n";
       ctr++;                       // Add one to the count,
                                    // after each printf()
     } while (ctr < 10);            // Print again if fewer
                                    // than 10 times

   return 0;
────3:1──
┌─[■]─────────────────────────── Message ══════════════════2═[↑]─┐
 Compiling ..\..\CPP\C12CNT1.CPP:
•Error ..\..\CPP\C12CNT1.CPP 3: Unable to open include file 'ISTREAM.H'
 Error ..\..\CPP\C12CNT1.CPP 9: Undefined symbol 'cout'

F1 Help  Space View source  ◄┘ Edit source  F10 Menu
```

Figure 2.3. The compiler reporting a program error.

When you get an error message (or more than one), you must return to the program editor and correct the error. If you don't understand the error, you might have to check your reference manual or scour your program's source code until you find the offending code line.

Getting the Bugs Out

One of the first computers, owned by the military, refused to print some important data one day. After its programmers tried for many hours to find the problem in the program, a programmer by the name of Grace Hopper decided to check the printer.

She found a small moth lodged between two important wires. When she removed the moth, the printer started working perfectly (although the moth did not have the same luck).

Grace Hopper was an admiral from the Navy and, although she was responsible for developing many important computer concepts (she was the author of the original COBOL language), she might be best known for discovering the first computer bug.

Ever since Admiral Hopper discovered that moth, errors in computer programs have been known as *computer bugs*. When you test your programs, you might have to *debug* them—get the bugs (errors) out by correcting your typing errors or changing the logic so your program does exactly what you want it to do.

After you have typed your program correctly using the editor (and you get no compile errors), the program should run properly by asking for your first name, then printing it on-screen five times. After it prints your name for the fifth time, you hear the computer's bell ring.

This example helps to illustrate the difference between a program and its output. You must type the program (or load one from disk), then run the program to see its output.

Review Questions

The answers to the review questions are in Appendix B, "Answers to Review Questions."

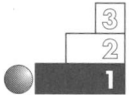

1. What is a program?

2. What are the two ways to obtain a program that does what you want?

3. True or false: Computers can think.

4. What is the difference between a program and its output?

5. What do you use for typing C++ programs into the computer?

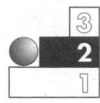

6. What filename extension do all C++ programs have?

7. Why is typing the program one of the *last* steps in the programming process?

8. What does the term *debug* mean?

9. Why is it important to write programs that are compatible with the AT&T C++?

10. True or false: You must link a program before compiling it.

Summary

After reading this chapter, you should understand the steps necessary to write a C++ program. You know that planning makes writing the program much easier, and that your program's instructions produce the output only after you run the program.

You also learned how to use your program editor and compiler. Some program editors are as powerful as word processors. Now that you know how to run C++ programs, it is time to start learning the C++ programming language.

Your First C++ Program

This chapter introduces you to some important C++ language commands and other elements. Before looking at the language more specifically, many people like to "walk through" a few simple programs to get an overall feel for what a C++ program involves. This is done here. The rest of the book covers these commands and elements more formally.

This chapter introduces the following topics:

♦ An overview of C++ programs and their structure

♦ Variables and literals

♦ Simple math operators

♦ Screen output format

This chapter introduces a few general tools you need to become familiar with the C++ programming language. The rest of the book concentrates on more specific areas of the actual language.

Looking at a C++ Program

Figure 3.1 shows the outline of a typical small C++ program. No C++ commands are shown in the figure. Although there is much more to a program than this outline implies, this is the general format of the beginning examples in this book.

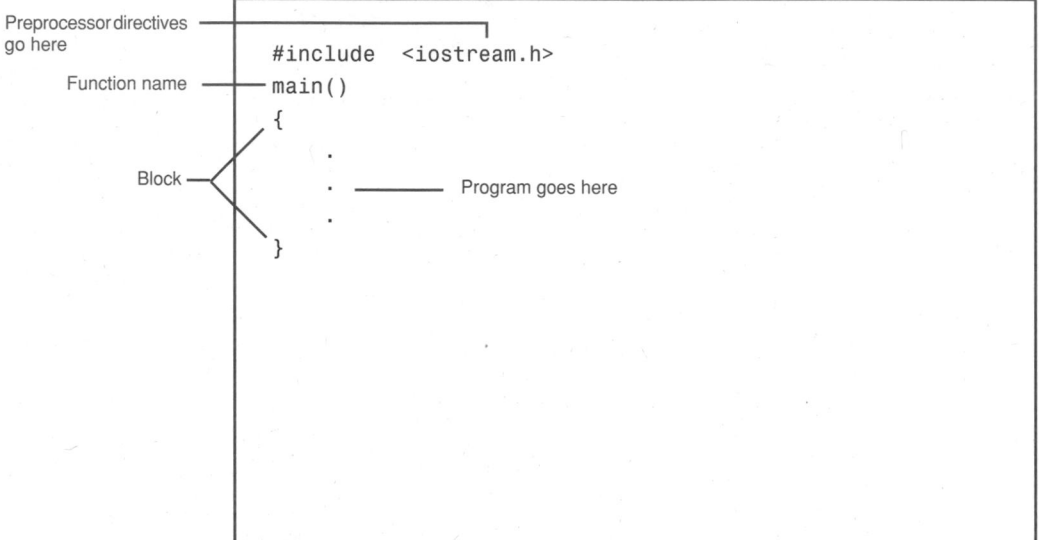

Figure 3.1. **A skeleton outline of a simple C++ program.**

To acquaint yourself with C++ programs as fast as possible, you should begin to look at a program in its entirety. The following is a listing of a simple example C++ program. It doesn't do much, but it enables you to see the general format of C++ programming. The next few sections cover elements from this and other programs. You might not understand everything in this program, even after finishing the chapter, but it is a good place to start.

```
// Filename: C3FIRST.CPP
// Initial C++ program that demonstrates the C++ comments
// and shows a few variables and their declarations.
```

```
#include <iostream.h>

main()
{
   int i, j;      // These three lines declare four variables.
   char c;
   float x;

   i = 4;         // i and j are both assigned integer literals.
   j = i + 7;
   c = 'A';       // All character literals are
                  // enclosed in single quotations.
   x = 9.087;     // x requires a floating-point value because it
                  // was declared as a floating-point variable.
   x = x * 4.5;   // Change what was in x with a formula.

   // Sends the values of the variables to the screen.
   cout <<  i << ", " << j << ", " << c << ", " << x << "\n";

   return 0;      // ALWAYS end programs and functions with return.
                  // The 0 returns to the operating system and
                  // usually indicates no errors occurred.
}
```

For now, familiarize yourself with this overall program. See if you can understand any part or all of it. If you are new to programming, you should know that the computer reads each line of the program, starting with the first line and working its way down, until it has completed all the instructions in the program. (Of course, you first have to compile and link the program, as described in Chapter 2, "What Is a Program?".)

The output of this program is minimal: It simply displays four values on-screen after performing some assignments and calculations of arbitrary values. Just concentrate on the general format at this point.

The Format of a C++ Program

C++ is a free-form language.

Unlike some other programming languages, such as COBOL, C++ is a *free-form* language, meaning that programming statements can start in any column of any line. You can insert blank lines in a program if you want. This sample program is called C3FIRST.CPP (you can find the name of each program in this book in the first line of each program listing). It contains several blank lines to help separate parts of the program. In a simple program such as this, the separation is not as critical as it might be in a longer, more complex program.

Generally, spaces in C++ programs are free-form as well. Your goal should not be to make your programs as compact as possible. Your goal should be to make your programs as readable as possible. For example, the C3FIRST.CPP program shown in the previous section could be rewritten as follows:

```
// Filename: C3FIRST.CPP Initial C++ program that demonstrates
// the C++ comments and shows a few variables and their
// declarations.
#include <iostream.h>
main(){int i,j;// These three lines declare four variables.
char c;float x;i=4;// i and j are both assigned integer literals.
j=i+7;c='A';// All character literals are enclosed in
//single quotations.
x=9.087;//x requires a floating-point value because it was
//declared as a floating-point variable.
x=x*4.5;//Change what was in x with a formula.
//Sends the values of the variables to the screen.
cout<<i<<", "<<j<<", "<<c<<", "<<x<<"\n";return 0;// ALWAYS
//end programs and functions with return. The 0 returns to
//the operating system and usually indicates no errors occurred.
}
```

To your C++ compiler, the two programs are exactly the same, and they produce exactly the same result. However, to people who have to read the program, the first style is much more readable.

Readability Is the Key

As long as programs do their job and produce correct output, who cares how well they are written? Even in today's world of fast computers and abundant memory and disk space, you should still care. Even if nobody else ever looks at your C++ program, you might have to change it at a later date. The more readable you make your program, the faster you can find what needs changing, and change it accordingly.

If you work as a programmer for a corporation, you can almost certainly expect to modify someone else's source code, and others will probably modify yours. In programming departments, it is said that long-term employees write readable programs. Given this new global economy and all the changes that face business in the years ahead, companies are seeking programmers who write for the future. Programs that are straightforward, readable, abundant with *white space* (separating lines and spaces), and devoid of hard-to-read "tricks" that create messy programs are the most desirable.

Use ample white space so you can have separate lines and spaces throughout your programs. Notice the first few lines of C3FIRST.CPP start in the first column, but the body of the program is indented a few spaces. This helps programmers "zero in" on the important code. When you write programs that contain several sections (called *blocks*), your use of white space helps the reader's eye follow and recognize the next indented block.

Uppercase Versus Lowercase

Use lowercase abundantly in C++!

Your uppercase and lowercase letters are much more significant in C++ than in most other programming languages. You can see that most of C3FIRST.CPP is in lowercase. The entire C++ language is in lowercase. For example, you must type the keywords int, char, and return in programs using lowercase characters. If you use uppercase letters, your C++ compiler would produce many errors and refuse to compile the program until you correct the errors. Appendix E, "Keyword and Function Reference," shows a list of every command in the C++ programming language. You can see that none of the commands have uppercase letters.

Many C++ programmers reserve uppercase characters for some words and messages sent to the screen, printer, or disk file; they use lowercase letters for almost everything else. There is, however, one exception to this rule in Chapter 4, "Variables and Literals," dealing with the const keyword.

Braces and `main()`

All C++ programs require the following lines:

```
main()
{
```

The statements that follow `main()` are executed first. The section of a C++ program that begins with `main()`, followed by an opening brace, {, is called the *main function*. A C++ program is actually a collection of functions (small sections of code). The function called `main()` is always required and always the first *function* executed.

> A C++ block is enclosed in two braces.

In the sample program shown here, almost the entire program is `main()` because the matching closing brace that follows `main()`'s opening brace is at the end of the program. Everything between two matching braces is called a *block*. You read more about blocks in Chapter 16, "Writing C++ Functions." For now, you only have to realize that this sample program contains just one function, `main()`, and the entire function is a single block because there is only one pair of braces.

> All executable C++ statements must end with a semi-colon (;).

All *executable* C++ statements must have a semicolon (;) after them so C++ is aware that the statement is ending. Because the computer ignores all comments, do *not* put semicolons after your comments. Notice that the lines containing `main()` and braces do not end with semicolons either, because these lines simply define the beginning and ending of the function and are not executed.

As you become better acquainted with C++, you learn when to include the semicolon and when to leave it off. Many beginning C++ programmers learn quickly when semicolons are required; your compiler certainly lets you know if you forget to include a semicolon where one is needed.

Figure 3.2 repeats the sample program shown in Figure 3.1. It contains additional markings to help acquaint you with these new terms as well as other items described in the remainder of this chapter.

```
                  ┌─ // Filename: C3FIRST.CPP
Comments ─────────┤  // Initial C++ program that demonstrates the C++ comments
                  └─ // and shows a few variables and their declarations.

Preprocessor directive ─── #include <iostream.h>

                     main()
Begin block ─────── {
                  ┌─    int i, j;     // These three lines declare four variables.
Variable declarations ┤   char c;
                  └─    float x;

                  ┌─    i = 4;        // i and j are both assigned integer literals.
                  │     j = i + 7;
                  │     c = '∧';      // All character literals are
                  │                   // enclosed in single quotations.
                  │     x = 9.087;    // x requires a floating-point value because it
                  │                   // was declared as a floating-point variable.
                  │     x = x * 4.5;  // Change what was in x with a formula.
                  │
                  │     // Sends the values of the variables to the screen.
Body of program ──┤   cout <<  i << ", " << j << ", " << c << ", " << x << "\n";
                  │
                  │     return 0;     // ALWAYS end programs and functions with return.
                  │                   // The 0 returns to the operating system and
                  └─                  // usually indicates no errors occurred.

End block ──────── }
```

Figure 3.2. The parts of the sample program.

Comments in C++

In Chapter 2, "What Is a Program?," you learned the difference between a program and its output. Most users of a program do not see the actual program; they see the output from the execution of the program's instructions. Programmers, on the other hand, look at the program listings, add new routines, change old ones, and update for advancements in computer equipment.

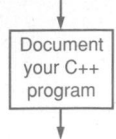

Document
your C++
program

Comments tell
people what the
program is doing.

As explained earlier, the readability of a program is important so you and other programmers can look through it easily. Nevertheless, no matter how clearly you write C++ programs, you can always enhance their readability by adding comments throughout.

Comments are messages that you insert in your C++ programs, explaining what is going on at that point in the program. For example, if you write a payroll program, you might put a comment before the check-printing routine that describes what is about to happen. You never put C++ language statements inside a comment, because a comment is a message for people—not computers. Your C++ compiler ignores all comments in every program.

> **NOTE:** C++ comments always begin with a // symbol and end at the end of the line.

Some programmers choose to comment several lines. Notice in the sample program, C3FIRST.CPP, that the first three lines are comment lines. The comments explain the filename and a little about the program.

Comments also can share lines with other C++ commands. You can see several comments sharing lines with commands in the C3FIRST.CPP program. They explain what the individual lines do. Use abundant comments, but remember who they're for: people, not computers. Use comments to help explain your code, but do not *over*comment. For example, even though you might not be familiar with C++, the following statement is easy: It prints "C++ By Example" on-screen.

```
cout << "C++ By Example"; // Print C++ By Example on-screen.
```

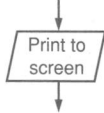

Print to
screen

This comment is redundant and adds nothing to your understanding of the line of code. It would be much better, in this case, to leave out the comment. If you find yourself almost repeating the C++ code, leave out that particular comment. Not every line of a C++ program should be commented. Comment only when code lines need explaining—in English—to the people looking at your program.

It does not matter if you use uppercase, lowercase, or a mixture of both in your comments because C++ ignores them. Most C++

programmers capitalize the first letter of sentences in comments, just as you would in everyday writing. Use whatever case seems appropriate for the letters in your message.

C++ can also use C-style comments. These are comments that begin with /* and end with */. For instance, this line contains a comment in the C *and* C++ style:

```
netpay = grosspay - taxes;   /* Compute take-home pay. */
```

Comment As You Go

Insert your comments as you write your programs. You are most familiar with your program logic at the time you are typing the program in the editor. Some people put off adding comments until after the program is written. More often than not, however, those comments are never added, or else they are written halfheartedly.

If you comment as you write your code, you can glance back at your comments while working on later sections of the program—instead of having to decipher the previous code. This helps you whenever you want to search for something earlier in the program.

Examples

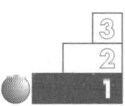

1. Suppose you want to write a C++ program that produces a fancy boxed title containing your name with flashing dots around it (like a marquee). The C++ code to do this might be difficult to understand. Before such code, you might want to insert the following comment so others can understand the code later:

```
// The following few lines draw a fancy box around
// a name, then display flashing dots around the
// name like a Hollywood movie marquee.
```

This would not tell C++ to do anything because a comment is not a command, but it would make the next few lines of code more understandable to you and others. The comment explains in English, for people reading the program, exactly what the program is getting ready to do.

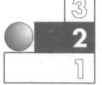

2. You should also put the disk filename of the program in one of the first comments. For example, in the C3FIRST.CPP program shown earlier, the first line is the beginning of a comment:

```
// Filename: C3FIRST.CPP
```

The comment is the first of three lines, but this line tells you in which disk file the program is stored. Throughout this book, programs have comments that include a possible filename under which the program can be stored. They begin with C*x*, where *x* is the chapter number in which they appear (for example, C6VARPR.CPP and C*10*LNIN.CPP). This method helps you find these programs when they are discussed in another section of the book.

TIP: It might be a good idea to put your name at the top of a program in a comment. If people have to modify your program at a later date, they first might want to consult with you, as the original programmer, before they change it.

Explaining the Sample Program

Now that you have an overview of a C++ program, its structure, and its comments, the rest of this chapter walks you through the entire sample program. Do not expect to become a C++ expert just by completing this section—that is what the rest of the book is for! For now, just sit back and follow this step-by-step description of the program code.

As described earlier, this sample program contains several comments. The first three lines of the program are comments:

```
// Filename: C3FIRST.CPP
// Initial C++ program that demonstrates the C++ comments
// and shows a few variables and their declarations.
```

This comment lists the filename and explains the purpose of the program. This is not the only comment in the program; others appear throughout the code.

The next line beginning with #include is called a preprocessor directive and is shown here:

```
#include <iostream.h>
```

This strange looking statement is not actually a C++ command, but is a directive that instructs the C++ compiler to load a file from disk into the middle of the current program. The only purpose for this discussion is to ensure that the output generated with cout works properly. Chapter 6, "Preprocessor Directives," more fully explains this directive.

The next two lines (following the blank separating line) are shown here:

```
main()
{
```

This begins the main() function. Basically, the main() function's opening and closing braces enclose the body of this program and main()'s instructions that execute. C++ programs often contain more than one function, but they *always* contain a function called main(). The main() function does not have to be the first one, but it usually is. The opening brace begins the first and only block of this program.

When a programmer compiles and runs this program, the computer looks for main() and starts executing whatever instruction follows main()'s opening brace. Here are the three lines that follow:

```
int i, j;     // These three lines declare four variables.
char c;
float x;
```

These three lines declare variables. A *variable declaration* describes variables used in a block of code. Variable declarations describe the program's data storage.

A C++ program processes data into meaningful results. All C++ programs include the following:

- ◆ Commands

- ◆ Data

Data comprises *variables* and *literals* (sometimes called constants). As the name implies, a *variable* is data that can change (become variable) as the program runs. A literal remains the same. In life, a variable might be your salary. It increases over time (if you are lucky). A literal would be your first name or social security number, because each remains with you throughout life and does not (naturally) change.

Chapter 4, "Variables and Literals," fully explains these concepts. However, to give you an overview of the sample program's elements, the following discussion explains variables and literals in this program.

C++ enables you to use several kinds of literals. For now, you simply have to understand that a C++ literal is any number, character, word, or phrase. The following are all valid C++ literals:

```
5.6
-45
'Q'
"Mary"
18.67643
0.0
```

As you can see, some literals are numeric and some are character-based. The single and double quotation marks around two of the literals, however, are not part of the actual literals. A single-character literal requires single quotation marks around it; a string of characters, such as `"Mary"`, requires double quotation marks.

Look for the literals in the sample program. You find these:

```
4
7
'A'
9.087
4.5
```

A variable is like a box inside your computer that holds something. That "something" might be a number or a character. You can have as many variables as needed to hold changing data. After you define a variable, it keeps its value until you change it or define it again.

Variables have names so you can tell them apart. You use the assignment operator, the equal sign (=), to assign values to variables. The following statement,

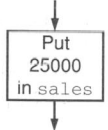

```
sales=25000;
```

puts the literal value 25000 into the variable named sales. In the sample program, you find the following variables:

```
i
j
c
x
```

The three lines of code that follow the opening brace of the sample program declare these variables. This variable declaration informs the rest of the program that two integer variables named i and j as well as a character variable called c and a floating-point variable called x appear throughout the program. The terms *integer* and *floating-point* basically refer to two different types of numbers: Integers are whole numbers, and floating-point numbers contain decimal points.

The next few statements of the sample program assign values to these variables.

```
i = 4;          // i and j are both assigned integer literals.
j = i + 7;
c = 'A';        // All character literals are
                // enclosed in single quotations.
x = 9.087;      // x requires a floating-point value because it
                // was declared as a floating-point variable.
x = x * 4.5;    // Change what was in x with a formula.
```

The first line puts 4 in the integer variable, i. The second line adds 7 to the variable i's value to get 11, which then is assigned to (or put into) the variable called j. The plus sign (+) in C++ works just like it does in mathematics. The other primary math operators are shown in Table 3.1.

Table 3.1. The primary math operators.

Operator	Meaning	Example
+	Addition	4 + 5
–	Subtraction	7 – 2
*	Multiplication	12 * 6
/	Division	48 / 12

The character literal A is assigned to the c variable. The number 9.087 is assigned to the variable called x, then x is immediately overwritten with a new value: itself (9.087) multiplied by 4.5. This helps illustrate why computer designers use an asterisk (*) for multiplication and not a lowercase x as people generally do to show multiplication; the computer would confuse the variable x with the multiplication symbol, x, if both were allowed.

> **TIP:** If mathematical operators are on the right side of the equal sign, the program completes the math before assigning the result to a variable.

The next line (after the comment) includes the following special—and, at first, confusing—statement:

```
cout <<  i << ", " << j << ", " << c << ", " << x << "\n";
```

When the program reaches this line, it prints the contents of the four variables on-screen. The important part of this line is that the four values for i, j, c, and x print on-screen.

The output from this line is

```
4, 11, ∧, 40.891499
```

Because this is the only cout in the program, this is the only output the sample program produces. You might think the program is rather long for such a small output. After you learn more about C++, you should be able to write more useful programs.

The cout is not a C++ command. You might recall from Chapter 2, "What Is a Program?," that C++ has no built-in input/output commands. The cout is an operator, described to the compiler in the #include file called iostream.h, and it sends output to the screen.

C++ also supports the printf() function for formatted output. You have seen one function already, main(), which is one for which you write the code. The C++ programming designers have already written the code for the printf function. At this point, you can think of printf as a command that outputs values to the screen, but it is actually a built-in function. Chapter 7, "Simple Input/Output" describes the printf function in more detail.

> **NOTE:** To differentiate printf from regular C++ commands, parentheses are used after the name, as in printf(). In C++, all function names have parentheses following them. Sometimes these parentheses have something between them, and sometimes they are blank.

Put a return statement at the end of each function.

The last two lines in the program are shown here:

```
return 0; // ALWAYS end programs and functions with return.
}
```

The `return` command simply tells C++ that this function is finished. C++ returns control to whatever was controlling the program before it started running. In this case, because there was only one function, control is returned either to DOS or to the C++ editing environment. C++ requires a return value. Most C++ programmers return a 0 (as this program does) to the operating system. Unless you use operating-system return variables, you have little use for a return value. Until you have to be more specific, always return a 0 from `main()`.

Actually, many `return` statements are optional. C++ would know when it reached the end of the program without this statement. It is a good programming practice, however, to put a `return` statement at the end of every function, including `main()`. Because some functions require a `return` statement (if you are returning values), it is better to get in the habit of using them, rather than run the risk of leaving one out when you really need it.

You will sometimes see parentheses around the `return` value, as in:

```
return (0); // ALWAYS end programs and functions with return.
```

The parentheses are unnecessary and sometimes lead beginning C++ students into thinking that `return` is a built-in function. However, the parentheses are recommended when you want to return an expression. You read more about returning values in Chapter 19, "Function Return Values and Prototypes."

The closing brace after the `return` does two things in this program. It signals the end of a block (begun earlier with the opening brace), which is the end of the `main()` function, and it signals the end of the program.

Review Questions

The answers to the review questions are in Appendix B, aptly named "Answers to Review Questions."

1. What must go before each comment in a C++ program?

2. What is a variable?

3. What is a literal?

4. What are four C++ math operators?

5. What operator assigns a variable its value? (*Hint:* It is called the assignment operator.)

6. True or false: A variable can consist of only two types: integers and characters.

7. What is the operator that writes output to the screen?

8. Is the following a variable name or a string literal?

```
city
```

9. What, if anything, is wrong with the following C++ statement?

```
RETURN;
```

Summary

This chapter focused on teaching you to write helpful and appropriate comments for your programs. You also learned a little about variables and literals, which hold the program's data. Without them, the term *data processing* would no longer be meaningful (there would be no data to process).

Now that you have a feel for what a C++ program looks like, it is time to begin looking at specifics of the commands. Starting with the next chapter, you begin to write your own programs. The next chapter picks up where this one left off; it takes a detailed look at literals and variables, and better describes their uses and how to choose their names.

Variables and Literals

To understand data processing with C++, you must understand how C++ creates, stores, and manipulates data. This chapter teaches you how C++ handles data by introducing the following topics:

♦ The concepts of variables and literals

♦ The types of C++ variables and literals

♦ Special literals

♦ Constant variables

♦ Naming and using variables

♦ Declaring variables

♦ Assigning values to variables

Garbage in, garbage out!

Now that you have seen an overview of the C++ programming language, you can begin writing C++ programs. In this chapter, you begin to write your own programs from scratch.

You learned in Chapter 3, "Your First C++ Program," that C++ programs consist of commands and data. Datum is the heart of all C++ programs; if you do not correctly declare or use variables and literals, your data are inaccurate and your results are going to be

69

inaccurate as well. A computer adage says the if you put garbage in, you are going to get garbage out. This is very true. People usually blame computers for mistakes, but the computers are not always at fault. Rather, their data are often not entered properly into their programs.

This chapter spends a long time focusing on numeric variables and numeric literals. If you are not a "numbers" person, do not fret. Working with numbers is the computer's job. You have to understand only how to tell the computer what you want it to do.

Variables

Variables have characteristics. When you decide your program needs another variable, you simply declare a new variable and C++ ensures that you get it. In C++, variable declarations can be placed anywhere in the program, as long as they are not referenced until after they are declared. To declare a variable, you must understand the possible characteristics, which follow.

◆ Each variable has a name.

◆ Each variable has a type.

◆ Each variable holds a value that you put there, by assigning it to that variable.

The following sections explain each of these characteristics in detail.

Naming Variables

Because you can have many variables in a single program, you must assign names to them to keep track of them. Variable names are unique, just as house addresses are unique. If two variables have the same name, C++ would not know to which you referred when you request one of them.

Variable names can be as short as a single letter or as long as 32 characters. Their names must begin with a letter of the alphabet but, after the first letter, they can contain letters, numbers, and underscore (_) characters.

> **TIP:** Spaces are not allowed in a variable name, so use the underscore character to separate parts of the name.

The following list of variable names are all valid:

```
salary   aug91_sales   i   index_age   amount
```

It is traditional to use lowercase letters for C++ variable names. You do not have to follow this tradition, but you should know that uppercase letters in variable names are different from lowercase letters. For example, each of the following four variables is viewed differently by your C++ compiler.

```
sales   Sales   SALES   sALES
```

Be very careful with the Shift key when you type a variable name. Do not inadvertently change the case of a variable name throughout a program. If you do, C++ interprets them as distinct and separate variables.

Do not give variables the same name as a command or built-in function.

Variables cannot have the same name as a C++ command or function. Appendix E, "Keyword and Function Reference," shows a list of all C++ command and function names.

The following are *invalid* variable names:

```
81_sales    Aug91+Sales    MY AGE    printf
```

> **TIP:** Although you can call a variable any name that fits the naming rules (as long as it is not being used by another variable in the program), you should always use meaningful variable names. Give your variables names that help describe the values they are holding.
>
> For example, keeping track of total payroll in a variable called `total_payroll` is much more descriptive than using the variable name `XYZ34`. Even though both names are valid, `total_payroll` is easier to remember and you have a good idea of what the variable holds by looking at its name.

71

Variable Types

Variables can hold different types of data. Table 4.1 lists the different types of C++ variables. For instance, if a variable holds an integer, C++ assumes no decimal point or fractional part (the part to the right of the decimal point) exists for the variable's value. A large number of types are possible in C++. For now, the most important types you should concentrate on are `char`, `int`, and `float`. You can append the prefix `long` to make some of them hold larger values than they would otherwise hold. Using the `unsigned` prefix enables them to hold only positive numbers.

Table 4.1. Some C++ variable types.

Declaration Name	Type
char	Character
unsigned char	Unsigned character
signed char	Signed character (same as `char`)
int	Integer
unsigned int	Unsigned integer
signed int	Signed integer (same as `int`)
short int	Short integer
unsigned short int	Unsigned short integer
signed short int	Signed short integer (same as `short int`)
long	Long integer
long int	Long integer (same as `long`)
signed long int	Signed long integer (same as `long int`)
unsigned long int	Unsigned long integer
float	Floating-point
double	Double floating-point
long double	Long double floating-point

The next section more fully describes each of these types. For now, you have to concentrate on the importance of declaring them before using them.

Declaring Variables

There are two places you can declare a variable:

♦ Before the code that uses the variable

♦ Before a function name (such as before `main()` in the program)

The first of these is the most common, and is used throughout much of this book. (If you declare a variable before a function name, it is called a *global* variable. Chapter 17, "Variable Scope," addresses the pros and cons of global variables.) To declare a variable, you must state its type, followed by its name. In the previous chapter, you saw a program that declared four variables in the following way.

Start of the `main()` *function.*
    Declare the variables i *and* j *as integers.*
    Declare the variable c *as a character.*
    Declare the variable x as a floating-point variable.

```
main()
{
   int i, j;     // These three lines declare four variables.
   char c;
   float x;
   // The rest of program follows.
```

This declares two integer variables named i and j. You have no idea what is inside those variables, however. You generally cannot assume a variable holds zero—or any other number—until you assign it a value. The first line basically tells C++ the following:

Declare all variables in a C++ program before you use them.

"I am going to use two integer variables somewhere in this program. Be expecting them. I want them named i and j. When I put a value into i or j, I ensure that the value is an integer."

Without such a declaration, you could not assign i or j a value later. All variables must be declared before you use them. This does not necessarily hold true in other programming languages, such as BASIC, but it does for C++. You could declare each of these two variables on its own line, as in the following code:

```
main()
{
    int i;
    int j;
    // The rest of program follows.
```

You do not gain any readability by doing this, however. Most C++ programmers prefer to declare variables of the same type on the same line.

The second line in this example declares a character variable called c. Only single characters should be placed there. Next, a floating-point variable called x is declared.

Examples

1. Suppose you had to keep track of a person's first, middle, and last initials. Because an initial is obviously a character, it would be prudent to declare three character variables to hold the three initials. In C++, you could do that with the following statement:

```
main()
{
    char first, middle, last;
    // The rest of program follows.
```

This statement could go after the opening brace of main(). It informs the rest of the program that you require these three character variables.

2. You could declare these three variables also on three separate lines, although it does not necessarily improve readability to do so. This could be accomplished with:

```
main()
{
   char first;
   char middle;
   char last;
   // The rest of program follows.
```

3. Suppose you want to keep track of a person's age and weight. If you want to store these values as whole numbers, they would probably go in integer variables. The following statement would declare those variables:

```
main()
{
   int age, weight;
   // The rest of program follows.
```

Looking at Data Types

You might wonder why it is important to have so many variable types. After all, a number is just a number. C++ has more data types, however, than almost all other programming languages. The variable's type is critical, but choosing the type among the many offerings is not as difficult as it might first seem.

The character variable is easy to understand. A character variable can hold only a single character. You cannot put more than a single character into a character variable.

> **NOTE:** Unlike many other programming languages, C++ does not have a string variable. Also, you cannot hold more than a single character in a C++ character variable. To store a string of characters, you must use an *aggregate* variable type that combines other fundamental types, such as an array. Chapter 5, "Character Arrays and Strings," explains this more fully.

Integers hold whole numbers. Although mathematicians might cringe at this definition, an integer is actually any number that does not contain a decimal point. All the following expressions are integers:

```
45     -932     0     12     5421
```

Floating-point numbers contain decimal points. They are known as *real* numbers to mathematicians. Any time you have to store a salary, a temperature, or any other number that might have a fractional part (a decimal portion), you must store it in a floating-point variable. All the following expressions are floating-point numbers, and any floating-point variable can hold them:

```
45.12   -2344.5432   0.00    .04594
```

Sometimes you have to keep track of large numbers, and sometimes you have to keep track of smaller numbers. Table 4.2 shows a list of ranges that each C++ variable type can hold.

CAUTION: All true AT&T C++ programmers know that they cannot count on using the exact values in Table 4.2 on every computer that uses C++. These ranges are typical on a PC, but might be much different on another computer. Use this table only as a guide.

Table 4.2. Typical ranges that C++ variables hold.

Type	Range*
char	−128 to 127
unsigned char	0 to 255
signed char	−128 to 127
int	−32768 to 32767
unsigned int	0 to 65535
signed int	−32768 to 32767
short int	−32768 to 32767
unsigned short int	0 to 65535

Type	Range*
signed short int	–32768 to 32767
long int	–2147483648 to 2147483647
signed long int	–2147483648 to 2147483647
float	–3.4E–38 to 3.4E+38
double	–1.7E–308 to 1.7E+308
long double	–3.4E–4932 to 1.1E+4932

* Use this table only as a guide; different compilers and different computers can have different ranges.

> **NOTE:** The floating-point ranges in Table 4.2 are shown in scientific notation. To determine the actual range, take the number before the *E* (meaning *Exponent*) and multiply it by 10 raised to the power after the plus sign. For instance, a floating-point number (type `float`) can contain a number as small as -3.4^{38}.

Notice that long integers and long doubles tend to hold larger numbers (and therefore, have a higher precision) than regular integers and regular double floating-point variables. This is due to the larger number of memory locations used by many of the C++ compilers for these data types. Again, this is usually—but not always—the case.

> **Do Not Over Type a Variable**
>
> If the long variable types hold larger numbers than the regular ones, you might initially want to use long variables for all your data. This would not be required in most cases, and would probably slow your program's execution.

As Appendix A, "Memory Addressing, Binary, and Hexadecimal Review," describes, the more memory locations used by data, the larger that data can be. However, every time your computer has to access more storage for a single variable (as is usually the case for long variables), it takes the CPU much longer to access it, calculate with it, and store it.

Use the long variables only if you suspect your data might overflow the typical data type ranges. Although the ranges differ between computers, you should have an idea of whether you numbers might exceed the computer's storage ranges. If you are working with extremely large (or extremely small and fractional) numbers, you should consider using the long variables.

Generally, all numeric variables should be signed (the default) unless you know for certain that your data contain only positive numbers. (Some values, such as age and distances, are always positive.) By making a variable an unsigned variable, you gain a little extra storage range (as explained in Appendix A, "Memory Addressing, Binary, and Hexadecimal Review"). That range of values must always be positive, however.

Obviously, you must be aware of what kinds of data your variables hold. You certainly do not always know exactly what each variable is holding, but you can have a general idea. For example, in storing a person's age, you should realize that a long integer variable would be a waste of space, because nobody can live to an age that can't be stored by a regular integer.

At first, it might seem strange for Table 4.2 to state that character variables can hold numeric values. In C++, integers and character variables frequently can be used interchangeably. As explained in Appendix A, "Memory Addressing, Binary, and Hexadecimal Review," each ASCII table character has a unique number that corresponds to its location in the table. If you store a number in a character variable, C++ treats the data as if it were the ASCII character that matched that number in the table. Conversely, you can store character data in an integer variable. C++ finds that character's ASCII number, and stores that number rather than the character. Examples that help illustrate this appear later in the chapter.

Designating Long, Unsigned, and Floating-Point Literals

When you type a number, C++ interprets its type as the smallest type that can hold that number. For example, if you print 63, C++ knows that this number fits into a signed integer memory location. It does not treat the number as a long integer, because 63 is not large enough to warrant a long integer literal size.

However, you can append a suffix character to numeric literals to override the default type. If you put an L at the end of an integer, C++ interprets that integer as a long integer. The number 63 is an integer literal, but the number 63L is a long integer literal.

Assign the U suffix to designate an unsigned integer literal. The number 63 is, by default, a signed integer literal. If you type 63U, C++ treats it as an unsigned integer. The suffix UL indicates an unsigned long literal.

C++ interprets all floating-point literals (numbers that contain decimal points) as double floating-point literals (double floating-point literals hold larger numbers than floating-point literals). This process ensures the maximum accuracy in such numbers. If you use the literal 6.82, C++ treats it as a double floating-point data type, even though it would fit in a regular float. You can append the floating-point suffix (F) or the long double floating-point suffix (L) to literals that contain decimal points to represent a floating-point literal or a long double floating-point literal.

You may rarely use these suffixes, but if you have to assign a literal value to an extended or unsigned variable, your literals might be a little more accurate if you add U, L, UL, or F (their lowercase equivalents work too) to their ends.

Assigning Values to Variables

Now that you know about the C++ variable types, you are ready to learn the specifics of assigning values to those variables. You do this with the *assignment* statement. The equal sign (=) is used for assigning values to variables. The format of the assignment statement is

Assign value of expression to variable

```
variable=expression;
```

The `variable` is any variable that you declared earlier. The `expression` is any variable, literal, expression, or combination that produces a resulting data type that is the same as the `variable`'s data type.

> **TIP:** Think of the equal sign as a left-pointing arrow. Loosely, the equal sign means you want to take the number, variable, or expression on the right side of the equal sign and put it into the variable on the left side of the equal sign.

Examples

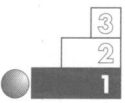

1. If you want to keep track of your current age, salary, and dependents, you could store these values in three C++ variables. You first declare the variables by deciding on correct types and good names for them. You then assign values to them. Later in the program, these values might change (for example, if the program calculates a new pay increase for you).

   Good variable names include `age`, `salary`, and `dependents`. To declare these three variables, the first part of the `main()` function would look like this:

```
// Declare and store three values.
main()
{
   int age;
   float salary;
   int dependents;
```

Notice that you do not have to declare all integer variables together. The next three statements assign values to the variables.

```
age=32;
salary=25000.00;
dependents=2;
// Rest of program follows.
```

This example is not very long and doesn't do much, but it illustrates the using and assigning of values to variables.

2. Do not put commas in values that you assign to variables. Numeric literals should never contain commas. The following statement is invalid:

```
salary=25,000.00;
```

3. You can assign variables or mathematical expressions to other variables. Suppose, earlier in a program, you stored your tax rate in a variable called `tax_rate`, then decided to use your tax rate for your spouse's rate as well. At the proper point in the program, you would code the following:

```
spouse_tax_rate = tax_rate;
```

(Adding spaces around the equal sign is acceptable to the C++ compiler, but you do not have to do so.) At this point in the program, the value in `tax_rate` is copied to a new variable named `spouse_tax_rate`. The value in `tax_rate` is still there after this line finishes. The variables were declared earlier in the program.

If your spouse's tax rate is 40 percent of yours, you can assign an expression to the spouse's variable, as in:

```
spouse_tax_rate = tax_rate * .40;
```

Any of the four mathematical symbols you learned in the previous chapter, as well as the additional ones you learn later in the book, can be part of the expression you assign to a variable.

4. If you want to assign character data to a character variable, you must enclose the character in single quotation marks. All C++ character literals must be enclosed in single quotation marks.

The following section of a program declares three variables, then assigns three initials to them. The initials are character literals because they are enclosed in single quotation marks.

```
main()
{
    char first, middle, last;
    first = 'G';
    middle = 'M';
    last = 'P';
    // Rest of program follows.
```

Because these are variables, you can reassign their values later if the program warrants it.

CAUTION: Do not mix types. C enables programmers to do this, but C++ does not. For instance, in the `middle` variable presented in the previous example, you could not have stored a floating-point literal:

```
middle = 345.43244;    // You cannot do this!
```

If you did so, `middle` would hold a strange value that would seem to be meaningless. Make sure that values you assign to variables match the variable's type. The only major exception to this occurs when you assign an integer to a character variable, or a character to an integer variable, as you learn shortly.

Literals

As with variables, there are several types of C++ literals. Remember that a literal does not change. Integer literals are whole numbers that do not contain decimal points. Floating-point literals are numbers that contain a fractional portion (a decimal point with an optional value to the right of the decimal point).

Assigning Integer Literals

You already know that an integer is any whole number without a decimal point. C++ enables you to assign integer literals to variables, use integer literals for calculations, and print integer literals using the cout operator.

An octal integer literal contains a leading 0, and a hexadecimal literal contains a leading 0x.

A regular integer literal cannot begin with a leading 0. To C++, the number 012 is not the number twelve. If you precede an integer literal with a 0, C++ interprets it as an *octal* literal. An octal literal is a base-8 number. The octal numbering system is not used much in today's computer systems. The newer versions of C++ retain octal capabilities for compatibility with previous versions.

A special integer in C++ that is still greatly used today is the base-16, or *hexadecimal*, literal. Appendix A, "Memory Addressing, Binary, and Hexadecimal Review," describes the hexadecimal numbering system. If you want to represent a hexadecimal integer literal, add the 0x prefix to it. The following numbers are hexadecimal numbers:

```
0x10     0x2C4     0xFFFF     0X9
```

Notice that it does not matter if you use a lowercase or uppercase letter x after the leading zero, or an uppercase or lowercase hexadecimal digit (for hex numbers A through F). If you write business-application programs in C++, you might think you never have the need for using hexadecimal, and you might be correct. For a complete understanding of C++ and your computer in general, however, you should become a little familiar with the fundamentals of hexadecimal numbers.

Table 4.3 shows a few integer literals represented in their regular decimal, hexadecimal, and octal notations. Each row contains the same number in all three bases.

Table 4.3. **Integer literals represented in three bases.**

Decimal (Base 10)	Hexadecimal (Base 16)	Octal (Base 8)
16	0x10	020
65536	0x10000	0100000
25	0x19	031

NOTE: Floating-point literals can begin with a leading zero, for example, 0.7. They are properly interpreted by C++. Only integers can be hexadecimal or octal literals.

Your Computer's Word Size Is Important

If you write many system programs that use hexadecimal numbers, you probably want to store those numbers in *unsigned* variables. This keeps C++ from improperly interpreting positive numbers as negative numbers.

For example, if your computer stores integers in 2-byte words (as most PCs do), the hexadecimal literal 0xFFFF represents either –1 or 65535, depending on how the sign bit is interpreted. If you declared an unsigned integer, such as

```
unsigned_int i_num = 0xFFFF;
```

C++ knows you want it to use the sign bit as data and not as the sign. If you declared the same value as a signed integer, however, as in

```
int i_num = 0xFFFF;   /* The word "signed" is optional.*/
```

C++ thinks this is a negative number (–1) because the sign bit is on. (If you were to convert 0xFFFF to binary, you would get sixteen *1*s.) Appendix A, "Memory Addressing, Binary, and Hexadecimal Review," discusses these concepts in more detail.

Assigning String Literals

A string literal is always enclosed in double quotation marks.

One type of C++ literal, called the *string literal*, does not have a matching variable. A string literal is always enclosed in double quotation marks. Here are examples of string literals:

```
"C++ Programming"   "123"   " "   "4323 E. Oak Road"   "x"
```

Any string of characters between double quotation marks—even a single character—is considered to be a string literal. A single space, a word, or a group of words between double quotation marks are all C++ string literals.

If the string literal contains only numeric digits, it is *not* a number; it is a string of numeric digits that you cannot use to perform mathematics. You can perform math only on numbers, not on string literals.

> **NOTE:** A string literal is *any* character, digit, or group of characters enclosed in double quotation marks. A character literal is any character enclosed in single quotation marks.

The double quotation marks are never considered part of the string literal. The double quotation marks surround the string and simply inform your C++ compiler that the code is a string literal and not another type of literal.

It is easy to print string literals. Simply put the string literals in a cout statement. The following code prints a string literal to the screen:

The following code prints the string literal, C++ By Example.

```
cout << "C++ By Example";
```

Examples

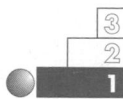

1. The following program displays a simple message on-screen. No variables are needed because no datum is stored or calculated.

```
// Filename: C4ST1.CPP
// Display a string on-screen.

#include <iostream.h>
main()
{
    cout << "C++ programming is fun!";
    return 0;
}
```

Remember to make the last line in your C++ program (before the closing brace) a `return` statement.

2. You probably want to label the output from your programs. Do not print the value of a variable unless you also print a string literal that describes that variable. The following program computes sales tax for a sale and prints the tax. Notice a message is printed first that tells the user what the next number means.

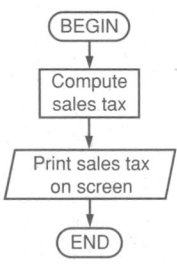

```
// Filename: C4ST2.CPP
// Compute sales tax and display it with an appropriate
message.

#include <iostream.h>
main()
{
    float sale, tax;
    float tax_rate = .08;    // Sales tax percentage

    // Determine the amount of the sale.
    sale = 22.54;

    // Compute the sales tax.
    tax = sale * tax_rate;

    // Print the results.
    cout << "The sales tax is " << tax << "\n";

    return 0;
}
```

Here is the output from the program:

```
The sales tax is 1.8032
```

You later learn how to print accurately to two decimal places to make the cents appear properly.

String-Literal Endings

An additional aspect of string literals sometimes confuses beginning C++ programmers. All string literals end with a zero. You do not see the zero, but C++ stores the zero at the end of the string in memory. Figure 4.1 shows what the string `"C++ Program"` looks like in memory.

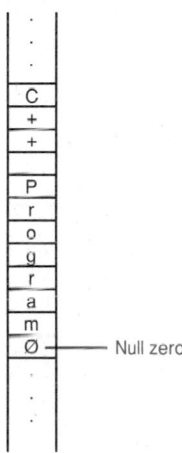

Figure 4.1. In memory, a string literal always ends with 0.

You do not have to worry about putting the zero at the end of a string literal; C++ does it for you every time it stores a string. If your program contained the string `"C++ Program"`, for example, the compiler would recognize it as a string literal (from the double quotation marks) and store the zero at the end.

All string literals end in a null zero (also called binary zero or ASCII zero).

The zero is important to C++. It is called the *string delimiter*. Without it, C++ would not know where the string literal ended in memory. (Remember that the double quotation marks are not stored as part of the string, so C++ cannot use them to determine where the string ends.)

The string-delimiting zero is not the same as the character zero. If you look at the ASCII table in Appendix C, "ASCII Table," you can see that the first entry, ASCII number 0, is the *null* character. (If you are unfamiliar with the ASCII table, you should read Appendix A, "Memory Addressing, Binary, and Hexadecimal Review," for a brief description.) This string-delimiting zero is different from the from the character '0', which has an ASCII value of 48.

As explained in Appendix A, "Memory Addressing, Binary, and Hexadecimal Review," all memory locations in your computer actually hold bit patterns for characters. If the letter *A* is stored in memory, an *A* is not actually there; the binary bit pattern for the ASCII *A* (01000001) is stored there. Because the binary bit pattern for the null zero is 00000000, the string-delimiting zero is also called a *binary zero*.

To illustrate this further, Figure 4.2 shows the bit patterns for the following string literal when stored in memory: "I am 30".

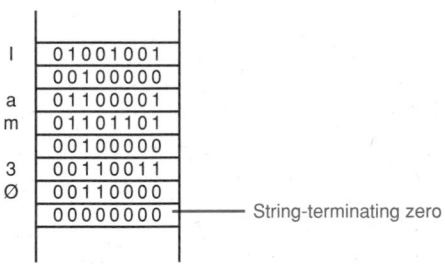

Figure 4.2. The bit pattern showing that a null zero and a character zero are different.

Figure 4.2 shows how a string is stored in your computer's memory at the binary level. It is important for you to recognize that the character 0, inside the number 30, is not the same zero (at the bit level) as the string-terminating null zero. If it were, C++ would think this string ended after the 3, which would be incorrect.

This is a fairly advanced concept, but you truly have to understand it before continuing. If you are new to computers, reviewing the material in Appendix A, "Memory Addressing, Binary, and Hexadecimal Review," will help you understand this concept.

String Lengths

The length of a string literal does not include the null binary zero.

Many times, your program has to know the length of a string. This becomes critical when you learn how to accept string input from the keyboard. The length of a string is the number of characters up to, but not including, the delimiting null zero. Do *not* include the null character in that count, even though you know C++ adds it to the end of the string.

Examples

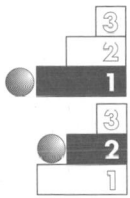

1. The following are all string literals:

   `"0"`   `"C"`   `"A much longer string literal"`

2. The following table shows some string literals and their corresponding string lengths.

String	Length
`"C"`	1
`"0"`	21
`"Hello"`	5
`""`	0
`"30 oranges"`	10

Assigning Character Literals

All C character literals should be enclosed in single quotation marks. The single quotation marks are not part of the character, but they serve to delimit the character. The following are valid C++ character literals:

`'w'` `'W'` `'C'` `'7'` `'*'` `'='` `'.'` `'K'`

C++ does not append a null zero to the end of character literals. You should know that the following are different to C++.

`'R'`   and   `"R"`

`'R'` is a single character literal. It is one character long, because *all* character literals (and variables) are one character long. `"R"` is a string literal because it is delimited by double quotation marks. Its length is also one, but it includes a null zero in memory so C++ knows where the string ends. Due to this difference, you cannot mix character literals and character strings. Figure 4.3 shows how these two literals are stored in memory.

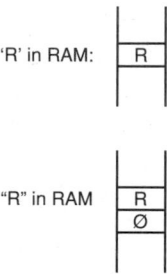

Figure 4.3.   The difference in memory between `'R'` as a character literal and `"R"` as a string literal.

All the alphabetic, numeric, and special characters on your keyboard can be character literals. Some characters, however, cannot be represented with your keyboard. They include some of the higher ASCII characters (such as the Spanish Ñ). Because you do not have keys for every character in the ASCII table, C++ enables you to represent these characters by typing their ASCII hexadecimal number inside single quotation marks.

For example, to store the Spanish Ñ in a variable, look up its hexadecimal ASCII number from Appendix C, "ASCII Table." You find that it is A5. Add the prefix \x to it and enclose it in single quotation marks, so C++ will know to use the special character. You could do that with the following code:

```
char sn='\xA5'; // Puts the Spanish Ñ into a variable called sn.
```

This is the way to store (or print) any character from the ASCII table, even if that character does not have a key on your keyboard.

The single quotation marks still tell C++ that a *single* character is inside the quotation marks. Even though `'\xA5'` contains four characters inside the quotation marks, those four characters represent a single character, not a character string. If you were to include those four characters inside a string *literal*, C++ would treat `\xA5` as a single character in the string. The following string literal,

```
"An accented a is \xA0"
```

is a C++ string that is 18 characters, not 21 characters. C++ interprets the `\xA0` character as the á, just as it should.

> **CAUTION:** If you are familiar with entering ASCII characters by typing their ASCII numbers with the Alt-keypad combination, do not do this in your C++ programs. They might work on your computer (not all C++ compilers support this), but your program might not be portable to another computer's C++ compiler.

Any character preceded by a backslash, \, (such as these have been) is called an *escape sequence,* or *escape character.* Table 4.4 shows some additional escape sequences that come in handy when you want to print special characters.

> **TIP:** Include `"\n"` in a cout if you want to skip to the next line when printing your document.

Table 4.4. Special C++ escape-sequence characters.

Escape Sequence	Meaning
\a	Alarm (the terminal's bell)
\b	Backspace
\f	Form feed (for the printer)

continues

Table 4.4. Continued.

Escape Sequence	Meaning
\n	Newline (carriage return and line feed)
\r	Carriage return
\t	Tab
\v	Vertical tab
\\	Backslash (\)
\?	Question mark
\'	Single quotation mark
\"	Double quotation mark
\000	Octal number
\xhh	Hexadecimal number
\0	Null zero (or binary zero)

Math with C++ Characters

Because C++ links characters so closely with their ASCII numbers, you can perform arithmetic on character data. The following section of code,

```
char c;
c = 'T' + 5;      // Add five to the ASCII character.
```

actually stores a *Y* in c. The ASCII value of the letter *T* is 84. Adding 5 to 84 produces 89. Because the variable c is not an integer variable, but is a character variable, C++ adds the ASCII character for 89, not the actual number.

Conversely, you can store character literals in integer variables. If you do, C++ stores the matching ASCII number for that character. The following section of code

```
int i='P';
```

> does not put a letter *P* in i because i is not a character variable. C++ assigns the number 80 in the variable because 80 is the ASCII number for the letter *P*.

Examples

1. To print two names on two different lines, include the \n between them.

   Print the name Harry; drop the cursor down to a new line and print Jerry.

   ```
   cout << "Harry\nJerry";
   ```

   When the program reaches this line, it prints

   ```
   Harry
   Jerry
   ```

   You also could separate the two names by appending more of the cout operator, such as:

   ```
   cout << "Harry" << "\n" << "Jerry";
   ```

   Because the \n only takes one byte of storage, you can output it as a character literal by typing '\n' in place of the preceding "\n".

2. The following short program rings the bell on your computer by assigning the \a escape sequence to a variable, then printing that variable.

   ```
   // Filename: C4BELL.CPP
   // Rings the bell
   #include <iostream.h>
   main()
   {
      char bell='\a';
      cout << bell;   // No newline needed here.
      return 0;
   }
   ```

Constant Variables

The term *constant variable* might seem like a contradiction. After all, a constant never changes and a variable holds values that change. In C++ terminology, you can declare variables to be constants with the `const` keyword. Throughout your program, the constants act like variables; you can use a constant variable anywhere you can use a variable, but you cannot change constant variables. To declare a constant, put the keyword `const` in front of the variable declaration, for instance:

```
const int days_of_week = 7;
```

C++ offers the `const` keyword as an improvement of the `#define` preprocessor directive that C uses. Although C++ supports `#define` as well, `const` enables you to specify constant values with specific data types.

The `const` keyword is appropriate when you have data that does not change. For example, the mathematical π is a good candidate for a constant. If you accidently attempt to store a value in a constant, C++ will let you know. Most C++ programmers choose to type their constant names in uppercase characters to distinguish them from regular variables. This is the one time when uppercase reigns in C++.

> **NOTE:** This book reserves the name *constant* for C++ program constants declared with the `const` keyword. The term *literal* is used for numeric, character, and string data values. Some books choose to use the terms constant and literal interchangeably, but in C++, the difference can be critical.

Example

Suppose a teacher wanted to compute the area of a circle for the class. To do so, the teacher needs the value of π (mathematically, π is approximately 3.14159). Because π remains constant, it is a good candidate for a const keyword, as the following program shows:

Comment for the program filename and description.

   Declare a constant value for π.

   Declare variables for radius and area.

Compute and print the area for both radius values.

```cpp
// Filename: C4AREAC.CPP
// Computes a circle with radius of 5 and 20.
#include <iostream.h>
main()
{
   const float PI=3.14159;
   float radius = 5;
   float area;

   area = radius * radius * PI;  // Circle area calculation
   cout << "The area is " << area << " with a radius of 5.\n";

   radius = 20;     // Compute area with new radius.
   area = radius * radius * PI;
   cout << "The area is " << area << " with a radius of 20.\n";

   return 0;
}
```

Review Questions

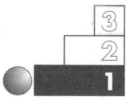

The answers to the review questions are in Appendix B.

1. Which of the following variable names are valid?

   my_name   89_sales   sales_89   a-salary

2. Which of the following literals are characters, strings, integers, and floating-point literals?

   0   -12.0   "2.0"   "X"   'X'   65.4   -708   '0'

3. How many variables do the following statements declare, and what are their types?

```
int i, j, k;
char c, d, e;
float x=65.43;
```

4. With what do all string literals end?

5. True or false: An unsigned variable can hold a larger value than a signed variable.

6. How many characters of storage does the following literal take?

```
'\x41'
```

7. How is the following string stored at the bit level?

```
"Order 10 of them."
```

8. How is the following string (called a *null string*) stored at the bit level? (*Hint:* The length is zero, but there is still a terminating character.)

```
""
```

9. What is wrong with the following program?

```
#include <iostream.h>
main()
{
    const int age=35;
    cout << age << "\n";

    age = 52;
    cout << age << "\n";
    return 0;
}
```

Review Exercises

Now that you have learned some basic C++ concepts, the remainder of the book will include this section of review exercises so you can practice your programming skills.

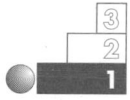

1. Write the C++ code to store three variables: your weight (you can fib), height in feet, and shoe size. Declare the variables, then assign their values in the body of your program.

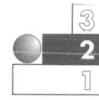

2. Rewrite your program from Exercise 1, adding proper cout statements to print the values to the screen. Use appropriate messages (by printing string literals) to describe the numbers that are printed.

3. Write a program that stores a value and prints each type of variable you learned in this chapter.

4. Write a program that stores a value into every type of variable C++ allows. You must declare each variable at the beginning of your program. Give them values and print them.

Summary

A firm grasp of C++'s fundamentals is critical to a better understanding of the more detailed material that follows. This is one of the last general-topic chapters in the book. You learned about variable types, literal types, how to name variables, how to assign variable values, and how to declare constants. These issues are *critical* to understanding the remaining concepts in C++.

This chapter taught you how to store almost every type of literal into variables. There is no string variable, so you cannot store string literals in string variables (as you can in other programming languages). However, you can "fool" C++ into *thinking* it has a string variable by using a character array to hold strings. You learn this important concept in the next chapter.

Character Arrays
and Strings

Even though C++ has no string variables, you can act as if C++ has them by using character arrays. The concept of arrays might be new to you, but this chapter explains how easy they are to declare and use. After you declare these arrays, they can hold character strings—just as if they were real string variables. This chapter includes

- ♦ Character arrays

- ♦ Comparison of character arrays and strings

- ♦ Examples of character arrays and strings

After you master this chapter, you are on your way to being able to manipulate almost every type of variable C++ offers. Manipulating characters and words is one feature that separates your computer from a powerful calculator; this capability gives computers true data-processing capabilities.

Character Arrays

A string literal can be stored in an array of characters.

Almost every type of data in C++ has a variable, but there is no variable for holding character strings. The authors of C++ realized that you need some way to store strings in variables, but instead of storing them in a string variable (as some languages such as BASIC or Pascal do) you must store them in an *array* of characters.

If you have never programmed before, an array might be new to you. An array is a list (sometimes called a *table*) of variables, and most programming languages allow the use of such lists. Suppose you had to keep track of the sales records of 100 salespeople. You could make up 100 variable names and assign a different salesperson's sales record to each one.

All those different variable names, however, are difficult to track. If you were to put them in an array of floating-point variables, you would have to keep track of only a single name (the array name) and reference each of the 100 values by a numeric subscript.

The last few chapters of this book cover array processing in more detail. However, to work with character string data in your early programs, you have to become familiar with the concept of *character arrays*.

Because a string is simply a list of one or more characters, a character array is the perfect place to hold strings of information. Suppose you want to keep track of a person's full name, age, and salary in variables. The age and salary are easy because there are variable types that can hold such data. The following code declares those two variables:

```
int age;
float salary;
```

You have no string variable to hold the name, but you can create an appropriate array of characters (which is actually one or more character variables in a row in memory) with the following declaration:

```
char name[15];
```

This reserves a character array. An array declaration always includes brackets ([ ]) that declare the space for the array. This array is 15 characters long. The array name is name. You also can assign a value to the character array at the time you declare the array. The following declaration statement not only declares the character array, but also assigns the name "Michael Jones" at the same time:

Declare the character array called name *as 15 characters long, and assign* Michael Jones *to the array.*

```
char name[15]="Michael Jones";
```

Figure 5.1 shows what this array looks like in memory. Each of the 15 boxes of the array is called an *element.* Notice the null zero (the string-terminating character) at the end of the string. Notice also that the last character of the array contains no data. You filled only the first 14 elements of the array with the data and the data's null zero. The 15th element actually has a value in it—but whatever follows the string's null zero is not a concern.

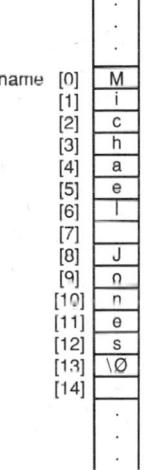

name [0] M
[1] i
[2] c
[3] h
[4] a
[5] e
[6] l
[7]
[8] J
[9] o
[10] n
[11] e
[12] s
[13] \0
[14]

Figure 5.1. A character array after being declared and assigned a string value.

You can access individual elements in an array, or you can access the array as a whole. This is the primary advantage of an array over the use of many differently named variables. You can assign values to the individual array elements by putting the elements' location, called a *subscript,* in brackets, as follows:

```
name[3]='k';
```

This overwrites the h in the name Michael with a k. The string now looks like the one in Figure 5.2.

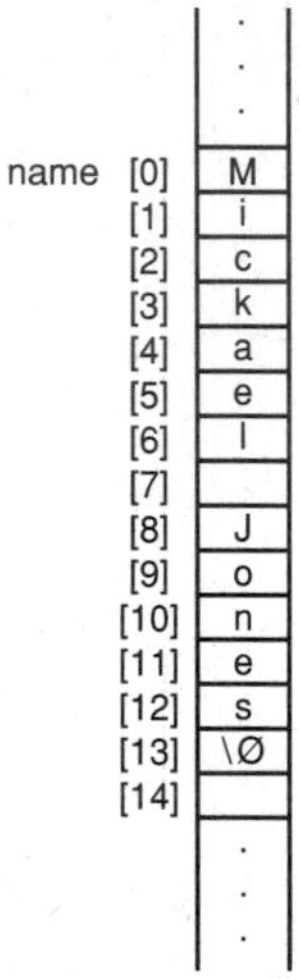

Figure 5.2. The array contents (see Figure 5.1) after changing one of the elements.

All array subscripts begin at 0.

All array subscripts start at zero. Therefore, to overwrite the first element, you must use 0 as the subscript. Assigning name[3] (as is done in Figure 5.2) changes the value of the fourth element in the array.

You can print the entire string—or, more accurately, the entire array—with a single cout statement, as follows:

```
cout << name;
```

Notice when you print an array, you do not include brackets after the array name. You must be sure to reserve enough characters in the array to hold the entire string. The following line,

```
char name[5]="Michael Jones";
```

is incorrect because it reserves only five characters for the array, whereas the name and its null zero require 14 characters. However, C++ does give you an error message for this mistake (illegal initialization).

> **CAUTION:** Always reserve enough array elements to hold the string, plus its null-terminating character. It is easy to forget the null character, but don't do it!

If your string contains 13 characters, it also must have a 14th for the null zero or it will never be treated like a string. To help eliminate this error, C++ gives you a shortcut. The following two character array statements are the same:

```
char horse[9]="Stallion";
```

and

```
char horse[]="Stallion";
```

If you assign a value to a character array at the same time you declare the array, C++ counts the string's length, adds one for the null zero, and reserves the array space for you.

If you do not assign a value to an array at the time it is declared, you cannot declare it with empty brackets. The following statement,

```
char people[];
```

does not reserve any space for the array called people. Because you did not assign a value to the array when you declared it, C++ assumes this array contains zero elements. Therefore, you have no room to put values in this array later. Most compilers generate an error if you attempt this.

Character Arrays Versus Strings

In the previous section, you saw how to put a string in a character array. Strings can exist in C++ only as string *literals,* or as stored information in character arrays. At this point, you have only to understand that strings must be stored in character arrays. As you read through this book and become more familiar with arrays and strings, however, you should become more comfortable with their use.

NOTE: Strings must be stored in character arrays, but not all character arrays contain strings.

Look at the two arrays shown in Figure 5.3. The first one, called cara1, is a character array, but it does not contain a string. Rather than a string, it contains a list of several characters. The second array, called cara2, contains a string because it has a null zero at its end.

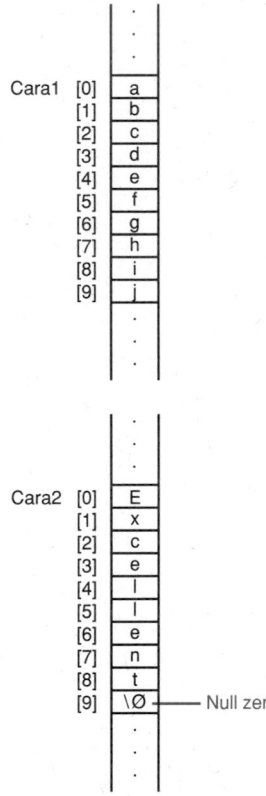

Figure 5.3. Two character arrays: Cara1 contains characters, and Cara2 contains a character string.

You could initialize these arrays with the following assignment statements.

Declare the array cara1 *with 10 individual characters.*
Declare the array cara2 *with the character string* "Excellent".

```
char cara1[10]={'a', 'b', 'c', 'd', 'e', 'f', 'g', 'h', 'i',
                'j'};
char cara2[10]="Excellent";
```

If you want to put only individual characters in an array, you must enclose the list of characters in braces, as shown. You could initialize cara1 later in the program, using assignment statements, as the following code section does.

Initialize each element of array

```
char cara1[10];
cara1[0]='a';
cara1[1]='b';
cara1[2]='c';
cara1[3]='d';
cara1[4]='e';
cara1[5]='f';
cara1[6]='g';
cara1[7]='h';
cara1[8]='i';
cara1[9]='j';    // Last element possible with subscript of nine.
```

Because the cara1 character array does not contain a null zero, it does not contain a string of characters. It does contain characters that can be stored in the array—and used individually—but they cannot be treated in a program as if they were a string.

> **CAUTION:** You cannot assign string values to character arrays in a regular assignment statement, except when you first declare the character arrays.

Because a character array is not a string variable (it can be used only to hold a string), it cannot go on the left side of an equal (=) sign. The program that follows is invalid:

```
#include <iostream.h>
main()
{
   char petname[20];       // Reserve space for the pet's name.
   petname = "Alfalfa";    // INVALID!
   cout << petname;        // The program will never get here.
   return;
}
```

Because the pet's name was not assigned *at the time the character array was declared,* it cannot be assigned a value later. The following is allowed, however, because you can assign values individually to a character array:

```
#include <iostream.h>
main()
{
   char petname[20];    // Reserve space for the pet's name.
   petname[0]='A';   // Assign values one element at a time.
   petname[1]='l';
   petname[2]='f';
   petname[3]='a';
   petname[4]='l';
   petname[5]='f';
   petname[6]='a';
   petname[7]='\0';   // Needed to ensure this is a string!
   cout <<petname;    // Now the pet's name prints properly.
   return;
}
```

The petname character array now holds a string because the last character is a null zero. How long is the string in petname? It is seven characters long because the length of a string never includes the null zero.

You cannot assign more than 20 characters to this array because its reserved space is only 20 characters. However, you can store any string of 19 (leaving one for the null zero) or fewer characters to the array. If you assign the "Alfalfa" string in the array as shown, and then assign a null zero to petname[3] as in:

```
petname[3]='\0';
```

the string in petname is now only three characters long. You have, in effect, shortened the string. There are still 20 characters reserved for petname, but the data inside it is the string "Alf" ending with a null zero.

There are many other ways to assign a value to a string. You can use the strcpy() function, for example. This is a built-in function that enables you to copy a string literal in a string. To copy the "Alfalfa" pet name into the petname array, you type:

```
strcpy(petname, "Alfalfa");  // Copies Alfalfa into the array.
```

The strcpy() function puts string literals in string arrays.

The strcpy() ("string copy") function assumes that the first value in the parentheses is a character array name, and that the second value is a valid string literal or another character array that holds a string. You must be sure that the first character array in the parentheses is long enough (in number of reserved elements) to hold whatever string you copy into it.

> **NOTE:** Place an #include <string.h> line before the main() function in programs that use strcpy() or any other built-in string functions mentioned in this book. Your compiler supplies the string.h file to help the strcpy() function work properly. The #include files such as iostream.h and string.h will be further explained as you progress through this book.

Other methods of initializing arrays are explored throughout the rest of this book.

Examples

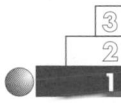

1. Suppose you want to keep track of your aunt's name in a program so you can print it. If your aunt's name is Ruth Ann Cooper, you have to reserve at least 16 elements—15 to hold the name and one to hold the null character. The following statement properly reserves a character array to hold her name:

```
char aunt_name[16];
```

2. If you want to put your aunt's name in the array at the same time you reserve the array space, you could do it like this:

```
char aunt_name[16]="Ruth Ann Cooper";
```

You could also leave out the array size and allow C++ to count the number needed:

```
char aunt_name[]="Ruth Ann Cooper";
```

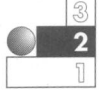

3. Suppose you want to keep track of the names of three friends. The longest name is 20 characters (including the null zero). You simply have to reserve enough character-array space to hold each friend's name. The following code does the trick:

```
char friend1[20];
char friend2[20];
char friend3[20];
```

These array declarations should appear toward the top of the block, along with any integer, floating-point, or character variables you have to declare.

4. The next example asks the user for a first and last name. Use the cin operator (the opposite of cout) to retrieve data from the keyboard. Chapter 7, "Simple I/O," more fully explains the cout and cin operators. The program then prints the user's initials on-screen by printing the first character of each name in the array. The program must print each array's 0 subscript because the first subscript of any array begins at 0, not 1.

```
// Filename: C5INIT.CPP
// Print the user's initials.
#include <iostream.h>
main()
{
   char first[20];    // Holds the first name
   char last[20];     // Holds the last name

   cout << "What is your first name? \n";
   cin >> first;
```

```
cout << "What is your last name? \n";
cin >> last;

// Print the initials
cout << "Your initials are " << first[0] << " "
     << last[0];
return 0;
}
```

5. The following program takes your three friends' character arrays and assigns them string values by using the three methods shown in this chapter. Notice the extra #include file used with the string function strcpy().

```
// Filename: C5STR.CPP
// Store and initialize three character arrays for three
friends.

#include <iostream.h>
#include <string.h>
main()
{
   // Declare all arrays and initialize the first one.
   char friend1[20]="Jackie Paul Johnson";
   char friend2[20];
   char friend3[20];

// Use a function to initialize the second array.
   strcpy(friend2, "Julie L. Roberts");

   friend3[0]='A';   // Initialize the last,
   friend3[1]='d';   // an element at a time.
   friend3[2]='a';
   friend3[3]='m';
   friend3[4]=' ';
   friend3[5]='G';
   friend3[6]='.';
   friend3[7]=' ';
   friend3[8]='S';
   friend3[9]='m';
   friend3[10]='i';
```

BEGIN

Initialize
friend1 array

Copy string
to friend2

Copy characters
to friend3

Print all
three arrays

END

```
    friend3[11]='t';
    friend3[12]='h';
    friend3[13]='\0';

    // Print all three names.
    cout << friend1 << "\n";
    cout << friend2 << "\n";
    cout << friend3 << "\n";
    return 0;
}
```

The last method of initializing a character array with a string—one element at a time—is not used as often as the other methods.

Review Questions

The answers to the review questions are in Appendix B.

1. How would you declare a character array called `my_name` that holds the following string literal?

   `"This is C++"`

2. How long is the string in Question 1?

3. How many bytes of storage does the string in Question 1 take?

4. With what do all string literals end?

5. How many variables do the following statements declare, and what are their types?

   ```
   char name[25];
   char address[25];
   ```

6. True or false: The following statement assigns a string literal to a character array.

   ```
   myname[]="Kim Langston";
   ```

7. True or false: The following declaration puts a string in the character array called `city`.

```
char city[]={'M', 'i', 'a', 'm', 'i', '\0'};
```

8. True or false: The following declaration puts a string in the character array called `city`.

```
char city[]={'M', 'i', 'a', 'm', 'i'};
```

Review Exercises

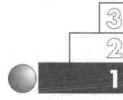

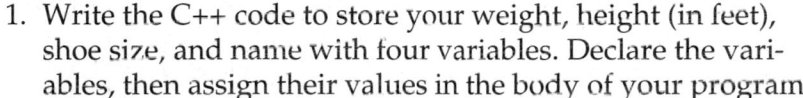

1. Write the C++ code to store your weight, height (in feet), shoe size, and name with four variables. Declare the variables, then assign their values in the body of your program.

2. Rewrite the program in Exercise 1, adding proper `printf()` statements to print the values. Use appropriate messages (by printing string literals) to describe the printed values.

3. Write a program to store and print the names of your two favorite television programs. Store these programs in two character arrays. Initialize one of the strings (assign it the first program's name) at the time you declare the array. Initialize the second value in the body of the program with the `strcpy()` function.

4. Write a program that puts 10 different initials in 10 elements of a single character array. Do not store a null zero. Print the list backward, one initial on each line.

Summary

This has been a short, but powerful chapter. You learned about character arrays that hold strings. Even though C++ has no string variables, character arrays can hold string literals. After you put a string in a character array, you can print or manipulate it as if it were a string.

Starting with the next chapter, you begin to hone the C++ skills you are building. Chapter 6, "Preprocessor Directives," introduces preprocessor directives, which are not actually part of the C++ language but help you work with your source code before your program is compiled.

Preprocessor Directives

As you might recall from Chapter 2, "What Is a Program?," the C++ compiler routes your programs through a *preprocessor* before it compiles them. The preprocessor can be called a "pre-compiler" because it preprocesses and prepares your source code for compiling before your compiler receives it.

Because this *preprocess* is so important to C++, you should familiarize yourself with it before learning more specialized commands in the language. Regular C++ commands do not affect the preprocessor. You must supply special non-C++ commands, called *preprocessor directives*, to control the preprocessor. These directives enable you, for example, to modify your source code before the code reaches the compiler. To teach you about the C++ preprocessor, this chapter

♦ Defines preprocessor directives

♦ Introduces the `#include` preprocessor directive

♦ Introduces the `#define` preprocessor directive

♦ Provides examples of both

Almost every proper C++ program contains preprocessor directives. This chapter teaches you the two most common: #include and #define.

Understanding Preprocessor Directives

Preprocessor directives are commands that you supply to the preprocessor. All preprocessor directives begin with a pound sign (#). Never put a semicolon at the end of preprocessor directives, because they are preprocessor commands and not C++ commands. Preprocessor directives typically begin in the first column of your source program. They can begin in any column, of course, but you should try to be consistent with the standard practice and start them in the first column wherever they appear. Figure 6.1 illustrates a program that contains three preprocessor directives.

```
// Filename: C6PRE.CPP
// C++ program that demonstrates preprocessor directives.

#include <iostream.h>
#define AGE 28
#define MESSAGE "Hello, world"

main()
{
   int i = 10, age;   // i is assigned a value at declaration
                      // age is still UNDEFINED

   age = 5;           // Defines the variable, age, as five.

   i = i * AGE;       // AGE is not the same as the variable, age.

   cout << i << " " << age << " " << AGE << "\n";  // 280 5 28
   cout << MESSAGE;   // Prints "Hello world".

   return 0;
}
```

Preprocessor directives

Figure 6.1. Program containing three preprocessor directives.

Preprocessor directives temporarily change your source code.

Preprocessor directives cause your C++ preprocessor to change your source code, but these changes last only as long as the compilation. When you look at your source code again, the preprocessor is finished with your file and its changes are no longer in the file. Your preprocessor does not in any way compile your program or change your actual C++ commands. This concept confuses some beginning C++ students, but just remember that your program has yet to be compiled when your preprocessor directives execute.

It has been said that a preprocessor is nothing more than a text-editor on your program. This analogy holds true throughout this chapter.

The #include Directive

The #include preprocessor directive merges a disk file into your source program. Remember that a preprocessor directive does nothing more than a word processing command does to your program; word processors also are capable of file merging. The format of the #include preprocessor directive follows:

```
#include <filename>
```

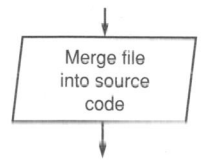

Merge file into source code

or

```
#include "filename"
```

In the #include directive, the *filename* must be an ASCII text file (as your source file must be) located somewhere on a disk. To better illustrate this rule, it might help to leave C++ for just a moment. The following example shows the contents of two files on disk. One is called OUTSIDE and the other is called INSIDE.

These are the contents of the OUTSIDE file:

```
Now is the time for all good men

#include <INSIDE>

to come to the aid of their country.
```

The INSIDE file contains the following:

```
A quick brown fox jumped
over the lazy dog.
```

Assume you can run the OUTSIDE file through the C++ preprocessor, which finds the #include directive and replaces it with the entire file called INSIDE. In other words, the C++ preprocessor directive merges the INSIDE file into the OUTSIDE file—at the #include location—and OUTSIDE expands to include the merged text. After the preprocessing ends, OUTSIDE looks like this:

```
Now is the time for all good men

A quick brown fox jumped
over the lazy dog.

to come to the aid of their country.
```

The INSIDE file remains on disk in its original form. Only the file containing the #include directive is changed. This change is only temporary; that is, OUTSIDE is expanded by the included file only for as long as it takes to compile the program.

A few real-life examples might help, because the OUTSIDE and INSIDE files are not C++ programs. You might want to include a file containing common code that you frequently use. Suppose you print your name and address quite often. You can type the following few lines of code in every program that prints your name and address:

```
cout << "Kelly Jane Peterson\n";
cout << "Apartment #217\n";
cout << "4323 East Skelly Drive\n";
cout << "New York, New York\n";
cout << "            10012\n";
```

Instead of having to retype the same five lines again and again, you type them once and save them in a file called MYADD.C. From then on, you only have to type the single line:

```
#include <myadd.c>
```

This not only saves typing, but it also maintains consistency and accuracy. (Sometimes this kind of repeated text is known as a *boilerplate*.)

You usually can use angled brackets, <>, or double quotation marks, "", around the included filename with the same results. The angled brackets tell the preprocessor to look for the *include* file in a default include directory, set up by your compiler. The double quotation marks tell the preprocessor first to look for the include file in the directory where the source code is stored, and then, to look for it in the system's include directory.

Most of the time, you do see angled brackets around the included filename. If you want to include sections of code in other programs, be sure to store that code in the system's include directory (if you use angled brackets).

Even though #include works well for inserted source code, there are other ways to include common source code that are more efficient. You learn about one technique, called writing *external functions*, in Chapter 16, "Writing C++ Functions."

This source code #include example serves well to explain what the #include preprocessor directive does. Despite this fact, #include seldom is used to include source code text, but is more often used to include special system files called *header* files. These system files help C++ interpret the many built-in functions that you use. Your C++ compiler comes with its own header files. When you (or your system administrator) installed your C++ compiler, these header files were automatically stored on your hard drive in the system's include directory. Their filenames always end in *.h* to differentiate them from regular C++ source code.

The most common header file is named iostream.h. This file gives your C++ compiler needed information about the built-in cout and cin operators, as well as other useful built-in routines that perform input and output. The name *"iostream.h"* stands for *input/output stream header*.

At this point, you don't have to understand the iostream.h file. You only have to place this file before main() in every program you write. It is rare that a C++ program does not need the iostream.h file. Even when the file is not needed, including it does no harm. Your programs can work without iostream.h as long as they do not use

> The #include directive is most often used for system header files.

an input or output operator defined there. Nevertheless, your programs are more accurate and hidden errors come to the surface much faster if you include this file.

Throughout this book, whenever a new built-in function is described, the function's matching header file is included. Because almost every C++ program you write includes a cout to print to the screen, almost every program contains the following line:

Include the built-in C++ header file called iostream.h.

```
#include <iostream.h>
```

In the last chapter, you saw the strcpy() function. Its header file is called string.h. Therefore, if you write a program that contains strcpy(), include its matching header file at the same time you include <iostream.h>. These appear on separate lines, such as:

```
#include <iostream.h>
#include <string.h>
```

The order of your include files does not matter as long as you include the files before the functions that need them. Most C++ programmers include all their needed header files before main().

These header files are simply text files. If you like, find a header file such as stdio.h on your hard drive and look at it. The file might seem complex at this point, but there is nothing "hidden" about it. Don't change the header file in any way while looking at it. If you do, you might have to reload your compiler to restore the file.

Examples

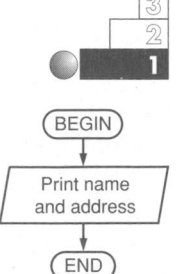

1. The following program is short. It includes the name-and-address printing routine described earlier. After printing the name and address, it ends.

```
// Filename: C6INC1.CPP
// Illustrates the #include preprocessor directives.
#include <iostream.h>
```

```
main()
{
#include "myadd.c"
return 0;
}
```

The double quotation marks are used because the file called MYADD.C is stored in the same directory as the source file. Remember that if you type this program into your computer (after typing and saving the MYADD.C file) and then compile your program, the MYADD.C file is included only as long as it takes to compile the program. Your compiler does not see this file. Your compiler acts as if you have typed the following:

```
// Filename: C6INCL1.CPP
// Illustrates the #include preprocessor directive.
#include <iostream.h>
main()
{
cout("Kelly Jane Peterson\n";
cout("Apartment #217\n";
cout("4323 East Skelly Drive\n";
cout("New York, New York\n";
cout("            10012\n";
return 0;
}
```

This explains what is meant by a preprocessor. The changes are made to your source code before it's compiled. Your original source code is restored as soon as the compile is finished. When you look at your program again, it appears as originally typed, with the `#include` statement.

2. The following program copies a message into a character array and prints it to the screen. Because the `cout` and `strcpy()` built-in functions are used, both of their header files are included.

```
// Filename: C6INCL3.CPP
// Uses two header files.

#include <iostream.h>
#include <string.h>

main()
{
    char message[20];
    strcpy(message, "This is fun!");
    cout << message;
    return 0;
}
```

The #define **Directive**

The #define preprocessor directive is used in C++ program-ming, although not nearly as frequently as it is in C. Due to the const keyword (in C++) that enables you to define variables as constants, #define is not used as much in C++. Nevertheless, #define is useful for compatibility to C programs you are converting to C++. The #define directive might seem strange at first, but it is similar to a search-and-replace command on a word processor. The format of #define follows:

#define *ARGUMENT1 argument2*

The #define directive replaces every occurrence of a first argument with a second argument.

where *ARGUMENT1* is a single word containing no spaces. Use the same naming rules for the #define statement's first argument as for vari-ables (see Chapter 4, "Variables and Literals"). For the first argu-ment, it is traditional to use uppercase letters—one of the only uses of uppercase in the entire C++ language. At least one space separates *ARGUMENT1* from *argument2*. The *argument2* can be any character, word, or phrase; it also can contain spaces or anything else you can type on the keyboard. Because #define is a preprocessor directive and not a C++ command, do not put a semicolon at the end of its expression.

The #define preprocessor directive replaces the occurrence of *ARGUMENT1* everywhere in your program with the contents of *argument2.* In most cases, the #define directive should go before main() (along with any #include directives). Look at the following #define directive:

Define the AGELIMIT literal to 21.

```
#define AGELIMIT 21
```

If your program includes one or more occurrences of the term AGELIMIT, the preprocessor replaces every one of them with the number 21. The compiler then reacts as if you actually had typed 21 rather than AGELIMIT, because the preprocessor changes all occurrences of AGELIMIT to 21 before your compiler reads the source code. But, again, the change is only temporary. After your program is compiled, you see it as you originally typed it, with #define and AGELIMIT still intact.

AGELIMIT is not a variable, because variables are declared and assigned values only at the time when your program is compiled and run. The preprocessor changes your source file before the time it is compiled.

The #define directive creates defined literals.

You might wonder why you would ever have to go to this much trouble. If you want 21 everywhere AGELIMIT occurs, you could type 21 to begin with! But the advantage of using #define rather than literals is that if the age limit ever changes (perhaps to 18), you have to change only one line in the program, not every single occurrence of the literal 21.

Because #define enables you easily to define and change literals, the replaced arguments of the #define directive are sometimes called *defined literals.* (C programmers say that #define "defines constants," but C++ programmers rarely use the word "constant" unless they are discussing the use of const.) You can define any type of literal, including string literals. The following program contains a defined string literal that replaces a string in two places.

```
// Filename: C6DEF1.CPP
// Defines a string literal and uses it twice.

#include <iostream.h>
#define MYNAME "Phil Ward"

main()
```

```
{
    char name[]=MYNAME;
    cout << "My name is " << name << "\n";    // Prints the array.
    cout << "My name is " << MYNAME << "\n"; // Prints the
                                             // defined literal.
    return 0;
}
```

The first argument of #define is in uppercase to distinguish it from variable names in the program. Variables are usually typed in lowercase. Although your preprocessor and compiler will not confuse the two, other users who look at your program can more quickly scan through and tell which items are defined literals and which are not. They will know when they see an uppercase word (if you follow the recommended standard for this first #define argument) to look at the top of the program for its actual defined value.

The fact that defined literals are not variables is even more clear in the following program. This program prints five values. Try to guess what those five values are before you look at the answer following the program.

```
// Filename: C6DEF2.CPP
// Illustrates that #define literals are not variables.

#include <iostream.h>

#define X1 b+c
#define X2 X1 + X1
#define X3 X2 * c + X1 - d
#define X4 2 * X1 + 3 * X2 + 4 * X3

main()
{
    int b = 2;      // Declares and initializes four variables.
    int c = 3;
    int d = 4;
    int e = X4;
    // Prints the values.
    cout << e << ", " << X1 << ", " << X2;
    cout << ", " << X3 << ", " << X4 << "\n";
    return 0;
}
```

The output from this program is

```
44    5    10    17    44
```

If you treated X1, X2, X3, and X4 as variables, you would not receive the correct answers. X1 through X4 are not variables; they are defined literals. Before your program is compiled, the preprocessor reads the first line and changes every occurrence of X1 to b+c. This occurs before the next #define is processed. Therefore, after the first #define, the source code looks like this:

```
// Filename: C6DEF2.CPP
// Illustrates that #define literals are not variables.

#include <iostream.h>

#define X2 b+c + b+c
#define X3 X2 * c + b+c - d
#define X4 2 * b+c + 3 * X2 + 4 * X3

main()
{
   int b=2;      // Declares and initializes four variables.
   int c=3;
   int d=4;
   int e=X4;

   // Prints the values.
   cout << e << ", " << b+c << ", " << X2;
   cout << ", " << X3 << ", " << X4 << "\n";
   return 0;
}
```

After the first #define finishes, the second one takes over and changes every occurrence of X2 to b+c + b+c. Your source code at that point becomes:

```
// Filename: C6DEF2.CPP
// Illustrates that #define literals are not variables.

#include <iostream.h>
```

```
#define X3 b+c + b+c * c + b+c - d
#define X4 2 * b+c + 3 * b+c + b+c + 4 * X3

main()
{
   int b=2;      // Declares and initializes four variables.
   int c=3;
   int d=4;
   int e=X4;

   // Prints the values.
   cout << e << ", " << b+c << ", " << b+c + b+c;
   cout << ", " << X3 << ", " << X4 << "\n";
   return 0;
}
```

After the second #define finishes, the third one takes over and changes every occurrence of X3 to b+c + b+c * c + b+c - d. Your source code then becomes:

```
// Filename: C6DEF2.CPP
// Illustrates that #define literals are not variables.

#include <iostream.h>

#define X4 2 * b+c + 3 * b+c + b+c + 4 * b+c + b+c * c + b+c - d

main()
{
   int b=2;      // Declares and initializes four variables.
   int c=3;
   int d=4;
   int e=X4;

   // Prints the values.
   cout << e << ", " << b+c << ", " << b+c + b+c;
   cout << ", " << b+c + b+c * c + b+c - d
        << ", " << X4 << "\n";
   return 0;
}
```

The source code is growing rapidly! After the third #define finishes, the fourth and last one takes over and changes every occurrence of X4 to 2 * b+c + 3 * b+c + b+c + 4 * b+c + b+c * c + b+c - d. Your source code at this last point becomes:

```
// Filename: C6DEF2.CPP
// Illustrates that #define literals are not variables.

#include <iostream.h>

main()
{
   int b=2;      // Declares and initializes four variables.
   int c=3;
   int d=4;
   int e=2 * b+c + 3 * b+c + b+c + 4 * b+c + b+c * c + b+c - d;


   // Prints the values.
   cout << e << ", " << b+c << ", " << b+c + b+c;
   cout << ", " << b+c + b+c * c + b+c - d
        << ", " << 2 * b+c + 3 * b+c + b+c + 4 * b+c +
        b+c * c + b+c - d << "\n";
   return 0;
}
```

This is what your compiler actually reads. You did not type this complete listing; you typed the original listing (shown first). The preprocessor expanded your source code into this longer form, just as if you had typed it this way.

This is an extreme example, but it serves to illustrate how #define works on your source code and doesn't define any variables. The #define behaves like a word processor's search-and-replace command. Due to #define's behavior, you can even rewrite the C++ language!

If you are used to BASIC, you might be more comfortable typing PRINT rather than C++'s cout when you want to print on-screen. If so, the following #define statement,

```
#define PRINT cout
```

enables you to print in C++ with these statements:

```
PRINT << "This is a new printing technique\n";
PRINT << "I could have used cout instead."\n;
```

This works because by the time your compiler reads the program, it reads only the following:

```
cout << "This is a new printing technique\n";
cout << "I could have used cout instead."\n;
```

In the next chapter, "Simple Input/Output," you learn about two functions sometimes used for input and output called `printf()` and `scanf()`. You can just as easily redefine function names using `#define` as you did with `cout`.

Also, remember that you cannot replace a defined literal if it resides in another string literal. For example, you cannot use the following `#define` statement:

```
#define AGE
```

to replace information in this `cout`:

```
cout << "AGE";
```

because AGE is a string literal, and it prints literally just as it appears inside the double quotation marks. The preprocessor can replace only defined literals that do not appear in quotation marks.

Do Not Overdo `#define`

Many early C programmers enjoyed redefining parts of the language to suit whatever they were used to in another language. The `cout` to `PRINT` example was only one example of this. You can redefine virtually any C++ statement or function to "look" any way you like.

There is a danger to this, however, so be wary of using `#define` for this purpose. Your redefining the language becomes confusing to others who modify your program later. Also, as you become more familiar with C++, you will naturally use the true

---

C++ language more and more. When you are comfortable with C++, older programs that you redefined will be confusing—even to you!

If you are programming in C++, use the language conventions that C++ provides. Shy away from trying to redefine commands in the language. Think of the #define directive as a way to define numeric and string literals. If those literals ever change, you have to change only one line in your program. "Just say no" to any temptation to redefine commands and built-in functions. Better yet, modify any older C code that uses #define, and replace the #define preprocessor directive with the more useful const command.

Examples

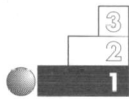

1. Suppose you want to keep track of your company's target sales amount of $55,000.00. That target amount has not changed for the previous two years. Because it probably will not change soon (sales are flat), you decide to start using a defined literal to represent this target amount. Then, if target sales do change, you just have to change the amount on the #define line to:

```
#define TARGETSALES 55000.00
```

which defines a floating-point literal. You can then assign TARGETSALES to floating-point variables and print its value, just as if you had typed 55000.00 throughout your program, as these lines show:

```
amt = TARGETSALES
cout << TARGETSALES;
```

2. If you find yourself defining the same literals in many programs, file the literals on disk and include them. Then, you don't have to type your defined literals at the beginning

of every program. If you store these literals in a file called MYDEFS.C in your program's directory, you can include the file with the following #include statement:

```
#include "mydefs.c"
```

(To use angled brackets, you have to store the file in your system's include directory.)

3. Defined literals are appropriate for array sizes. For example, suppose you declare an array for a customer's name. When you write the program, you know you don't have a customer whose name is longer than 22 characters (including the null). Therefore, you can do this:

```
#define CNMLENGTH 22
```

When you define the array, you can use this:

```
char cust_name[CNMLENGTH]
```

Other statements that need the array size also can use CNMLENGTH.

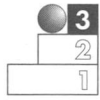

4. Many C++ programmers define a list of error messages. Once they define the messages with an easy-to-remember name, they can print those literals if an error occurs and still maintain consistency in their programs. The following error messages (or a similar form) often appear at the beginning of C++ programs.

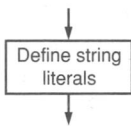

Define string literals

```
#define DISKERR "Your disk drive seems not to be working"
#define PRNTERR "Your printer is not responding"
#define AGEERR  "You cannot enter an age that small"
#define NAMEERR "You must enter a full name"
```

Review Questions

The answers to the review questions are in Appendix B.

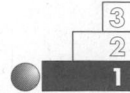

1. True or false: You can define variables with the preprocessor directives.

2. Which preprocessor directive merges another file into your program?

3. Which preprocessor directive defines literals throughout your program?

4. True or false: You can define character, string, integer, and floating-point literals with the `#define` directive.

5. Which happens first: your program is compiled or preprocessed?

6. What C++ keyword is used to replace the `#define` preprocessor directive?

7. When do you use the angled brackets in an `#include`, and when do you use double quotation marks?

8. Which are easier to change: defined literals or literals that you type throughout a program? Why?

9. Which header file should you include in almost every C++ program you write?

10. True or false: The `#define` in the following:

    ```
    #define MESSAGE "Please press Enter to continue..."
    ```

    changes this statement:

    ```
    cout << "MESSAGE";
    ```

11. What is the output from the following program?

    ```
    // Filename: C6EXER.C

    #include <iostream.h>
    #define AMT1 a+a+a
    #define AMT2 AMT1 · AMT1

    main()
    {
       int a=1;
       cout << "Amount is " << AMT2 << "\n";
       return 0;
    }
    ```

Even if you get this right, you will appreciate the side effects of `#define`. The `const` keyword (discussed in Chapter 4, "Variables and Literals") before a constant variable has none of the side effects that `#define` has.

Review Exercises

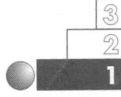

1. Write a program that prints your name to the screen. Use a defined literal for the name. Do not use a character array, and don't type your actual name inside the `cout`.

2. Suppose your boss wanted you to write a program that produced an "exception report." If the company's sales are less than $100,000.00 or more than $750,000.00, your boss wants your program to print the appropriate message. You learn how to produce these types of reports later in the book, but for now just write the `#define` statements that define these two floating-point literals.

3. Write the `cout` statements that print your name and birth date to the screen. Store these statements in their own file. Write a second program that includes the first file and prints your name and birth date. Be sure also to include <iostream.h>, because the included file contains `cout` statements.

4. Write a program that defines the ten digits, 0 through 9, as literals ZERO through NINE. Add these ten defined digits and print the result.

Summary

This chapter taught you the `#include` and `#define` preprocessor directives. Despite the fact that these directives are not executed, they temporarily change your source code by merging and defining literals into your program.

The next chapter, "Simple Input/Output," explains input and output in more detail. There are ways to control precision when using cin and cout, as well as built-in functions that format input and output.

Simple Input/Output

You have already seen the cout operator. It prints values to the screen. There is much more to cout than you have learned. Using cout and the screen (the most common output device), you can print information any way you want it. Your programs also become much more powerful if you learn to receive input from the keyboard. cin is an operator that mirrors the cout. Instead of sending output values to the screen, cin accepts values that the user types at the keyboard.

The cout and cin operators offer the new C++ programmer input and output operators they can use with relative ease. Both of these operators have a limited scope, but they give you the ability to send output from and receive input to your programs. There are corresponding functions supplied with all C++ compilers called printf() and scanf(). These functions are still used by C++ programmers due to their widespread use in regular C programs.

This chapter introduces you to

♦ The cout operator

♦ Control operators

♦ The cin operator

◆ The `printf()` output function

◆ The `scanf()` input function

You will be surprised at how much more advanced your programs can be after you learn these input/output operators.

The cout Operator

cout sends output to the screen.

The `cout` operator sends data to the standard output device. The standard output device is usually the screen; you can, however, redirect standard output to another device. If you are unfamiliar with device redirection at the operating system level, don't worry, you learn more about it in this book. At this point, `cout` sends all output to the screen.

The format of the `cout` is different from those of other C++ commands. The format for `cout` is

```
cout << data [ << data ];
```

The *data* placeholder can be variables, literals, expressions, or a combination of all three.

Printing Strings

To print a string constant, simply type the string constant after the `cout` operator. For example, to print the string, The rain in Spain, you would simply type this:

Print the sentence "The rain in Spain" to the screen.

```
cout << "The rain in Spain";
```

You must remember, however, that `cout` does not perform an automatic carriage return. This means the screen's cursor appears directly after the last printed character and subsequent `cout`s begin thereafter.

To better understand this concept, try to predict the output from the following three `cout` operators:

```
cout << "Line 1";
cout << "Line 2";
cout << "Line 3";
```

These operators produce the following output:

```
Line 1Line 2Line 3
```

which is probably not what you intended. Therefore, you must include the newline character, \n, whenever you want to move the cursor to the next line. The following three cout operators produce a three-line output:

```
cout << "Line 1\n";
cout << "Line 2\n";
cout << "Line 3\n";
```

The output from these couts is

```
Line 1
Line 2
Line 3
```

The \n character sends the cursor to the next line no matter where you insert it. The following three cout operators also produce the correct three-line output:

```
cout << "Line 1";
cout << "\nLine 2\n";
cout "Line 3";
```

The second cout prints a newline before it prints anything else. It then prints its string followed by another newline. The third string prints on the third line.

You also can print strings stored in character arrays by typing the array name inside the cout. If you were to store your name in an array defined as:

```
char my_name[ ] = "Lyndon Harris";
```

you could print the name with the following cout:

```
cout << my_name;
```

The following section of code prints three string literals on three different lines:

```
cout << "Nancy Carson\n";
cout << "1213 Oak Street\n";
cout << "Fairbanks, Alaska\n";
```

The cout is often used to label output. Before printing an age, amount, salary, or any other numeric data, you should print a string constant that tells the user what the number means. The following cout tells the user that the next number printed is an age. Without this cout, the user would not know what the number represented.

```
cout << "Here is the age that was found in our files:";
```

You can print a blank line by printing two newline characters, \n, next to each other after your string, as in:

```
cout << "Prepare the invoices...\n\n";
```

Examples

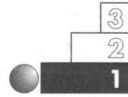

1. The following program stores a few values in three variables, then prints the results:

```
// Filename: C7PRNT1.CPP
// Prints values in variables.

#include <iostream.h>

main()
{
  char first = 'E';      // Store some character, integer,
  char middle = 'W';      // and floating-point variable.
  char last = 'C';
  int age = 32;
  int dependents = 2;
  float salary = 25000.00;
  float bonus = 575.25;

  // Prints the results.
  cout << first << middle << last;
```

```
    cout << age << dependents;
    cout << salary << bonus;
    return 0;
}
```

2. The last program does not help the user. The output is not labeled, and it prints on a single line. Here is the same program with a few messages included and some newline characters placed where needed:

```
// Filename: C7PRNT2.CPP
// Prints values in variables with appropriate labels.

#include <iostream.h>

main()
{
    char first = 'E';        // Store some character, integer,
    char middle = 'W';        // and floating-point variable.
    char last = 'C';
    int age = 32;
    int dependents = 2;
    float salary = 25000.00;
    float bonus = 575.25;

    // Prints the results.
    cout << "Here are the initials:\n";
    cout << first << middle << last <<"\n";
    cout << "The age and number of dependents are\n";
    cout << age << "    " << dependents << "\n\n";
    cout << "The salary and bonus are\n";
    cout << salary << ' ' << bonus;
    return 0;
}
```

The output from this program appears below:

```
Here are the initials:
EWC
The age and number of dependents are
32    2
```

```
The salary and bonus are
25000 575.25
```

The first floating-point values do not print with zeros, but the number is correct. The next section shows you how to set the number of leading and trailing zeros.

3. If you have to print a table of numbers, you can use the \t tab character to do so. Place the tab character between each of the printed numbers. The following program prints a list of team names and number of hits for the first three weeks of the season:

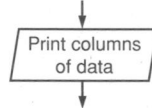

Print columns of data

```
// Filename: C7TEAM.CPP
// Prints a table of team names and hits for three weeks.

#include <iostream.h>

main()
{
   cout << "Parrots\tRams\tKings\tTitans\tChargers\n";
   cout << "3\t5\t3\t1\t0\n";
   cout << "2\t5\t1\t0\t1\n";
   cout << "2\t6\t4\t3\t0\n";
   return 0;
}
```

This program produces the table shown below. You can see that even though the names are different widths, the numbers print correctly beneath them. The \t character forces the next name or value to the next tab position (every eight characters).

Parrots	Rams	Kings	Titans	Chargers
3	5	3	1	0
2	5	1	0	1
2	6	4	3	0

Control Operators

You have already seen the need for additional program-output control. All floating-point numbers print with too many decimal places for most applications. What if you want to print only dollars and cents (two decimal places), or print an average with a single decimal place?

You can specify how many print positions to use in printing a number. For example, the following cout prints the number 456, using three positions (the length of the data):

```
cout << 456;
```

If the 456 were stored in an integer variable, it would still use three positions to print because the number of digits printed is three. However, you can specify how many positions to print. The following cout prints the number 456 in five positions (with two leading spaces):

```
cout << setw(5) << setfill(' ') << 456;
```

You typically use the setw manipulator when you want to print data in uniform columns. Be sure to include the iomanip.h header file in any programs that use manipulators because iomanip.h describes how the setw works to the compiler.

The following program shows you the importance of the width number. Each cout output is described in the comment to its left.

```
// Filename: C7MOD1.CPP
// Illustrates various integer width cout modifiers.

#include <iostream.h>
#include <iomanip.h>

main()
{                                   // The output appears below.
   cout << 456 << 456 << 456 << "\n";   // Prints 456456456
   cout << setw(5) << 456 << setw(5) << 456 << setw(5) <<
        456 << "\n";                // Prints 456  456  456
   cout << setw(7) << 456 << setw(7) << 456 << setw(7) <<
        456 << " \n";         // Prints 456    456    456
   return 0;
}
```

When you use a `setw` manipulator inside a conversion character, C++ right-justifies the number by the width you specify. When you specify an eight-digit width, C++ prints a value inside those eight digits, padding the number with leading blanks if the number does not fill the whole width.

> **NOTE:** If you do not specify a width large enough to hold the number, C++ ignores your width request and prints the number in its entirety.

You can control the width of strings in the same manner with the `setw` manipulator. If you don't specify enough width to output the full string, C++ ignores the width. The mailing list application in the back of this book uses this technique to print names on mailing labels.

> **NOTE:** `setw()` becomes more important when you print floating-point numbers.

`setprecision(2)` prints a floating-point number with two decimal places. If C++ has to round the fractional part, it does so. The following `cout`:

```
cout << setw(6) << setprecision(2) << 134.568767;
```

produces the following output:

```
134.57
```

Without the `setw` or `setprecision` manipulators, C++ would have printed:

```
134.568767
```

> **TIP:** When printing floating-point numbers, C++ always prints the entire portion to the left of the decimal (to maintain as much accuracy as possible) no matter how many positions you specify. Therefore, many C++ programmers ignore the `setw` manipulator for floating-point numbers and only specify the precision, as in `setprecision(2)`.

Examples

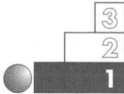

1. If you want to control the width of your data, use a `setw` manipulator. The following program is a revision of the C7TEAM.CPP shown earlier. Instead of using the tab character, `\t`, which is limited to eight spaces, this program uses the width specifier to set the tabs. It ensures that each column is 10 characters wide.

```
// Filename: C7TEAMMD.CPP
// Prints a table of team names and hits for three weeks
// using width-modifying conversion characters.

#include <iostream.h>
#include <iomanip.h>

main()
{
  cout << setw(10) << "Parrots" << setw(10) <<
        "Rams" << setw(10) << "Kings" << setw(10) <<
        "Titans" << setw(10) << "Chargers" << "\n";
  cout << setw(10) << 3 << setw(10) << 5 <<
          setw(10) << 2 << setw(10) << 1 <<
          setw(10) << 0 << "\n";
  cout << setw(10) << 2 << setw(10) << 5 <<
          setw(10) << 1 << setw(10) << 0 <<
          setw(10) << 1 << "\n";
  cout << setw(10) << 2 << setw(10) << 6 <<
          setw(10) << 4 << setw(10) << 3 <<
          setw(10) << 0 << "\n";
  return 0;
}
```

2. The following program is a payroll program. The output is in "dollars and cents" because the dollar amounts print properly to two decimal places.

```
// Filename: C7PAY1.CPP
// Computes and prints payroll data properly in dollars
// and cents.
```

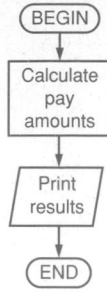

```
#include <iostream.h>
#include <iomanip.h>

main()
{
  char emp_name[ ] = "Larry Payton";
  char pay_date[ ] = "03/09/92";
  int hours_worked = 43;
  float rate = 7.75;          // Pay per hour
  float tax_rate = .32;       // Tax percentage rate
  float gross_pay, taxes, net_pay;

  // Computes the pay amount.
  gross_pay = hours_worked * rate;
  taxes = tax_rate * gross_pay;
  net_pay = gross_pay - taxes;

  // Prints the results.
  cout << "As of: " << pay_date << "\n";
  cout << emp_name << " worked " << hours_worked <<
       " hours\n";
  cout << "and got paid " << setw(2) << setprecision(2)
       << gross_pay << "\n";
  cout << "After taxes of: " << setw(6) << setprecision(2)
       << taxes << "\n";
  cout << "his take-home pay was $" << setw(8) <<
          setprecision(2) << net_pay << "\n";
  return 0;
}
```

The output from this program follows. Remember that the floating-point variables still hold the full precision (to six decimal places), as they did in the previous program. The modifying setw manipulators only affect how the variables are output, not what is stored in them.

```
As of: 03/09/92
Larry Payton worked 43 hours
and got paid 333.25
After taxes of: 106.64
his take-home pay was $226.61
```

3. Most C++ programmers do not use the setw manipulator when printing dollars and cents. Here is the payroll program again that uses the shortcut floating-point width method. Notice the previous three cout statements include no setw manipulator. C++ automatically prints the full number to the left of the decimal and prints only two places to the right.

```cpp
// Filename: C7PAY2.CPP
// Computes and prints payroll data properly
// using the shortcut modifier.

#include <iostream.h>
#include <iomanip.h>

main()
{
  char emp_name[ ] = "Larry Payton";
  char pay_date[ ] = "03/09/92";
  int hours_worked = 43;
  float rate = 7.75;          // Pay per hour
  float tax_rate = .32;       // Tax percentage rate
  float gross_pay, taxes, net_pay;

  // Computes the pay amount.
  gross_pay = hours_worked * rate;
  taxes = tax_rate * gross_pay;
  net_pay = gross_pay - taxes;

  // Prints the results.
  cout << "As of: " << pay_date << "\n";
  cout << emp_name << " worked " << hours_worked <<
          " hours\n";
  cout << "and got paid " << setprecision(2) << gross_pay
          << "\n";
  cout << "After taxes of: " << setprecision(2) << taxes
          << "\n";
  cout << "his take-home pay was " << setprecision(2) <<
          net_pay << "\n";
  return 0;
}
```

This program's output is the same as the previous program's.

The cin Operator

You now understand how C++ represents data and variables, and you know how to print the data. There is one additional part of programming you have not seen: inputting data to your programs.

Until this point, you have not inputted data into a program. All data you worked with was assigned to variables in the program. However, this is not always the best way to transfer data to your programs; you rarely know what your data is when you write your programs. The data is known only when you run the programs (or another user runs them).

The cin operator stores keyboard input in variables.

The cin operator is one way to input from the keyboard. When your programs reach the line with a cin, the user can enter values directly into variables. Your program can then process those variables and produce output. Figure 7.1 illustrates the difference between cout and cin.

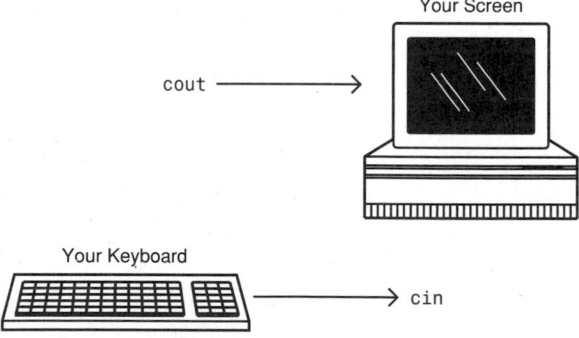

Figure 7.1. The actions of cout and cin.

The cin Function Fills Variables with Values

There is a major difference between cin and the assignment statements (such as i = 17;). Both fill variables with values. However, the assignment statement assigned specific values to variables at programming time. When you run a program with assignment statements, you know from the program's listing exactly what values go into the variables because you wrote the program specifically to store those values. Every time you run the program, the results are exactly the same because the same values are *assigned* to the same variables.

You have no idea, when you write programs that use cin, what values will be assigned to the cin's variables because their values are not known until the program runs and the user enters those values. This means you have a more flexible program that can be used by a variety of people. Every time the program is run, different results are created, depending on the values typed at each cin in the program.

The cin has its drawbacks. Therefore, in the next few chapters you will use cin until you learn more powerful (and flexible) input methods. The cin operator looks much like cout. It contains one or more variables that appear to the right of the operator name. The format of the cin is

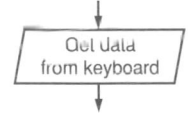

Get data
from keyboard

```
cin >> value [>> values];
```

The iostream.h header file contains the information C++ needs to use cin, so include it when using cin.

NOTE: The cin operator uses the same manipulators (setw and setprecision) as the cout operator.

As mentioned earlier, cin poses a few problems. The cin operator requires that your user type the input *exactly* as cin expects it. Because you cannot control the user's typing, this cannot be ensured. You might want the user to enter an integer value followed by a floating-point value and your `cin` operator call might expect it too, but your user might decide to enter something else! If this happens, there is not much you can do because the resulting input is incorrect and your C++ program has no reliable method for testing user accuracy. Before every `cin`, print a prompt that explains exactly what you expect the user to type.

The `cin` operator requires that the user type correct input. This is not always possible to guarantee!

For the next few chapters, you can assume that the user knows to enter the proper values, but for your "real" programs, read on for better methods to receive input, starting with Chapter 21, "Device and Character Input/Output."

Examples

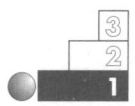

1. If you wanted a program that computed a seven percent sales tax, you could use the `cin` statement to figure the sales, compute the tax, and print the results as the following program shows:

```
// Filename: C7SLTX1.CPP
// Prompt for a sales amount and print the sales tax.

#include <iostream.h>
#include <iomanip.h>

main()
{
  float total_sale;     // User's sale amount goes here.
  float stax;

  // Display a message for the user.
  cout << "What is the total amount of the sale? ";

  // Receive the sales amount from user.
  cin >> total_sale;

  // Calculate sales tax.
  stax = total_sale * .07;
```

BEGIN

Prompt for
sale amount

Get amount
from keyboard

Calculate
sales tax

Print
sales
tax

END

```
cout << "The sales tax for " << setprecision(2) <<
        total_sale << " is " << setprecision (2) << stax;
return 0;
}
```

Because the first `cout` does not contain a newline character, `\n`, the user's response to the prompt appears to the right of the question mark.

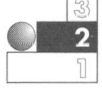

2. When inputting keyboard strings into character arrays with `cin`, you are limited to receiving one word at a time. The `cin` does not enable you to type more than one word in a single character array at a time. The following program asks the user for his or her first and last name. The program has to store those two names in two different character arrays because `cin` cannot input both names at once. The program then prints the names in reverse order.

```
// Filename: C7PHON1.CPP
// Program that requests the user's name and prints it
// to the screen as it would appear in a phone book.

#include <iostream.h>
#include <iomanip.h>

main()
{
  char first[20], last[20];

  cout << "What is your first name? ";
  cin >> first;
  cout << "What is your last name? ";
  cin >> last;
  cout << "\n\n";        // Prints two blank lines.
  cout << "In a phone book, your name would look like this:\n";
  cout << last << ", " << first;
  return 0;
}
```

3. Suppose you want to write a program that does simple addition for your seven-year-old daughter. The following program prompts her for two numbers. The program then waits for her to type an answer. When she gives her answer, the program displays the correct result so she can see how well she did.

```cpp
// Filename: C7MATH.CPP
// Program to help children with simple addition.
// Prompt child for two values after printing
// a title message.
#include <iostream.h>
#include <iomanip.h>

main()
{
  int num1, num2, ans;
  int her_ans;

  cout << "*** Math Practice ***\n\n\n";
  cout << "What is the first number? ";
  cin >> num1;
  cout << "What is the second number? ";
  cin >> num2;

  // Compute answer and give her a chance to wait for it.
  ans = num1 + num2;

  cout << "\nWhat do you think is the answer? ";
  cin >> her_ans;     // Nothing is done with this.

  // Prints answer after a blank line.
  cout << "\n" << num1 << " plus " << num2 << " is "
       << ans << "\n\nHope you got it right!";
  return 0;
}
```

printf() **and** scanf()

Before C++, C programmers had to rely on function calls to perform input and output. Two of those functions, printf() and scanf(), are still used frequently in C++ programs, although cout and cin have advantages over them. printf() (like cout) prints values to the screen and scanf() (like cin) inputs values from the keyboard. printf() requires a controlling format string that describes the data you want to print. Likewise, scanf() requires a controlling format string that describes the data the program wants to receive from the keyboard.

> **NOTE:** cout is the C++ replacement to printf() and cin is the C++ replacement to scanf().

Because you are concentrating on C++, this chapter only briefly covers printf() and scanf(). Throughout this book, a handful of programs use these functions to keep you familiar with their format. printf() and scanf() are not obsolete in C++, but their use will diminish dramatically when programmers move away from C and to C++. cout and cin do not require controlling strings that describe their data; cout and cin are intelligent enough to know how to treat data. Both printf() and scanf() are limited—especially scanf()—but they do enable your programs to send output and to receive input.

The printf() **Function**

The printf() function sends output to the screen.

printf() sends data to the standard output device, which is generally the screen. The format of printf() is different from those of regular C++ commands. The values that go inside the parentheses vary, depending on the data you are printing. However, as a general rule, the following printf() format holds true:

```
printf(control_string [, one or more values]);
```

Notice printf() always requires a *control_string*. This is a string, or a character array containing a string, that determines how the rest of the values (if any are listed) print. These values can be variables, literals, expressions, or a combination of all three.

> **TIP:** Despite its name, `printf()` sends output to the screen and not to the printer.

The easiest data to print with `printf()` are strings. To print a string constant, you simply type that string constant inside the `printf()` function. For example, to print the string The rain in Spain, you would simply type the following:

Print the phrase `"The rain in Spain"` *to the screen.*

```
printf("The rain in Spain");
```

`printf()`, like `cout`, does *not* perform an automatic carriage return. Subsequent `printf()`s begin next to that last printed character. If you want a carriage return, you must supply a newline character, as so:

```
printf("The rain in Spain\n");
```

You can print strings stored in character arrays also by typing the array name inside the `printf()`. For example, if you were to store your name in an array defined as:

```
char my_name[] = "Lyndon Harris";
```

you could print the name with this `printf()`:

```
printf(my_name);
```

You must include the stdio.h header file when using `printf()` and `scanf()` because stdio.h determines how the input and output functions work in the compiler. The following program assigns a message in a character array, then prints that message.

```
// Filename: C7PS2.CPP
// Prints a string stored in a character array.
#include <stdio.h>
main()
{
   char message[] = "Please turn on your printer";
   printf(message);
   return 0;
}
```

Conversion Characters

Inside most `printf()` control strings are *conversion characters*. These special characters tell `printf()` exactly how the data (following the characters) are to be interpreted. Table 7.1 shows a list of common conversion characters. Because any type of data can go inside the `printf()`'s parentheses, these conversion characters are required any time you print more than a single string constant. If you don't want to print a string, the string constant must contain at least one of the conversion characters.

Table 7.1. Common `printf()` conversion characters.

Conversion Character	Output
%s	String of characters (until null zero is reached)
%c	Character
%d	Decimal integer
%f	Floating-point numbers
%u	Unsigned integer
%x	Hexadecimal integer
%%	Prints a percent sign (%)

Note: You can insert an 1 (lowercase 1) or L before the integer and floating-point conversion characters (such as %1d and %Lf) to indicate that a long integer or long double floating-point is to be printed.

NOTE: Characters other than those shown in the table print exactly as they appear in the control string.

When you want to print a numeric constant or variable, you must include the proper conversion character inside the `printf()` control string. If i, j, and k are integer variables, you cannot print them with the `printf()` that follows.

```
printf(i,j,k);
```

Because `printf()` is a function and not a command, this `printf()` function has no way of knowing what type the variables are. The results are unpredictable, and you might see garbage on your screen—if anything appears at all.

When you print numbers, you must first print a control string that includes the format of those numbers. The following `printf()` prints a string. In the output from this line, a string appears with an integer (`%d`) and a floating-point number (`%f`) printed inside that string.

```
printf("I am Betty, I am %d years old, and I make %f\n",
       35, 34050.25);
```

This produces the following output:

```
I am Betty, I am 35 years old, and I make 34050.25
```

Figure 7.2 shows how C interprets the control string and the variables that follow. Be sure you understand this example before moving on. It is the foundation of the `printf()` function.

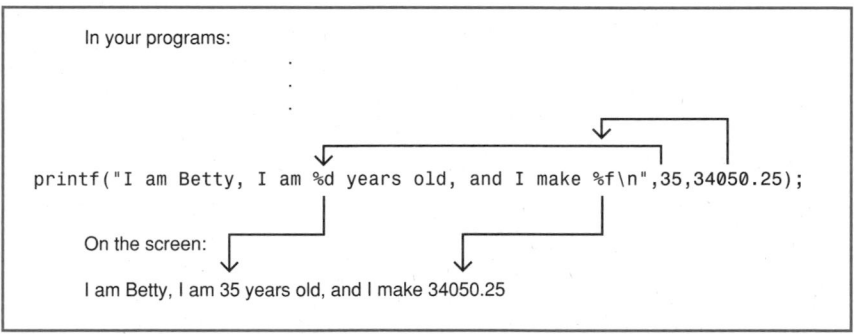

Figure 7.2. **Control string in action.**

You also can print integer and floating-point variables in the same manner.

Examples

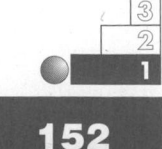

1. The following program stores a few values in three variables, then prints the results.

```
// Filename: C7PRNTF.CPP
// Prints values in variables with appropriate labels.
#include <stdio.h>

main()
{
    char first='E';          // Store some character, integer,
    char middle='W';         // and floating-point variable.
    char last='C';
    int age=32;
    int dependents=2;
    float salary=25000.00;
    float bonus=575.25;

    /* Prints the results. */
    printf("Here are the initials\n");
    printf("%c%o%c\n\n", first, middle, last);
    printf("The age and number of dependents are\n");
    printf("%d   %d\n\n", age, dependents);
    printf("The salary and bonus are\n");
    printf("%f %f", salary, bonus);
    return 0;
}
```

The output from this program is

```
Here are the initials
EWC

The age and number of dependents are
32    2

The salary and bonus are
25000.000000 575.250000
```

2. The floating-point values print with too many zeros, of course, but the numbers are correct. You can limit the number of leading and trailing zeros that is printed by adding a width specifier in the control string. For instance, the following `printf()` prints the salary and bonus with two decimal places:

```
printf("%.2f %.2f", salary, bonus);
```

Make sure your printed values match the control string supplied with them. The `printf()` function cannot fix problems resulting from mismatched values and control strings. Don't try to print floating-point values with character-string control codes. If you list five integer variables in a `printf()`, be sure to include five `%d` conversion characters in the `printf()` as well.

Printing ASCII Values

There is one exception to the rule of printing with matching conversion characters. If you want to print the ASCII value of a character, you can print that character (whether it is a constant or a variable) with the integer `%d` conversion character. Instead of printing the character, `printf()` prints the matching ASCII number for that character.

Conversely, if you print an integer with a `%c` conversion character, you see the character that matches that integer's value from the ASCII table.

The following `printf()`s illustrate this fact:

```
printf("%c", 65);  // Prints the letter A.
printf("%d", 'A'); // Prints the number 65.
```

The `scanf()` Function

The `scanf()` function stores keyboard input to variables.

The `scanf()` function reads input from the keyboard. When your programs reach the line with a `scanf()`, the user can enter values directly into variables. Your program can then process the variables and produce output.

The `scanf()` function looks much like `printf()`. It contains a control string and one or more variables to the right of the control string. The control string informs C++ exactly what the incoming keyboard values look like, and what their types are. The format of `scanf()` is

```
scanf(control_string, one or more values);
```

The scanf() control_string uses almost the same conversion characters as the printf() control_string, with two slight differences. You should never include the newline character, \n, in a scanf() control string. The scanf() function "knows" when the input is finished when the user presses Enter. If you supply an additional newline code, scanf() might not terminate properly. Also, always put a beginning space inside every scanf() control string. This does not affect the user's input, but scanf() sometimes requires it to work properly. Later examples in this chapter clarify this fact.

The scanf() function requires that your user type accurately. This is not always possible to guarantee!

As mentioned earlier, scanf() poses a few problems. The scanf() function requires that your user type the input exactly the way control_string specifies. Because you cannot control your user's typing, this cannot always be ensured. For example, you might want the user to enter an integer value followed by a floating-point value (your scanf() control string might expect it too), but your user might decide to enter something else! If this happens, there is not much you can do. The resulting input is incorrect, but your C program has no reliable method for testing user accuracy before your program is run.

> **CAUTION:** The user's keyboard input values *must* match, in number and type, the control string contained in each scanf().

Another problem with scanf() is not as easy for beginners to understand as the last. The scanf() function requires that you use pointer variables, not regular variables, in its parentheses. Although this sounds complicated, it doesn't have to be. You should have no problem with scanf()'s pointer requirements if you remember these two simple rules:

1. Always put an ampersand (&) before variable names inside a scanf().

2. Never put an ampersand (&) before an array name inside a scanf().

Despite these strange scanf() rules, you can learn this function quickly by looking at a few examples.

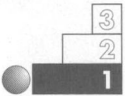

Examples

1. If you want a program that computes a seven percent sales tax, you could use the `scanf()` statement to receive the sales, compute the tax, and print the results as the following program shows.

```
// Filename: C7SLTXS.CPP
// Compute a sales amount and print the sales tax.
#include <stdio.h>
main()
{
   float total_sale;    // User's sale amount goes here.
   float stax;

   // Display a message for the user.
   printf("What is the total amount of the sale? ");

   // Compute the sales amount from user.
   scanf(" %f", &total_sale);    // Don't forget the beginning
                                 // space and an &.

   stax = total_sale * .07;  // Calculate the sales tax.

   printf("The sales tax for %.2f is %.2f", total_sale, stax);
   return 0;
}
```

If you run this program, the program waits for you to enter a value for the total sale. Remember to use the ampersand in front of the `total_sale` variable when you enter it in the `scanf()` function. After pressing the Enter key, the program calculates the sales tax and prints the results.

If you entered 10.00 as the sale amount, you would receive the following output :

```
The sales tax for 10.00 is 0.70
```

2. Use the string `%s` conversion character to input keyboard strings into character arrays with `scanf()`. As with `cin`, you are limited to inputting one word at a time, because you

cannot type more than one word into a single character array with scanf(). The following program is similar to C7PHON1.CPP except the scanf() function, rather than cin, is used. It must store two names in two different character arrays, because scanf() cannot input both names at once. The program then prints the names in reverse order.

```
// Filename: C7PHON2.CPP
// Program that requests the user's name and prints it
// to the screen as it would appear in a phone book.
#include <stdio.h>
main()
{
    char first[20], last[20];
    printf("What is your first name? ");
    scanf(" %s", first);
    printf("What is your last name? ");
    scanf(" %s", last);
    printf("\n\n");    // Prints two blank lines.
    printf("In a phone book, your name would look like"
            "this:\n");
    printf("%s, %s", last, first);
    return 0;
}
```

3. How many values are entered with the following scanf(), and what are their types?

```
scanf(" %d %d %f %s", &i, &j, &k, l);
```

Review Questions

The answers to the Review Questions are in Appendix B.

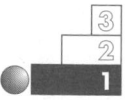

1. What is the difference between cout and cin?

2. Why is a prompt message important before using cin for input?

3. How many values do you enter with the following `cin`?

```
cin >> i >> j >> k >> l;
```

4. Because they both assign values to variables, is there any difference between assigning values to variables and using `cin` to give them values?

5. True or false: The `%s` conversion character is usually not required in `printf()` control strings.

6. Which types of variables do not require the ampersand (&) character in `scanf()` functions?

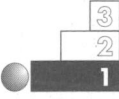

7. What is the output produced by the following `cout`?

```
cout << "The backslash \"\\\" character is special";
```

8. What is the result of the following `cout`?

```
cout << setw(8) << setprecision(3) << 123.456789;
```

Review Exercises

1. Write a program that prompts the user for his or her name and weight. Store these values in separate variables and print them on-screen.

2. Assume you are a college professor and have to average grades for 10 students. Write a program that prompts you for 10 different grades, then displays an average of them.

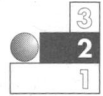

3. Modify the program in Exercise 2 to ask for each student's name as well as her grade. Print the grade list to the screen, with each student's name and grade in two columns. Make sure the columns align by using a `setw` manipulator on the grade. At the bottom, print the average of the grades. (*Hint:* Store the 10 names and 10 grades in different variables with different names.) This program is easy, but takes thirty or so lines, plus appropriate comments and prompts. Later, you learn ways to streamline this program.

4. This exercise tests your understanding of the backslash conversion character: Write a program that uses cout operators to produce the following picture on-screen:

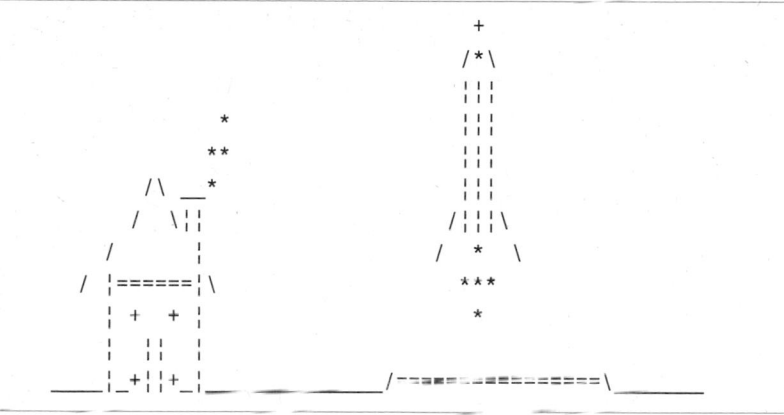

Summary

You now can print almost anything to the screen. By studying the manipulators and how they behave, you can control your output more thoroughly than ever before. Also, because you can receive keyboard values, your programs are much more powerful. No longer do you have to know your data values when you write the program. You can ask the user to enter values into variables with cin.

You have the tools to begin writing programs that fit the data processing model of INPUT->PROCESS->OUTPUT. This chapter concludes the preliminary discussion of the C++ language. This part of the book attempted to give you an overview of the language and to teach you enough of the language elements so you can begin writing helpful programs.

Chapter 8, "Using C++ Math Operators and Precedence," begins a new type of discussion. You learn how C++'s math and relational operators work on data, and the importance of the precedence table of operators.

Part II

Using C++ Operators

Using C++ Math Operators and Precedence

If you are dreading this chapter because you don't like math—relax, C++ does all your math for you! It is a misconception that you have to be good at math to understand how to program computers. In fact, programming practice assumes the opposite is true! Your computer is your "slave," to follow your instructions, and to do all the calculations for you. This chapter explains how C++ computes by introducing you to

♦ Primary math operators

♦ Order of operator precedence

♦ Assignment statements

♦ Mixed data type calculations

♦ Type casting

Many people who dislike math actually enjoy learning how the computer handles it. After learning the math operators and a few simple ways in which C++ uses them, you should feel comfortable using calculations in your programs. Computers are fast, and they can perform math operations much faster than you can!

C++'s Primary Math Operators

A C++ *math operator* is a symbol used for adding, subtracting, multiplying, dividing, and other operations. C++ operators are not always mathematical in nature, but many are. Table 8.1 lists these operator symbols and their primary meanings.

Table 8.1. C++ primary operators.

Symbol	Meaning
*	Multiplication
/	Division and Integer Division
%	Modulus or Remainder
+	Addition
-	Subtraction

Most of these operators work in the familiar way you expect them to. Multiplication, addition, and subtraction produce the same results (and the division operator *usually* does) as those produced with a calculator. Table 8.2 illustrates four of these simple operators.

Table 8.2. Typical operator results.

Formula	Result
4 * 2	8
64 / 4	16
80 - 15	65
12 + 9	21

Table 8.2 contains examples of *binary operations* performed with the four operators. Don't confuse binary operations with *binary numbers.* When an operator is used between two literals, variables, or a combination of both, it is called a *binary operator* because it operates using two values. When you use these operators (when assigning their results to variables, for example), it does not matter in C++ whether you add spaces to the operators or not.

> **CAUTION:** For multiplication, use the asterisk (*), *not* an x as you might normally do. An x cannot be used as the multiplication sign because C++ uses x as a variable name. C++ interprets x as the value of a variable called x.

The Unary Operators

A *unary operator* operates on, or affects, a single value. For instance, you can assign a variable a positive or negative number by using a unary + or –.

Examples

1. The following section of code assigns four variables a positive or a negative number. The plus and minus signs are all unary because they are not used between two values.

The variable a is assigned a negative 25 value.
The variable b is assigned a positive 25 value.
The variable c is assigned a negative a value.
The variable d is assigned a positive b value.

```
a = -25;// Assign 'a' a negative 25.
b = +25;// Assign 'b' a positive 25 (+ is not needed).
c = -a; // Assign 'c' the negative of 'a' (-25).
d = +b; // Assign 'd' the positive of 'b' (25, + not needed).
```

2. You generally do not have to use the unary plus sign. C++ assumes a number or variable is positive, even if it has no plus sign. The following four statements are equivalent to the previous four, except they do not contain plus signs.

```
a = -25;   // Assign 'a' a negative 25.
b =  25;   // Assign 'b' a positive 25.
c = -a;    // Assign 'c' the negative of 'a' (-25).
d =  b;    // Assign 'd' the positive of 'b' (25).
```

3. The unary negative comes in handy when you want to negate a single number or variable. The negative of a negative is positive. Therefore, the following short program assigns a negative number (using the unary –) to a variable, then prints the negative of that same variable. Because it had a negative number to begin with, the cout produces a positive result.

```
// Filename: C8NEG.CPP
// The negative of a variable that contains a negative value.
#include <iostream.h>
main()
{
    signed int temp=-12;   // 'signed' is not needed because
                           //      it is the default.
    cout << -temp << "\n"; // Produces a 12 on-screen.

    return 0;
}
```

The variable declaration does not need the *signed* prefix, because all integer variables are signed by default.

4. If you want to subtract the negative of a variable, make sure you put a space before the unary minus sign. For example, the following line:

```
new_temp + new_temp- -inversion_factor;
```

temporarily negates the inversion_factor and subtracts that negated value from new_temp.

Division and Modulus

The division sign, /, and the modulus operator, %, might behave in ways unfamiliar to you. They're as easy to use, however, as the other operators you have just seen.

The modulus (%) computes remainders in division.

The forward slash (/) is always used for division. However, it produces an integer called divide if integer values (literals, variables, or a combination of both) appear on both sides of the slash. If there is a remainder, C++ discards it.

The percent sign (%) produces a *modulus*, or a *remainder*, of an integer division. It requires that integers be on both sides of the symbol, or it does not work.

Examples

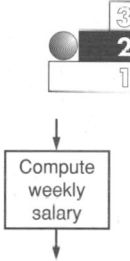

Compute weekly salary

1. Suppose you want to compute your weekly pay. The following program asks for your yearly pay, divides it by 52, and prints the results to two decimal places.

```
// Filename: C8DIV.CPP
// Displays user's weekly pay.
#include <stdio.h>
main()
{
   float weekly, yearly;
   printf("What is your annual pay? ");  // Prompt user.
   scanf("%f", &yearly);

   weekly = yearly/52;   // Computes the weekly pay.
   printf("\n\nYour weekly pay is $%.2f", weekly);
   return 0;
}
```

Because a floating-point number is used in the division, C++ produces a floating-point result. Here is a sample output from such a program:

```
What is your annual pay? 38000.00
Your weekly pay is $730.77
```

Because this program used `scanf()` and `printf()` (to keep you familiar with both ways of performing input and output), the stdio.h header file is included rather than iostream.h.

2. Integer division does not round its results. If you divide two integers and the answer is not a whole number, C++ ignores the fractional part. The following `printf()`s help show this. The output that results from each `printf()` appears in the comment to the right of each line.

```
printf("%d \n", 10/2);      // 5  (no remainder)
printf("%d \n", 300/100);   // 3  (no remainder)
printf("%d \n", 10/3);      // 3  (discarded remainder)
printf("%d \n", 300/165);   // 1  (discarded remainder)
```

The Order of Precedence

Understanding the math operators is the first of two steps toward understanding C++ calculations. You must also understand the *order of precedence*. The order of precedence (sometimes called the *math hierarchy* or *order of operators*) determines exactly how C++ computes formulas. The precedence of operators is exactly the same concept you learned in high school algebra courses. (Don't worry, this is the easy part of algebra!) To see how the order of precedence works, try to determine the result of the following simple calculation:

```
2 + 3 * 2
```

If you said 10, you are not alone; many people respond with 10. However, 10 is correct only if you interpret the formula from the left. What if you calculated the multiplication first? If you took the value of `3 * 2` and got an answer of 6, then added the 2, you receive an answer of 8—which is exactly the same answer that C++ computes (and happens to be the correct way)!

C++ performs multiplication, division, and modulus *before* addition and subtraction.

C++ always performs multiplication, division, and modulus first, then addition and subtraction. Table 8.3 shows the order of the operators you have seen so far. Of course, there are many more levels to C++'s precedence table of operators than the ones shown in Table 8.3. Unlike most computer languages, C++ has 20 levels of precedence. Appendix D, "C++ Precedence Table," contains the complete precedence table. Notice in this appendix that multiplication, division, and modulus reside on level 8, one level higher than level 9's addition and subtraction. In the next few chapters, you learn how to use the remainder of this precedence table in your C++ programs.

Table 8.3. Order of precedence for primary operators.

Order	Operator
First	Multiplication, division, modulus remainder (*, /, %)
Second	Addition, subtraction (+, -)

Examples

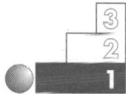

1. It is easy to follow C++'s order of operators if you follow the intermediate results one at a time. The three calculations in Figure 8.1 show you how to do this.

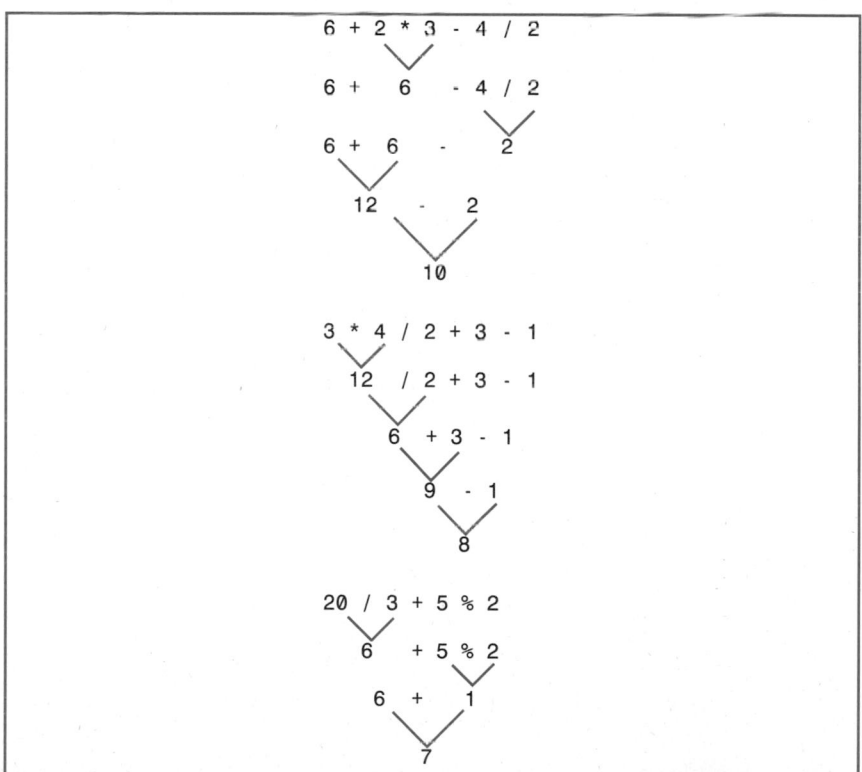

Figure 8.1. C++'s order of operators with lines indicating precedence.

2. Looking back at the order of precedence table, you might notice that multiplication, division, and modulus are on the same level. This implies there is no hierarchy on that level. If more than one of these operators appear in a calculation, C++ performs the math from the left. The same is true of addition and subtraction—C++ performs the operation on the extreme left first.

Figure 8.2 illustrates an example showing this process.

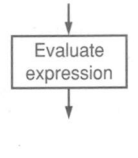

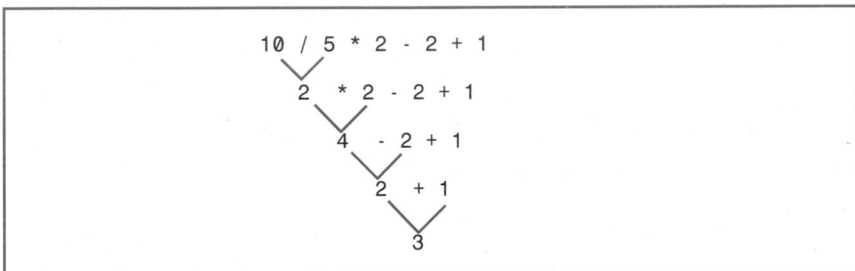

Figure 8.2. C++'s order of operators from the left, with lines indicating precedence.

Because the division appears to the left of the multiplication, it is computed first.

You now should be able to follow the order of these C++ operators. You don't have to worry about the math because C++ does the actual work. However, you should understand this order of operators so you know how to structure your calculations. Now that you have mastered this order, it's time to learn how you can override it with parentheses!

Using Parentheses

If you want to override the order of precedence, you can add parentheses to the calculation. The parentheses actually reside on a level above the multiplication, division, and modulus in the precedence table. In other words, any calculation in parentheses—whether it is addition, subtraction, division, or whatever—is always calculated before the rest of the line. The other calculations are then performed in their normal operator order.

Parentheses override the usual order of math.

The first formula in this chapter, 2 + 3 * 2, produced an 8 because the multiplication was performed before addition. However, by adding parentheses around the addition, as in (2 + 3) * 2, the answer becomes 10.

In the precedence table shown in Appendix D, "C++ Precedence Table," the parentheses reside on level 3. Because they are higher than the other levels, the parentheses take precedence over multiplication, division, and all other operators.

Examples

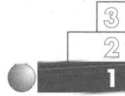

1. The calculations shown in Figure 8.3 illustrate how parentheses override the regular order of operators. These are the same three formulas shown in the previous section, but their results are calculated differently because the parentheses override the normal order of operators.

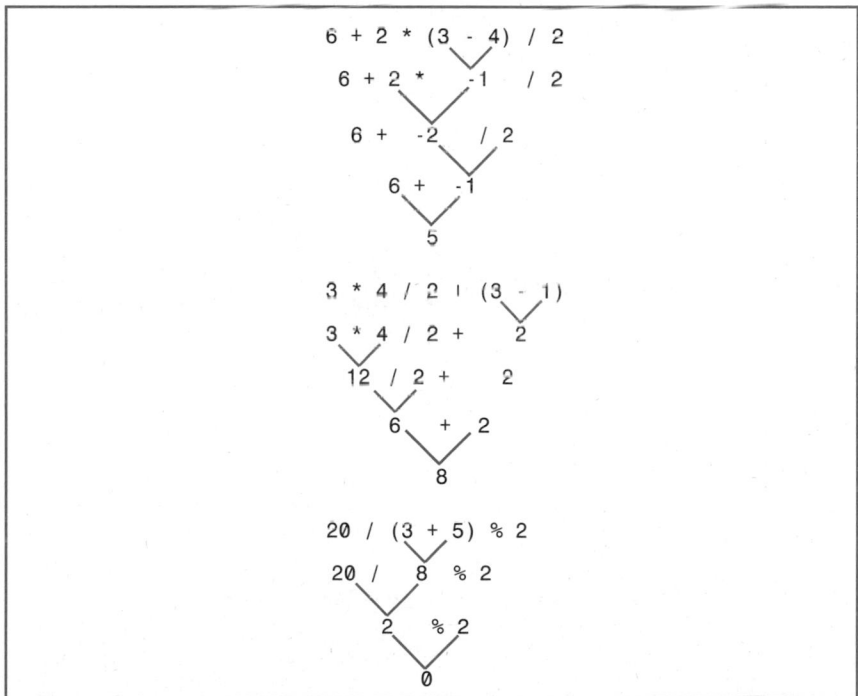

Figure 8.3. Example of parentheses as the highest precedence level with lines indicating precedence.

2. If an expression contains parentheses-within-parentheses, C++ evaluates the innermost parentheses first. The expressions in Figure 8.4 illustrate this.

```
5 * (5 + (6 - 2) + 1)

5 * (5 +    4    + 1)

5 *    (9    + 1)

5 *    10

50
```

Figure 8.4. Precedence example of parentheses-within-parentheses with lines indicating precedence.

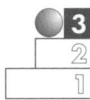

3. The following program produces an incorrect result, even though it looks as if it will work. See if you can spot the error!

Comments to identify your program.
Include the header file iostream.h so cout *works.*
Declare the variables avg, grade1, grade2, *and* grade3 *as floating-point variables.*
The variable avg *becomes equal to* grade3 *divided by 3.0 plus* grade2 *plus* grade1.
Print to the screen The average is *and the average of the three grade variables.*
Return to the operating system.

```
// Filename: C8AVG1.CPP
// Compute the average of three grades.
#include <iostream.h>
main()
{
    float avg, grade1, grade2, grade3;

    grade1 = 87.5;
    grade2 = 92.4;
    grade3 = 79.6;
```

```
    avg = grade1 + grade2 + grade3 / 3.0;
    cout << "The average is " << avg << "\n";
    return 0;
}
```

The problem is that division is performed first. Therefore, the third grade is divided by 3.0 first, then the other two grades are added to that result. To correct this problem, you simply have to add one set of parentheses, as shown in the following:

```
// Filename: C8AVG2.CPP
// Compute the average of three grades.
#include <iostream.h>
main()
{
    float avg, grade1, grade2, grade3;

    grade1 = 87.5;
    grade2 = 92.4;
    grade3 = 79.6;

    avg = (grade1 + grade2 + grade3) / 3.0;
    cout << "The average is " << avg << "\n";
    return 0;
}
```

TIP: Use plenty of parentheses in your C++ programs to clarify the order of operators, even when you don't have to override their default order. Using parentheses makes the calculations easier to understand later, when you might have to modify the program.

Shorter Is Not Always Better

When you program computers for a living, it is much more important to write programs that are easy to understand than programs that are short or include tricky calculations.

Maintainability is the computer industry's word for the changing and updating of programs previously written in a simple style. The business world is changing rapidly, and the programs companies have used for years must often be updated to reflect this changing environment. Businesses do not always have the resources to write programs from scratch, so they usually modify the ones they have.

Years ago when computer hardware was much more expensive, and when computer memories were much smaller, it was important to write small programs, which often meant relying on clever, individualized tricks and shortcuts. Unfortunately, such programs are often difficult to revise, especially if the original programmers leave and someone else (you!) must modify the original code.

Companies are realizing the importance of spending time to write programs that are easy to modify and that do not rely on tricks, or "quick and dirty" routines that are hard to follow. You can be a much more valuable programmer if you write clean programs with ample white space, frequent remarks, and straightforward code. Use parentheses in formulas if it makes the formulas clearer, and use variables for storing results in case you need the same answer later in the program. Break long calculations into several smaller ones.

Throughout the remainder of this book, you can read tips on writing maintainable programs. You and your colleagues will appreciate these tips when you incorporate them in your own C++ programs.

The Assignment Statements

In C++, the assignment operator, =, behaves differently from what you might be used to in other languages. So far, you have used it to assign values to variables, which is consistent with its use in most other programming languages.

However, the assignment operator also can be used in other ways, such as multiple assignment statements and compound assignments, as the following sections illustrate.

Multiple Assignments

If two or more equal signs appear in an expression, each performs an assignment. This fact introduces a new aspect of the precedence order you should understand. Consider the following expression:

```
a=b=c=d=e=100;
```

This might at first seem confusing, especially if you know other computer languages. To C++, the equal sign always means: Assign the value on the right to the variable on the left. This right-to-left order is described in Appendix D's precedence table. The third column in the table is labeled *Associativity*, which describes the direction of the operation. The assignment operator associates from the right, whereas some of the other C++ operators associate from the left.

Because the assignment associates from the right, the previous expression assigns 100 to the variable named e. This assignment produces a value, 100, for the expression. In C++, all expressions produce values, typically the result of assignments. Therefore, 100 is assigned to the variable d. The value, 100, is assigned to c, then to b, and finally to a. The old values of these variables are replaced by 100 after the statement finishes.

Because C++ does not automatically set variables to zero before you use them, you might want to do so before you use the variables with a single assignment statement. The following section of variable declarations and initializations is performed using multiple assignment statements.

```
main()
{
    int ctr, num_emp, num_dep;
    float sales, salary, amount;

    ctr=num_emp=num_dep=0;
    sales=salary=amount=0;
    // Rest of program follows.
```

In C++, you can include the assignment statement almost anywhere in a program, even in another calculation. For example, consider this statement:

```
value = 5 + (r = 9 - c);
```

which is a perfectly legal C++ statement. The assignment operator resides on the first level of the precedence table, and always produces a value. Because its associativity is from the right, the r is assigned 9 - c because the equal sign on the extreme right is evaluated first. The subexpression (r = 9 - c) produces a value (and places that value in r), which is then added to 5 before storing the answer in value.

Example

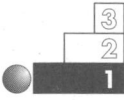

Because C++ does not initialize variables to zero before you use them, you might want to include a multiple assignment operator to do so before using the variables. The following section of code ensures that all variables are initialized before the rest of the program uses them.

```
main()
{
    int num_emp, dependents, age;
    float salary, hr_rate, taxrate;

    // Initialize all variables to zero.
    num_emp=dependents=age=hours=0;
    salary=hr_rate=taxrate=0.0;

    // Rest of program follows.
```

Compound Assignments

Many times in programming, you might want to update the value of a variable. In other words, you have to take a variable's current value, add or multiply that value by an expression, then reassign it to the original variable. The following assignment statement demonstrates this process:

```
salary=salary*1.2;
```

This expression multiplies the old value of salary by 1.2 (in effect, raising the value in salary by 20 percent), then reassigns it to salary. C++ provides several operators, called *compound operators,* that you can use any time the same variable appears on both sides of the equal sign. The compound operators are shown in Table 8.4.

Table 8.4. C++'s compound operators.

Operator	Example	Equivalent
+=	bonus+=500;	bonus=bonus+500;
-=	budget-=50;	budget=budget-50;
*=	salary*=1.2;	salary=salary*1.2;
/=	factor/=.50;	factor=factor/.50;
%=	daynum%=7;	daynum=daynum%7;

The compound operators are low in the precedence table. They typically are evaluated last or near-last.

Examples

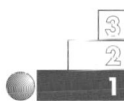

1. You have been storing your factory's production amount in a variable called prod_amt, and your supervisor has just informed you that a new addition has to be applied to the production value. You could code this update in a statement, as follows:

```
prod_amt = prod_amt + 2.6;  // Add 2.6 to current production.
```

Instead of using this formula, use C++'s compound addition operator by coding it like this:

```
prod_amt += 2.6;  // Add 2.6 to current production.
```

2. Suppose you are a high school teacher who wants to raise your students' grades. You gave a test that was too difficult, and the grades were not what you expected. If you had stored each of the student's grades in variables named grade1, grade2, grade3, and so on, you can update the grades in a program with the following section of compound assignments.

```
grade1*=1.1;        // Increase each student's grade by 10.
percent.
grade2*=1.1;
grade3*=1.1;
// Rest of grade changes follow.
```

3. The precedence of the compound operators requires important consideration when you decide how to code compound assignments. Notice from Appendix D, "C++ Precedence Table," that the compound operators are on level 19, much lower than the regular math operators. This means you must be careful how you interpret them.

For example, suppose you want to update the value of a `sales` variable with this formula:

`4-factor+bonus`

You can update the `sales` variable with the following statement:

`sales = *4 - factor + bonus;`

This statement adds the quantity `4-factor+bonus` to `sales`. Due to operator precedence, this statement is not the same as the following one:

`sales = sales *4 - factor + bonus;`

Because the `*=` operator is much lower in the precedence table than `*` or `-`, it is performed last, and with right-to-left associativity. Therefore, the following are equivalent, from a precedence viewpoint:

`sales *= 4 - factor + bonus;`

and

`sales = sales * (4 - factor + bonus);`

Mixing Data Types in Calculations

You can mix data types in C++. Adding an integer and a floating-point value is mixing data types. C++ generally converts the smaller of the two types into the other. For instance, if you add a double to an integer, C++ first converts the integer into a double value, then performs the calculation. This method produces the most accurate result possible. The automatic conversion of data types is only temporary; the converted value is back in its original data type as soon as the expression is finished.

C++ attempts to convert the smaller data type to the larger one in a mixed data-type expression.

If C++ converted two different data types to the smaller value's type, the higher-precision value is *truncated,* or shortened, and accuracy is lost. For example, in the following short program, the floating-point value of sales is added to an integer called bonus. Before C++ computes the answer, it converts bonus to floating-point, which results in a floating-point answer.

```
// Filename: C8DATA.CPP
// Demonstrate mixed data type in an expression.
#include <stdio.h>
main()
{
   int bonus=50;
   float salary=1400.50;
   float total;

   total=salary+bonus;  // bonus becomes floating-point
                        // but only temporarily.
   printf("The total is %.2f", total);
   return 0;
}
```

Type Casting

Most of the time, you don't have to worry about C++'s automatic conversion of data types. However, problems can occur if you mix unsigned variables with variables of other data types. Due to differences in computer architecture, unsigned variables do not always convert to the larger data type. This can result in loss of accuracy, and even incorrect results.

You can override C++'s default conversions by specifying your own temporary type change. This process is called *type casting.* When you type cast, you temporarily change a variable's data type from its declared data type to a new one. There are two formats of the type cast. They are

```
(data type) expression
```

and

```
data type(expression)
```

where *data type* can be any valid C++ data type, such as int or float, and the *expression* can be a variable, literal, or an expression that combines both. The following code temporarily type casts the integer variable age into a double floating-point variable, so it can be multiplied by the double floating-point factor. Both formats of the type cast are illustrated.

The variable age_factor *is assigned the value of the variable* age *(now treated like a double floating-point variable) multiplied by the variable* factor.

```
age_factor = (double)age * factor;   // Temporarily change age
                                     // to double.
```

The second way of type casting adds the parentheses around the variable rather than the data type, as so:

```
age_factor = double(age) * factor;   // Temporarily change age
                                     // to double.
```

NOTE: Type casting by adding the parentheses around the expression and not the data type is new to C++. C programmers do not have the option—they must put the data type in parentheses. The second method "feels" like a function call and seems to be more natural for this language. Therefore, becoming familiar with the second method will clarify your code.

Examples

1. Suppose you want to verify the interest calculation used by your bank on a loan. The interest rate is 15.5 percent, stored as .155 in a floating-point variable. The amount of interest you owe is computed by multiplying the interest rate by the amount of the loan balance, then multiplying that by the number of days in the year since the loan originated. The following program finds the daily interest rate by dividing the annual interest rate by 365, the number of days in a year. C++ must convert the integer 365 to a floating-point literal automatically, because it is used in combination with a floating-point variable.

```cpp
// Filename: C8INT1.CPP
// Calculate interest on a loan.
#include <stdio.h>
main()
{
    int days=45;   // Days since loan origination.
    float principle = 3500.00; // Original loan amount
    float interest_rate=0.155;    // Annual interest rate
    float daily_interest;    // Daily interest rate

    daily_interest=interest_rate/365; // Compute floating-
                                      // point value.

    // Because days is int, it too is converted to float.
    daily_interest - principle * daily_interest * days;
    principle+=daily_interest;//Update principle with interest.
    printf("The balance you owe is %.2f\n", principle);
    return 0;
}
```

The output of this program follows:

```
The balance you owe is 3566.88
```

2. Instead of having C++ perform the conversion, you might want to type cast all mixed expressions to ensure they convert to your liking. Here is the same program as in the first example, except type casts are used to convert the integer literals to floating-points before they are used.

```
// Filename: C8INT2.CPP
// Calculate interest on a loan using type casting.
#include <stdio.h>
main()
{
    int days=45;  // Days since loan origination.
    float principle = 3500.00;   // Original loan amount
    float interest_rate=0.155;   // Annual interest rate
    float daily_interest;        // Daily interest rate

    daily_interest=interest_rate/float(365);  // Type cast days
                                              // to float.

    // Because days is integer, convert it to float also.
    daily_interest = principle * daily_interest * float(days);
    principle+=daily_interest;// Update principle with interest.
    printf("The balance you owe is %.2f", principle);
    return 0;
}
```

The output from this program is exactly the same as the previous one.

Review Questions

The answers to the review questions are in Appendix B.

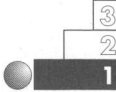

1. What is the result for each of the following expressions?

a. 1 + 2 * 4 / 2

b. (1 + 2) * 4 / 2

c. 1 + 2 * (4 / 2)

2. What is the result for each of the following expressions?

   a. `9 % 2 + 1`

   b. `(1 + (10 - (2 + 2)))`

3. Convert each of the following formulas into its C++ assignment equivalents.

   a. $a = \dfrac{3 + 3}{4 + 4}$

   b. `x = (a - b)*(a - c)2`

   c. $f = \dfrac{a2}{b3}$

   d. $d = \dfrac{(8 - x2)}{(x - 9)} - \dfrac{(4 * 2 - 1)}{x3}$

4. Write a short program that prints the area of a circle, when its radius equals 4 and π equals 3.14159. (*Hint:* The area of a circle is computed by π * radius^2.)

5. Write the assignment and `printf()` statements that print the remainder of 100/3.

Review Exercises

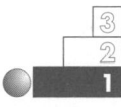

1. Write a program that prints each of the first eight powers of 2 (21, 22, 23,...28). Please write comments and include your name at the top of the program. Print string literals that describe each answer printed. The first two lines of your output should look like this:

```
2 raised to the first power is 2
2 raised to the second power is 4
```

2. Change C8PAY.CPP so it computes and prints a bonus of 15 percent of the gross pay. Taxes are not to be taken out of the bonus. After printing the four variables, gross_pay, tax_rate, bonus, and gross_pay, print a check on-screen that looks like a printed check. Add string literals so it prints the check-holder and put your name as the payer at the bottom of the check.

3. Store the weights and ages of three people in variables. Print a table, with titles, of the weights and ages. At the bottom of the table, print the averages.

4. Assume that a video store employee works 50 hours. He is paid $4.50 for the first 40 hours, time-and-a-half (1.5 times the regular pay rate) for the first five hours over 40, and double-time pay for all hours over 45. Assuming a 28 percent tax rate, write a program that prints his gross pay, taxes, and net pay to the screen. Label each amount with appropriate titles (using string literals) and add appropriate comments in the program.

Summary

You now understand C++'s primary math operators and the importance of the precedence table. Parentheses group operations so they can override the default precedence levels. Unlike some other programming languages, every operator in C++ has a meaning, no matter where it appears in an expression. This fact enables you to use the assignment operator (the equal sign) in the middle of other expressions.

When you perform math with C++, you also must be aware of how C++ interprets data types, especially when you mix them in the same expression. Of course, you can temporarily type cast a variable or literal so you can override its default data type.

This chapter has introduced you to a part of the book concerned with C++ operators. The following two chapters (Chapter 9, "Relational Operators," and Chapter 10, "Logical Operators") extend this introduction to include relational and logical operators. They enable you to compare data and compute accordingly.

Relational Operators

Sometimes you won't want every statement in your C++ program to execute every time the program runs. So far, every program in this book has executed from the top and has continued, line-by-line, until the last statement completes. Depending on your application, you might not always want this to happen.

Programs that don't always execute by rote are known as *data-driven* programs. In data driven programs, the data dictates what the program does. You would not want the computer to print every employee's paychecks for every pay period, for example, because some employees might be on vacation, or they might be paid on commission and not have made a sale during that period. Printing paychecks with zero dollars is ridiculous. You want the computer to print checks only for employees who have worked.

This chapter shows you how to create data-driven programs. These programs do not execute the same way every time. This is possible through the use of *relational* operators that *conditionally* control other statements. Relational operators first "look" at the literals and variables in the program, then operate according to what they "find." This might sound like difficult programming, but it is actually straightforward and intuitive.

This chapter introduces you to

◆ Relational operators

◆ The `if` statement

◆ The `else` statement

Not only does this chapter introduce these comparison commands, but it prepares you for much more powerful programs, possible once you learn the relational operators.

Defining Relational Operators

Relational operators compare data.

In addition to the math operators you learned in Chapter 8, "Using C++ Math Operators and Precedence," there are also operators that you use for data comparisons. They are called *relational operators*, and their task is to compare data. They enable you to determine whether two variables are equal, not equal, and which one is less than the other. Table 9.1 lists each relational operator and its meaning.

Table 9.1. The relational operators.

Operator	Description
==	Equal to
>	Greater than
<	Less than
>=	Greater than or equal to
<=	Less than or equal to
!=	Not equal to

The six relational operators form the foundation of data comparison in C++ programming. They always appear with two literals, variables, expressions (or some combination of these), one on each side of the operator. These relational operators are useful and you should know them as well as you know the +, -, *, /, and % mathematical operators.

> **NOTE:** Unlike many programming languages, C++ uses a double equal sign (==) as a test for equality. The single equal sign (=) is reserved for assignment of values.

Examples

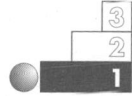

1. Assume that a program initializes four variables as follows:

```
int a=5;
int b=10;
int c=15;
int d=5;
```

The following statements are then True:

a is equal to d, so a == d

b is less than c, so b < c

c is greater than a, so c > a

b is greater than or equal to a, so b >= a

d is less than or equal to b, so d <= b

b is not equal to c, so b != c

These are not C++ statements; they are statements of comparison (*relational logic*) between values in the variables. Relational logic is easy.

Relational logic always produces a *True* or *False* result. In C++, unlike some other programming languages, you can directly use the True or False result of relational operators inside other expressions. You will soon learn how to do this; but for now, you have to understand only that the following True and False evaluations are correct:

♦ A True relational result evaluates to 1.

♦ A False relational result evaluates to 0.

Each of the statements presented earlier in this example evaluates to a 1, or True, result.

2. If you assume the same values as stated for the previous example's four variables, each of the value's statements is False (0):

```
a == b
b > c

d < a

d > a

a != d

b >= c

c <= b
```

Study these statements to see why each is False and evaluates to 0. The variables a and d, for example, are exactly equal to the same value (5), so neither is greater or less than the other.

You use relational logic in everyday life. Think of the following statements:

"The generic butter costs less than the name brand."

"My child is younger than Johnny."

"Our salaries are equal."

"The dogs are not the same age."

Each of these statements can be either True or False. There is no other possible answer.

Watch the Signs!

Many people say they are "not math-inclined" or "not logical," and you might be one of them. But, as mentioned in Chapter 8, you do not have to be good in math to be a good computer programmer. Neither should you be frightened by the term "relational logic," because you just saw how you use it in everyday life. Nevertheless, symbols confuse some people.

The two primary relational operators, *less than* (<) and *greater than* (>), are easy to remember. You probably learned this concept in school, but might have forgotten it. Actually, their signs tell you what they mean.

The arrow points to the lesser of the two values. Notice how, in the previous Example 1, the arrow (the point of the < or >) always points to the lesser number. The larger, open part of the arrow points to the larger number.

The relation is False if the arrow is pointing the wrong way. In other words, 4 > 9 is False because the operator symbol is pointing to the 9, which is not the lesser number. In English this statement says, "4 is greater than 9," which is clearly false.

The if Statement

You incorporate relational operators in C++ programs with the if statement. Such an expression is called a *decision statement* because it tests a relationship—using the relational operators—and, based on the test's result, makes a decision about which statement to execute next.

The if statement appears as follows:

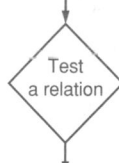

Test a relation

```
if (condition)
  { block of one or more C++ statements }
```

The *condition* includes any relational comparison, and it must be enclosed in parentheses. You saw several relational comparisons earlier, such as a==d, c<d, and so on. The *block of one or more C++ statements* is any C++ statement, such as an assignment or printf(), enclosed in braces. The block of the if, sometimes called the *body* of the if statement, is usually indented a few spaces for readability. This enables you to see, at a glance, exactly what executes if *condition* is True.

If only one statement follows the `if`, the braces are not required (but it is always good to include them). The block executes only if `condition` is True. If `condition` is False, C++ ignores the block and simply executes the next appropriate statement in the program that follows the `if` statement.

The `if` statement makes a decision.

Basically, you can read an `if` statement in the following way: "If the condition is True, perform the block of statements inside the braces. Otherwise, the condition must be False; so do not execute that block, but continue executing the remainder of the program as though this `if` statement did not exist."

The `if` statement is used to make a decision. The block of statements following the `if` executes if the decision (the result of the relation) is True, but the block does not execute otherwise. As with relational logic, you also use if logic in everyday life. Consider the statements that follow.

"If the day is warm, I will go swimming."

"If I make enough money, we will build a new house."

"If the light is green, go."

"If the light is red, stop."

Each of these statements is *conditional.* That is, if *and only if* the condition is true do you perform the activity.

CAUTION: Do not type a semicolon after the parentheses of the relational test. Semicolons appear after each statement inside the block.

Expressions as the Condition

C++ interprets any nonzero value as True, and zero always as False. This enables you to insert regular nonconditional expressions in the `if` logic. To understand this concept, consider the following section of code:

```
main()

{

    int age=21;    // Declares and assigns age as 21.

    if (age=85)

    {  cout << "You have lived through a lot!"; }

    // Remaining program code goes here.
```

At first, it might seem as though the `printf()` does not execute, but it does! Because the code line used a regular assignment operator (=) (not a relational operator, ==), C++ performs the assignment of 85 to age. This, as with all assignments you saw in Chapter 8, "Using C++ Math Operators and Precedence," produces a value for the expression of 85. Because 85 is nonzero, C++ interprets the `if` condition as True and then performs the body of the `if` statement.

Confusing the relational equality test (==) with the regular assignment operator (=) is a common error in C++ programs, and the nonzero True test makes this bug even more difficult to find.

The designers of C++ didn't intend for this to confuse you. They want you to take advantage of this feature whenever you can. Instead of putting an assignment before an `if` and testing the result of that assignment, you can combine the assignment and `if` into a single statement.

Test your understanding of this by considering this: Would C++ interpret the following condition as True or False?

```
if (10 == 10 == 10)...
```

Be careful! At first glance, it seems True; but C++ interprets it as False! Because the == operator associates from the left, the program compares the first 10 to the second. Because they are equal, the result is 1 (for True) and the 1 is then compared to the third 10—which results in a 0 (for False)!

Examples

1. The following are examples of valid C++ `if` statements.

If (the variable `sales` is greater than `5000`), then the variable `bonus` becomes equal to `500`.

```
if (sales > 5000)
    { bonus = 500; }
```

If this is part of a C++ program, the value inside the variable `sales` determines what happens next. If `sales` contains more than `5000`, the next statement that executes is the one inside the block that initializes `bonus`. If, however, `sales` contains `5000` or less, the block does not execute, and the line following the `if`'s block executes.

If (the variable `age` is less than or equal to `21`) then print `You are a minor.` to the screen and go to a new line, print `What is your grade?` to the screen, and accept an integer from the keyboard.

```
if (age <= 21)
    { cout << "You are a minor.\n";
      cout << "What is your grade? ";
      cin >> grade; }
```

If the value in `age` is less than or equal to `21`, the lines of code within the block execute next. Otherwise, C++ skips the entire block and continues with the remaining program.

If (the variable `balance` is greater than the variable `low_balance`), then print `Past due!` to the screen and move the cursor to a new line.

```
if (balance > low_balance)
    {cout << "Past due!\n"; }
```

If the value in `balance` is more than that in `low_balance`, execution of the program continues at the block and the message "`Past due!`" prints on-screen. You can compare two variables to each other (as in this example), or a variable to a literal (as in the previous examples), or a literal to a literal (although this is rarely done), or a literal to any expression in place of any variable or literal. The following `if` statement shows an expression included in the `if`.

If (the variable pay *multiplied by the variable* tax_rate *equals the variable* minimum*), then the variable* low_salary *is assigned* 1400.60.

```
If (pay * tax_rate == minimum)
   { low_salary = 1400.60; }
```

The precedence table of operators in Appendix D, "C++ Precedence Table," includes the relational operators. They are at levels 11 and 12, lower than the other primary math operators. When you use expressions such as the one shown in this example, you can make these expressions much more readable by enclosing them in parentheses (even though C++ does not require it). Here is a rewrite of the previous if statement with ample parentheses:

If (the variable pay *(multiplied by the variable* tax_rate*) equals the variable* minimum*), then the variable* low_salary *is assigned* 1400.60.

```
If ((pay * tax_rate) == minimum)
   { low_salary - 1400.60; }
```

2. The following is a simple program that computes a salesperson's pay. The salesperson receives a flat rate of $4.10 per hour. In addition, if sales are more than $8,500, the salesperson also receives an additional $500 as a bonus. This is an introductory example of conditional logic, which depends on a relation between two values, sales and $8500.

```cpp
// Filename: C9PAY1.CPP
// Calculates a salesperson's pay based on his or her sales.
#include <iostream.h>
#include <stdio.h>
main()
{
   char sal_name[20];
   int hours;
   float total_sales, bonus, pay;

   cout << "\n\n";        // Print two blank lines.
   cout << "Payroll Calculation\n";
   cout << "------------------\n";
```

```
// Ask the user for needed values.
cout << "What is salesperson's last name? ";
cin >> sal_name;
cout << "How many hours did the salesperson work? ";
cin >> hours;
cout << "What were the total sales? ";
cin >> total_sales;

bonus = 0;      // Initially, there is no bonus.

// Compute the base pay.
pay = 4.10 * (float)hours;   // Type casts the hours.

// Add bonus only if sales were high.
if (total_sales > 8500.00)
   { bonus = 500.00; }

printf("%s made $%.2f \n", sal_name, pay);
printf("and got a bonus of $%.2f", bonus);

   return 0;
}
```

This program uses cout, cin, and printf() for its input and output. You can mix them. Include the appropriate header files if you do (stdio.h and iostream.h).

The following output shows the result of running this program twice, each time with different input values. Notice that the program does two different things: It computes a bonus for one employee, but doesn't for the other. The $500 bonus is a direct result of the if statement. The assignment of $500 to bonus executes only if the value in total_sales is more than $8500.

```
Payroll Calculation
- - - - - - - - - - - - - - - - - -
What is salesperson's last name? Harrison
How many hours did the salesperson work? 40
What were the total sales? 6050.64
Harrison made $164.00
and got a bonus of $0.00
```

```
Payroll Calculation
------------------
What is salesperson's last name? Robertson
How many hours did the salesperson work? 40
What were the total sales? 9800
Robertson made $164.00
and got a bonus of $500.00
```

3. When programming the way users input data, it is wise to program *data validation* on the values they type. If they enter a bad value (for instance, a negative number when the input cannot be negative), you can inform them of the problem and ask them to reenter the data.

Not all data can be validated, of course, but most of it can be checked for reasonableness. For example, if you write a student record-keeping program, to track each student's name, address, age, and other pertinent data, you can check whether the age falls in a reasonable range. If the user enters 213 for the age, you know the value is incorrect. If the user enters -4 for the age, you know this value is also incorrect. Not all erroneous input for age can be checked, however. If the user is 21, for instance, and types 22, your program has no way of knowing whether this is correct, because 22 falls in a reasonable age range for students.

The following program is a routine that requests an age, and makes sure it is more than 10. This is certainly not a foolproof test (because the user can still enter incorrect ages), but it takes care of extremely low values. If the user enters a bad age, the program asks for it again inside the if statement.

```
// Filename: C9AGE.CPP
// Program that ensures age values are reasonable.
#include <stdio.h>
main()
{
    int age;

    printf("\nWhat is the student's age? ");
    scanf(" %d", &age);   // With scanf(), remember the &
```

BEGIN

Get age

Is age < 10? — No

Yes

Print error

END

```
    if (age < 10)
      { printf("%c", '\x07');   // BEEP
        printf("*** The age cannot be less than 10 ***\n");
        printf("Try again...\n\n");
        printf("What is the student's age? ");
        scanf(" %d", &age);
      }

    printf("Thank you. You entered a valid age.");
    return 0;
}
```

This routine can also be a section of a longer program. You learn later how to prompt repeatedly for a value until a valid input is given. This program takes advantage of the bell (ASCII 7) to warn the user that a bad age was entered. Because the \a character is an escape sequence for the alarm (see Chapter 4, "Variables and Literals" for more information on escape sequences), \a can replace the \x07 in this program.

If the entered age is less than 10, the user receives an error message. The program beeps and warns the user about the bad age before asking for it again.

The following shows the result of running this program. Notice that the program "knows," due to the if statement, whether age is more than 10.

```
What is the student's age? 3
*** The age cannot be less than 10 ***
Try again...

What is the student's age? 21
Thank you. You entered a valid age.
```

4. Unlike many languages, C++ does not include a square math operator. Remember that you "square" a number by multiplying it times itself (3*3, for example). Because many computers do not allow for integers to hold more than the square of 180, the following program uses if statements to make sure the number fits as an integer.

The program takes a value from the user and prints its square—unless it is more than 180. The message * Square is not allowed for numbers over 180 * appears on-screen if the user types a huge number.

```cpp
// Filename: C9SQR1.CPP
// Print the square of the input value
// if the input value is less than 180.
#include <iostream.h>
main()
{
    int num, square;

    cout << "\n\n";   // Print two blank lines.
    cout << "What number do you want to see the square of? ";
    cin >> num;

    if (num <= 180)
    { square = num * num;
      cout << "The square of " << num << " is " <<
             square << "\n";
    }

    if (num > 180)
    { cout << '\x07';    // BEEP
    cout << "\n* Square is not allowed for numbers over 180 *";
    cout << "\nRun this program again trying a smaller value.";
    }

    cout << "\nThank you for requesting square roots.\n";
    return 0;
}
```

The following output shows a couple of sample runs with this program. Notice that both conditions work: If the user enters a number less than 180, the calculated square appears, but if the user enters a larger number, an error message appears.

```
What number do you want to see the square of? 45

The square of 45 is 2025
Thank you for requesting square roots.

What number do you want to see the square of? 212

* Square is not allowed for numbers over 180 *
Run this program again trying a smaller value.
Thank you for requesting square roots.
```

You can improve this program with the else statement, which you learn later in this chapter. This code includes a redundant check of the user's input. The variable num must be checked once to print the square if the input number is less than or equal to 180, and checked again for the error message if it is greater than 180.

5. The value of 1 and 0 for True and False, respectively, can help save you an extra programming step, which you are not necessarily able to save in other languages. To understand this, examine the following section of code:

```
commission = 0;    // Initialize commission

if (sales > 10000)
   { commission = 500.00; }

pay = net_pay + commission;    // Commission is 0 unless
                               // high sales.
```

You can make this program more efficient by combining the if's relational test because you know that if returns 1 or 0:

```
pay = net_pay + (commission = (sales > 10000) * 500.00);
```

This single line does what it took the previous four lines to do. Because the assignment on the extreme right has precedence, it is computed first. The program compares the variable sales to 10000. If it is more than 10000, a True result of 1 returns. The program then multiplies 1 by 500.00 and stores the result in commission. If, however, the sales were not more than 10000, a 0 results and the program receives 0 from multiplying 0 by 500.00.

Whichever value (500.00 or 0) the program assigns to commission is then added to net_pay and stored in pay.

The else Statement

The else statement never appears in a program without an if statement. This section introduces the else statement by showing you the popular if-else combination statement. Its format is

```
if (condition)
  { A block of 1 or more C++ statements }
else
  { A block of 1 or more C++ statements }
```

The first part of the if-else is identical to the if statement. If *condition* is True, the block of C++ statements following the if executes. However, if *condition* is False, the block of C++ statements following the else executes instead. Whereas the simple if statement determines what happens only when the *condition* is True, the if-else also determines what happens if the *condition* is False. No matter what the outcome is, the statement following the if-else executes next.

The following describes the nature of the if-else:

♦ If the *condition* test is True, the entire block of statements following the if executes.

♦ If the *condition* test is False, the entire block of statements following the else executes.

NOTE: You can also compare characters, in addition to numbers. When you compare characters, C++ uses the ASCII table to determine which character is "less than" the other (lower in the ASCII table). But you cannot compare character strings or arrays of character strings directly with relational operators.

Examples

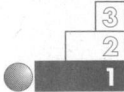

1. The following program asks the user for a number. It then prints whether or not the number is greater than zero, using the `if-else` statement.

```cpp
// Filename: C9IFEL1.CPP
// Demonstrates if-else by printing whether an
// input value is greater than zero or not.
#include <iostream.h>
main()
{
   int num;

   cout << "What is your number? ";
   cin >> num;    // Get the user's number.

   if (num > 0)
      { cout << "More than 0\n"; }
   else
      { cout << "Less or equal to 0\n"; }

   // No matter what the number was, the following executes.
   cout << "\n\nThanks for your time!\n";
   return 0;
}
```

There is no need to test for both possibilities when you use an `else`. The `if` tests whether the number is greater than zero, and the `else` automatically handles all other possibilities.

2. The following program asks the user for his or her first name, then stores it in a character array. The program checks the first character of the array to see whether it falls in the first half of the alphabet. If it does, an appropriate message is displayed.

```cpp
// Filename: C9IFEL2.CPP
// Tests the user's first initial and prints a message.
#include <iostream.h>
main()
{
```

```
char last[20];    // Holds the last name.
cout << "What is your last name? ";
cin >> last;

// Test the initial
if (last[0] <= 'P')
   { cout << "Your name is early in the alphabet.\n";}
else
   { cout << "You have to wait a while for "
          << "YOUR name to be called!\n";}
return 0;
}
```

Notice that because the program is comparing a character array element to a character literal, you must enclose the character literal inside single quotation marks. The data type on each side of each relational operator must match.

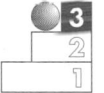

3. The following program is a more complete payroll routine than the other one. It uses the if statement to illustrate how to compute overtime pay. The logic goes something like this:

If employees work 40 hours or fewer, they are paid regular pay (their hourly rate times the number of hours worked). If employees work between 40 and 50 hours, they receive one-and-a-half times their hourly rate for those hours over 40, in addition to their regular pay for the first 40. All hours over 50 are paid at double the regular rate.

```
// Filename: C9PAY2.CPP
// Compute the full overtime pay possibilities.
#include <iostream.h>
#include <stdio.h>
main()
{
   int hours;
   float dt, ht, rp, rate, pay;

   cout << "\n\nHow many hours were worked? ";
   cin >> hours;
   cout << "\nWhat is the regular hourly pay? ";
   cin >> rate;
```

```
// Compute pay here
// Double-time possibility
if (hours > 50)
   { dt = 2.0 * rate * (float)(hours - 50);
     ht = 1.5 * rate * 10.0;}   // Time + 1/2 for 10 hours.
else
   { dt = 0.0; }// Either none or double for hours over 50.

// Time and a half.
if (hours > 40)
   { ht = 1.5 * rate * (float)(hours - 40); }

// Regular Pay
if (hours >= 40)
   { rp = 40 * rate; }
else
   { rp = (float)hours * rate; }

pay = dt + ht + rp;    // Add three components of payroll.

printf("\nThe pay is %.2f", pay);
return 0;
}
```

4. The block of statements following the if can contain any valid C++ statement—even another if statement! This sometimes is handy, as the following example shows.

You can even use this program to award employees for their years of service to your company. In this example, you are giving a gold watch to those with more than 20 years of service, a paperweight to those with more than 10 years, and a pat on the back to everyone else!

```
// Filename: C9SERV.CPP
// Prints a message depending on years of service.
#include <iostream.h>
main()
{
   int yrs;
   cout << "How many years of service? ";
   cin >> yrs;    // Determine the years they have worked.
```

```
        if (yrs > 20)
           { cout << "Give a gold watch\n"; }
        else
           { if (yrs > 10)
             { cout << "Give a paper weight\n"; }
             else
                { cout << "Give a pat on the back\n"; }
           }
        return 0;
}
```

Don't rely on the `if` within an `if` to handle too many conditions, because more than three or four conditions can add confusion. You might mess up your logic, such as: "If this is True, and if this is also True, then do something; but if not that, but something else is True, then..." (and so on). The `switch` statement that you learn about in a later chapter handles these types of multiple `if` selections much better than a long `if` within an `if` statement does.

Review Questions

The answers to the review questions are in Appendix B.

1. Which operator tests for equality?

2. State whether each of these relational tests is True or False:

   a. `4 >= 5`

   b. `4 == 4`

   c. `165 >= 165`

   d. `0 != 25`

3. True or false: `C++ is fun` prints on-screen when the following statement executes.

```
if (54 <= 54)
   { printf("C++ is fun"); }
```

4. What is the difference between an `if` and an `if-else` statement?

5. Does the following `printf()` execute?

```
if (3 != 4 != 1)
   { printf("This will print"); }
```

6. Using the ASCII table (see Appendix C, "ASCII Table"), state whether these character relational tests are True or False:

   a. `'C' < 'c'`

   b. `'0' > '0'`

   c. `'?' > ')'`

Review Exercises

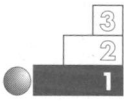

1. Write a weather-calculator program that asks for a list of the previous five days' temperatures, then prints `Brrrr!` every time a temperature falls below freezing.

2. Write a program that asks for a number and then prints the square and cube (the number multiplied by itself three times) of the number you input, if that number is more than 1. Otherwise, the program does not print anything.

3. In a program, ask the user for two numbers. Print a message telling how the first one relates to the second. In other words, if the user enters 5 and 7, your program prints "5 is less than 7."

4. Write a program that prompts the user for an employee's pre-tax salary and prints the appropriate taxes. The taxes are 10 percent if the employee makes less than $10,000; 15 percent if the employee earns $10,000 up to, but not including, $20,000; and 20 percent if the employee earns $20,000 or more.

Summary

You now have the tools to write powerful data-checking programs. This chapter showed you how to compare literals, variables, and combinations of both by using the relational operators. The `if` and the `if-else` statements rely on such data comparisons to determine which code to execute next. You can now *conditionally execute* statements in your programs.

The next chapter takes this one step further by combining relational operators to create logical operators (sometimes called *compound conditions*). These logical operators further improve your program's capability to make selections based on data comparisons.

Logical Operators

C++'s *logical operators* enable you to combine relational operators into more powerful data-testing statements. The logical operators are sometimes called *compound relational operators*. As C++'s precedence table shows, relational operators take precedence over logical operators when you combine them. The precedence table plays an important role in these types of operators, as this chapter emphasizes.

This chapter introduces you to

♦ The logical operators

♦ How logical operators are used

♦ How logical operators take precedence

This chapter concludes your study of the conditional testing that C++ enables you to perform, and it illustrates many examples of if statements in programs that work on compound conditional tests.

Defining Logical Operators

There may be times when you have to test more than one set of variables. You can combine more than one relational test into a *compound relational test* by using C++'s logical operators, as shown in Table 10.1.

Table 10.1. Logical operators.

Operator	Meaning
&&	AND
¦¦	OR
!	NOT

The first two logical operators, && and ¦¦, never appear by themselves. They typically go between two or more relational tests.

Logical operators enable the user to compute compound relational tests.

Table 10.2 shows you how each logical operator works. These tables are called *truth tables* because they show you how to achieve True results from an if statement that uses these operators. Take some time to study these tables.

Table 10.2. Truth tables.

The AND (&&) truth table
(Both sides must be True)

True	AND	True = True
True	AND	False = False
False	AND	True = False
False	AND	False = False

The OR (¦¦) truth table
(One or the other side must be True)

True	OR	True = True
True	OR	False = True
False	OR	True = True
False	OR	False = False

The NOT (!) truth table
(Causes an opposite relation)

NOT	True = False
NOT	False = True

Logical Operators and Their Uses

The True and False on each side of the operators represent a relational `if` test. The following statements, for example, are valid `if` tests that use logical operators (sometimes called *compound relational operators*).

If the variable a is less than the variable b, and the variable c is greater than the variable d, then print Results are invalid. to the screen.

```
if ((a < b) && (c > d))
    { cout << "Results are invalid."; }
```

The variable a must be less than b and, at the same time, c must be greater than d for the `printf()` to execute. The `if` statement still requires parentheses around its complete conditional test. Consider this portion of a program:

```
if ((sales > 5000) || (hrs_worked > 81))
    { bonus=500; }
```

The `sales` must be more than 5000, or the `hrs_worked` must be more than 81, before the assignment executes.

The ¦¦ is sometimes called *inclusive OR*. Here is a program segment that includes the not (!) operator:

```
if (!(sales < 2500))
    { bonus = 500; }
```

If `sales` is greater than or equal to 2500, `bonus` is initialized. This illustrates an important programming tip: Use `!` sparingly. Or, as some professionals so wisely put it: "Do not use `!` or your programs will not be `!`(unclear)." It is much clearer to rewrite the previous example by turning it into a positive relational test:

```
if (sales >= 2500)
  { bonus 500; }
```

But the `!` operator is sometimes helpful, especially when testing for end-of-file conditions for disk files, as you learn in Chapter 30, "Sequential Files." Most the time, however, you can avoid using `!` by using the reverse logic shown in the following:

`!(var1 == var2)` is the same as `(var1 != var2)`

`!(var1 <= var2)` is the same as `(var1 > var2)`

`!(var1 >= var2)` is the same as `(var1 < var2)`

`!(var1 != var2)` is the same as `(var1 == var2)`

`!(var1 > var2)` is the same as `(var1 <= var2)`

`!(var1 < var2)` is the same as `(var1 >= var2)`

Notice that the overall format of the `if` statement is retained when you use logical operators, but the relational test expands to include more than one relation. You even can have three or more, as in the following statement:

```
if ((a == B) && (d == f) ¦¦ (l = m) ¦¦ !(k <> 2)) ...
```

This is a little too much, however, and good programming practice dictates using *at most* two relational tests inside a single `if` statement. If you have to combine more than two, use more than one `if` statement to do so.

As with other relational operators, you also use the following logical operators in everyday conversation.

"If my pay is high and my vacation time is long, we can go to Italy this summer."

"If you take the trash out or clean your room, you can watch TV tonight."

"If you aren't good, you'll be punished."

Internal Truths

The True or False results of relational tests occur internally at the bit level. For example, take the `if` test:

```
if (a == 6) ...
```

to determine the truth of the relation, (a==6). The computer takes a binary 6, or 00000110, and compares it, bit-by-bit, to the variable a. If a contains 7, a binary 00000111, the result of this *equal* test is False, because the right bit (called the *least-significant bit*) is different.

C++'s Logical Efficiency

C++ attempts to be more efficient than other languages. If you combine multiple relational tests with one of the logical operators, C++ does not always interpret the full expression. This ultimately makes your programs run faster, but there are dangers! For example, if your program is given the conditional test:

```
if ((5 > 4) ¦¦ (sales < 15) && (15 != 15))...
```

C++ only evaluates the first condition, (5 > 4), and realizes it does not have to look further. Because (5 > 4) is True and because ¦¦ (OR) anything that follows it is still True, C++ does not bother with the rest of the expression. The same holds true for the following statement:

```
if ((7 < 3) && (age > 15) && (initial == 'D'))...
```

Here, C++ evaluates only the first condition, which is False. Because the && (AND) anything else that follows it is also False, C++ does not interpret the expression to the right of (7 < 3). Most of the time, this doesn't pose a problem, but be aware that the following expression might not fulfill your expectations:

```
if ((5 > 4) ¦¦ (num = 0))...
```

The (num = 0) assignment never executes, because C++ has to interpret only (5 > 4) to determine whether the entire expression is True or False. Due to this danger, do not include assignment expressions in the same condition as a logical test. The following single if condition:

```
if ((sales > old_sales) ¦¦ (inventory_flag = 'Y'))...
```

should be broken into two statements, such as:

```
inventory_flag) = 'Y';
if ((sales > old_sales) ¦¦ (inventory_flag))...
```

so the inventory_flag is always assigned the 'Y' value, no matter how the (sales > old_sales) expression tests.

Examples

1. The summer Olympics are held every four years during each year that is divisible evenly by 4. The U.S. Census is taken every 10 years, in each year that is evenly divisible by 10. The following short program asks for a year, and then tells the user if it is a year of the summer Olympics, a year of the census, or both. It uses relational operators, logical operators, and the modulus operator to determine this output.

```
// Filename: C10YEAR.CPP
// Determines if it is Summer Olympics year,
// U.S. Census year, or both.
#include <iostream.h>
main()
{
   int year;
   // Ask for a year
   cout << "What is a year for the test? ";
   cin >> year;

   // Test the year
   if (((year % 4)==0) && ((year % 10)==0))
     { cout << "Both Olympics and U.S. Census!";
       return 0; }  // Quit program, return to operating
                    // system.
   if ((year % 4)==0)
     { cout << "Summer Olympics only"; }
   else
     { if ((year % 10)==0)
         { cout << "U.S. Census only"; }
     }
   return 0;
}
```

2. Now that you know about compound relations, you can write an age-checking program like the one called C9AGE.CPP presented in Chapter 9, "Relational Operators." That program ensured the age would be above 10. This is another way you can validate input for reasonableness.

The following program includes a logical operator in its `if` to determine whether the age is greater than 10 and less than 100. If either of these is the case, the program concludes that the user did not enter a valid age.

```cpp
// Filename: C10AGE.CPP
// Program that helps ensure age values are reasonable.
#include <iostream.h>
main()
{
   int age;

   cout << "What is your age? ";
   cin >> age;
   if ((age < 10) || (age > 100))
     { cout << " \x07 \x07 \n";    // Beep twice
       cout << "*** The age must be between 10 and"
                   "100 ***\n"; }
   else
      { cout << "You entered a valid age."; }
   return 0;
}
```

3. The following program could be used by a video store to calculate a discount, based on the number of rentals people transact as well as their customer status. Customers are classified either R for *Regular* or S for *Special*. Special customers have been members of the rental club for more than one year. They automatically receive a 50-cent discount on all rentals. The store also holds "value days" several times a year. On value days, all customers receive the 50-cent discount. Special customers do not receive an additional 50 cents off during value days, because every day is a discount for them.

The program asks for each customer's status and whether or not it is a value day. It then uses the || relation to test for the discount. Even before you started learning C++, you would probably have looked at this problem with the following idea in mind.

"If a customer is Special or if it is a value day, deduct 50 cents from the rental."

That's basically the idea of the `if` decision in the following program. Even though Special customers do not receive an additional discount on value days, there is one final `if` test for them that prints an extra message at the bottom of the screen's indicated billing.

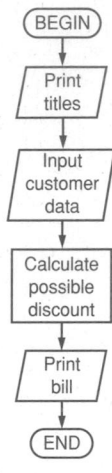

BEGIN

Print titles

Input customer data

Calculate possible discount

Print bill

END

```cpp
// Filename: C10VIDEO.CPP
// Program that computes video rental amounts and gives
// appropriate discounts based on the day or customer status.
#include <iostream.h>
#include <stdio.h>
main()
{
    float tape_charge, discount, rental_amt;
    char first_name[15];
    char last_name[15];
    int num_tapes;
    char val_day, sp_stat;

    cout << "\n\n *** Video Rental Computation ***\n";
    cout << "      -----------------------\n";
    // Underline title

    tape_charge = 2.00;
    // Before-discount tape fee-per tape.

    // Receive input data.
    cout << "\nWhat is customer's first name? ";
    cin >> first_name;
    cout << "What is customer's last name? ";
    cin >> last_name;

    cout << "\nHow many tapes are being rented? ";
    cin >> num_tapes;

    cout << "Is this a Value day (Y/N)? ";
    cin >> val_day;

    cout << "Is this a Special Status customer (Y/N)? ";
    cin >> sp_stat;
    // Calculate rental amount.
```

```
    discount = 0.0;    // Increase discount if they are eligible.
      if ((val_day == 'Y') || (sp_stat == 'Y'))
        { discount = 0.5;
           rental_amt=(num_tapes*tape_charge)
                      (discount*num_tapes); }


      // Print the bill.
      cout << "\n\n** Rental Club **\n\n";
      cout << first_name << " " << last_name << " rented "
          << num_tapes << " tapes\n";
      printf("The total was %.2f\n", rental_amt);
      printf("The discount was %.2f per tape\n", discount);
      // Print extra message for Special Status customers.
      if (sp_stat == 'Y')
         { cout << "\nThank them for being a Special "
               << "Status customer\n";}
      return 0;
}
```

The output of this program appears below. Notice that Special customers have the extra message at the bottom of the screen. This program, due to its if statements, performs differently depending on the data entered. No discount is applied for Regular customers on nonvalue days.

```
*** Video Rental Computation ***
    --------------     ----

What is customer's first name? Jerry
What is customer's last name? Parker

How many tapes are being rented? 3
Is this a Value day (Y/N)? Y
Is this a Special Status customer (Y/N)? Y

** Rental Club **

Jerry Parker rented 3 tapes
The total was 4.50
The discount was 0.50 per tape

Thank them for being a Special Status customer
```

Logical Operators and Their Precedence

The math precedence order you read about in Chapter 8, "Using C++ Math Operators and Precedence," did not include the logical operators. To be complete, you should be familiar with the entire order of precedence, as presented in Appendix D, "C++ Precedence Table."

You might wonder why the relational and logical operators are included in a precedence table. The following statement helps show you why:

```
if ((sales < min_sal * 2 && yrs_emp > 10 * sub) ...
```

Without the complete order of operators, it is impossible to determine how such a statement would execute. According to the precedence order, this `if` statement executes as follows:

```
if ((sales < (min_sal * 2)) && (yrs_emp > (10 * sub))) ...
```

This still might be confusing, but it is less so. The two multiplications are performed first, followed by the relations < and >. The `&&` is performed last because it is lowest in the precedence order of operators.

To avoid such ambiguous problems, be sure to use ample parentheses—even if the default precedence order is your intention. It is also wise to resist combining too many expressions inside a single `if` relational test.

Notice that `¦¦` (OR) has lower precedence than `&&` (AND). Therefore, the following `if` tests are equivalent:

```
if ((first_initial=='A') && (last_initial=='G') ¦¦ (id==321)) ...
if (((first_initial=='A') && (last_initial=='G')) ¦¦ (id==321)) ...
```

The second is clearer, due to the parentheses, but the precedence table makes them identical.

Review Questions

The answers to the review questions are in Appendix B.

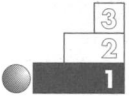

1. What are the three logical operators?

2. The following compound relational tests produce True or False comparisons. Determine which are True and which are False.

   a. ! (True ¦¦ False)

   b. (True && False) && (False ¦¦ True)

   c. ! (True && False)

   d. True ¦¦ (False && False) ¦¦ False

3. Given the statement:

   ```
   int i=12, j=10, k=5;
   ```

   What are the results (True or False) of the following statements? (*Hint:* Remember that C++ interprets any nonzero statement as True.)

   a. i && j

   b. 12 - i ¦¦ k

   c. j != k && i != k

4. What is the value printed in the following program? (*Hint:* Don't be misled by the assignment operators on each side of the ¦¦.)

   ```
   // Filename: C10LOGO.CPP
   // Logical operator test
   #include <iostream.h>
   main()
   {
      int f, g;

      g = 5;
      f = 8;
      if ((g = 25) ¦¦ (f = 35))
   ```

```
    { cout << "g is " << g << " and f got changed to " << f; }
  return 0;
}
```

5. Using the precedence table, determine whether the following statements produce a True or False result. After this, you should appreciate the abundant use of parentheses!

   a. `5 == 4 + 1 ¦¦ 7 * 2 != 12 - 1 && 5 == 8 / 2`

   b. `8 + 9 != 6 - 1 ¦¦ 10 % 2 != 5 + 0`

   c. `17 - 1 > 15 + 1 && 0 + 2 != 1 == 1 ¦¦ 4 != 1`

   d. `409 * 0 != 1 * 409 + 0 ¦¦ 1 + 8 * 2 >= 17`

6. Does the following `cout` execute?

```
if (!0)
  { cout << "C++ By Example \n"; }
```

Review Exercises

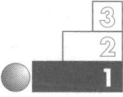

1. Write a program (by using a single compound `if` statement) to determine whether the user enters an odd positive number.

2. Write a program that asks the user for two initials. Print a message telling the user if the first initial falls alphabetically before the second.

3. Write a number-guessing game. Assign a value to a variable called `number` at the top of the program. Give a prompt that asks for five guesses. Receive the user's five guesses with a single `scanf()` for practice with `scanf()`. Determine whether any of the guesses match the `number` and print an appropriate message if one does.

4. Write a tax-calculation routine, as follows: A family pays no tax if its income is less than $5,000. It pays a 10 percent tax if its income is $5,000 to $9,999, inclusive. It pays a 20 percent tax if the income is $10,000 to $19,999, inclusive. Otherwise, it pays a 30 percent tax.

Summary

This chapter extended the `if` statement to include the `&&`, `||`, and `!` logical operators. These operators enable you to combine several relational tests into a single test. C++ does not always have to look at every relational operator when you combine them in an expression.

This chapter concludes the explanation of the `if` statement. The next chapter explains the remaining regular C++ operators. As you saw in this chapter, the precedence table is still important to the C++ language. Whenever you are evaluating expressions, keep the precedence table in the back of your mind (or at your fingertips) at all times!

Additional C++ Operators

C++ has several other operators you should learn besides those you learned in Chapters 9 and 10. In fact, C++ has more operators than most programming languages. Unless you become familiar with them, you might think C++ programs are cryptic and difficult to follow. C++'s heavy reliance on its operators and operator precedence produces the efficiency that enables your programs to run more smoothly and quickly.

This chapter teaches you the following:

♦ The ?: conditional operator

♦ The ++ increment operator

♦ The -- decrement operator

♦ The sizeof operator

♦ The (,) comma operator

♦ The Bitwise Operators (&, ¦, and ^)

Most the operators described in this chapter are unlike those found in any other programming language. Even if you have programmed in other languages for many years, you still will be surprised by the power of these C++ operators.

The Conditional Operator

The conditional operator is a ternary operator.

The *conditional operator* is C++'s only *ternary* operator, requiring three operands (as opposed to the unary's single-and the binary's double-operand requirements). The conditional operator is used to replace `if-else` logic in some situations. The conditional operator is a two-part symbol, `?:`, with a format as follows:

```
conditional_expression ? expression1 : expression2;
```

The `conditional_expression` is any expression in C++ that results in a True (nonzero) or False (zero) answer. If the result of `conditional_expression` is True, `expression1` executes. Otherwise, if the result of `conditional_expression` is False, `expression2` executes. Only one of the expressions following the question mark ever executes. Only a single semicolon appears at the end of `expression2`. The internal expressions, such as `expression1`, do not have a semicolon. Figure 11.1 illustrates the conditional operator more clearly.

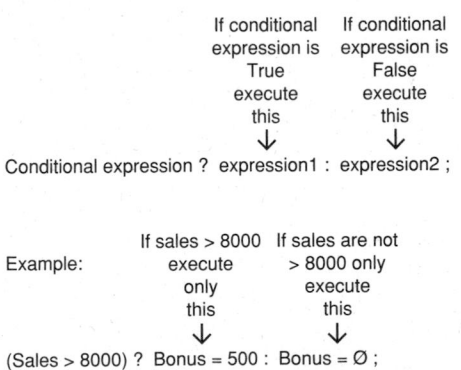

Figure 11.1. **Format of the conditional operator.**

If you require simple if-else logic, the conditional operator usually provides a more direct and succinct method, although you should always prefer readability over compact code.

To glimpse the conditional operator at work, consider the section of code that follows.

```
if (a > b)
   { ans = 10; }
else
   { ans = 25; }
```

You can easily rewrite this kind of if-else code by using a single conditional operator.

If the variable a *is greater than the variable* b, *make the variable* ans *equal to 10; otherwise, make* ans *equal to 25.*

```
a > b ? (ans = 10) : (ans = 25);
```

Although parentheses are not required around conditional_expression to make it work, they usually improve readability. This statement's readability is improved by using parentheses, as follows:

```
(a > b) ? (ans = 10) : (ans = 25);
```

Because each C++ expression has a value—in this case, the value being assigned—this statement could be even more succinct, without loss of readability, by assigning ans the answer to the left of the conditional:

```
ans = (a > b) ? (10) : (25);
```

This expression says: If a is greater than b, assign 10 to ans; otherwise, assign 25 to ans. Almost any if-else statement can be rewritten as a conditional, and vice versa. You should practice converting one to the other to familiarize yourself with the conditional operator's purpose.

> **NOTE:** Any valid if C++ statement also can be a conditional_expression, including all relational and logical operators as well as any of their possible combinations.

Examples

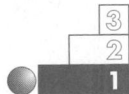

1. Suppose you are looking over your early C++ programs, and you notice the following section of code.

```
if (production > target)
   { target *= 1.10; }
else
   { target *= .90; }
```

You should realize that such a simple `if-else` statement can be rewritten using a conditional operator, and that more efficient code results. You can therefore change it to the following single statement.

```
(production > target) ? (target *= 1.10) : (target *= .90);
```

2. Using a conditional operator, you can write a routine to find the minimum value between two variables. This is sometimes called a *minimum routine.* The statement to do this is

```
minimum = (var1 < var2) ? var1 : var2;
```

If `var1` is less than `var2`, the value of `var1` is assigned to `minimum`. If `var2` is less, the value of `var2` is assigned to `minimum`. If the variables are equal, the value of `var2` is assigned to `minimum`, because it does not matter which is assigned.

3. A *maximum routine* can be written just as easily:

```
maximum = (var1 > var2) ? var1 : var2;
```

4. Taking the previous examples a step further, you can also test for the sign of a variable. The following conditional expression assigns –1 to the variable called `sign` if `testvar` is less than 0; 0 to `sign` if `testvar` is zero; and +1 to `sign` if `testvar` is 1 or more.

```
sign = (testvar < 0) ? -1 : (testvar > 0);
```

It might be easy to spot why the less-than test results in a –1, but the second part of the expression can be confusing. This works well due to C++'s 1 and 0 (for True and False, respectively) return values from a relational test. If `testvar` is 0 or greater, `sign` is assigned the answer (`testvar > 0`). The value of (testvar > 0) is 1 if True (therefore, testvar is more than 0) or 0 if testvar is equal to 0.

The preceding statement shows C++'s efficient conditional operator. It might also help you understand if you write the statement using typical if-else logic. Here is the same problem written with a typical if-else statement:

```
if (testvar < 0)
    { sign = -1; }
else
    { sign = (testvar > 0); }    // testvar can only be
                                 // 0 or more here.
```

The Increment and Decrement Operators

The ++ operator adds 1 to a variable. The −− operator subtracts 1 from a variable.

C++ offers two unique operators that add or subtract 1 to or from variables. These are the *increment* and *decrement* operators: ++ and --. Table 11.1 shows how these operators relate to other types of expressions you have seen. Notice that the ++ and - can appear on either side of the modified variable. If the ++ or -- appears on the left, it is known as a *prefix* operator. If the operator appears on the right, it is a *postfix* operator.

Table 11.1. The ++ and -- operators.

Operator	Example	Description	Equivalent Statements	
++	i++;	postfix	i = i + 1;	i += 1;
++	++i;	prefix	i = i + 1;	i += 1;
-	i--;	postfix	i = i - 1;	i -= 1;
--	--i;	prefix	i = i - 1;	i -= 1;

Any time you have to add 1 or subtract 1 from a variable, you can use these two operators. As Table 11.1 shows, if you have to increment or decrement only a single variable, these operators enable you to do so.

Increment and Decrement Efficiency

The increment and decrement operators are straightforward, efficient methods for adding 1 to a variable and subtracting 1 from a variable. You often have to do this during counting or processing loops, as discussed in Chapter 12, "The `while` Loop" and beyond.

These two operators compile directly into their assembly language equivalents. Almost all computers include, at their lowest binary machine-language commands, increment and decrement instructions. If you use C++'s increment and decrement operators, you ensure that they compile to these low-level equivalents.

If, however, you code expressions to add or subtract 1 (as you do in other programming languages), such as the expression `i = i - 1`, you do not actually ensure that C++ compiles this instruction in its efficient machine-language equivalent.

Whether you use prefix or postfix does not matter—if you are incrementing or decrementing single variables on lines by themselves. However, when you combine these two operators with other operators in a single expression, you must be aware of their differences. Consider the following program section. Here, all variables are integers because the increment and decrement operators work only on integer variables.

Make a equal to 6. Increment a, subtract 1 from it, then assign the result to b.

```
a = 6;
b = ++a - 1;
```

What are the values of a and b after these two statements finish? The value of a is easy to determine: it is incremented in the second statement, so it is 7. However, b is either 5 or 6 depending on when the variable a increments. To determine when a increments, consider the following rule:

♦ If a variable is incremented or decremented with a *prefix* operator, the increment or decrement occurs *before* the variable's value is used in the remainder of the expression.

♦ If a variable is incremented or decremented with a *postfix* operator, the increment or decrement occurs *after* the variable's value is used in the remainder of the expression.

In the previous code, a contains a prefix increment. Therefore, its value is first incremented to 7, then 1 is subtracted from 7, and the result (6) is assigned to b. If a postfix increment is used, as in

```
a = 6;
b = a++ - 1;
```

a is 6, therefore, 5 is assigned to b because a does not increment to 7 until after its value is used in the expression. The precedence table in Appendix D, "C++ Precedence Table," shows that prefix operators contain much higher precedence than almost every other operator, especially low-precedence postfix increments and decrements.

> **TIP:** If the order of prefix and postfix confuses you, break your expressions into two lines of code and type the increment or decrement before or after the expression that uses it.

By taking advantage of this tip, you can now rewrite the previous example as follows:

```
a = 6;
b = a - 1;
a++;
```

There is now no doubt as to when a is incremented: a increments after b is assigned to a-1.

Even parentheses cannot override the postfix rule. Consider the following statement.

```
x = p + (((amt++)));
```

There are too many unneeded parentheses here, but even the redundant parentheses are not enough to increment amt before adding its value to p. Postfix increments and decrements *always* occur after their variables are used in the surrounding expression.

> **CAUTION:** Do not attempt to increment or decrement an expression. You can apply these operators only to variables. The following expression is invalid:
>
> ```
> sales = ++(rate * hours);   // Not allowed!!
> ```

Examples

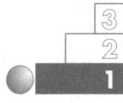

1. As you should with all other C++ operators, keep the precedence table in mind when you evaluate expressions that increment and decrement. Figures 11.2 and 11.3 show you some examples that illustrate these operators.

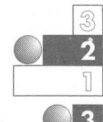

2. The precedence table takes on even more meaning when you see a section of code such as that shown in Figure 11.3.

3. Considering the precedence table—and, more importantly, what you know about C++'s relational efficiencies—what is the value of the ans in the following section of code?

```
int i=1, j=20, k=-1, l=0, m=1, n=0, o=2, p=1;
ans = i || j-- && k++ || ++l && ++m || n-- & !o || p--;
```

This, at first, seems to be extremely complicated. Nevertheless, you can simply glance at it and determine the value of ans, as well as the ending value of the rest of the variables.

Recall that when C++ performs a relation || (or), it ignores the right side of the || if the left value is True (any nonzero value is True). Because any nonzero value is True, C++ does

not evaluate the values on the right. Therefore, C++ performs this expression as shown:

```
ans = i || j-- && k++ || ++l && ++m || n-- & !o || p--;
             |
          1  (TRUE)
```

```
    int i=1;
    int j=2;
    int k=3;
    ans = i++ * j - --k;
                      |
        i++ * j -    2
            \/
          2    -   2
                \/
                0

    ans = 0, then i increments by 1 to its final value of 2.

    int i=1;
    int j=2;
    int k=3;
    ans = ++i * j - k--;
            |
          2  ^ j - k--
            \/
          4     - k--
               \/
               1

    ans = 1, then k decrements by 1 to its final value of 2.
```

Figure 11.2. C++ operators incrementing (above) and decrementing
(below) by order of precedence.

```
int i=0;
int j=-1;
int k=0;
int m=1
ans = i++ && ++j ¦¦ k ¦¦ m++;
                |
    i++ &&  0  ¦¦ k ¦¦ m++
             \ /
              0       ¦¦ k ¦¦ m++
                       \ /
                        0        ¦¦ m++
                                  \ /
                                   1

ans = 1, then i increments by 1 to its final value of 1,
and m increments by 1 to its final value of 2.
```

Figure 11.3. Another example of C++ operators and their precedence.

NOTE: Because i is True, C++ evaluates the entire expression as True and ignores all code after the first ¦¦. Therefore, *every other increment and decrement expression is ignored.* Because C++ ignores the other expressions, only ans is changed by this expression. The other variables, j through p, are never incremented or decremented, even though several of them contain increment and decrement operators. If you use relational operators, be aware of this problem and break out all increment and decrement operators into statements by themselves, placing them on lines before the relational statements that use their values.

The sizeof Operator

There is another operator in C++ that does not look like an operator at all. It looks like a built-in function, but it is called the `sizeof` operator. In fact, if you think of `sizeof` as a function call, you might not become confused because it works in a similar way. The format of `sizeof` follows:

Determine
size of
data

`sizeof data`

or

`sizeof(data type)`

The `sizeof` operator is unary, because it operates on a single value. This operator produces a result that represents the size, in bytes, of the *data* or *data type* specified. Because most data types and variables require different amounts of internal storage on different computers, the `sizeof` operator enables programs to maintain consistency on different types of computers.

> **TIP:** Most C++ programmers use parentheses around the `sizeof` argument, whether that argument is *data* or *data type*. Because you *must* use parentheses around *data type* arguments and you *can* use them around *data* arguments, it doesn't hurt to always use them.

The `sizeof` operator returns its argument's size in bytes.

The `sizeof` operator is sometimes called a *compile-time operator*. At compile time, rather than runtime, the compiler replaces each occurrence of `sizeof` in your program with an unsigned integer value. Because `sizeof` is used more in advanced C++ programming, this operator is better utilized later in the book for performing more advanced programming requirements.

If you use an array as the `sizeof` argument, C++ returns the number of bytes you originally reserved for that array. Data inside the array have nothing to do with its returned `sizeof` value—even if it's only a character array containing a short string.

Examples

1. Suppose you want to know the size, in bytes, of floating-point variables for your computer. You can determine this by entering the keyword `float` in parentheses—after `sizeof`—as shown in the following program.

```
// Filename: C11SIZE1.CPP
// Prints the size of floating-point values.
#include <iostream.h>
main()
{
   cout << "The size of floating-point variables on \n";
   cout << "this computer is " << sizeof(float) << "\n";
   return 0;
}
```

This program might produce different results on different computers. You can use any valid data type as the sizeof argument. On most PCs, this program probably produces this output:

```
The size of floating-point variables on
this computer is: 4
```

The Comma Operator

Another C++ operator, sometimes called a *sequence point*, works a little differently. This is the *comma operator* (,), which does not directly operate on data, but produces a left-to-right evaluation of expressions. This operator enables you to put more than one expression on a single line by separating each one with a comma.

You already saw one use of the sequence point comma when you learned how to declare and initialize variables. In the following section of code, the comma separates statements. Because the comma associates from the left, the first variable, i, is declared and initialized before the second variable.

```
main()
{
   int i=10, j=25;
   // Remainder of the program follows.
```

However, the comma is *not* a sequence point when it is used inside function parentheses. Then it is said to *separate* arguments, but it is not a sequence point. Consider the `printf()` that follows.

```
printf("%d %d %d", i, i++, ++i);
```

Many results are possible from such a statement. The commas serve only to separate arguments of the `printf()`, and do not generate the left-to-right sequence that they otherwise do when they aren't used in functions. With the statement shown here, you are not ensured of *any* order! The postfix `i++` might possibly be performed before the prefix `++i`, even though the precedence table does not require this. Here, the order of evaluation depends on how your compiler sends these arguments to the `printf()` function.

> **TIP:** Do not put increment operators or decrement operators in function calls because you cannot predict the order in which they execute.

Examples

1. You can put more than one expression on a line, using the comma as a sequence point. The following program does this.

```cpp
// Filename: C11COM1.CPP
// Illustrates the sequence point.
#include <iostream.h>
main()
{
    int num, sq, cube;
    num = 5;

    // Calculate the square and cube of the number.
    sq = (num * num), cube = (num * num * num);

    cout << "The square of " << num << " is " << sq <<
            " and the cube is " << cube;
    return 0;
}
```

This is not necessarily recommended, however, because it doesn't add anything to the program and actually decreases its readability. In this example, the square and cube are probably better computed on two separate lines.

2. The comma enables some interesting statements. Consider the following section of code.

```
i = 10
j = (i = 12, i + 8);
```

When this code finishes executing, j has the value of 20—even though this is not necessarily clear. In the first statement, i is assigned 10. In the second statement, the comma causes i to be assigned a value of 12, then j is assigned the value of i + 8, or 20.

3. In the following section of code, ans is assigned the value of 12, because the assignment *before* the comma is performed first. Despite this right-to-left associativity of the assignment operator, the comma's sequence point forces the assignment of 12 to x before x is assigned to ans.

```
ans = (y = 8, x = 12);
```

When this fragment finishes, y contains 8, x contains 12, and ans also contains 12.

Bitwise Operators

The *bitwise operators* manipulate internal representations of data and not just "values in variables" as the other operators do. These bitwise operators require an understanding of Appendix A's binary numbering system, as well as a computer's memory. This section introduces the bitwise operators. The bitwise operators are used for advanced programming techniques and are generally used in much more complicated programs than this book covers.

Some people program in C++ for years and never learn the bitwise operators. Nevertheless, understanding them can help you improve a program's efficiency and enable you to operate at a more advanced level than many other programming languages allow.

Bitwise Logical Operators

There are four bitwise logical operators, and they are shown in Table 11.2. These operators work on the binary representations of integer data. This enables systems programmers to manipulate internal bits in memory and in variables. The bitwise operators are not just for systems programmers, however. Application programmers also can improve their programs' efficiency in several ways.

Table 11.2. Bitwise logical operators.

Operator	Meaning
&	Bitwise AND
¦	Bitwise inclusive OR
^	Bitwise exclusive OR
~	Bitwise 1's complement

Bitwise operators make bit-by-bit comparisons of internal data.

Each of the bitwise operators makes a bit-by-bit comparison of internal data. Bitwise operators apply only to character and integer variables and constants, and not to floating-point data. Because binary numbers consist of 1s and 0s, these 1s and 0s (called *bits*) are compared to each other to produce the desired result for each bitwise operator.

Before you study the examples, you should understand Table 11.3. It contains truth tables that describe the action of each bitwise operator on an integer's—or character's—internal-bit patterns.

Table 11.3. Truth tables.

Bitwise AND (&)

```
0 & 0 = 0

0 & 1 = 0

1 & 0 = 0

1 & 1 = 1
```

continues

Table 11.3. Continued.

Bitwise inclusive OR (¦)

```
0 ¦ 0 = 0

0 ¦ 1 = 1

1 ¦ 0 = 1

1 ¦ 1 = 1
```

Bitwise exclusive OR (^)

```
0 ^ 0 = 0

0 ^ 1 = 1

1 ^ 0 = 1

1 ^ 1 = 0
```

Bitwise 1's complement (~)

```
~0 = 1

~1 = 0
```

In bitwise truth tables, you can replace the 1 and 0 with True and False, respectively, if it helps you to understand the result better. For the bitwise AND (&) truth table, both bits being compared by the & operator must be True for the result to be True. In other words, "True AND True results in True."

> **TIP:** By replacing the 1s and 0s with True and False, you might be able to relate the bitwise operators to the regular logical operators, && and ¦¦, that you use for if comparisons.

For bitwise ^, one side *or* the other—but not both—must be 1.

The ¦ bitwise operator is sometimes called the *bitwise inclusive OR* operator. If one side of the ¦ operator is 1 (True)—or if both sides are 1—the result is 1 (True).

The ^ operator is called *bitwise exclusive OR*. It means that either side of the ^ operator must be 1 (True) for the result to be 1 (True), but both sides cannot be 1 (True) at the same time.

The ~ operator, called *bitwise 1's complement*, reverses each bit to its opposite value.

> **NOTE:** Bitwise 1's complement does *not* negate a number. As Appendix A, "Memory Addressing, Binary, and Hexadecimal Review," shows, most computers use a 2's complement to negate numbers. The bitwise 1's complement reverses the bit pattern of numbers, but it doesn't add the additional 1 as the 2's complement requires.

You can test and change individual bits inside variables to check for patterns of data. The following examples help to illustrate each of the four bitwise operators.

Examples

1. If you apply the bitwise & operator to numerals 9 and 14, you receive a result of 8. Figure 11.4 shows you why this is so. When the binary values of 9 (1001) and 14 (1110) are compared on a bitwise & basis, the resulting bit pattern is 8 (1000).

```
  1   0   0   1   (9)
  ↓   ↓   ↓   ↓
  &   &   &   &
  1   1   1   0   (14)
= 1   0   0   0   (8)
```

Figure 11.4. Performing bitwise & on 9 and 14.

In a C++ program, you can code this bitwise comparison as follows.

Make result *equal to the binary value of 9 (1001) ANDed to the binary value of 14 (1110).*

```
result = 9 & 14;
```

The `result` variable holds 8, which is the result of the bitwise `&`. The 9 (binary 1001) or 14 (binary 1110)—or both—also can be stored in variables with the same result.

2. When you apply the bitwise | operator to the numbers 9 and 14, you get 15. When the binary values of 9 (1001) and 14 (1110) are compared on a bitwise | basis, the resulting bit pattern is 15 (1111). `result`'s bits are 1 (True) in every position where a 1 appears in both numbers.

In a C++ program, you can code this bitwise comparison as follows:

```
result = 9 | 14;
```

The `result` variable holds 15, which is the result of the bitwise |. The 9 or 14 (or both) also can be stored in variables.

3. The bitwise ^ applied to 9 and 14 produces 7. Bitwise ^ sets the resulting bits to 1 if one number or the other's bit is 1, but not if both of the matching bits are 1 at the same time.

In a C++ program, you can code this bitwise comparison as follows:

```
result = 9 ^ 14;
```

The `result` variable holds 7 (binary 0111), which is the result of the bitwise ^. The 9 or 14 (or both) also can be stored in variables with the same result.

4. The bitwise ~ simply negates each bit. It is a unary bitwise operator because you can apply it to only a single value at any one time. The bitwise ~ applied to 9 results in 6, as shown in Figure 11.5.

```
~ 1  0  0  1  (9)
= 0  1  1  0  (6)
```

Figure 11.5. Performing bitwise ~ on the number 9.

In a C++ program, you can code this bitwise operation like this:

```
result = ~9;
```

The `result` variable holds 6, which is the result of the bitwise ~. The 9 can be stored in a variable with the same result.

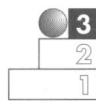

5. You can take advantage of the bitwise operators to perform tests on data that you cannot do as efficiently in other ways.

   For example, suppose you want to know if the user typed an odd or even number (assuming integers are being input). You can use the modulus operator (%) to determine whether the remainder—after dividing the input value by 2—is 0 or 1. If the remainder is 0, the number is even. If the remainder is 1, the number is odd.

   The bitwise operators are more efficient than other operators because they directly compare bit patterns without using any mathematical operations.

   Because a number is even if its bit pattern ends in a 0 and odd if its bit pattern ends in 1, you also can test for odd or even numbers by applying the bitwise & to the data and to a binary 1. This is more efficient than using the modulus operator. The following program informs users if their input value is odd or even using this technique.

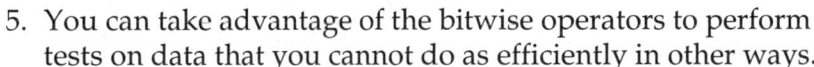

Identify the file and include the input/output header file. This program tests for odd or even input. You need a place to put the user's number, so declare the `input` variable as an integer.

Ask the user for the number to be tested. Put the user's answer in `input`. Use the bitwise operator, &, to test the number. If the bit on the extreme right in `input` is 1, tell the user that the number is odd. If the bit on the extreme right in `input` is 0, tell the user that the number is even.

Test if odd or even

```
// Filename: C11ODEV.CPP
// Uses a bitwise & to determine whether a
// number is odd or even.
#include <iostream.h>
main()
{
```

```
    int input;                    // Will hold user's number
    cout << "What number do you want me to test? ";
    cin >> input;

    if (input & 1)                // True if result is 1;
                                  // otherwise it is false (0)
        { cout << "The number " << input << " is odd\n"; }
    else
        { cout << "The number " << input << " is even\n"; }
    return 0;
}
```

6. The only difference between the bit patterns for uppercase and lowercase characters is bit number 5 (the third bit from the left, as shown in Appendix A, "Memory Addressing, Binary, and Hexadecimal Review"). For lowercase letters, bit 5 is a 1. For uppercase letters, bit 5 is a 0. Figure 11.6 shows how *A* and *B* differ from *a* and *b* by a single bit.

Only bit 6   ASCII A is 01000001   (hex 41, decimal 65)
is different   ASCII a is 01100001   (hex 61, decimal 97)

Only bit 6   ASCII B is 01000010   (hex 42, decimal 66)
is different   ASCII b is 01100010   (hex 62, decimal 98)

Figure 11.6. Bitwise difference between two uppercase and two lowercase ASCII letters.

To convert a character to uppercase, you have to turn off (change to a 0) bit number 5. You can apply a bitwise & to the input character and 223 (which is 11011111 in binary) to turn off bit 5 and convert any input character to its uppercase equivalent. If the number is already in uppercase, this bitwise & does not change it.

The 223 (binary 11011111) is called a *bit mask* because it masks (just as masking tape masks areas not to be painted) bit 5 so it becomes 0, if it is not already. The following program does this to ensure that users typed uppercase characters when they were asked for their initials.

```
// Filename: C11UPCS1.CPP
// Converts the input characters to uppercase
// if they aren't already.
#include <iostream.h>
main()
{
   char first, middle, last;    // Will hold user's initials
   int bitmask=223;                         // 11011111 in binary

   cout << "What is your first initial? ";
   cin >> first;
   cout << "What is your middle initial? ";
   cin >> middle;
   cout << "What is your last initial? ";
   cin >> last;

   // Ensure that initials are in uppercase.
   first = first & bitmask;          // Turn off bit 5 if
   middle = middle & bitmask;        // it is not already
   last = last & bitmask;            // turned off.

   cout << "Your initials are " << first << " " <<
           middle << " " << last;
   return 0;
}
```

The following output shows what happens when two of the initials are typed with lowercase letters. The program converts them to uppercase before printing them again. Although there are other ways to convert to lowercase, none are as efficient as using the & bitwise operator.

```
What is your first initial? g
What is your middle initial? M
What is your last initial? p
Your initials are: G M P
```

Review Questions

The answers to the review questions are in Appendix B.

1. What set of statements does the conditional operator replace?

2. Why is the conditional operator called a "ternary" operator?

3. Rewrite the following conditional operator as an `if-else` statement.

   ```
   ans = (a == b) ? c + 2 : c + 3;
   ```

4. True or false: The following statements produce the same results.

   ```
   var++;
   ```

   and

   ```
   var = var + 1;
   ```

5. Why is using the increment and decrement operators more efficient than using the addition and subtraction operators?

6. What is a sequence point?

7. Can the output of the following code section be determined?

   ```
   age = 20;
   printf("You are now %d, and will be %d in one year",
           age, age++);
   ```

8. What is the output of the following program section?

   ```
   char name[20] = "Mike";
   cout << "The size of name is " << sizeof(name) << "\n";
   ```

9. What is the result of each of the following bitwise True-False expressions?

   a. `1 ^ 0 & 1 & 1 | 0`

   b. `1 & 1 & 1 & 1`

   c. `1 ^ 1 ^ 1 ^ 1`

   d. `~(1 ^ 0)`

Review Exercises

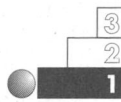

1. Write a program that prints the numerals from 1 to 10. Use ten different `cout`s and only one variable called `result` to hold the value before each `cout`. Use the increment operator to add 1 to `result` before each `cout`.

2. Write a program that asks users for their ages. Using a single `printf()` that includes a conditional operator, print on-screen the following if the input age is over 21,

   ```
   You are not a minor.
   ```

   or print this otherwise:

   ```
   You are still a minor.
   ```

   This `printf()` might be long, but it helps to illustrate how the conditional operator can work in statements where `if-else` logic does not.

3. Use the conditional operator—and no `if-else` statements—to write the following tax-calculation routine: A family pays no tax if its annual salary is less than $5,000. It pays a 10 percent tax if the salary range begins at $5,000 and ends at $9,999. It pays a 20 percent tax if the salary range begins at $10,000 and ends at $19,999. Otherwise, the family pays a 30 percent tax.

4. Write a program that converts an uppercase letter to a lowercase letter by applying a bitmask and one of the bitwise logical operators. If the character is already in lowercase, do not change it.

Summary

Now you have learned almost every operator in the C++ language. As explained in this chapter, conditional, increment, and decrement are three operators that enable C++ to stand apart from many other programming languages. You must always be aware of the precedence table whenever you use these, as you must with all operators.

The `sizeof` and sequence point operators act unlike most others. The `sizeof` is a compile operator, and it works in a manner similar to the `#define` preprocessor directive because they are both replaced by their values at compile time. The sequence point enables you to have multiple statements on the same line—or in a single expression. Reserve the sequence point for declaring variables only because it can be unclear when it's combined with other expressions.

This chapter concludes the discussion on C++ operators. Now that you can compute just about any result you will ever need, it is time to discover how to gain more control over your programs. The next few chapters introduce control loops that give you repetitive power in C++.

The while Loop

The repetitive capabilities of computers make them good tools for processing large amounts of information. Chapters 12-15 introduce you to C++ constructs, which are the control and looping commands of programming languages. C++ constructs include powerful, but succinct and efficient, looping commands similar to those of other languages you already know.

The while loops enable your programs to repeat a series of statements, over and over, as long as a certain condition is always met. Computers do not get "bored" while performing the same tasks repeatedly. This is one reason why they are so important in business data processing.

This chapter teaches you the following:

♦ The while loop

♦ The concept of loops

♦ The do-while loop

♦ Differences between if and while loops

♦ The exit() function

♦ The break statement

♦ Counters and totals

After completing this chapter, you should understand the first of several methods C++ provides for repeating program sections. This chapter's discussion of loops includes one of the most important uses for looping: creating counter and total variables.

The while Statement

The while statement is one of several C++ *construct statements.* Each construct (from *construction*) is a programming language statement—or a series of statements—that controls looping. The while, like other such statements, is a *looping statement* that controls the execution of a series of other statements. Looping statements cause parts of a program to execute repeatedly, as long as a certain condition is being met.

The format of the while statement is

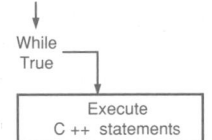

While
True

Execute
C ++ statements

```
while (test expression)
   { block of one or more C++ statements; }
```

The parentheses around *test expression* are required. As long as *test expression* is True (nonzero), the *block* of one or more C++ statements executes repeatedly until *test expression* becomes False (evaluates to zero). Braces are required before and after the body of the while loop, unless you want to execute only one statement. Each statement in the body of the while loop requires an ending semicolon.

The placeholder *test expression* usually contains relational, and possibly logical, operators. These operators provide the True-False condition checked in *test expression*. If *test expression* is False when the program reaches the while loop for the first time, the body of the while loop does not execute at all. Regardless of whether the body of the while loop executes no times, one time, or many times, the statements following the while loop's closing brace execute if *test expression* becomes False.

The body of a while loop executes repeatedly as long as test expression is True.

Because *test expression* determines when the loop finishes, the body of the while loop must change the variables used in *test expression*. Otherwise, *test expression* never changes and the while loop repeats forever. This is known as an *infinite loop,* and you should avoid it.

> **TIP:** If the body of the while loop contains only one statement, the braces surrounding it are not required. It is a good habit to enclose all while loop statements in braces, however, because if you have to add statements to the body of the while loop later, your braces are already there.

The Concept of Loops

You use the loop concept in everyday life. Any time you have to repeat the same procedure, you are performing a loop—just as your computer does with the while statement. Suppose you are wrapping holiday gifts. The following statements represent the looping steps (in while format) that you follow while gift-wrapping.

while (there are still unwrapped gifts)
{ Get the next gift;
Cut the wrapping paper;
Wrap the gift;
Put a bow on the gift;
Fill out a name card for the gift;
Put the wrapped gift with the others; }

Whether you have 3, 15, or 100 gifts to wrap, you use this procedure (loop) repeatedly until every gift is wrapped. For an example that is more easily computerized, suppose you want to total all the checks you wrote in the previous month. You could perform the following loop.

while (there are still checks from the last month to be totaled)
{ Add the amount of the next check to the total; }

The body of this pseudocode while loop has only one statement, but that single statement must be performed until you have added each one of the previous month's checks. When this loop ends (when no more checks from the previous month remain to be totaled), you have the result.

The body of a while loop can contain one or more C++ statements, including additional while loops. Your programs will be more readable if you indent the body of a while loop a few spaces to the right. The following examples illustrate this.

Examples

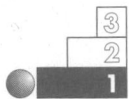

1. Some programs presented earlier in the book require user input with cin. If users do not enter appropriate values, these programs display an error message and ask the user to enter another value, which is an acceptable procedure.

   Now that you understand the while loop construct, however, you should put the error message inside a loop. In this way, users see the message continually until they type proper input values, rather than once.

   The following program is short, but it demonstrates a while loop that ensures valid keyboard input. It asks users whether they want to continue. You can incorporate this program into a larger one that requires user permission to continue. Put a prompt, such as the one presented here, at the bottom of a text screen. The text remains on-screen until the user tells the program to continue executing.

Identify the file and include the necessary header file. In this program, you want to ensure the user enters Y or N.
You have to store the user's answer, so declare the ans variable as a character. Ask the users whether they want to continue, and get the response. If the user doesn't type Y or N, ask the user for another response.

Continue asking
while answer
is not yes

```cpp
// Filename: C12WHIL1.CPP
// Input routine to ensure user types a
// correct response. This routine can be part
// of a larger program.
#include <iostream.h>
main()
{
    char ans;

    cout << "Do you want to continue (Y/N)? ";
    cin >> ans;                    // Get user's answer
```

```
    while ((ans != 'Y') && (ans != 'N'))
      { cout << "\nYou must type a Y or an N\n";  // Warn
                                                   // and ask
        cout << "Do you want to continue (Y/N)?"; // again.
        cin >> ans;
      }           // Body of while loop ends here.

    return 0;
}
```

Notice that the two `cin` functions do the same thing. You must use an initial `cin`, outside the `while` loop, to provide an answer for the `while` loop to check. If users type something other than Y or N, the program prints an error message, asks for another answer, then checks the new answer. This validation method is preferred over one where the reader only has one additional chance to succeed.

The `while` loop tests the test expression at the top of the loop. This is why the loop might never execute. If the test is initially False, the loop does not execute even once. The output from this program is shown as follows. The program repeats indefinitely, until the relational test is True (as soon as the user types either Y or N).

```
Do you want to continue (Y/N)? k

You must type a Y or an N
Do you want to continue (Y/N)? c

You must type a Y or an N
Do you want to continue (Y/N)? s

You must type a Y or an N
Do you want to continue (Y/N)? 5

You must type a Y or an N
Do you want to continue (Y/N)? Y
```

2. The following program is an example of an *invalid* `while` loop. See if you can find the problem.

```
// Filename: C12WHBAD.CPP
// Bad use of a while loop.
#include <iostream.h>
main()
{
   int a=10, b=20;
   while (a > 5)
      { cout << "a is " << a << ", and b is " << b << "\n";
        b = 20 + a; }
   return 0;
}
```

This while loop is an example of an infinite loop. It is vital that at least one statement inside the while changes a variable in the test expression (in this example, the variable a); otherwise, the condition is always True. Because the variable a does not change inside the while loop, this program will never end.

TIP: If you inadvertently write an infinite loop, you must stop the program yourself. If you use a PC, this typically means pressing Ctrl-Break. If you are using a UNIX-based system, your system administrator might have to stop your program's execution.

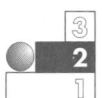

3. The following program asks users for a first name, then uses a while loop to count the number of characters in the name. This is a *string length program;* it counts characters until it reaches the null zero. Remember that the length of a string equals the number of characters in the string, not including the null zero.

```
// Filename: C12WHIL2.CPP
// Counts the number of letters in the user's first name.
#include <iostream.h>
main()
{
   char name[15];              // Will hold user's first name
```

```
int count=0;        // Will hold total characters in name

// Get the user's first name
cout << "What is your first name? ";
cin >> name;

while (name[count] > 0) // Loop until null zero reached.
   {  count++; }                      // Add 1 to the count.

cout << "Your name has " << count << " characters";
return 0;
}
```

The loop continues as long as the value of the next character in the name array is greater than zero. Because the last character in the array is a null zero, the test is False on the name's last character and the statement following the body of the loop continues.

> **NOTE:** A built-in string function called strlen() determines the length of strings. You learn about this function in Chapter 22, "Character, String, and Numeric Functions."

4. The previous string-length program's while loop is not as efficient as it could be. Because a while loop fails when its test expression is zero, there is no need for the greater-than test. By changing the test expression as the following program shows, you can improve the efficiency of the string length count.

```
// Filename: C12WHIL3.CPP
// Counts the number of letters in the user's first name.
#include <iostream.h>
main()
{
   char name[15];        // Will hold user's first name
   int count=0;      // Will hold total characters in name

   // Get the user's first name
```

```
cout << "What is your first name? ";
cin >> name;

while (name[count])  // Loop until null zero is reached.
   { count++; }                  // Add 1 to the count.

cout << "Your name has " << count << " characters";
return 0;
}
```

The do-while Loop

The body of the do-while loop executes at least once.

The do-while statement controls the do-while loop, which is similar to the while loop except the relational test occurs at the end (rather than beginning) of the loop. This ensures the body of the loop executes at least once. The do-while tests for a *positive relational test;* as long as the test is True, the body of the loop continues to execute.

The format of the do-while is

```
do
   { block of one or more C++ statements; }
while (test expression)
```

test expression must be enclosed in parentheses, just as it must in a while statement.

Examples

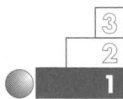

1. The following program is just like the first one you saw with the while loop (C12WHIL1.CPP), except the do-while is used. Notice the placement of *test expression*. Because this expression concludes the loop, user input does not have to appear before the loop and again in the body of the loop.

```
// Filename: C12WHIL4.CPP
// Input routine to ensure user types a
// correct response. This routine might be part
// of a larger program.
```

```
#include <iostream.h>
main()
{
   char ans;

   do
    { cout << "\nYou must type a Y or an N\n";    // Warn
                                                  // and ask
       cout << "Do you want to continue (Y/N) ?"; // again.
       cin >> ans; }            // Body of while loop
                                //    ends here.
    while ((ans != 'Y') && (ans != 'N'));

    return 0;
}
```

2. Suppose you are entering sales amounts into the computer to calculate extended totals. You want the computer to print the quantity sold, part number, and extended total (quantity times the price per unit), as the following program does.

Compute
extended
inventory
amount

```
// Filename: C12INV1.CPP
// Gets inventory information from user and prints
// an inventory detail listing with extended totals.
#include <iostream.h>
#include <iomanip.h>
main()
{
   int part_no, quantity;
   float cost, ext_cost;

   cout << "*** Inventory Computation ***\n\n";    // Title

   // Get inventory information.
   do
    { cout << "What is the next part number (-999 to end)? ";
      cin >> part_no;
      if (part_no != -999)
         { cout << "How many were bought? ";
           cin >> quantity;
           cout << "What is the unit price of this item? ";
```

```
            cin >> cost;
            ext_cost = cost * quantity;
            cout << "\n" << quantity << " of # " << part_no <<
                    " will cost " <<  setprecision(2) <<
                    ext_cost;
            cout << "\n\n\n";        // Print two blank lines.
        }
    } while (part_no != -999);         // Loop only if part
                                       //  number is not -999.


    cout << "End of inventory computation\n";
    return 0;
}
```

Here is the output from this program:

```
*** Inventory Computation ***

What is the next part number (-999 to end)? 213
How many were bought? 12
What is the unit price of this item? 5.66

12 of # 213 will cost 67.92


What is the next part number (-999 to end)? 92
How many were bought? 53
What is the unit price of this item? .23

53 of # 92 will cost 12.19


What is the next part number (-999 to end)? -999
End of inventory computation
```

The do-while loop controls the entry of the customer sales information. Notice the "trigger" that ends the loop. If the user enters –999 for the part number, the do-while loop quits because no part numbered –999 exists in the inventory.

However, this program can be improved in several ways. The invoice can be printed to the printer rather than the screen. You learn how to direct your output to a printer in Chapter 21, "Device and Character Input/Output." Also, the inventory total (the total amount of the entire order) can be computed. You learn how to total such data in the "Counters and Totals" section later in this chapter.

The if **Loop Versus the** while **Loop**

Some beginning programmers confuse the if statement with loop constructs. The while and do-while loops repeat a section of code multiple times, depending on the condition being tested. The if statement may or may not execute a section of code; if it does, it executes that section only once.

Use an if statement when you want to conditionally execute a section of code *once,* and use a while or do-while loop if you want to execute a section *more than once.* Figure 12.1 shows differences between the if statement and the two while loops.

```
if (conditional test)
    {
        /* Body of if statements */————————————  Body executes only
    }                                             once if test is true
                         ┌————————————————————  Test at top of loop.
while (conditional test)
    {
        /* Body of while statements */ —┐
    }                                   │
do                                      │        Body loops continuously
    {                                   │        as long as test is true.
        /* Body of do-while statements */ ┘
    } while (conditional test)
         └——————————————————————————————  Test at top of loop.
```

Figure 12.1. Differences between the if statement and the two while loops.

The `exit()` Function and `break` Statement

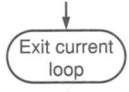

Exit program

C++ provides the `exit()` function as a way to leave a program early (before its natural finish). The format of `exit()` is

```
exit(status);
```

where *status* is an optional integer variable or literal. If you are familiar with your operating system's return codes, *status* enables you to test the results of C++ programs. In DOS, *status* is sent to the operating system's `errorlevel` *environment variable,* where it can be tested by batch files.

The `exit()` function provides an early exit from your program.

Many times, something happens in a program that requires the program's termination. It might be a major problem, such as a disk drive error. Perhaps users indicate that they want to quit the program—you can tell this by giving your users a special value to type with `cin` or `scanf()`. You can isolate the `exit()` function on a line by itself, or anywhere else that a C++ statement or function can appear. Typically, `exit()` is placed in the body of an `if` statement to end the program early, depending on the result of some relational test.

Always include the stdlib.h header file when you use `exit()`. This file describes the operation of `exit()` to your program. Whenever you use a function in a program, you should know its corresponding `#include` header file, which is usually listed in the compiler's reference manual.

The `break` statement ends the current loop.

Instead of exiting an entire program, however, you can use the `break` statement to exit the current loop. The format of `break` is

Exit current loop

```
break;
```

The `break` statement can go anywhere in a C++ program that any other statement can go, but it typically appears in the body of a `while` or `do-while` loop, used to leave the loop early. The following examples illustrate the `exit()` function and the `break` statement.

> **NOTE:** The `break` statement exits only the most current loop. If you have a `while` loop in another `while` loop, `break` exits only the internal loop.

Examples

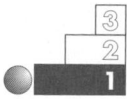

1. Here is a simple program that shows you how the `exit()` function works. This program looks as though it prints several messages on-screen, but it doesn't. Because `exit()` appears early in the code, this program quits immediately after `main()`'s opening brace.

```
// C12EXIT1.CPP
// Quits early due to exit() function.
#include <iostream.h>
#include <stdlib.h>                    // Required for exit().
main()
{
    exit(0);                 // Forces program to end here.

    cout << "C++ programming is fun.\n";
    cout << "I like learning C++ by example!\n";
    cout << "C++ is a powerful language that is " <<
            "not difficult to learn.";

    return 0;
}
```

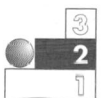

2. The `break` statement is not intended to be as strong a program exit as the `exit()` function. Whereas `exit()` ends the entire program, `break` quits only the loop that is currently active. In other words, `break` is usually placed inside a `while` or `do-while` loop to "simulate" a finished loop. The statement following the loop executes after a `break` occurs, but the program does not quit as it does with `exit()`.

The following program appears to print `C++ is fun!` until the user enters `N` to stop it. The message prints only once, however, because the `break` statement forces an early exit from the loop.

```
// Filename: C12BRK.CPP
// Demonstrates the break statement.
#include <iostream.h>
main()
```

```
{
   char user_ans;

   do
     { cout << "C++ is fun! \n";
       break;                          // Causes early exit.
       cout << "Do you want to see the message again (N/Y)? ";
       cin >> user_ans;
     } while (user_ans == 'Y');

   cout << "That's all for now\n";
   return 0;
}
```

This program always produces the following output:

```
C++ is fun!
That's all for now
```

You can tell from this program's output that the break statement does not allow the do-while loop to reach its natural conclusion, but causes it to finish early. The final cout prints because only the current loop—and not the entire program—exits with the break statement.

3. Unlike the previous program, break usually appears after an if statement. This makes it a *conditional* break, which occurs only if the relational test of the if statement is True.

A good illustration of this is the inventory program you saw earlier (C12INV1.CPP). Even though the users enter –999 when they want to quit the program, an additional if test is needed inside the do-while. The –999 ends the do-while loop, but the body of the do-while still needs an if test, so the remaining quantity and cost prompts are not given.

If you insert a break after testing for the end of the user's input, as shown in the following program, the do-while will not need the if test. The break quits the do-while as soon as the user signals the end of the inventory by entering –999 as the part number.

```
// Filename: C12INV2.CPP
// Gets inventory information from user and prints
// an inventory detail listing with extended totals.
#include <iostream.h>
#include <iomanip.h>
main()
{
   int part_no, quantity;
   float cost, ext_cost;

   cout << "*** Inventory Computation ***\n\n";   // Title

   // Get inventory information
   do
    { cout << "What is the next part number (-999 to end)? ";
      cin >> part_no;
      if (part_no == -999)
        { break; }                    // Exit the loop if
                                      // no more part numbers.
      cout << "How many were bought? ";
      cin >> quantity;
      cout << "What is the unit price of this item? ";
      cin >> cost;
      cout << "\n" << quantity << " of # " << part_no <<
           " will cost " << setprecision(2) << cost*quantity;
      cout << "\n\n\n";          // Print two blank lines.
    } while (part_no != 999);       // Loop only if part
                                    // number is not -999.

   cout << "End of inventory computation\n";
   return 0;
}
```

4. You can use the following program to control the two other programs. This program illustrates how C++ can pass information to DOS with exit(). This is your first example of a menu program. Similar to a restaurant menu, a C++ menu program lists possible user choices. The users decide what they want the computer to do from the menu's available options. The mailing list application in Appendix F, "The Mailing List Application," uses a menu for its user options.

This program returns either a 1 or a 2 to its operating system, depending on the user's selection. It is then up to the operating system to test the exit value and run the proper program.

```cpp
// Filename: C12EXIT2.CPP
// Asks user for his or her selection and returns
// that selection to the operating system with exit().
#include <iostream.h>
#include <stdlib.h>
main()
{
   int ans;

   do
     { cout << "Do you want to:\n\n";
       cout << "\t1. Run the word processor \n\n";
       cout << "\t2. Run the database program \n\n";
       cout << "What is your selection? ";
       cin >> ans;
     } while ((ans != 1) && (ans != 2));   // Ensures user
                                           // enters 1 or 2.
   exit(ans);   // Return value to operating system.
   return 0;    // Return does not ever execute due to exit().
}
```

Counters and Totals

Counting is important for many applications. You might have to know how many customers you have or how many people scored over a certain average in your class. You might want to count how many checks you wrote in the previous month with your computerized checkbook system.

Before you develop C++ routines to count occurrences, think of how you count in your own mind. If you were adding a total number of something, such as the stamps in your stamp collection or the number of wedding invitations you sent out, you would probably do the following:

Start at 0, and add 1 for each item being counted. When you are finished, you should have the total number (or the total count).

This is all you do when you count with C++: Assign 0 to a variable and add 1 to it every time you process another data value. The increment operator (++) is especially useful for counting.

Examples

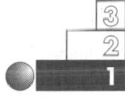

1. To illustrate using a counter, the following program prints "Computers are fun!" on-screen 10 times. You can write a program that has 10 cout statements, but that would not be efficient. It would also be too cumbersome to have 5000 cout statements, if you wanted to print that same message 5000 times.

By adding a while loop and a counter that stops after a certain total is reached, you can control this printing, as the following program shows.

```cpp
// Filename: C12CNT1.CPP
// Program to print a message 10 times.
#include <iostream.h>
main()
{
   int ctr = 0;    // Holds the number of times printed.

   do
     { cout << "Computers are fun!\n";
       ctr++;                      // Add one to the count,
                                   // after each cout.
     } while (ctr < 10);          // Print again if fewer
                                   // than 10 times.
   return 0;
}
```

The output from this program is shown as follows. Notice that the message prints exactly 10 times.

```
Computers are fun!
Computers are fun!
Computers are fun!
Computers are fun!
Computers are fun!
Computers are fun!
Computers are fun!
Computers are fun!
Computers are fun!
Computers are fun!
```

The heart of the counting process in this program is the statement that follows.

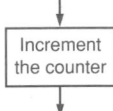

Increment
the counter

```
ctr++;
```

You learned earlier that the increment operator adds 1 to a variable. In this program, the counter variable is incremented each time the do-while loops. Because the only operation performed on this line is the increment of ctr, the prefix increment (++ctr) produces the same results.

2. The previous program not only added to the counter variable, but also performed the loop a specific number of times. This is a common method of conditionally executing parts of a program for a fixed number of times.

The following program is a password program. A password is stored in an integer variable. The user must correctly enter the matching password in three attempts. If the user does not type the correct password in that time, the program ends. This is a common method that dial-up computers use. They enable a caller to try the password a fixed number of times, then hang up the phone if that limit is exceeded. This helps deter people from trying hundreds of different passwords at any one sitting.

If users guess the correct password in three tries, they see the secret message.

```
// Filename: C12PASS1.CPP
// Program to prompt for a password and
// check it against an internal one.
#include <iostream.h>
#include <stdlib.h>
main()
{
   int stored_pass = 11862;
   int num_tries = 0;      // Counter for password attempts.
   int user_pass;

   while (num_tries < 3)              // Loop only three
                                      // times.
      { cout << "What is the password (You get 3 tries...)? ";
        cin >> user_pass;
        num_tries++;                        // Add 1 to counter.
        if (user_pass == stored_pass)
           { cout << "You entered the correct password.\n";
             cout << "The cash safe is behind the picture " <<
                     "of the ship.\n";
             exit(0);
           }
        else
           { cout << "You entered the wrong password.\n";
           if (num_tries == 3)
           { cout << "Sorry, you get no more chances"; }
           else
           { cout << "You get " << (3-num_tries) <<
                     " more tries...\n";}
        }
      }                                     // End of while loop.
   exit(0);
   return 0;
}
```

This program gives users three chances in case they type
some mistakes. After three unsuccessful attempts, the program quits without displaying the secret message.

3. The following program is a letter-guessing game. It includes a message telling users how many tries they made before guessing the correct letter. A counter counts the number of these tries.

```cpp
// Filename: C12GUES.CPP
// Letter-guessing game.
#include <iostream.h>
main()
{
   int tries = 0;
   char comp_ans, user_guess;

   // Save the computer's letter
   comp_ans = 'T';                    // Change to a different
                                      //     letter if desired.

   cout << "I am thinking of a letter...";
   do
     { cout << "What is your guess? ";
       cin >> user_guess;
       tries++;    // Add 1 to the guess-counting variable.
       if (user_guess > comp_ans)
          { cout << "Your guess was too high\n";
            cout << "\nTry again...";
          }
       if (user_guess < comp_ans)
          { cout << "Your guess was too low\n";
            cout << "\nTry again...";
          }
     } while (user_guess != comp_ans);  // Quit when a
                                        // match is found.

   // They got it right, let them know.
   cout << "*** Congratulations!  You got it right! \n";
   cout << "It took you only " << tries <<
          " tries to guess.";
   return 0;
}
```

Here is the output of this program:

```
I am thinking of a letter...What is your guess? E
Your guess was too low

Try again...What is your guess? X
Your guess was too high

Try again...What is your guess? H
Your guess was too low

Try again...What is your guess? O
Your guess was too low

Try again...What is your guess? U
Your guess was too high

Try again...What is your guess? Y
Your guess was too high

Try again...What is your guess? T
*** Congratulations!  You got it right!
It took you only 7 tries to guess.
```

Producing Totals

Writing a routine to add values is as easy as counting. Instead of adding 1 to the counter variable, you add a value to the total variable. For instance, if you want to find the total dollar amount of checks you wrote during December, you can start at nothing (0) and add the amount of every check written in December. Instead of building a count, you are building a total.

When you want C++ to add values, just initialize a total variable to zero, then add each value to the total until you have included all the values.

Examples

1. Suppose you want to write a program that adds your grades for a class you are taking. The teacher has informed you that you earn an *A* if you can accumulate over 450 points.

   The following program keeps asking you for values until you type –1. The –1 is a signal that you are finished entering grades and now want to see the total. This program also prints a congratulatory message if you have enough points for an *A*.

```
// Filename: C12GRAD1.CPP
// Adds grades and determines whether you earned an A.
#include <iostream.h>
include <iomanip.h>
main()
{
    float total_grade=0.0;
    float grade;              // Holds individual grades.

    do
    { cout << "What is your grade? (-1 to end) ";
      cin >> grade;
      if (grade >= 0.0)
        { total_grade += grade; }        // Add to total.
    } while (grade >= 0.0);     // Quit when -1 entered.

    // Control begins here if no more grades.
    cout << "\n\nYou made a total of " << setprecision(1) <<
            total_grade << " points\n";
    if (total_grade >= 450.00)
        { cout << "** You made an A!!"; }

    return 0;
}
```

Notice that the -1 response is not added to the total number of points. This program checks for the -1 before adding to total_grade. Here is the output from this program:

```
What is your grade? (-1 to end) 87.6
What is your grade? (-1 to end) 92.4
What is your grade? (-1 to end) 78.7
What is your grade? (-1 to end) -1

You made a total of   258.7 points
```

2. The following program is an extension of the grade-calculating program. It not only totals the points, but also computes their average.

To calculate the average grade, the program must first determine how many grades were entered. This is a subtle problem because the number of grades to be entered is unknown in advance. Therefore, every time the user enters a valid grade (not –1), the program must add 1 to a counter as well as add that grade to the total variable. This is a combination counting and totaling routine, which is common in many programs.

```cpp
// Filename: C12GRAD2.CPP
// Adds up grades, computes average,
// and determines whether you earned an A.
#include <iostream.h>
#include <iomanip.h>
main()
{
    float total_grade=0.0;
    float grade_avg = 0.0;
    float grade;
    int grade_ctr = 0;

    do
    { cout << "What is your grade? (-1 to end) ";
      cin >> grade;
      if (grade >= 0.0)
       { total_grade += grade;          // Add to total.
         grade_ctr ++; }                // Add to count.
    } while (grade >= 0.0);             // Quit when -1 entered.
```

```
// Control begins here if no more grades.
grade_avg = (total_grade / grade_ctr);       // Compute
                                             // average.
cout << "\nYou made a total of " << setprecision(1) <<
        total_grade << " points.\n";
cout << "Your average was " << grade_avg << "\n";
if (total_grade >= 450.0)
   { cout << "** You made an A!!"; }
return 0;
}
```

Below is the output of this program. Congratulations! You are on your way to becoming a master C++ programmer.

```
What is your grade? (-1 to end) 67.8
What is your grade? (-1 to end) 98.7
What is your grade? (-1 to end) 67.8
What is your grade? (-1 to end) 92.4
What is your grade? (-1 to end) -1

You made a total of 326.68 points.
Your average was 81.7
```

Review Questions

The answers to the review questions are in Appendix B.

1. What is the difference between the while loop and the do-while loop?

2. What is the difference between a total variable and a counter variable?

3. Which C++ operator is most useful for counting?

4. True or false: Braces are not required around the body of while and do-while loops.

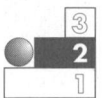

5. What is wrong with the following code?

```
while (sales > 50)
   cout << "Your sales are very good this month.\n";
   cout << "You will get a bonus for your high sales\n";
```

6. What file must you include as a header file if you use `exit()`?

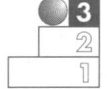

7. How many times does this `printf()` print?

```
int a=0;
do
   { printf("Careful \n");
     a++; }
while (a > 5);
```

8. How can you inform DOS of the program exit status?

9. What is printed to the screen in the following section of code?

```
a = 1;
while (a < 4)
   { cout << "This is the outer loop\n";
     a++;
     while (a <= 25)
        { break;
          cout << "This prints 25 times\n"; }
   }
```

Review Exercises

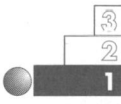

1. Write a program with a `do-while` loop that prints the numerals from 10 to 20 (inclusive), with a blank line between each number.

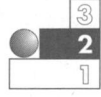

2. Write a weather-calculator program that asks for a list of the previous 10 days' temperatures, computes the average, and prints the results. You have to compute the total as the input occurs, then divide that total by 10 to find the average. Use a `while` loop for the 10 repetitions.

3. Rewrite the program in Exercise 2 using a do-while loop.

4. Write a program, similar to the weather calculator in Exercise 2, but generalize it so it computes the average of any number of days' temperatures. (*Hint:* You have to count the number of temperatures to compute the final average.)

5. Write a program that produces your own ASCII table on-screen. Don't print the first 31 characters because they are nonprintable. Print the codes numbered 32 through 255 by storing their numbers in integer variables and printing their ASCII values using printf() and the "%c" format code.

Summary

This chapter showed you two ways to produce a C++ loop: the while loop and the do-while loop. These two variations of while loops differ in where they test their *test condition* statements. The while tests at the beginning of its loop, and the do-while tests at the end. Therefore, the body of a do-while loop always executes at least once. You also learned that the exit() function and break statement add flexibility to the while loops. The exit() function terminates the program, and the break statement terminates only the current loop.

This chapter explained two of the most important applications of loops: counters and totals. Your computer can be a wonderful tool for adding and counting, due to the repetitive capabilities offered with while loops.

The next chapter extends your knowledge of loops by showing you how to create a *determinate* loop, called the for loop. This feature is useful when you want a section of code to loop for a specified number of times.

Part III

C++ Constructs

The for Loop

The for loop enables you to repeat sections of your program for a specific number of times. Unlike the while and do-while loops, the for loop is a *determinate loop*. This means when you write your program you can usually determine how many times the loop iterates. The while and do-while loops repeat only until a condition is met. The for loop does this and more: It continues looping until a count (or countdown) is reached.

After the final for loop count is reached, execution continues with the next statement, in sequence. This chapter focuses on the for loop construct by introducing

♦ The for statement

♦ The concept of for loops

♦ Nested for loops

The for loop is a helpful way of looping through a section of code when you want to count, or sum, specified amounts, but it does not replace the while and do-while loops.

The for Statement

The for statement encloses one or more C++ statements that form the body of the loop. These statements in the loop continuously repeat for a specified number of times. You, as the programmer, control the number of loop repetitions.

The format of the for loop is

```
for (start expression; test expression; count expression)
{ Block of one or more C++ statements; }
```

C++ evaluates the *start expression* before the loop begins. Typically, the *start expression* is an assignment statement (such as ctr=1;), but it can be any legal expression you specify. C++ evaluates *start expression* only once, at the top of the loop.

> **CAUTION:** Do not put a semicolon after the right parenthesis. If you do, the for loop interprets the body of the loop as zero statements long! It would continue looping—doing *nothing* each time—until the *test expression* becomes False.

The for loop iterates for a specified number of times.

Every time the body of the loop repeats, the *count expression* executes, usually incrementing or decrementing a variable. The *test expression* evaluates to True (nonzero) or False (zero), then determines whether the body of the loop repeats again.

> **TIP:** If only one C++ statement resides in the for loop's body, braces are not required, but they are recommended. If you add more statements, the braces are there already, reminding you that they are now needed.

The Concept of for Loops

You use the concept of for loops throughout your day-to-day life. Any time you have to repeat a certain procedure a specified number of times, that repetition becomes a good candidate for a computerized for loop.

To illustrate the concept of a for loop further, suppose you are installing 10 new shutters on your house. You must do the following steps for each shutter:

1. Move the ladder to the location of the shutter.

2. Take a shutter, hammer, and nails up the ladder.

3. Hammer the shutter to the side of the house.

4. Climb down the ladder.

You must perform each of these four steps exactly 10 times, because you have 10 shutters. After 10 times, you don't install another shutter because the job is finished. You are looping through a procedure that has several steps (the block of the loop). These steps are the body of the loop. It is not an endless loop because there are a fixed number of shutters; you run out of shutters only after you install all 10.

For a less physical example that might be more easily computerized, suppose you have to fill out three tax returns for each of your teenage children. (If you have three teenage children, you probably need more than a computer to help you get through the day!) For each child, you must perform the following steps:

1. Add the total income.

2. Add the total deductions.

3. Fill out a tax return.

4. Put it in an envelope.

5. Mail it.

You then must repeat this entire procedure two more times. Notice how the sentence before these steps began: *For each child.* This signals an idea similar to the for loop construct.

> **NOTE:** The for loop tests the *test expression* at the top of the loop. If the *test expression* is False when the for loop begins, the body of the loop never executes.

The Choice of Loops

Any loop construct can be written with a `for` loop, a `while` loop, or a `do-while` loop. Generally, you use the `for` loop when you want to count or loop a specific number of times, and reserve the `while` and `do-while` loops for looping until a False condition is met.

Examples

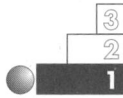

1. To give you a glimpse of the `for` loop's capabilities, this example shows you two programs: one that uses a `for` loop and one that does not. The first one is a counting program. Before studying its contents, look at the output. The results illustrate the `for` loop concept very well.

Identify the program and include the necessary header file. You need a counter, so make `ctr` an integer variable.

1. Add one to the counter.

2. If the counter is less than or equal to 10, print its value and repeat step one.

The program with a `for` loop follows:

```
// Filename: C13FOR1.CPP
// Introduces the for loop.
#include <iostream.h>
main()
{
    int ctr;
    for (ctr=1; ctr<=10; ctr++)      // Start ctr at one.
                                     // Increment through loop.
        { cout << ctr << "\n"; }     // Body of for loop.

    return 0;
}
```

This program's output is

```
1
2
3
4
5
6
7
8
9
10
```

Here is the same program using a do-while loop:

Identify the program and include the necessary header file. You need a counter, so make ctr an integer variable.

1. *Add one to the counter.*
2. *Print the value of the counter.*
3. *If the counter is less than or equal to 10, repeat step one.*

```cpp
// Filename: C13WHI1.CPP
// Simulating a for loop with a do-while loop.
#include <iostream.h>
main()
{
    int ctr=1;
    do
      { cout << ctr << "\n"; // Body of do-while loop.
        ctr++; }
    while (ctr <= 10);

    return 0;
}
```

Notice that the for loop is a cleaner way of controlling the looping process. The for loop does several things that require extra statements in a while loop. With for loops, you do not have to write extra code to initialize variables and increment or decrement them. You can see at a glance (in the expressions in the `for` statement) exactly how the loop executes, unlike the `do-while`, which forces you to look at the *bottom* of the loop to see how the loop stops.

2. Both of the following sample programs add the numbers from 100 to 200. The first one uses a `for` loop; the second one does not. The first example starts with a *start expression* bigger than 1, thus starting the loop with a bigger *count expression* as well.

This program has a `for` loop:

```
// Filename: C13FOR2.CPP
// Demonstrates totaling using a for loop.
#include <iostream.h>
main()
{
   int total, ctr;

   total = 0;              // Holds a total of 100 to 200.

   for (ctr=100; ctr<=200; ctr++)      // ctr is 100, 101,
                                       // 102,...200
     { total += ctr; }  // Add value of ctr to each iteration.

   cout << "The total is " << total << "\n";
   return 0;
}
```

The same program without a `for` loop follows:

```
// Filename: C13WHI2.CPP
// A totaling program using a do-while loop.
#include <iostream.h>
main()
{
   int total=0;            // Initialize total
   int num=100;            // Starting value

   do
     { total += num;       // Add to total
       num++;              // Increment counter
```

```
      } while (num <= 200);
   cout << "The total is " << total << "\n";;
   return 0;
}
```

Both programs produce this output:

```
The total is 15150
```

The body of the loop in both programs executes 101 times.
The starting value is 101, not 1 as in the previous example.
Notice that the `for` loop is less complex than the `do-while`
because the initialization, testing, and incrementing are
performed in the single `for` statement.

> **TIP:** Notice how the body of the `for` loop is indented. This is a
> good habit to develop because it makes it easier to see the
> beginning and ending of the loop's body.

3. The body of the `for` loop can have more than one statement.
   The following example requests five pairs of data values:
   children's first names and their ages. It prints the teacher
   assigned to each child, based on the child's age. This illustrates a `for` loop with `cout` functions, a `cin` function, and an `if`
   statement in its body. Because exactly five children are
   checked, the `for` loop ensures the program ends after the
   fifth child.

Get child's
name

Get child's
age

Print
child's
teacher

```
// Filename: C13FOR3.CPP
// Program that uses a loop to input and print
// the teacher assigned to each child.
#include <iostream.h>
main()
{
   char child[25];    // Holds child's first name
   int age;           // Holds child's age
   int ctr;           // The for loop counter variable

   for (ctr=1; ctr<=5; ctr++)
     { cout << "What is the next child's name? ";
```

```
        cin >> child;
        cout << "What is the child's age? ";
        cin >> age;
        if (age <= 5)
            { cout << "\n" << child << " has Mrs. "
                    << "Jones for a teacher\n"; }
        if (age == 6)
            { cout << "\n" << child << " has Miss "
                    << "Smith for a teacher\n"; }
        if (age >= 7)
            { cout << "\n" << child << " has Mr. "
                    << "Anderson for a teacher\n"; }
    }  // Quits after 5 times

    return 0;
}
```

Below is the output from this program. You can improve this program even more after learning the switch statement in the next chapter.

```
What is the next child's name? Joe
What is the child's age? 5

Joe has Mrs. Jones for a teacher
What is the next child's name? Larry
What is the child's age? 6

Larry has Miss Smith for a teacher
What is the next child's name? Julie
What is the child's age? 9

Julie has Mr. Anderson for a teacher
What is the next child's name? Manny
What is the child's age? 6

Manny has Miss Smith for a teacher
What is the next child's name? Lori
What is the child's age? 5

Lori has Mrs. Jones for a teacher
```

4. The previous examples used an increment as the *count expression.* You can make the `for` loop increment the loop variable by any value. It does not have to increment by 1.

The following program prints the even numbers from 1 to 20. It then prints the odd numbers from 1 to 20. To do this, two is added to the counter variable (rather than one, as shown in the previous examples) each time the loop executes.

```cpp
// Filename: C13EVOD.CPP
// Prints the even numbers from 1 to 20,
// then the odd numbers from 1 to 20.
#include <iostream.h>
main()
{
   int num;                          // The for loop variable

   cout << "Even numbers below 21\n";          // Title
   for (num=2; num<=20; num+=2)
     { cout << num << " "; }  // Prints every other number.

   cout << "\nOdd numbers below 20\n";   // A second title
   for (num-1; num<=20; num+=2)
     { cout << num << " "; }  // Prints every other number.

   return 0;
}
```

There are two loops in this program. The body of each one consists of a single `printf()` function. In the first half of the program, the loop variable, `num`, is 2 and not 1. If it were 1, the number 1 would print first, as it does in the odd number section.

The two `cout` statements that print the titles are not part of either loop. If they were, the program would print a title before each number. The following shows the result of running this program.

```
Even numbers below 21
2 4 6 8 10 12 14 16 18 20
Odd numbers below 20
1 3 5 7 9 11 13 15 17 19
```

5. You can decrement the loop variable as well. If you do, the value is subtracted from the loop variable each time through the loop.

   The following example is a rewrite of the counting program. It produces the reverse effect by showing a countdown.

```
// Filename: C13CNTD1.CPP
// Countdown to the liftoff.
#include <iostream.h>
main()
{
   int ctr;

   for (ctr=10; ctr!=0; ctr--)
     { cout << ctr << "\n"; }    // Print ctr as it
                                 // counts down.
   cout << "*** Blast off! ***\n";
   return 0;
}
```

   When decrementing a loop variable, the initial value should be larger than the end value being tested. In this example, the loop variable, ctr, counts down from 10 to 1. Each time through the loop (each iteration), ctr is decremented by one. You can see how easy it is to control a loop by looking at this program's output, as follows.

```
10
 9
 8
 7
 6
 5
 4
 3
```

```
      2
      1
 *** Blast Off! ***
```

TIP: This program's `for` loop test illustrates a redundancy that you can eliminate, thanks to C++. The `test expression`, `ctr!=0;` tells the `for` loop to continue looping until `ctr` is not equal to zero. However, if `ctr` becomes zero (a False value), there is no reason to add the additional `!=0` (except for clarity). You can rewrite the `for` loop as

```
for (ctr=10; ctr; ctr--)
```

without loss of meaning. This is more efficient and such an integral part of C++ that you should become comfortable with it. There is little loss of clarity once you adjust to it.

6. You also can make a `for` loop test for something other than a literal value. The following program combines much of what you have learned so far. It asks for student grades and computes an average. Because there might be a different number of students each semester, the program first asks the user for the number of students. Next, the program iterates until the user enters an equal number of scores. It then computes the average based on the total and the number of student grades entered.

```cpp
// Filename: C13FOR4.CPP
// Computes a grade average with a for loop.
#include <iostream.h>
#include <iomanip.h>
main()
{
   float grade, avg;
   float total=0.0;
   int num;               // Total number of grades.
   int loopvar;           // Used to control the for loop

   cout << "\n*** Grade Calculation ***\n\n";  // Title
```

```
cout << "How many students are there? ";
cin >> num;      // Get total number to enter

for (loopvar=1; loopvar<=num; loopvar++)
   { cout << "\nWhat is the next student's grade? ";
     cin >> grade;
     total += grade;  }      // Keep a running total

avg = total / num;
cout << "\n\nThe average of this class is " <<
        setprecision(1) << avg;
return 0;
}
```

Due to the `for` loop, the total and the average calculations do not have to be changed if the number of students changes.

7. Because characters and integers are so closely associated in C++, you can increment character variables in a `for` loop. The following program prints the letters *A* through *Z* with a simple `for` loop.

Print each letter of alphabet

```
// Filename: C13FOR5.CPP
// Prints the alphabet with a simple for loop.
#include <iostream.h>
main()
{
   char letter;

   cout << "Here is the alphabet:\n";
   for (letter='A'; letter<='Z'; letter++) // Loops A to Z
      { cout << " " << letter; }

   return 0;
}
```

This program produces the following output:

```
Here is the alphabet:
A B C D E F G H I J K L M N O P Q R S T U V W X Y Z
```

8. A `for` expression can be a blank, or *null expression.* In the following `for` loop, all the expressions are blank:

```
for (;;)
   { printf("Over and over..."); }
```

This `for` loop iterates forever. Although you should avoid infinite loops, your program might dictate that you make a `for` loop expression blank. If you already initialized the *start expression* earlier in the program, you are wasting computer time to repeat it in the `for` loop—and C++ does not require it.

The following program omits the *start expression* and the *count expression*, leaving only the `for` loop's *test expression*. Most the time, you have to omit only one of them. If you use a `for` loop without two of its expressions, consider replacing it with a `while` loop or a `do while` loop.

```
// Filename: C13FOR6.CPP
// Uses only the test expression in
// the for loop to count by fives.
#include <iostream.h>
main()
{
   int num=5;                              // Starting value

   cout << "\nCounting by 5s. \n";         // Title
   for (; num<=100;)  // Contains only the test expression.
     { cout << num << "\n";
       num+=5;     // Increment expression outside the loop.
     }                               // End of the loop's body

   return 0;
}
```

The output from this program follows:

```
Counting by 5s:
5
10
15
```

```
        20
        25
        30
        35
        40
        45
        50
        55
        60
        65
        70
        75
        80
        85
        90
        95
       100
```

Nested for Loops

Any C++ statement can go inside the body of a for loop—even another for loop! When you put a loop in a loop, you are creating a *nested loop.* The clock in a sporting event works like a nested loop. You might think this is stretching the analogy a little far, but it truly works. A football game counts down from 15 minutes to 0. It does this four times. The first countdown loops from 15 to 0 (for each minute). That countdown is nested in another that loops from 1 to 4 (for each of the four quarters).

Use nested loops when you want to repeat a loop more than once.

If your program has to repeat a loop more than one time, it is a good candidate for a nested loop. Figure 13.1 shows two outlines of nested loops. You can think of the inside loop as looping "faster" than the outside loop. In the first example, the inside for loop counts from 1 to 10 before the outside loop (the variable out) can finish its first iteration. When the outside loop finally does iterate a second time, the inside loop starts over.

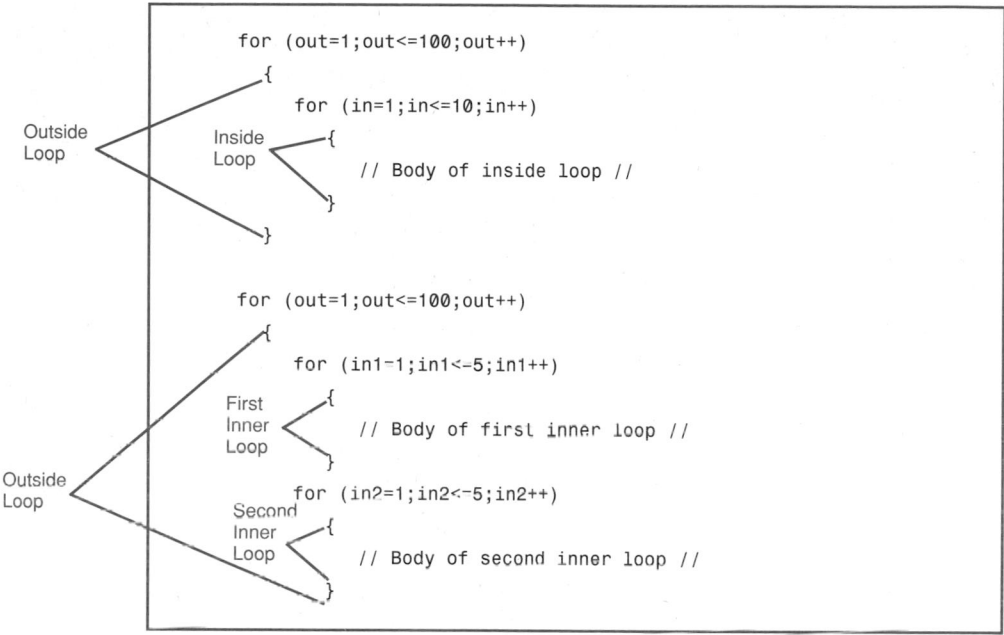

```
          for (out=1;out<=100;out++)
        {
            for (in=1;in<=10;in++)
Outside    Inside    {
Loop       Loop          // Body of inside loop //
        }
          }


          for (out=1;out<=100;out++)
        {
            for (in1=1;in1<=5;in1++)
First        {
Inner            // Body of first inner loop //
Loop         }
            for (in2=1;in2<=5;in2++)
Outside   Second
Loop      Inner    {
          Loop         // Body of second inner loop //
             }
```

Figure 13.1. Outlines of two nested loops.

The second nested loop outline shows two loops in an outside loop. Both of these loops execute in their entirety before the outside loop finishes its first iteration. When the outside loop starts its second iteration, the two inside loops repeat again.

Notice the order of the braces in each example. The inside loop *always* finishes, and therefore its ending brace must come before the outside loop's ending brace. Indention makes this much clearer because you can align the braces of each loop.

Nested loops become important when you use them for array and table processing in Chapter 23, "Introducing Arrays."

NOTE: In nested loops, the inside loop (or loops) execute completely before the outside loop's next iteration.

Examples

1. The following program contains a loop in a loop—a nested loop. The inside loop counts and prints from 1 to 5. The outside loop counts from 1 to 3. The inside loop repeats, in its entirety, three times. In other words, this program prints the values 1 to 5 and does so three times.

```cpp
// Filename: C13NEST1.CPP
// Print the numbers 1-5 three times.
// using a nested loop.
#include <iostream.h>
main()
{
    int times, num;   // Outer and inner for loop variables

    for (times=1; times<=3; times++)
    {
        for (num=1; num<=5; num++)
            { cout << num; }            // Inner loop body
        cout << "\n";
    }                                   // End of outer loop

    return 0;
}
```

The indention follows the standard of for loops; every statement in each loop is indented a few spaces. Because the inside loop is already indented, its body is indented another few spaces. The program's output follows:

```
12345
12345
12345
```

2. The outside loop's counter variable changes each time through the loop. If one of the inside loop's control variables is the outside loop's counter variable, you see effects such as those shown in the following program.

```
// Filename: C13NEST2.CPP
// An inside loop controlled by the outer loop's
// counter variable.
#include <iostream.h>
main()
{
   int outer, inner;

   for (outer=5; outer>=1; outer--)
     { for (inner=1; inner<=outer; inner++)
          { cout << inner; }    // End of inner loop.
     cout << "\n";
     }
     return 0;
}
```

The output from this program follows. The inside loop repeats five times (as outer counts down from 5 to 1) and prints from five numbers to one number.

```
12345
1234
123
12
1
```

The following table traces the two variables through this program. Sometimes you have to "play computer" when learning a new concept such as nested loops. By executing a line at a time and writing down each variable's contents, you create this table.

The outer variable	The inner variable
5	1
5	2
5	3
5	4
5	5
4	1
4	2

continues

The outer variable	The inner variable
4	3
4	4
3	1
3	2
3	3
2	1
2	2
1	1

Tip for Mathematicians

The `for` statement is identical to the mathematical summation symbol. When you write programs to simulate the summation symbol, the `for` statement is an excellent candidate. A nested `for` statement is good for double summations.

For example, the following summation

```
i = 30
Σ (i / 3 * 2)
i = 1
```

can be rewritten as

```
total = 0;
for (i=1; i<=30; i++)
    { total += (i / 3 * 2); }
```

4. A factorial is a mathematical number used in probability theory and statistics. A factorial of a number is the multiplied product of every number from 1 to the number in question.

For example, the factorial of 4 is 24 because $4 \times 3 \times 2 \times 1 = 24$. The factorial of 6 is 720 because $6 \times 5 \times 4 \times 3 \times 2 \times 1 = 720$. The factorial of 1 is 1 by definition.

Nested loops are good candidates for writing a factorial number-generating program. The following program asks the user for a number, then prints the factorial of that number.

```cpp
// Filename: C13FACT.CPP
// Computes the factorial of numbers through
// the user's number.
#include <iostream.h>
main()
{
   int outer, num, fact, total;

   cout << "What factorial do you want to see? ";
   cin >> num;

   for (outer=1; outer <= num; outer++)
     { total = 1;   // Initialize total for each factorial.
       for (fact=1; fact<= outer; fact++)
         { total *= fact; }      // Compute each factorial.
     }

   cout << "The factorial for " << num << " is "
        << total;

   return 0;
}
```

The following shows the factorial of seven. You can run this program, entering different values when asked, and see various factorials. Be careful: factorials multiply quickly. (A factorial of 11 won't fit in an integer variable.)

```
What factorial do you want to see? 7
The factorial for 7 is 5040
```

Review Questions

The answers to the review questions are in Appendix B.

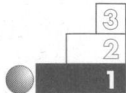

1. What is a loop?

2. True or false: The body of a `for` loop contains at most one statement.

3. What is a nested loop?

4. Why might you want to leave one or more expressions out of the `for` statement's parentheses?

5. Which loop "moves" fastest: the inner loop or the outer loop?

6. What is the output from the following program?

```
for (ctr=10; ctr>=1; ctr-=3)
   { cout << ctr << "\n"; }
```

7. True or false: A `for` loop is better to use than a `while` loop when you know in advance exactly how many iterations a loop requires.

8. What happens when the `test expression` becomes False in a `for` statement?

9. True or false: The following program contains a valid nested loop.

```
for (i=1; i<=10; i++);
  { for (j=1; j<=5; j++)
      { cout << i << j; }
  }
```

10. What is the output of the following section of code?

```
i=1;
start=1;
end=5;
step=1;
```

```
for (; start>=end;)
  { cout << i << "\n";
    start+=step;
    end--;}
```

Review Exercises

1. Write a program that prints the numerals 1 to 15 on-screen. Use a for loop to control the printing.

2. Write a program to print the numerals 15 to 1 on-screen. Use a for loop to control the printing.

3. Write a program that uses a for loop to print every odd number from 1 to 100.

4. Write a program that asks the user for her or his age. Use a for loop to print "Happy Birthday!" for every year of the user's age.

5. Write a program that uses a for loop to print the ASCII characters from 32 to 255 on-screen. (*Hint:* Use the %c conversion character to print integer variables.)

6. Using the ASCII table numbers, write a program to print the following output, using a nested for loop. (*Hint:* The outside loop should loop from 1 to 5, and the inside loop's start variable should be 65, the value of ASCII *A*.)

```
A
AB
ABC
ABCD
ABCDE
```

Summary

This chapter taught you how to control loops. Instead of writing extra code around a while loop, you can use the for loop to control the number of iterations at the time you define the loop. All for loops contain three parts: a *start expression,* a *test expression,* and a *count expression.*

You have now seen C++'s three loop constructs: the while loop, the do-while loop, and the for loop. They are similar, but behave differently in how they test and initialize variables. No loop is better than the others. The programming problem should dictate which loop to use. The next chapter (Chapter 14, "Other Loop Options") shows you more methods for controlling your loops.

Other Loop Options

Now that you have mastered the looping constructs, you should learn some loop-related statements. This chapter teaches the concepts of *timing loops*, which enable you to slow down your programs. Slowing program execution can be helpful if you want to display a message for a fixed period of time or write computer games with slower speeds so they are at a practical speed for recreational use.

You can use two additional looping commands, the `break` and `continue` statements, to control the loops. These statements work with `while` loops and `for` loops.

This chapter introduces you to the following:

♦ Timing loops

♦ The `break` statement with `for` loops

♦ The `continue` statement with `for` loops

When you master these concepts, you will be well on your way toward writing powerful programs that process large amounts of data.

Timing Loops

Computers are fast, and at times you would probably like them to be even faster. Sometimes, however, you want to slow down the computer. Often, you have to slow the execution of games because the computer's speed makes the game unplayable. Messages that appear on-screen many times clear too fast for the user to read if you don't delay them.

A nested loop is a perfect place for a *timing loop,* which simply cycles through a `for` or `while` loop many times. The larger the end value of the `for` loop, the longer the time in which the loop repeats.

A nested loop is appropriate for displaying error messages to your user. If the user requested a report—but had not entered enough data for your program to print the report—you might print a warning message on-screen for a few seconds, telling users that they cannot request the report yet. After displaying the message for a few seconds, you can clear the message and give the user another chance. (The example program in Appendix F, "The Mailing List Application," uses timing loops to display error messages.)

Timing loops make the computer wait.

There is no way to determine how many iterations a timing loop takes for one second (or minute or hour) of delay because computers run at different speeds. You therefore have to adjust your timing loop's end value to set the delay to your liking.

Examples

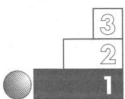

1. Timing loops are easy to write—simply put an empty `for` loop inside the program. The following program is a rewritten version of the countdown program (C13CNTD1.CPP) you saw in Chapter 13. Each number in the countdown is delayed so the countdown does not seem to take place instantly. (Adjust the delay value if this program runs too slowly or too quickly on your computer.)

Identify the program and include the input/output header file. You need a counter and a delay, so make `cd` *and* `delay` *integer variables. Start the counter at 10, and start the* `delay` *at 1.*

1. *If the* `delay` *is less than or equal to 30,000, add 1 to its value and repeat step one.*

2. *Print the value of the counter.*

3. *If the counter is greater than or equal to 0, subtract 1 from its value and repeat step one.*

Print a blast-off message.

```
// Filename: C14CNTD1.CPP
// Countdown to the liftoff with a delay.
#include <iostream.h>
main()
{
   int cd, delay;

   for (cd=10; cd>-0; cd--)
   { { for (delay=1; delay <=30000; delay++); }  // Delay
                                              // program.
      cout << cd << "\n";          // Print countdown value.
   }                                   // End of outer loop
   cout << "Blast off!!! \n";
   return 0;
}
```

2. The following program asks users for their ages. If a user enters an age less than 0, the program beeps (by printing an alarm character, \a), then displays an error message for a few seconds by using a nested timing loop. Because an integer does not hold a large enough value (on many computers) for a long timing loop, you must use a nested timing loop. (Depending on the speed of your computer, adjust the numbers in the loop to display the message longer or shorter.)

The program uses a rarely seen printf() conversion character, \r, inside the loop. As you might recall from Chapter 7, "Simple Input and Output," \r is a carriage-return character. This conversion character moves the cursor to the beginning of the current line, enabling the program to print blanks on that same line. This process overwrites the error message and it appears as though the error disappears from the screen after a brief pause.

```
// Filename: C14TIM.CPP
// Displays an error message for a few seconds.
#include <stdio.h>
main()
{
    int outer, inner, age;

    printf("What is your age? ");
    scanf(" %d", &age);

    while (age <= 0)
      { printf("*** Your age cannot be that small! ***");
        // Timing loop here
        for (outer=1; outer<=30000; outer++)
            { for (inner=1; inner<=500; inner++); }
        // Erase the message
        printf("\r\n\n");
        printf("What is your age? ");
        scanf(" %d", &age);   // Ask again
      }

    printf("\n\nThanks, I did not think you would actually tell");
    printf("me your age!");
    return 0;
}
```

NOTE: Notice the inside loop has a semicolon (;) after the `for` statement—with no loop body. There is no need for a loop body here because the computer is only cycling through the loop to waste some time.

The break and for Statements

The `for` loop was designed to execute for a specified number of times. On rare occasions, you might want the `for` loop to quit before the counting variable has reached its final value. As with while loops, you use the break statement to quit a for loop early.

The break statement is nested in the body of the for loop. Programmers rarely put break on a line by itself, and it almost always comes after an if test. If the break were on a line by itself, the loop would always quit early, defeating the purpose of the for loop.

Examples

1. The following program shows what can happen when C++ encounters an *unconditional* break statement (one not pre-ceeded by an if statement).

   Identify the program and include the input/output header files. You need a variable to hold the current number, so make num an integer variable. Print a "Here are the numbers" message.

   1. *Make num equal to 1. If num is less than or equal to 20, add one to it each time through the loop.*

   2. *Print the value of num.*

   3. *Break out of the loop.*

   Print a goodbye message.

```cpp
// Filename: C14BRAK1.CPP
// A for loop defeated by the break statement.
#include <iostream.h>
main()
{
   int num;

   cout << "Here are the numbers from 1 to 20\n";
   for(num=1; num<=20; num++)
     { cout << num << "\n";
       break;  } // This line exits the for loop immediately.

   cout << "That's all, folks!";
   return 0;
}
```

The following shows you the result of running this program. Notice the `break` immediately terminates the `for` loop. The `for` loop might as well not be in this program.

```
Here are the numbers from 1 to 20
1
That's all, folks!
```

2. The following program is an improved version of the preceding example. It asks users if they want to see another number. If they do, the `for` loop continues its next iteration. If they don't, the `break` statement terminates the `for` loop.

```cpp
// Filename: C14BRAK2.CPP
// A for loop running at the user's request.
#include <iostream.h>
main()
{
    int num;    // Loop counter variable
    char ans;

    cout << "Here are the numbers from 1 to 20\n";

    for (num=1; num<=20; num++)
      { cout << num << "\n";
        cout << "Do you want to see another (Y/N)? ";
        cin >> ans;
        if ((ans == 'N') || (ans == 'n'))
          { break; }    // Will exit the for loop
                        // if user wants to.
    }

    cout << "\nThat's all, folks!\n";
    return 0;
}
```

The following display shows a sample run of this program. The `for` loop prints 20 numbers, as long as the user does not answer N to the prompt. Otherwise, the `break` terminates the `for` loop early. The statement after the body of the loop always executes next if the `break` occurs.

```
Here are the numbers from 1 to 20
1
Do you want to see another (Y/N)? Y
2
Do you want to see another (Y/N)? Y
3
Do you want to see another (Y/N)? Y
4
Do you want to see another (Y/N)? Y
5
Do you want to see another (Y/N)? Y
6
Do you want to see another (Y/N)? Y
7
Do you want to see another (Y/N)? Y
8
Do you want to see another (Y/N)? Y
9
Do you want to see another (Y/N)? Y
10
Do you want to see another (Y/N)? N

That's all, folks!
```

If you nest one loop inside another, the break terminates the "most active" loop (the innermost loop in which the break statement resides).

3. Use the *conditional* break (an if statement followed by a break) when you are missing data. For example, when you process data files or large amounts of user data-entry, you might expect 100 input numbers and receive only 95. You can use a break to terminate the for loop before it iterates the 96th time.

Suppose the teacher that used the grade-averaging program in the preceding chapter (C13FOR4.CPP) entered an incorrect total number of students. Maybe she typed 16, but there are only 14 students. The previous for loop looped 16 times, no matter how many students there are, because it relies on the teacher's count.

The following grade averaging program is more sophisticated than the last one. It asks the teacher for the total number of students, but if the teacher wants, she can enter –99 as a student's score. The –99 is not averaged; it is used as a trigger value to break out of the for loop before its normal conclusion.

```cpp
// Filename: C14BRAK3.CPP
// Computes a grade average with a for loop,
// allowing an early exit with a break statement.
#include <iostream.h>
#include <iomanip.h>
main()
{
    float grade, avg;
    float total=0.0;
    int num, count=0; // Total number of grades and counter
    int loopvar;                  // Used to control for loop

    cout << "\n*** Grade Calculation ***\n\n";     // Title
    cout << "How many students are there? ";
    cin >> num;                  // Get total number to enter.

    for (loopvar=1; loopvar<=num; loopvar++)
       { cout << "\nWhat is the next student's " <<
                  "grade? (-99 to quit) ";
         cin >> grade;
         if (grade < 0.0)                  // A negative number
                                           //    triggers break.
            { break; }                 // Leave the loop early.
         count++;
         total += grade;  }            // Keep a running total.

    avg = total / count;
    cout << "\n\nThe average of this class is "<<
            setprecision(1) << avg;
    return 0;
}
```

Notice that grade is tested for less than 0, not –99.0. You cannot reliably use floating-point values to compare for equality (due to their bit-level representations). Because no grade is negative, *any* negative number triggers the break statement. The following shows how this program works.

```
*** Grade Calculation ***

How many students are there? 10

What is the next student's grade? (-99 to quit) 87

What is the next student's grade? (-99 to quit) 97

What is the next student's grade? (-99 to quit) 67

What is the next student's grade? (-99 to quit) 89

What is the next student's grade? (-99 to quit) 94

What is the next student's grade? (-99 to quit) -99


The average of this class is: 86.8
```

The continue Statement

The continue statement causes C++ to skip all remaining statements in a loop.

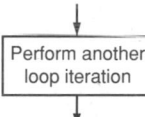

Perform another loop iteration

The break statement exits a loop early, but the continue statement forces the computer to perform another iteration of the loop. If you put a continue statement in the body of a for or a while loop, the computer ignores any statement in the loop that follows continue.

The format of continue is

```
continue;
```

You use the continue statement when data in the body of the loop is bad, out of bounds, or unexpected. Instead of acting on the bad data, you might want to go back to the top of the loop and try another data value. The following examples help illustrate the use of the continue statement.

> **TIP:** The continue statement forces a new iteration of any of the three loop constructs: the for loop, the while loop, and the do-while loop.

Figure 14.1 shows the difference between the break and continue statements.

```
for (i=0;i<=10;i++)
    {
        break;
        printf("Loop it\n");/*never prints!*/
    }

/*Rest of program */
```
break terminates loop immediately

```
for (i=0;i<=10;i++)
    {
        continue;
        printf("Loop it\n");/*never prints!*/
    }

/*Rest of program*/
```
continue causes loop to perform another iteration

Figure 14.1. The difference between break and continue.

Examples

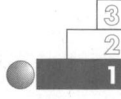

1. Although the following program seems to print the numbers 1 through 10, each followed by "C++ Programming," it does not. The continue in the body of the for loop causes an early finish to the loop. The first cout in the for loop executes, but the second does not—due to the continue.

```
// Filename: C14CON1.CPP
// Demonstrates the use of the continue statement.
#include <iostream.h>
main()
{
   int ctr;

   for (ctr=1; ctr<=10; ctr++)      // Loop 10 times.
     {  cout << ctr << " ";
        continue;          // Causes body to end early.
        cout << "C++ Programming\n";
     }
   return 0;
}
```

This program produces the following output:

```
1 2 3 4 5 6 7 8 9 10
```

On some compilers, you receive a warning message when you compile this type of program. The compiler recognizes that the second cout is *unreachable* code—it never executes due to the continue statement.

Because of this fact, most programs do not use a continue, except after an if statement. This makes it a conditional continue statement, which is more useful. The following two examples demonstrate the conditional use of continue.

2. This program asks users for five lowercase letters, one at a time, and prints their uppercase equivalents. It uses the ASCII table (see Appendix C, "ASCII Table") to ensure that users type lowercase letters. (These are the letters whose ASCII numbers range from 97 to 122.) If users do not type a lowercase letter, the program ignores the mistake with the continue statement.

```
// Filename: C14CON2.CPP
// Prints uppercase equivalents of five lowercase letters.
#include <iostream.h>
main()
```

```
{
    char letter;
    int ctr;

    for (ctr=1; ctr<=5; ctr++)
      { cout << "Please enter a lowercase letter ";
        cin >> letter;
        if ((letter < 97) || (letter > 122))  // See if
                                        // out-of-range.
            { continue; }               // Go get another
         letter -= 32;    // Subtract 32 from ASCII value.
                                        // to get uppercase.
         cout << "The uppercase equivalent is " <<
                 letter << "\n";
      }
    return 0;
}
```

Due to the continue statement, only lowercase letters are converted to uppercase.

3. Suppose you want to average the salaries of employees in your company who make over $10,000 a year, but you have only their monthly gross pay figures. The following program might be useful. It prompts for each monthly employee salary, annualizes it (multiplying by 12), and computes an average. The continue statement ensures that salaries less than or equal to $10,000 are ignored in the average calculation. It enables the other salaries to "fall through."

If you enter -1 as a monthly salary, the program quits and prints the result of the average.

```
// Filename: C14CON3.CPP
// Average salaries over $10,000
#include <iostream.h>
#include <iomanip.h>
main()
{
    float month, year;       // Monthly and yearly salaries
    float avg=0.0, total=0.0;
    int count=0;
```

```
do
   { cout << "What is the next monthly salary (-1) " <<
           "to quit)? ";
     cin >> month;
     if ((year=month*12.00) <= 10000.00)  // Do not add
        { continue; }                     // low salaries.
     if (month < 0.0)
        { break; }              // Quit if user entered -1.
     count++;                   // Add 1 to valid counter.
     total += year;        // Add yearly salary to total.
   } while (month > 0.0);

   avg = total / (float)count;         // Compute average.
   cout << "\n\nThe average of high salaries " <<
           "is $" << setprecision(2) << avg;
   return 0;
}
```

Notice this program uses both a continue and a break statement. The program does one of three things, depending on each user's input. It adds to the total, continues another iteration if the salary is too low, or exits the while loop (and the average calculation) if the user types a -1.

The following display is the output from this program:

```
What is the next monthly salary (-1 to quit)? 500.00
What is the next monthly salary (-1 to quit)? 2000.00
What is the next monthly salary (-1 to quit)? 750.00
What is the next monthly salary (-1 to quit)? 4000.00
What is the next monthly salary (-1 to quit)? 5000.00
What is the next monthly salary (-1 to quit)? 1200.00
What is the next monthly salary (-1 to quit)? -1


The average of high salaries is $36600.00
```

Review Questions

The answers to the review questions are in Appendix B.

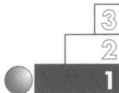

1. For what do you use timing loops?

2. Why do timing loop ranges have to be adjusted for different types of computers?

3. Why do `continue` and `break` statements rarely appear without an `if` statement controlling them?

4. What is the output from the following section of code?

```
for (i=1; i<=10; i++)
   { continue;
     cout << "***** \n";
   }
```

5. What is the output from the following section of code?

```
for (i=1; i<=10; i++)
   { cout << "***** \n";
     break;
   }
```

6. To perform a long timing loop, why do you generally have to use a nested loop?

Review Exercises

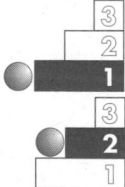

1. Write a program that prints `c++ is fun` on-screen for ten seconds. (*Hint:* You might have to adjust the timing loop.)

2. Make the program in Exercise 1 flash the message `c++ is fun` for ten seconds. (*Hint:* You might have to use several timing loops.)

3. Write a grade averaging program for a class of 20 students. Ignore any grade less than 0 and continue until all 20 student grades are entered, or until the user types –99 to end the program early.

4. Write a program that prints the numerals from 1 to 14 in one column. To the right of the even numbers, print each number's square. To the right of the odd numbers, print each number's cube (the number raised to its third power).

Summary

In this chapter, you learned several additional ways to use and modify your program's loops. By adding timing loops, `continue` statements, and `break` statements, you can better control how each loop behaves. Being able to exit early (with the `break` statement) or continue the next loop iteration early (with the `continue` statement) gives you more freedom when processing different types of data.

The next chapter (Chapter 15, "The `switch` and `goto` Statements") shows you a construct of C++ that does not loop, but relies on the `break` statement to work properly. This is the `switch` statement, and it makes your program choices much easier to write.

The switch and goto **Statements**

This chapter focuses on the switch statement. It also improves the if and else-if constructs by streamlining the multiple-choice decisions your programs make. The switch statement does not replace the if statement, but it is better to use switch when your programs must perform one of many different actions.

The switch and break statements work together. Almost every switch statement you use includes at least one break statement in the body of the switch. To conclude this chapter—and this section of the book on C++ constructs—you learn the goto statement, although it is rarely used.

This chapter introduces the following:

◆ The switch statement used for selection

◆ The goto statement used for branching from one part of your program to another

If you have mastered the if statement, you should have little trouble with the concepts presented here. By learning the switch statement, you should be able to write menus and multiple-choice data-entry programs with ease.

The switch Statement

Use the switch statement when your program makes a multiple-choice selection.

The switch statement is sometimes called the *multiple-choice statement*. The switch statement enables your program to choose from several alternatives. The format of the switch statement is a little longer than the format of other statements you have seen. Here is the switch statement:

Select a block of statements based on a condition

```
switch (expression)
    { case (expression1): { one or more C++ statements; }
      case (expression2): { one or more C++ statements; }
      case (expression3): { one or more C++ statements; }
      .
      .
      .
      default: { one or more C++ statements; }
    }
```

The *expression* can be an integer expression, a character, a literal, or a variable. The *sub*expressions (*expression1, expression2,* and so on) can be any other integer expression, character, literal, or variable. The number of case expressions following the switch line is determined by your application. The *one or more C++ statements* is any block of C++ code. If the block is only one statement long, you do not need the braces, but they are recommended.

The default line is optional; most (but not all) switch statements include the default. The default line does not have to be the last line of the switch body.

If *expression* matches *expression1*, the statements to the right of *expression1* execute. If *expression* matches *expression2*, the statements to the right of *expression2* execute. If none of the expressions match the switch *expression,* the default case block executes. The case expression does not need parentheses, but the parentheses sometimes make the value easier to find.

TIP: Use a break statement after each case block to keep execution from "falling through" to the remaining case statements.

Using the `switch` statement is easier than its format might lead you to believe. Anywhere an `if-else-if` combination of statements can go, you can usually put a clearer `switch` statement. The `switch` statement is much easier to follow than an `if-in-an-if-in-an-if` statement, as you have had to write previously.

However, the `if` and `else-if` combinations of statements are not difficult to follow. When the relational test that determines the choice is complex and contains many `&&` and `||` operators, the `if` statement might be a better candidate. The `switch` statement is preferred whenever multiple-choice possibilities are based on a single literal, variable, or expression.

> **TIP:** Arrange `case` statements in the most-often to least-often executed order to improve your program's speed.

The following examples clarify the `switch` statement. They compare the `switch` statement to `if` statements to help you see the difference.

Examples

1. Suppose you are writing a program to teach your child how to count. Your program will ask the child for a number. It then beeps (rings the computer's alarm bell) as many times as necessary to match that number.

   The following program assumes the child presses a number key from 1 to 5. This program uses the `if-else-if` combination to accomplish this counting-and-beeping teaching method.

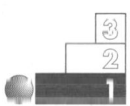

   Identify the program and include the necessary header file. You want to sound a beep and move the cursor to the next line, so define a global variable called BEEP *that does this. You need a variable to hold the user's answer, so make* num *an integer variable.*

   Ask the user for a number. Assign the user's number to num. *If* num *is 1, call* BEEP *once. If* num *is 2, call* BEEP *twice. If* num *is 3, call* BEEP *three times. If* num *is 4, call* BEEP *four times. If* num *is 5, call* BEEP *five times.*

```
// Filename: C15BEEP1.CPP
// Beeps a designated number of times.
#include <iostream.h>

// Define a beep cout to save repeating printf()s
// throughout the program.
#define BEEP cout << "\a \n"
main()
{
   int num;

   // Request a number from the child
   // (you might have to help).
   cout << "Please enter a number ";
   cin >> num;

   // Use multiple if statements to beep.
   if (num == 1)
     { BEEP; }
   else if (num == 2)
         { BEEP; BEEP; }
       else if (num == 3)
               { BEEP; BEEP; BEEP; }
             else if (num == 4)
                     { BEEP; BEEP; BEEP; BEEP; }
                   else if (num == 5)
                           { BEEP; BEEP; BEEP; BEEP; BEEP; }
   return 0;
}
```

No beeps are sounded if the child enters something other than 1 through 5. This program takes advantage of the #define preprocessor directive to define a shortcut to an alarm cout function. In this case, the BEEP is a little clearer to read, as long as you remember that BEEP is not a command, but is replaced with the cout everywhere it appears.

One drawback to this type of if-in-an-if program is its readability. By the time you indent the body of each if and else, the program is too far to the right. There is no room for more than five or six possibilities. More importantly, this type of logic is difficult to follow. Because it involves a multiple-choice selection, a switch statement is much better to use, as you can see with the following, improved version.

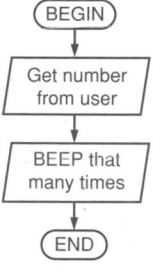

```cpp
// Filename: C15BEEP2.CPP
// Beeps a certain number of times using a switch.
#include <iostream.h>

// Define a beep cout to save repeating couts
// throughout the program.
#define BEEP cout << "\a \n"
main()
{
   int num;

   // Request from the child (you might have to help).
   cout << "Please enter a number ";
   cin >> num;

   switch (num)
   { case (1): { BEEP;
                 break; }
     case (2): { BEEP; BEEP;
                 break; }
     case (3): { BEEP; BEEP; BEEP;
                 break; }
     case (4): { BEEP; BEEP; BEEP; BEEP;
                 break; }
     case (5): { BEEP; BEEP; BEEP; BEEP; BEEP;
                 break; }
   }
   return 0;
}
```

This example is much clearer than the previous one. The value of num controls the execution—only the case that matches num executes. The indention helps separate each case.

If the child enters a number other than 1 through 5, no beeps are sounded because there is no case expression to match any other value and there is no default case.

Because the BEEP preprocessor directive is so short, you can put more than one on a single line. This is not a requirement, however. The block of statements following a case can also be more than one statement long.

If more than one case expression is the same, only the first expression executes.

2. If the child does not enter a 1, 2, 3, 4, or 5, nothing happens in the previous program. What follows is the same program modified to take advantage of the default option. The default block of statements executes if none of the previous cases match.

```
// Filename: C15BEEP3.CPP
// Beeps a designated number of times using a switch.
#include <iostream.h>

// Define a beep cout to save repeating couts
// throughout the program.
#define BEEP cout << "\a \n"
main()
{
    int num;

 // Request a number from the child (you might have to help).
    cout << "Please enter a number ";
    cin >> num;

    switch (num)
    { case (1): { BEEP;
                  break; }
      case (2): { BEEP; BEEP;
                  break; }
      case (3): { BEEP; BEEP; BEEP;
                  break; }
      case (4): { BEEP; BEEP; BEEP; BEEP;
                  break; }
      case (5): { BEEP; BEEP; BEEP; BEEP; BEEP;
                  break; }
      default:  { cout << "You must enter a number from " <<
                          "1 to 5\n";
```

```
                    cout << "Please run this program again\n";
                    break; }
        }
    return 0;
}
```

The break at the end of the default case might seem redundant. After all, no other case statements execute by "falling through" from the default case. It is a good habit to put a break after the default case anyway. If you move the default higher in the switch (it doesn't have to be the last switch option), you are more inclined to move the break with it (where it is then needed).

3. To show the importance of using break statements in each case expression, here is the same beeping program without any break statements.

```cpp
// Filename: C15BEEP4.CPP
// Incorrectly beeps using a switch.
#include <iostream.h>

// Define a beep printf() to save repeating couts
// throughout the program.
#define BEEP cout << "\a \n"
main()
{
    int num;

    // Request a number from the child
    // (you might have to help).
    cout << "Please enter a number ";
    cin >> num;

    switch (num)                          // Warning!
    { case (1): { BEEP; }      // Without a break, this code
      case (2): { BEEP; BEEP; }     // falls through to the
      case (3): { BEEP; BEEP; BEEP; } // rest of the beeps!
      case (4): { BEEP; BEEP; BEEP; BEEP; }
      case (5): { BEEP; BEEP; BEEP; BEEP; BEEP; }
      default:  { cout << "You must enter a number " <<
                        "from 1 to 5\n";
```

```
                            cout << "Please run this program again\n"; }
    }
    return 0;
}
```

If the user enters a 1, the program beeps 15 times! The `break` is not there to stop the execution from falling through to the other cases. Unlike other programming languages such as Pascal, C++'s `switch` statement requires that you insert `break` statements between each `case` if you want only one `case` executed. This is not necessarily a drawback. The trade-off of having to specify `break` statements gives you more control in how you handle specific `cases`, as shown in the next example.

4. This program controls the printing of end-of-day sales totals. It first asks for the day of the week. If the day is Monday through Thursday, a daily total is printed. If the day is a Friday, a weekly total and a daily total are printed. If the day happens to be the end of the month, a monthly sales total is printed as well.

In a real application, these totals would come from the disk drive rather than be assigned at the top of the program. Also, rather than individual sales figures being printed, a full daily, weekly, and monthly report of many sales totals would probably be printed. You are on your way to learning more about expanding the power of your C++ programs. For now, concentrate on the `switch` statement and its possibilities.

Each type of report for sales figures is handled through a hierarchy of `case` statements. Because the daily amount is the last `case`, it is the only report printed if the day of the week is Monday through Thursday. If the day of the week is Friday, the second `case` prints the weekly sales total and then falls through to the daily total (because Friday's daily total must be printed as well). If it is the end of the month, the first `case` executes, falling through to the weekly total, then to the daily sales total as well. Other languages that do not offer this "fall through" flexibility are more limiting.

```
// Filename: C15SALE.CPP
// Prints daily, weekly, and monthly sales totals.
#include <iostream.h>
#include <stdio.h>

main()
{
    float daily=2343.34;      // Later, these figures
    float weekly=13432.65;    // come from a disk file
    float monthly=43468.97;   // instead of being assigned
                              // as they are here.
    char ans;
    int day;          // Day value to trigger correct case.


    // Month is assigned 1 through 5 (for Monday through
    // Friday) or 6 if it is the end of the month. Assume
    // a weekly and a daily prints if it is the end of the
    // month, no matter what the day is.
    cout << "Is this the end of the month? (Y/N) ";
    cin >> ans;
    if ((ans=='Y') || (ans=='y'))
      { day=6; }                             // Month value
    else
      { cout << "What day number, 1 through 5 (for Mon-Fri)" <<
               " is it? ";
        cin >> day; }


    switch (day)
      { case (6): printf("The monthly total is %.2f \n",
                         monthly);
        case (5): printf("The weekly total is %.2f \n",
                         weekly);
        default:  printf("The daily total is %.2f \n", daily);
      }
    return 0;
}
```

5. The order of the case statements is not fixed. You can rearrange the statements to make them more efficient. If only one or two cases are being selected most of the time, put those cases near the top of the switch statement.

For example, in the previous program, most of the company's reports are daily, but the daily option is third in the case statements. By rearranging the case statements so the daily report is at the top, you can speed up this program because C++ does not have to scan two case expressions that it rarely executes.

```cpp
// Filename: C15DEPT1.CPP
// Prints message depending on the department entered.
#include <iostream.h>
main()
{
   char choice;

   do   // Display menu and ensure that user enters a
        // correct option.
     { cout << "\nChoose your department: \n";
       cout << "S - Sales \n";
       cout << "A - Accounting \n";
       cout << "E - Engineering \n";
       cout << "P - Payroll \n";
       cout << "What is your choice? ";
       cin >> choice;
       // Convert choice to uppercase (if they
       // entered lowercase) with the ASCII table.
       if ((choice>=97) && (choice<=122))
         { choice -= 32; }          // Subtract enough to make
                                    // uppercase.
     } while ((choice!='S')&&(choice!='A')&&
              (choice!='E')&&(choice!='P'));

   // Put Engineering first because it occurs most often.
   switch (choice)
   { case ('E') : { cout << "\n Your meeting is at 2:30";
                    break; }
     case ('S') : { cout << "\n Your meeting is at 8:30";
                    break; }
     case ('A') : { cout << "\n Your meeting is at 10:00";
                    break; }
     case ('P') : { cout << "\n Your meeting has been " <<
                         "canceled";
```

```
                      break; }
     }
     return 0;
}
```

The goto **Statement**

Early programming languages did not offer the flexible constructs that C++ gives you, such as for loops, while loops, and switch
statements. Their only means of looping and comparing was with
the goto statement. C++ still includes a goto, but the other constructs
are more powerful, flexible, and easier to follow in a program.

The goto causes
execution to jump to
some statement
other than the
next one.

The goto statement causes your program to jump to a different
location, rather than execute the next statement in sequence. The
format of the goto statement is

goto *statement label*

A *statement label* is named just as variables are (see Chapter 4,
"Variables and Literals"). A *statement label* cannot have the same
name as a C++ command, a C++ function, or another variable in the
program. If you use a goto statement, there must be a *statement label*
elsewhere in the program to which the goto branches. Execution then
continues at the statement with the *statement label*.

The *statement label* precedes a line of code. Follow all *statement
labels* with a colon (:) so C++ recognizes them as labels, not
variables. You have not seen statement labels in the C++ programs
so far in this book because none of the programs needed them. A
statement label is optional unless you have a goto statement.

The following four lines of code each has a different *statement
label*. This is not a program, but individual lines that might be
included in a program. Notice that the *statement labels* are on the left.

```
pay: cout << "Place checks in the printer \n";

Again: cin >> name;

EndIt: cout << "That is all the processing. \n";

CALC: amount = (total / .5) * 1.15;
```

The statement labels are not intended to replace comments, although their names reflect the code that follows. Statement labels give goto statements a tag *to go to*. When your program finds the goto, it branches to the statement labeled by the *statement label*. The program then continues to execute sequentially until the next goto changes the order again (or until the program ends).

> **TIP:** Use identifying line labels. A repetitive calculation deserves a label such as CalcIt and not x15z. Even though both are allowed, the first one is a better indication of the code's purpose.

Use goto Judiciously

The goto is not considered a good programming statement when overused. There is a tendency, especially for beginning programmers, to include too many goto statements in a program. When a program branches all over the place, it becomes difficult to follow. Some people call programs with many goto statements "spaghetti code."

To eliminate goto statements and write better structured programs, use the other looping and switch constructs seen in the previous few chapters.

The goto is not necessarily a bad statement—if used judiciously. Starting with the next chapter, you begin to break your programs into smaller modules called functions, and the goto becomes less and less important as you write more and more functions.

For now, become familiar with goto so you can understand programs that use it. Some day, you might have to correct the code of someone who used the goto.

Examples

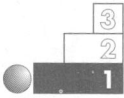

1. The following program has a problem that is a direct result of the goto, but it is still one of the best illustrations of the goto statement. The program consists of an *endless loop* (or an *infinite* loop). The first three lines (after the opening brace) execute, then the goto in the fourth line causes execution to loop back to the beginning and repeat the first three lines. The goto continues to do this until you press Ctrl-Break or ask your system administrator to cancel the program.

Identify the program and include the input/output header file. You want to print a message, but split it over three lines. You want the message to keep repeating, so label the first line, then use a goto to jump back to that line.

```
// Filename: C15GOTO1.CPP
// Program to show use of goto. This program ends
// only when the user presses Ctrl-Break.
#include <iostream.h>
main()
{
   Again: cout << "This message \n";
   cout << "\t keeps repeating \n";
   cout << "\t\t over and over \n";

   goto Again;    // Repeat continuously.

   return 0;
}
```

Notice the *statement label* (Again in the previous example) has a colon to separate it from the rest of the line, but there is not a colon with the label at the goto statement. Here is the result of running this program.

```
This message
        keeps repeating
                over and over
This message
        keeps repeating
                over and over
```

```
This message
        keeps repeating
                over and over
This message
        keeps repeating
                over and over
This message
        keeps repeating
                over and over
This message
        keeps repeating
                over and over
This message
        keeps repeating
                over and over
This message
```

2. It is sometimes easier to read your program's code when you write the statement labels on separate lines. Remember that writing maintainable programs is the goal of every good programmer. Making your programs easier to read is a prime consideration when you write them. The following program is the same repeating program shown in the previous example, except the statement label is placed on a separate line.

```cpp
// Filename: C15GOTO2.CPP
// Program to show use of goto. This program ends
// only when the user presses Ctrl-Break.
#include <iostream.h>
main()
{

Again:
   cout << "This message \n";
   cout << "\t keeps repeating \n";
   cout << "\t\t over and over \n";

   goto Again;    // Repeat continuously

   return 0;
}
```

The line following the statement label is the one that executes next, after control is passed (by the goto) to the label.

Of course, these are silly examples. You probably don't want to write programs with infinite loops. The goto is a statement best preceded with an if; this way the goto eventually stops branching without intervention from the user.

3. The following program is one of the worst-written programs ever! It is the epitome of spaghetti code! However, do your best to follow it and understand its output. By understanding the flow of this output, you can hone your understanding of the goto. You might also appreciate the fact that the rest of this book uses the goto only when needed to make the program clearer.

```cpp
// Filename: C15GOTO3.CPP
// This program demonstrates the overuse of goto.
#include <iostream.h>
main()
{
    goto Here;

    First:
    cout << "A \n";
    goto Final;

    There:
    cout << "B \n";
    goto First;

    Here:
    cout << "C \n";
    goto There;

    Final:
    return 0;
}
```

At first glance, this program appears to print the first three letters of the alphabet, but the goto statements make them print in the reverse order, *C, B, A*. Although the program is not a well-designed program, some indention of the lines without statement labels make it a little more readable. This enables you to quickly separate the statement labels from the remaining code, as you can see from the following program.

```cpp
// Filename: C15GOTO4.CPP
// This program demonstrates the overuse of goto.
#include <iostream.h>
main()
{
    goto Here;

First:
    cout << "A \n";
    goto Final;

There:
    cout << "B \n";
    goto First;

Here:
    cout << "C \n";
    goto There;

Final:
    return 0;
}
```

This program's listing is slightly easier to follow than the previous one, even though both do the same thing. The remaining programs in this book with statement labels also use such indention.

You certainly realize that this output is better produced by the following three lines.

```cpp
cout << "C \n";
cout << "B \n";
cout << "A \n";
```

The goto warning is worth repeating: Use goto sparingly and only when its use makes your program more readable and maintainable. Usually, you can use much better commands.

Review Questions

The answers to the review questions are in Appendix B.

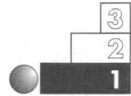

1. How does goto change the order in which a program normally executes?

2. What statement can substitute for an if-else-if construct?

3. Which statement almost always ends each case statement in a switch?

4. True or false: The order of your case statements has no bearing on the efficiency of your program.

5. Rewrite the following section of code using a switch statement.

```
if (num == 1)
    { cout << "Alpha"; }
else if (num == 2)
        { cout << "Beta"; }
    else if (num == 3)
            { cout << "Gamma"; }
        else
            { cout << "Other"; }
```

6. Rewrite the following program using a do-while loop.

```
Ask:
    cout << "What is your first name? ";
    cin >> name;
    if ((name[0] < 'A') ¦¦ (name[0] > 'Z'))
        { goto Ask; }   // Keep asking until the user
                        // enters a valid letter.
```

Review Exercises

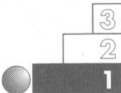

1. Write a program using the switch statement that asks users for their age, then prints a message saying "You can vote!" if they are 18, "You can adopt!" if they are 21, or "Are you really that young?" for any other age.

2. Write a menu-driven program for your local TV cable company. Here is how to assess charges: If you are within 20 miles outside the city limits, you pay $12.00 per month; 21 to 30 miles outside the city limits, you pay $23.00 per month; 31 to 50 miles outside the city limits, you pay $34.00. No one outside 50 miles receives the service. Prompt the users with a menu for their residence's distance from the city limits.

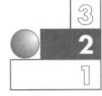

3. Write a program that calculates parking fees for a multilevel parking garage. Ask whether the driver is in a car or a truck. Charge the driver $2.00 for the first hour, $3.00 for the second, and $5.00 for more than 2 hours. If it is a truck, add $1.00 to the total fee. (*Hint:* Use one switch and one if statement.)

4. Modify the previous parking problem so the charge depends on the time of day the vehicle is parked. If the vehicle is parked before 8 a.m., charge the fees in Exercise 3. If the vehicle is parked after 8 a.m. and before 5 p.m., charge an extra usage fee of 50 cents. If the vehicle is parked after 5 p.m., deduct 50 cents from the computed price. You must prompt users for the starting time in a menu, as follows.

```
1. Before 8 a.m.
2. Before 5 p.m.
3. After 5 p.m.
```

Summary

You now have seen the switch statement and its options. With it, you can improve the readability of a complicated if-else-if selection. The switch is especially good when several outcomes are possible, based on the user's choice.

The goto statement causes an unconditional branch, and can be difficult to follow at times. The goto statement is not used much now, and you can almost always use a better construct. However, you should be acquainted with as much C++ as possible in case you have to work on programs others have written.

This ends the section on program control. The next section introduces user-written functions. So far, you have been using C++'s built-in functions, such as strcpy() and printf(). Now it's time to write your own.

Writing C++ Functions

Computers never become bored. They perform the same input, output, and computations your program requires—for as long as you want them to do it. You can take advantage of their repetitive natures by looking at your programs in a new way: as a series of small routines that execute whenever you need them, however many times you require.

This chapter approaches its subject a little differently than the previous chapters do. It concentrates on teaching you to write your own *functions*, which are *modules* of code that you execute and control from the main() function. So far, the programs in this book have consisted of a single long function called main(). As you learn here, the main() function's primary purpose is to control the execution of other functions that follow it.

This chapter introduces the following:

♦ The need for functions

♦ How to trace functions

♦ How to write functions

♦ How to call and return from functions

This chapter stresses the use of *structured programming*, sometimes called *modular programming*. C++ was designed in a way that the programmer can write programs in several modules rather than in one long block. By breaking the program into several smaller routines (*functions*), you can isolate problems, write correct programs faster, and produce programs that are easier to maintain.

Function Basics

When you approach an application that has to be programmed, it is best not to sit down at the keyboard and start typing. Rather, first *think* about the program and what it is supposed to do. One of the best ways to attack a program is to start with the overall goal, then divide this goal into several smaller tasks. You should never lose sight of the overall goal, but think also of how individual pieces can fit together to accomplish such a goal.

When you finally do sit down to begin coding the problem, continue to think in terms of those pieces fitting together. Don't approach a program as if it were one giant problem; rather, continue to write those small pieces individually.

This does not mean you must write separate programs to do everything. You can keep individual pieces of the overall program together—if you know how to write functions. Then you can use the same functions in many different programs.

C++ programs should consist of many small functions.

C++ programs are not like BASIC or FORTRAN programs. C++ was designed to force you to think in a modular, or subroutine-like, functional style. Good C++ programmers write programs that consist of many small functions, even if their programs execute one or more of these functions only once. Those functions work together to produce a program quicker and easier than if the program had to be written from scratch.

> **TIP:** Rather than code one long program, write several smaller routines, called functions. One of those functions must be called main(). The main() function is always the first to execute. It doesn't have to be first in a program, but it usually is.

Breaking Down Problems

If your program does very much, break it into several functions. Each function should do only *one* primary task. For example, if you were writing a C++ program to retrieve a list of characters from the keyboard, alphabetize them, then print them to the screen, you could—but shouldn't—write all these instructions in one big `main()` function, as the following C++ *skeleton* (program outline) shows:

```
main()
{
   // :
   // C++ code to retrieve a list of characters.
   // :
   // C++ code to alphabetize the characters.
   // :
   // C++ code to print the alphabetized list on-screen.
   // :
   return 0;
}
```

This skeleton is *not* a good way to write this program. Even though you can type this program in only a few lines of code, it is much better to begin breaking every program into distinct tasks so this process becomes a habit to you. You should not use `main()` to do everything—in fact, use `main()` to do very little except call each of the functions that does the actual work.

A better way to organize this program is to write a separate function for each task the program is supposed to do. This doesn't mean that each function has to be only one line long. Rather, it means you make every function a building block that performs only one distinct task in the program.

The following program outline shows you a better way to write the program just described:

```
main()
{
   getletters();    // Calls a function to retrieve the numbers.
   alphabetize();   // Calls a function to alphabetize
                    // letters.
```

Call three
functions

```
    printletters();  // Calls a function to print letters
                     // on-screen.
    return 0;        // Returns to the operating system.
}

getletters()
{
    // :
    // C++ code to get a list of characters.
    // :
    return 0;   // Returns to main().
}

alphabetize()
{
    // :
    // C++ code to alphabetize the characters
    // :
    return 0;   // Returns to main().
}

printletters()
{
    // :
    // C++ code to print the alphabetized list on-screen
    // :
    return 0;   // Returns to main().
}
```

The program outline shows you a much better way of writing this program. It takes longer to type, but it's much more organized. The only action the `main()` function takes is to control the other functions by calling them in a certain order. Each separate function executes its instructions, then returns to `main()`, whereupon `main()` calls the next function until no more functions remain. The `main()` function then returns control of the computer to the operating system.

Do not be too concerned about the 0 that follows the `return` statement. C++ functions return values. So far, the functions you've seen have returned zero, and that return value has been ignored.

Chapter 19, "Function Return Values and Prototypes," describes how you can use the return value for programming power.

> **TIP:** A good rule of thumb is that a function should not be more than one screen in length. If it is longer, you are probably doing too much in one function and should therefore break it into two or more functions.

The main() function is usually a calling function that controls the remainder of the program.

The first function called main() is what you previously used to hold the entire program. From this point, in all but the smallest of programs, main() simply controls other functions that do the work.

These listings are not examples of real C++ programs; instead, they are skeletons, or outlines, of programs. From these outlines, it is easier to develop the actual full program. Before going to the keyboard to write a program such as this, know that there are four distinct sections: a primary function-calling main() function, a keyboard data-entry function, an alphabetizing function, and a printing function.

Never lose sight of the original programming problem. (Using the approach just described, you never will!) Look again at the main() calling routine in the preceding program. Notice that you can glance at main() and get a feel for the overall program, without the remaining statements getting in the way. This is a good example of structured, modular programming. A large programming problem is broken into distinct, separate modules called functions, and each function performs one primary job in a few C++ statements.

More Function Basics

Little has been said about naming and writing functions, but you probably understand much of the goals of the previous listing already. C++ functions generally adhere to the following rules:

1. Every function must have a name.

2. Function names are made up and assigned by the programmer (you!) following the same rules that apply to naming

variables: They can contain up to 32 characters, they must begin with a letter, and they can consist of letters, numbers, and the underscore (_) character.

3. All function names have one set of parentheses immediately following them. This helps you (and C++) differentiate them from variables. The parentheses may or may not contain something. So far, all such parentheses in this book have been empty (you learn more about functions in Chapter 18, "Passing Values").

4. The body of each function, starting immediately after the closing parenthesis of the function name, must be enclosed by braces. This means a block containing one or more state-ments makes up the body of each function.

> **TIP:** Use meaningful function names. `Calc_balance()` is more descriptive than `xy3()`.

Although the outline shown in the previous listing is a good example of structured code, it can be improved by using the under-score character (_) in the function names. Do you see how `get_letters()` and `print_letters()` are much easier to read than are `getletters()` and `printletters()`?

> **CAUTION:** Be sure to use the underscore character (_) and not the hyphen (-) when naming functions and variables. If you use a hyphen, C++ produces misleading error messages.

All programs must have a `main()` function.

The following listing shows you an example of a C++ function. You can already tell quite a bit about this function. You know, for instance, that it isn't a complete program because it has no `main()` function. (All programs must have a `main()` function.) You know also that the function name is `calc_it` because parentheses follow this name. These parentheses happen to have something in them (you learn more about this in Chapter 18). You know also that the body of the function is enclosed in a block of braces. Inside that block is a *smaller* block, the body of a `while` loop. Finally, you recognize that the `return` statement is the last line of the function.

```
calc_it(int n)
{
    // Function to print the square of a number.
    int square;

    while (square <= 250)
      { square = n * n;
        cout << "The square of " << n <<
                " is " << square << "\n";
        n++; }      // A block in the function.

    return 0;
}
```

> **TIP:** Not all functions require a `return` statement for their last line, but it is recommended that you always include one because it helps to show your intention to return to the calling function at that point. Later in the book, you learn that the `return` is required in certain instances. For now, develop the habit of including a `return` statement.

Calling and Returning Functions

You have been reading much about "function calling" and "returning control." Although you might already understand these phrases from their context, you can probably learn them better through an illustration of what is meant by a function call.

A function call is like a temporary program detour.

A function call in C++ is like a detour on a highway. Imagine you are traveling along the "road" of the primary function called `main()` and then run into a function-calling statement. You must temporarily leave the `main()` function and execute the function that was called. After that function finishes (its `return` statement is reached), program control reverts to main(). In other words, when you finish a detour, you return to the "main" route and continue the trip. Control continues as main() calls other functions.

> **NOTE:** Generally, the primary function that controls function calls and their order is called a *calling function*. Functions controlled by the calling function are called the *called functions.*

A complete C++ program, with functions, will make this concept clear. The following program prints several messages to the screen. Each message printed is determined by the order of the functions. Before worrying too much about what this program does, take a little time to study its structure. Notice that there are three functions defined in the program: main(), next_fun(), and third_fun(). A fourth function is used also, but it is the built-in C++ printf() function. The three defined functions appear sequentially. The body of each is enclosed in braces, and each has a return statement at its end.

As you will see from the program, there is something new following the #include directive. The first line of every function that main() calls is listed here and also appears above the actual function. C++ requires these *prototypes.* For now, just ignore them and study the overall format of multiple-function programs. Chapter 19, "Function Return Values and Prototypes, " explains prototypes.

```
// C16FUN1.CPP
// The following program illustrates function calls.
#include <stdio.h>
next_fun();  // Prototypes.
third_fun();

main()  // main() is always the first C++ function executed.
{
   printf("First function called main() \n");
   next_fun();            // Second function is called here.
   third_fun();            // This function is called here.
   printf("main() is completed \n");      // All control
                                          // returns here.
```

```
    return 0;                       // Control is returned to
                                    //the operating system.
}                                   // This brace concludes main().

next_fun()                                   // Second function.
                                    // Parentheses always required.
{
   printf("Inside next_fun() \n");      // No variables are
                                    // defined in the program.
   return 0;             // Control is now returned to main().
}

third_fun()               // Last function in the program.
{
   printf("Inside third_fun() \n");
   return 0;                // Always return from all functions.
}
```

The output of this program follows:

```
First function called main()
Inside next_fun()
Inside third_fun()
main() is completed
```

Figure 16.1 shows a tracing of this program's execution. Notice that main() controls which of the other functions is called, as well as the order of the calling. Control *always* returns to the calling function after the called function finishes.

To call a function, simply type its name—including the parentheses—and follow it with a semicolon. Remember that semicolons follow all executable statements in C++, and a function call (sometimes called a *function invocation*) is an executable statement. The execution is the function's code being called. Any function can call any other function. In the previous program, main() is the only function that calls other functions.

Now you can tell that the following statement is a function call:

```
print_total();
```

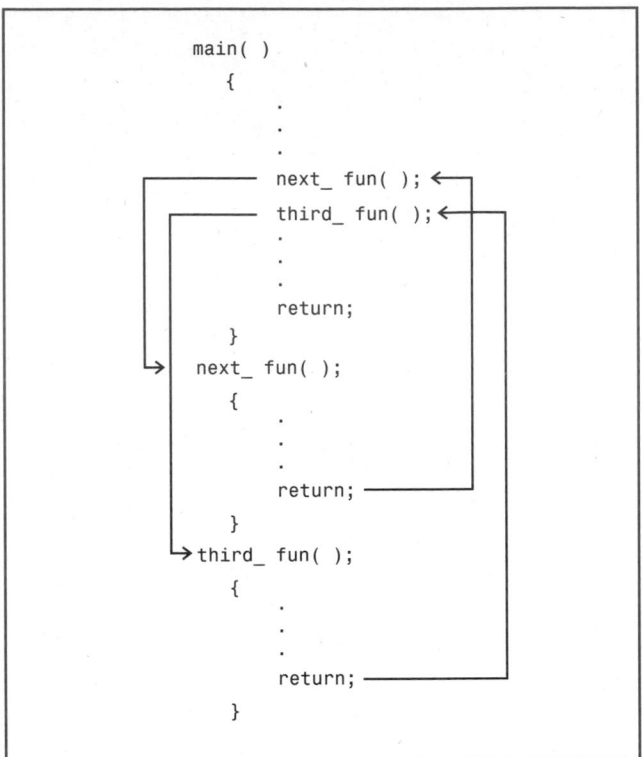

Figure 16.1. Tracing function calls.

Because `print_total` is not a C++ command or built-in function name, it must be a variable or a written function's name. Only function names end with the parentheses, so it must be a function call or the start of a function's code. Of the last two possibilities, it must be a call to a function because it ends with a semicolon. If it didn't have a semicolon, it would have to be the start of a function definition.

When you define a function (by typing the function name and its subsequent code inside braces), you *never* follow the name with a semicolon. Notice in the previous program that `main()`, `next_fun()`, and `third_fun()` have no semicolons when they appear in the body of the program. A semicolon follows their names only in `main()`, where these functions are called.

> **CAUTION:** Never define a function in another function. All function code must be listed sequentially, throughout the program. A function's closing brace *must* appear before another function's code can be listed.

Examples

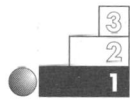

1. Suppose you are writing a program that does the following. First, it asks users for their departments. Then, if they are in accounting, they receive the accounting department's report. If they are in engineering, they receive the engineering department's report. Finally, if they are in marketing, they receive the marketing department's report.

   The skeleton of such a program follows. The code for `main()` is shown in its entirety, but only a skeleton of the other functions is shown. The `switch` statement is a perfect function-calling statement for such multiple-choice selections.

```cpp
// Skeleton of a departmental report program.
#include <iostream.h>
main()
{
   int choice;

   do
     { cout << "Choose your department from the " <<
             "following list\n";
       cout << "\t1. Accounting \n";
       cout << "\t2. Engineering \n";
       cout << "\t3. Marketing \n";
       cout << "What is your choice? ";
       cin >> choice;
     } while ((choice<1) || (choice>3));  // Ensure 1, 2,
                                          // or 3 is chosen.

   switch choice
   { case(1): { acct_report(); // Call accounting function.
```

```
                    break; }              // Don't fall through.
        case(2): { eng_report(); // Call engineering function.
                    break; }
        case(3): { mtg_report();   // Call marketing function.
                    break; }
      }
    return 0;  // Program returns to the operating
               // system when finished.
}

acct_report()
{
   // :
   // Accounting report code goes here.
   // :
   return 0;
}

eng_report()
{
   // :
   // Engineering report code goes here.
   // :
   return 0;
}

mtg_report()
{
   // :
   // Marketing report code goes here.
   // :
   return 0;
}
```

The bodies of switch statements normally contain function calls. You can tell that these case statements execute functions. For instance, acct_report(); (which is the first line of the first case) is not a variable name or a C++ command. It is the name of a function defined later in the program. If users enter 1 at the menu, the function called acct_report() executes. When it finishes, control returns to the first case body, and its `break` statement causes the `switch` statement to end. The `main()` function returns to DOS (or to your integrated C++ environment if you are using one) when its `return` statement executes.

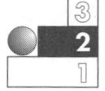

2. In the previous example, the `main()` routine is not very modular. It displays the menu, but not in a separate function, as it should. Remember that `main()` does very little except control the other functions, which do all the work.

Here is a rewrite of this sample program, with a fourth function to print the menu to the screen. This is truly a modular example, with each function performing a single task. Again, the last three functions are shown only as skeleton code because the goal here is simply to illustrate function calling and returning.

```
// Second skeleton of a departmental report program.
#include <iostream.h>
main()
{
    int choice;

    do
       { menu_print();  // Call function to print the menu.
         cin >> choice;
       } while ((choice<1) || (choice>3));   // Ensure 1, 2,
                                             // or 3 is chosen.
    switch choice
    { case(1): { acct_report(); // Call accounting function.
                 break; }              // Don't fall through.
      case(2): { eng_report(); // Call engineering function.
                 break; }
      case(3): { mtg_report();   // Call marketing function.
                 break; }
    }
    return 0;  // Program returns to the operating system
               // when finished.
}

menu_print()
{
```

```
      cout << "Choose your department from the following"
              "list\n";
      cout << "\t1. Accounting \n";
      cout << "\t2. Engineering \n";
      cout << "\t3. Marketing \n";
      cout << "What is your choice? ";
      return 0;    // Return to main().
   }

acct_report()
{
   // :
   // Accounting report code goes here.
   // :
   return 0;
}

eng_report()
{
   // :
   // Engineering report code goes here.
   // :
   return 0;
}

mtg_report()
{
   // :
   // Marketing report code goes here.
   // :
   return 0;
}
```

The menu-printing function doesn't have to follow main(). Because it's the first function called, however, it seems best to define it there.

3. Readability is the key, so programs broken into separate functions result in better written code. You can write and test each function, one at a time. After you write a general outline of the program, you can list a bunch of function calls in main(), and define their skeletons after main().

The body of each function initially should consist of a single return statement, so the program compiles in its skeleton format. As you complete each function, you can compile and test the program. This enables you to develop more accurate programs faster. The separate functions enable others (who might later modify your program) to find the particular function easily and without affecting the rest of the program.

Another useful habit, popular with many C++ programmers, is to separate functions from each other with a comment consisting of a line of asterisks (*) or dashes (-). This makes it easy, especially in longer programs, to see where a function begins and ends. What follows is another listing of the previous program, but now with its four functions more clearly separated by this type of comment line.

```cpp
// Third skeleton of a departmental report program.
#include <iostream.h>
main()
{
   int choice;

   do
     {  menu_print();   // Call function to print the menu.
        cin >> choice;
     } while ((choice<1) || (choice>3));   // Ensure 1, 2,
                                           // or 3 is chosen.
   switch choice
   { case(1): { acct_report(); // Call accounting function.
                break; }                // Don't fall through.
     case(2): { eng_report(); // Call engineering function.
                break; }
     case(3): { mtg_report();   // Call marketing function.
                break; }
   }
   return 0;   // Program returns to the operating system
               // when finished.
}


//**********************************************************
menu_print()
```

```
{
    cout << "Choose your department from the following"
            "list\n";
    cout << "\t1. Accounting \n";
    cout << "\t2. Engineering \n";
    cout << "\t3. Marketing \n";
    cout << "What is your choice? ";
    return 0;    // Return to main().
}

//**********************************************************
acct_report()
{
    // :
    // Accounting report code goes here.
    // :
    return 0;
}

//**********************************************************
eng_report()
{
    // :
    // Engineering report code goes here.
    // :
    return 0;
}

//**********************************************************
mtg_report()
{
    // :
    // Marketing report code goes here.
    // :
    return 0;
}
```

Due to space limitations, not all program listings in this book separate the functions in this manner. You might find, however, that your listings are easier to follow if you put these separating comments between your functions. The application in Appendix F, "The Mailing List Application," for example, uses these types of comments to separate its functions.

4. You can execute a function more than once simply by calling it from more than one place in a program. If you put a function call in the body of a loop, the function executes repeatedly until the loop finishes.

The following program prints the message C++ is Fun! several times on-screen—forward and backward—using functions. Notice that main() does not make every function call. The second function, name_print(), calls the function named reverse_print(). Trace the execution of this program's couts.

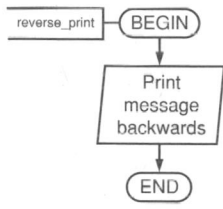

```
// Filename: C16FUN2.CPP
// Prints C++ is Fun! several times on-screen.
#include <iostream.h>
name_print();
reverse_print();
one_per_line();

main()
{
    int ctr;   // To control loops

    for (ctr=1; ctr<=5; ctr++)
      { name_print(), }              // Calls function five times.

    one_per_line();                  // Calls the program's last
                                     // function once.
    return 0;
}

//**********************************************************
name_print()
{
    // Prints C++ is Fun! across a line, separated by tabs.
    cout << "C++ is Fun!\tC++ is Fun!\tC++ is Fun!
            \tC++ is Fun!\n";
    cout << "C++  i s  F u n !\tC++  i s  F u n ! " <<
            "\tC++  i s  F u n !\n";
```

```
    reverse_print();        // Call next function from here.
    return 0;                        // Returns to main().
}


//*********************************************************
reverse_print()
{
    // Prints several C++ is Fun! messages,
    //    in reverse, separated by tabs.
    cout << "!nuF si ++C\t!nuF si ++C\t!nuF si ++C\t\n";

    return 0;                        // Returns to name_print().
}


//*********************************************************
one_per_line()
{
    // Prints C++ is Fun! down the screen.
    cout << "C++\n \ni\ns\n \nF\nu\nn\n!\n";
    return 0;    // Returns to main()
}
```

Here is the output from this program:

```
C++ is Fun!     C++ is Fun!     C++ is Fun!     C++ is Fun!
C++ i s  F u n !       C++  i s  F u n !  C++  i s  F u n !
!nuF si ++C      !nuF si ++C     !nuF si ++C
C++ is Fun!     C++ is Fun!     C++ is Fun!     C++ is Fun!
C++ i s  F u n !       C++  i s  F u n !  C++  i s  F u n !
!nuF si ++C      !nuF si ++C     !nuF si ++C
C++ is Fun!     C++ is Fun!     C++ is Fun!     C++ is Fun!
C++ i s  F u n !       C++  i s  F u n !  C++  i s  F u n !
!nuF si ++C      !nuF si ++C     !nuF si ++C
C++ is Fun!     C++ is Fun!     C++ is Fun!     C++ is Fun!
C++ i s  F u n !       C++  i s  F u n !  C++  i s  F u n !
!nuF si ++C      !nuF si ++C     !nuF si ++C
C++ is Fun!     C++ is Fun!     C++ is Fun!     C++ is Fun!
C++ i s  F u n !       C++  i s  F u n !  C++  i s  F u n !
!nuF si ++C      !nuF si ++C     !nuF si ++C
C++
```

```
i
s
F
u
n
!
```

Review Questions

The answers to the review questions are in Appendix B.

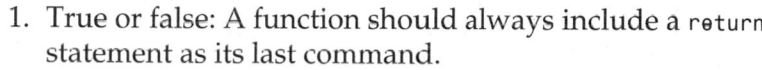

1. True or false: A function should always include a `return` statement as its last command.

2. What is the name of the first function executed in a C++ program?

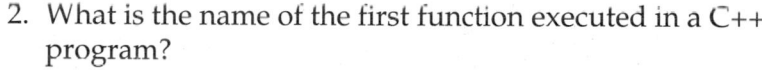

3. Which is better: one long function or several smaller functions? Why?

4. How do function names differ from variable names?

5. How can you use comments to help visually separate functions?

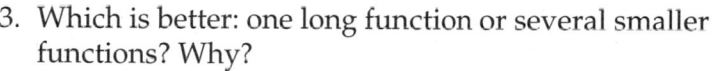

6. What is wrong with the following program section?

```cpp
calc_it()
{
   cout << "Getting ready to calculate the square of 25 \n";

   sq_25()
   {
      cout << "The square of 25 is " << (25*25);
      return 0;
   }

   cout << "That is a big number! \n";
   return 0;
}
```

7. Is the following a variable name, a function call, a function definition, or an expression?

```
scan_names();
```

8. True or false: The following line in a C++ program is a function call.

```
cout << "C++ is Fun! \n";
```

Summary

You have now been exposed to truly structured programs. Instead of typing a long program, you can break it into separate functions. This method isolates your routines so surrounding code doesn't clutter your program and add confusion.

Functions introduce just a little more complexity, involving the way variable values are recognized by the program's functions. The next chapter (Chapter 17, "Variable Scope") shows you how variables are handled between functions, and helps strengthen your structured programming skills.

Part IV

Variable Scope and
Modular Programming

Variable Scope

The concept of *variable scope* is most important when you write functions. Variable scope determines which functions recognize certain variables. If a function recognizes a variable, the variable is *visible* to that function. Variable scope protects variables in one function from other functions that might overwrite them. If a function doesn't need access to a variable, that function shouldn't be able to see or change the variable. In other words, the variable should not be "visible" to that particular function.

This chapter introduces you to

♦ Global and local variables

♦ Passing arguments

♦ Automatic and static variables

♦ Passing parameters

The previous chapter introduced the concept of using a different function for each task. This concept is much more useful when you learn about local and global variable scope.

Global Versus Local Variables

If you have programmed only in BASIC, the concept of local and global variables might be new to you. In many interpreted versions of BASIC, all variables are *global*, meaning the entire program knows each variable and has the capability to change any of them. If you use a variable called SALES at the top of the program, even the last line in the program can use SALES. (If you don't know BASIC, don't despair—there will be one less habit you have to break!)

Global variables can be dangerous. Parts of a program can inadvertently change a variable that shouldn't be changed. For example, suppose you are writing a program that keeps track of a grocery store's inventory. You might keep track of sales percentages, discounts, retail prices, wholesale prices, produce prices, dairy prices, delivered prices, price changes, sales tax percentages, holiday markups, post-holiday markdowns, and so on.

The huge number of prices in such a system is confusing. When writing a program to keep track of every price, it would be easy to mistakenly call both the dairy prices d_prices and the delivered prices d_prices. Either C++ will not enable you to do this (you can't define the same variable twice) or you will overwrite a value used for something else. Whatever happens, keeping track of all these different—but similarly named—prices makes this program confusing to write.

Global variables are visible across many program functions.

Global variables can be dangerous because code can inadvertently overwrite a variable initialized elsewhere in the program. It is better to make every variable *local* in your programs. Then, only functions that should be able to change the variables can do so.

Local variables are visible only in the block where they are defined.

Local variables can be seen (and changed) only from the function in which they are defined. Therefore, if a function defines a variable as local, that variable's scope is protected. The variable cannot be used, changed, or erased by any other function without special programming that you learn about shortly.

If you use only one function, main(), the concept of local and global is academic. You know from Chapter 16, "Writing C++ Functions," however, that single-function programs are not recommended. It is best to write modular, structured programs made up of many smaller functions. Therefore, you should know how to define variables as local to only those functions that use them.

Defining Variable Scope

When you first learned about variables in Chapter 4, "Variables and Literals," you learned you can define variables in two places:

♦ Before they are used inside a function

♦ Before a function name, such as main()

All examples in this book have declared variables with the first method. You have yet to see an example of the second method. Because most these programs have consisted entirely of a single main() function, there has been no reason to differentiate the two methods. It is only after you start using several functions in one program that these two variable definition methods become critical.

The following rules, specific to local and global variables, are important:

♦ A variable is local *if and only if* you define it after the opening brace of a block, usually at the top of a function.

♦ A variable is global *if and only if* you define it outside a function.

All variables you have seen so far have been local. They have all been defined immediately after the opening braces of main(). Therefore, they have been local to main(), and only main() can use them. Other functions have no idea these variables even exist because they belong to main() only. When the function (or block) ends, all its local variables are destroyed.

> **TIP:** All local variables disappear (lose their definition) when their block ends.

Global variables are visible from their definition through the remainder of the program.

Global variables are visible ("known") from their point of definition to the end of the program. If you define a global variable, *any* line throughout the rest of the program—no matter how many functions and code lines follow it—is able to use that global variable.

Examples

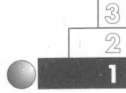

1. The following section of code defines two local variables, i and j.

```
main()
{
   int i, j;                  // Local because they're
                              // defined after the brace.
   // Rest of main() goes here.
}
```

These variables are visible to main() and not to any other function that might follow or be called by main().

2. The following section of code defines two global variables, g and h.

```
#include <iostream.h>
int g, h;                    // Global because they're
                             // defined before a function.
main()
{
   // main()'s code goes here.
}
```

It doesn't matter whether your #include lines go before or after global variable declarations.

3. Global variables can appear before any function. In the following program, main() uses no variables. However, both of the two functions after main() can use sales and profit because these variables are global.

```
// Filename: C17GLO.CPP
// Program that contains two global variables.
#include <iostream.h>
do_fun();
third_fun();  // Prototype discussed later.
main()
{
   cout << "No variables defined in main() \n\n";
   do_fun();                     // Call the first function.
```

```
      return 0;
}

float sales, profit;              // Two global variables.
do_fun()
{
   sales = 20000.00;        // This variable is visible
                            // from this point down.
   profit = 5000.00;        // As is this one. They are
                            // both global.

   cout << "The sales in the second function are " <<
           sales << "\n";
   cout << "The profit in the second function is " <<
           profit << "\n\n";

   third_fun();             // Call the third function to
                            // show that globals are visible.
   return 0;
}

third_fun()
{
   cout << "In the third function: \n";
   cout << "The sales in the third function are " <<
           sales << "\n";
   cout << "The profit in the third function is " <<
           profit << "\n";
   // If sales and profit were local, they would not be
   // visible by more than one function.
   return 0;
}
```

Notice that the main() function can never use sales and profit because they are not visible to main()—even though they are global. Remember, global variables are visible only from their point of definition downward in the program. Statements that appear before global variable definitions cannot use those variables. Here is the result of running this program.

```
No variables defined in main()

The sales in the second function are 20000
The profit in the second function is 5000

In the third function:
The sales in the third function are 20000
The profit in the third function is 5000
```

> **TIP:** Declare all global variables at the top of your programs. Even though you can define them later (between any two functions), you can find them faster if you declare them at the top.

4. The following program uses both local and global variables. It should now be obvious to you that j and p are local and i and z are global.

```cpp
// Filename: C17GLLO.CPP
// Program with both local and global variables.
// Local Variables      Global Variables
//      j, p                i, z
#include <iostream.h>
pr_again();  // Prototype

int i = 0;                  // Global variable because it's
                            //  defined outside main().
main()
{
   float p ;                        // Local to main() only.
   p = 9.0;                 // Puts value in global variable.
   cout << i << ", " << p << "\n";    // Prints global i
                                      //  and local p.
   pr_again();                      // Calls next function.
   return 0;                        // Returns to DOS.

}
```

```
float z = 9.0;              // Global variable because it's
                           //  defined before a function.
pr_again()
{
   int j = 5;               // Local to only pr_again().
   cout << j << ", " << z;    // This can't print p!.
   cout << ", " << i << "\n";
   return 0;                      // Return to main().
 }
```

Even though j is defined in a function that main() calls, main() cannot use j because j is local to pr_again(). When pr_again() finishes, j is no longer defined. The variable z is global from its point of definition down. This is why main() cannot print z. Also, the function pr_again() cannot print p because p is local to main() only.

Make sure you can recognize local and global variables before you continue. A little study here makes the rest of this chapter easy to understand.

5. Two variables can have the same name, as long as they are local to two different functions. They are distinct variables, even though they are named identically.

The following short program uses two variables, both named age. They have two different values, and they are considered to be two different variables. The first age is local to main(), and the second age is local to get_age().

```
// Filename: C17LOC1.CPP
// Two different local variables with the same name.
#include <iostream.h>
get_age();  // Prototype
main()
{
   int age;
   cout << "What is your age? ";
   cin >> age;

   get_age();                 // Call the second function.
   cout << "main()'s age is still " << age << "\n";
```

```
    return 0;
}

get_age()
{
    int age;                    // A different age. This one
                                //  is local to get_age().
    cout << "What is your age again? ";
    cin >> age;
    return 0;
}
```

Variables local to `main()` cannot be used in another function that `main()` calls.

The output of this program follows. Study this output carefully. Notice that main()'s last cout does not print the newly changed age. Rather, it prints the age known to main()—the age that is *local* to main(). Even though they are named the same, main()'s age has nothing to do with get_age()'s age. They might as well have two different variable names.

```
What is your age? 28
What is your age again? 56
main()'s age is still 28
```

You should be careful when naming variables. Having two variables with the same name is misleading. It would be easy to become confused while changing this program later. If these variables truly have to be separate, name them differently, such as old_age and new_age, or ag1 and ag2. This helps you remember that they are different.

6. There are a few times when overlapping local variable names does not add confusion, but be careful about overdoing it. Programmers often use the same variable name as the counter variable in a for loop. For example, the two local variables in the following program have the same name.

```
// Filename: C17LOC2.CPP
// Using two local variables with the same name
```

```
// as counting variables.
#include <iostream.h>
do_fun();  // Prototype
main()
{
   int ctr;                               // Loop counter.
   for (ctr=0; ctr<=10; ctr++)
      { cout << "main()'s ctr is " << ctr << "\n"; }
   do_fun();                        // Call second function.

   return 0;
}

do_fun()
{
   int otr;
   for (ctr=10; ctr>=0; ctr--)
      { cout << "do_fun()'s ctr is " << ctr << "\n"; }
   return 0;                        // Return to main().
}
```

Although this is a nonsense program that simply prints 0 through 10 and then prints 10 through 0, it shows that using ctr for both function names is not a problem. These variables do not hold important data that must be processed; rather, they are for loop-counting variables. Calling them both ctr leads to little confusion because their use is limited to controlling for loops. Because a for loop initializes and increments variables, the one function never relies on the other function's ctr to do anything.

7. Be careful about creating local variables with the same name in the same function. If you define a local variable early in a function and then define another local variable with the same name inside a new block, C++ uses only the innermost variable, until its block ends.

The following example helps clarify this confusing problem. The program contains one function with three local variables. See if you can find these three variables.

```
// Filename: C17MULI.CPP
// Program with multiple local variables called i.
#include <iostream.h>
main()
{
  int i;                               // Outer i
  i = 10;

  { int i;                             // New block's i
    i = 20;                   // Outer i still holds a 10.
    cout << i << " " << i  << "\n";       // Prints 20 20.

    { int i;     // Another new block and local variable.
      i = 30;                      // Innermost i only.
      cout << i << " " << i <<
              " " << i << "\n";       // Prints 30 30 30.
    }                   // Innermost i is now gone forever.


  }        // Second i is gone forever (its block ended).

  cout << i << " " << i << " " <<
          i << "\n";                  // Prints 10 10 10.
  return 0;
}                      // main() ends and so do its variables.
```

All local variables are local to the block in which they are defined. This program has three blocks, each one nested within another. Because you can define local variables immediately after an opening brace of a block, there are three distinct i variables in this program.

The local i disappears completely when its block ends (when the closing brace is reached). C++ always prints the variable that it interprets as the most local—the one that resides within the innermost block.

Use Global Variables Sparingly

You might be asking yourself, "Why do I have to understand global and local variables?" At this point, that is an understandable question, especially if you have been programming mostly in BASIC. Here is the bottom line: Global variables can be *dangerous*. Code can inadvertently overwrite a variable that was initialized in another place in the program. It is better to have every variable in your program be *local to the function that has to access it.*

Read the last sentence again. Even though you now know how to make variables global, you should avoid doing so! Try to never use another global variable. It might seem easier to use global variables when you write programs having more than one function: If you make every variable used by every function global, you never have to worry whether one is visible or not to any given function. On the other hand, a function can accidentally change a global variable when that was not your intention. If you keep variables local only to functions that need them, you protect their values, and you also keep your programs fully modular.

The Need for Passing Variables

You just learned the difference between local and global variables. You saw that by making your variables local, you protect their values because the function that sees the variable is the only one that can modify it.

What do you do, however, if you have a local variable you want to use in *two or more* functions? In other words, you might need a variable to be both added from the keyboard in one function and printed in another function. If the variable is local only to the first function, how can the second one access it?

You have two solutions if more than one function has to share a variable. One, you can declare the variable globally. This is not a good idea because you want only those two functions to have access to the variable, but all functions have access to it when it's global. The other alternative—and the better one by far—is to *pass* the local variable from one function to another. This has a big advantage: The variable is only known to those two functions. The rest of the program still has no access to it.

> **CAUTION:** Never pass a global variable to a function. There is no reason to pass global variables anyway because they are already visible to all functions.

You pass an argument when you pass one local variable to another function.

When you pass a local variable from one function to another, you *pass an argument* from the first function to the next. You can pass more than one argument (variable) at a time, if you want several local variables to be sent from one function to another. The receiving function *receives a parameter* (variable) from the function that sends it. You shouldn't worry too much about what you call them—either arguments or parameters. The important thing to remember is that you are sending local variables from one function to another.

> **NOTE:** You have already passed arguments to parameters when you passed data to the cout operator. The literals, variables, and expressions in the cout parentheses are arguments. The built-in cout function receives these values (called parameters on the receiving end) and displays them.

A little more terminology is needed before you see some examples. When a function passes an argument, it is called the *calling function*. The function that receives the argument (called a parameter when it is received) is called the *receiving function*. Figure 17.1 explains these terms.

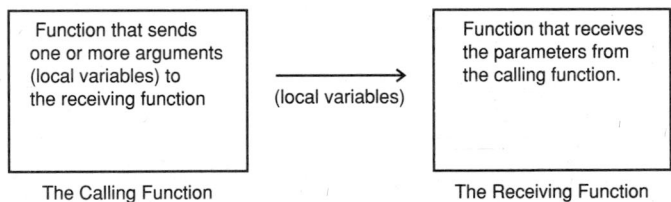

Figure 17.1. The calling and receiving functions.

If a function name has empty parentheses, nothing is being passed to it.

To pass a local variable from one function to another, you must place the local variable in parentheses in both the calling function and the receiving function. For example, the local and global

examples presented earlier did not pass local variables from main()
to do_fun(). If a function name has empty parentheses, nothing is
being passed to it. Given this, the following line passes two variables, total and discount, to a function called do_fun().

```
do_fun(total, discount);
```

It is sometimes said that a variable or function is *defined*. This
has nothing to do with the #define preprocessor directive, which
defines literals. You define variables with statements such as the
following:

```
int i, j;
int m=9;
float x;
char ara[] = "Tulsa";
```

These statements tell the program that you need these variables
to be reserved. A function is defined when the C++ compiler reads
the first statement in the function that describes the name and when
it reads any variables that might have been passed to that function
as well. Never follow a function definition with a semicolon, but
always follow the statement that calls a function with a semicolon.

> **NOTE:** To some C++ purists, a variable is only declared when
> you write int i; and only truly defined when you assign it a
> value, such as i=7;. They say that the variable is both declared
> and defined when you declare the variable and assign it a value
> at the same time, such as int i=7;.

The following program contains two function definitions,
main() and pr_it().

*To practice passing a variable to a function, declare i as an integer variable
and make it equal to five. The passing (or calling) function is main(), and
the receiving function is pr_it(). Pass the i variable to the pr_it()
function, then go back to main().*

```
main()                      // The main() function definition.
{
  int i=5;                  // Defines an integer variable.
  pr_it(i);                 // Calls the pr_it().
                            // function and passes it i.

  return 0;                 // Returns to the operating system.
}


pr_it(int i)                // The pr_it() function definition.
{
    cout << i << "\n";      // Calls the cout operator.
    return 0;               // Returns to main().
}
```

Because a passed parameter is treated like a local variable in the receiving function, the cout in pr_it() prints a 5, even though the main() function initialized this variable.

When you pass arguments to a function, the receiving function is not aware of the data types of the incoming variables. Therefore, you must include each parameter's data type in front of the parameter's name. In the previous example, the definition of pr_it() (the first line of the function) contains the type, int, of the incoming variable i. Notice that the main() calling function does not have to indicate the variable type. In this example, main() already knows the type of variable i (an integer); only pr_it() has to know that i is an integer.

> **TIP:** Always declare the parameter types in the receiving function. Precede each parameter in the function's parentheses with int, float, or whatever each passed variable's data type is.

Examples

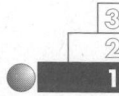

1. Here is a main() function that contains three local variables. main() passes one of these variables to the first function and two of them to the second function.

```cpp
// Filename: C17LOC3.CPP
// Pass three local variables to functions.
#include <iostream.h>
#include <iomanip.h>
pr_init(char initial);   // Prototypes discussed later.
pr_other(int age, float salary);

main()
{
   char initial;           // Three variables local to
                           // main().
   int age;
   float salary;

   // Fill these variables in main().
   cout << "What is your initial? ";
   cin >> initial;
   cout << "What is your age? ";
   cin >> age;
   cout << "What is your salary? ";
   cin >> salary;

   pr_init(initial);               // Call pr_init() and
                                   // pass it initial.
   pr_other(age, salary);          // Call pr_other() and
                                   // pass it age and salary.

   return 0;
}

pr_init(char initial)           // Never put a semicolon in
                                // the function definition.
{
   cout << "Your initial is " << initial << "\n";
   return 0;                              // Return to main().
}

pr_other(int age, float salary) // Must type both parameters.
{
   cout << "You look young for " << age << "\n";
   cout << "And " << setprecision(2) << salary <<
```

```
          " is a LOT of money!";
     return 0;                             // Return to main().
   }
```

2. A receiving function can contain its own local variables.
   As long as the names are not the same, these local variables
   do not conflict with the passed ones. In the following program, the second function receives a passed variable from
   main() and defines its own local variable called price_per.

```cpp
// Filename: C17LOC4.CPP
// Second function has its own local variable.
#include <iostream.h>
#include <iomanip.h>
compute_sale(int gallons); // Prototypes discussed later.

main()
{
   int gallons;

   cout << "Richard's Paint Service \n";
   cout << "How many gallons of paint did you buy? ";
   cin >> gallons;            // Get gallons in main().

   compute_sale(gallons);     // Compute total in function.
   return 0;
}

compute_sale(int gallons)
{
   float price_per = 12.45;   // Local to compute_sale().

   cout << "The total is " << setprecision(2) <<
           (price_per*(float)gallons) << "\n";
        // Had to type cast gallons because it was integer.
   return 0;                             // Return to main().
}
```

3. The following sample code lines test your skill at recognizing calling functions and receiving functions. Being able
   to recognize the difference is half the battle of understanding
   them.

```
do_it()
```

The preceding fragment must be the first line of a new function because it does not end with a semicolon.

```
do_it2(sales);
```

This line calls a function called `do_it2()`. The calling function passes the variable called `sales` to `do_it2()`.

```
pr_it(float total)
```

The preceding line is the first line of a function that receives a floating-point variable from another function that called it. All receiving functions must specify the type of each variable being passed.

```
pr_them(float total, int number)
```

This is the first line of a function that receives two variables—one is a floating-point variable and the other is an integer. This line cannot be calling the function `pr_them` because there is no semicolon at the end of the line.

Automatic Versus Static Variables

The terms *automatic* and *static* describe what happens to local variables when a function returns to the calling procedure. By default, all local variables are automatic, meaning that they are erased when their function ends. You can designate a variable as automatic by prefixing its definition with the term `auto`. The `auto` keyword is optional with local variables because they are automatic be default.

The two statements after `main()`'s opening brace declare automatic local variables:

```
main()
{
    int i;
    auto float x;
    // Rest of main() goes here.
```

Because `auto` is the default, you did not have to include the term `auto` with `x`.

> **NOTE:** C++ programmers rarely use the `auto` keyword with local variables because they are automatic by default.

Automatic variables are local and disappear when their function ends.

The opposite of an automatic variable is a static variable. All global variables are static and, as mentioned, all static variables retain their values. Therefore, if a local variable is static, it too retains its value when its function ends—in case the function is called a second time. To declare a variable as static, place the `static` keyword in front of the variable when you define it. The following code section defines three variables, `i`, `j`, and `k`. The variable `i` is automatic, but `j` and `k` are static.

```
my_fun()            // Start of new function definition.
{
    int i;
    static j=25;    // Both j and k are static variables.
    static k=30;
```

If local variables are static, their values remain in case the function is called again.

Always assign an initial value to a static variable when you declare it, as shown here in the last two lines. This initial value is placed in the static variable only the first time `my_fun()` executes. If you don't assign a static variable an initial value, C++ initializes it to zero.

> **TIP:** Static variables are good to use when you write functions that keep track of a count or add to a total. If the counting or totaling variables were local and automatic, their values would disappear when the function finished—destroying the totals.

Automatic and Static Rules for Local Variables

Local automatic variables disappear when their block ends. All local variables are automatic by default. You can prefix a variable (when you define it) with the auto keyword, or you can omit it; the variable is still automatic and its value is destroyed when its local block ends.

Local static variables do not lose their values when their function ends. They remain local to that function. When the function is called after the first time, the static variable's value is still in place. You declare a static variable by placing the static keyword before the variable's definition.

Examples

1. Consider this program:

```
// Filename: C17STA1.CPP
// Tries to use a static variable
// without a static declaration.
#include <iostream.h>
triple_it(int ctr);

main()
{
   int ctr;                       // Used in the for loop to
                                  // call a function 25 times.
   for (ctr=1; ctr<=25; ctr++)
     { triple_it(ctr); }         // Pass ctr to a function
                                  // called triple_it().
   return 0;
}

triple_it(int ctr)
{
   int total=0, ans;             // Local automatic variables.
```

```
// Triples whatever value is passed to it
// and adds the total.

ans = ctr * 3;                    // Triple number passed.
total += ans;   // Add triple numbers as this is called.

cout << "The number " << ctr << " multiplied by 3 is "
    << ans << "\n";

if (total > 300)
  { cout << "The total of triple numbers is over 300 \n"; }
return 0;
}
```

This is a nonsense program that doesn't do much, yet you might sense something is wrong. The program passes numbers from 1 to 25 to the function called `triple_it`. The function triples the number and prints it.

The variable called `total` is initially set to 0. The idea here is to add each tripled number and print a message when the total is larger than 300. However, the `cout` never executes. For each of the 25 times that this subroutine is called, `total` is reset to 0. The `total` variable is an automatic variable, with its value erased and initialized every time its procedure is called. The next example corrects this.

2. If you want `total` to retain its value after the procedure ends, you must make it static. Because local variables are automatic by default, you have to include the `static` keyword to override this default. Then the value of the `total` variable is retained each time the subroutine is called.

The following corrects the mistake in the previous program.

```
// Filename: C17STA2.CPP
// Uses a static variable with the static declaration.
#include <iostream.h>
triple_it(int ctr);

main()
```

```
   {
      int ctr;                          // Used in the for loop to
                                        //   call a function 25 times.
      for (ctr=1; ctr<=25; ctr++)
        { triple_it(ctr); }             // Pass ctr to a function
                                        // called triple_it().

      return 0;
   }

   triple_it(int ctr)
   {
      static int total=0;                 // Local and static
      int ans;                            // Local and automatic
      // total is set to 0 only the first time this
      // function is called.

      // Triples whatever value is passed to it and adds
      // the total.

      ans = ctr * 3;                   // Triple number passed.
      total += ans;   // Add triple numbers as this is called.

      cout << "The number " << ctr << " multiplied by 3 is "
           << ans << "\n";

      if (total > 300)
        { cout << "The total of triple numbers is over 300 \n"; }
      return 0;
   }
```

This program's output follows. Notice that the function's cout is triggered, even though total is a local variable. Because total is static, its value is not erased when the function finishes. When main() calls the function a second time, total's previous value (at the time you left the routine) is still there.

```
The number 1 multiplied by 3 is 3
The number 2 multiplied by 3 is 6
The number 3 multiplied by 3 is 9
The number 4 multiplied by 3 is 12
```

```
The number 5 multiplied by 3 is 15
The number 6 multiplied by 3 is 18
The number 7 multiplied by 3 is 21
The number 8 multiplied by 3 is 24
The number 9 multiplied by 3 is 27
The number 10 multiplied by 3 is 30
The number 11 multiplied by 3 is 33
The number 12 multiplied by 3 is 36
The number 13 multiplied by 3 is 39
The number 14 multiplied by 3 is 42
The number 15 multiplied by 3 is 45
The number 16 multiplied by 3 is 48
The number 17 multiplied by 3 is 51
The number 18 multiplied by 3 is 54
The number 19 multiplied by 3 is 57
The number 20 multiplied by 3 is 60
The number 21 multiplied by 3 is 63
The number 22 multiplied by 3 is 66
The number 23 multiplied by 3 is 69
The number 24 multiplied by 3 is 72
The number 25 multiplied by 3 is 75
```

This does not mean that local static variables become global. The main program cannot refer, use, print, or change `total` because it is local to the second function. Static simply means that the local variable's value is still there if the program calls the function again.

Three Issues of Parameter Passing

To have a complete understanding of programs with several functions, you have to learn three additional concepts:

◆ Passing arguments (variables) by value (also called "by copy")

◆ Passing arguments (variables) by address (also called "by reference")

◆ Returning values from functions

The first two concepts deal with the way local variables are passed and received. The third concept describes how receiving functions send values back to the calling functions. Chapter 18, "Passing Values," concludes this discussion by explaining these three methods for passing parameters and returning values.

Review Questions

The answers to the review questions are in Appendix B.

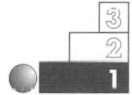

1. True or false: A function should always include a `return` statement as its last command, even though `return` is not required.

2. When a local variable is passed, is it called an argument or a parameter?

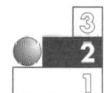

3. True or false: A function that is passed variables from another function cannot also have its own local variables.

4. What must appear inside the receiving function's parentheses, other than the variables passed to it?

5. If a function keeps track of a total or count every time it is called, should the counting or totaling variable be automatic or static?

6. When would you pass a global variable to a function? (Be careful—this might be a trick question!)

7. How many arguments are there in the following statement?

```
printf("The rain has fallen %d inches.", rainf);
```

Review Exercises

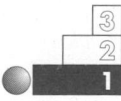

1. Write a program that asks, in `main()`, for the age of the user's dog. Write a second function called `people()` that computes the dog's age in human years (by multiplying the dog's age by seven).

2. Write a function that counts the number of times it is called. Name the function `count_it()`. Do not pass it anything. In the body of `count_it()`, print the following message:

```
The number of times this function has been called is: ##
```

where ## is the number. (*Hint:* Because the variable must be local, make it static and initialize it to zero when you first define it.)

3. The following program contains several problems. Some of these problems produce errors. One problem is not an error, but a bad location for a variable declaration. (*Hint:* Find all the global variables.) See if you can spot some of the problems, and rewrite the program so it works better.

```cpp
// Filename: C17BAD.CPP
// Program with bad uses of variable declarations.
#include <iostream.h>
#define NUM 10
do_var_fun();   // Prototypes discussed later.

char city[] = "Miami";
int count;

main()
{
    int abc;

    count = NUM;
    abc = 5;
    do_var_fun();

    cout << abc << " " << count << " " << pgm_var << " "
        << xyz;
    return 0;
}

int pgm_var = 7;

do_var_fun()
```

```
{
    char xyz = 'A';

    xyz = 'b';
    cout << xyz << " " << pgm_var << " " abc << " " << city;
    return 0;
}
```

Summary

Parameter passing is necessary because local variables are better than global. Local variables are protected in their own routines, but sometimes they must be shared with other routines. If local data are to remain in those variables (in case the function is called again in the same program), the variables should be static because otherwise their automatic values disappear.

Most the information in this chapter becomes more obvious as you use functions in your own programs. Chapter 18, "Passing Values," covers the actual passing of parameters in more detail and shows you two different ways to pass them.

Passing Values

C++ passes variables between functions using two different methods. The one you use depends on how you want the passed variables to be changed. This chapter explores these two methods. The concepts discussed here are not new to the C++ language. Other programming languages, such as Pascal, FORTRAN, and QBasic, pass parameters using similar techniques. A computer language must have the capability to pass information between functions before it can be called truly structured.

This chapter introduces you to the following:

♦ Passing variables by value

♦ Passing arrays by address

♦ Passing nonarrays by address

Pay close attention because most of the programs in the remainder of the book rely on the methods described in this chapter.

Passing by Value (by Copy)

The two wordings "passing by value" and "passing by copy" mean the same thing in computer terms. Some textbooks and C++ programmers state that arguments are passed *by value,* and some state that they are passed *by copy.* Both of these phrases describe one of the two methods by which arguments are passed to receiving functions. (The other method is called "by address," or "by reference." This method is covered later in the chapter.)

When an argument (local variable) is passed by value, a copy of the variable's value is sent to—and is assigned to—the receiving function's parameter. If more than one variable is passed by value, a copy of each of their values is sent to—and is assigned to—the receiving function's parameters.

Figure 18.1 shows the *passing by copy* in action. The value of i—not the variable—is passed to the called function, which receives it as a variable i. There are two variables called i, not one. The first is local to main(), and the second is local to pr_it(). They both have the same names, but because they are local to their respective functions, there is no conflict. The variable does not have to be called i in both functions, and because the value of i is sent to the receiving function, it does not matter what the receiving function calls the variable that receives this value.

When you pass by value, a copy of the variable's value is passed to the receiving function.

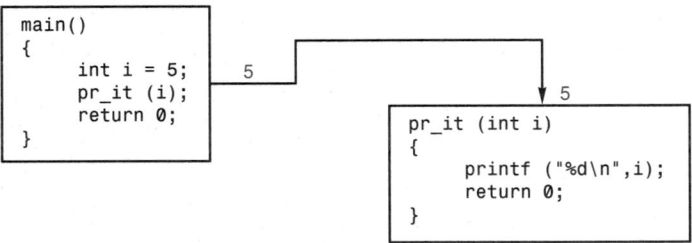

```
main()
{
        int i = 5;
        pr_it (i);
        return 0;
}
```

```
pr_it (int i)
{
        printf ("%d\n",i);
        return 0;
}
```

Figure 18.1. **Passing the variable i by value.**

In this case, when passing and receiving variables between functions, it is wisest to retain the same names. Even though they are not the same variables, they hold the same value. In this example, the value 5 is passed from main()'s i to pr_it()'s i.

Because a copy of i's value (and not the variable itself) is passed to the receiving function, if pr_it() changed i, it would be changing only its copy of i and not main()'s i. This fact truly separates functions and variables. You now have the technique for passing a copy of a variable to a receiving function, with the receiving function being unable to modify the calling function's variable.

All C++'s nonarray variables you have seen so far are passed by value. You do not have to do anything special to pass variables by value, except to pass them in the calling function's argument list and receive them in the receiving function's parameter list.

> **NOTE:** The default method for passing parameters is by value, as just described, unless you pass arrays. Arrays are always passed by the other method, by address, described later in the chapter.

Examples

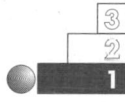

1. The following program asks users for their weight. It then passes that weight to a function that calculates the equivalent weight on the moon. Notice the second function uses the passed value, and calculates with it. After `weight` is passed to the second function, that function can treat `weight` as though it were a local variable.

Identify the program and include the necessary input/output file.

You want to calculate the user's weight on the moon. Because you have to hold the user's weight somewhere, declare the variable `weight` as an integer. You also need a function that does the calculations, so create a function called `moon()`.

Ask the user how much he or she weighs. Put the user's answer in `weight`. Now pass the user's weight to the `moon()` function, which divides the weight by six to determine the equivalent weight on the moon. Display the user's weight on the moon.

You have finished, so leave the `moon()` function, then leave the `main()` function.

```
// Filename: C18PASS1.CPP
// Calculate the user's weight in a second function.
#include <iostream.h>
moon(int weight);  // Prototypes discussed later.
```

```
main()
{
   int weight;                          // main()'s local weight.
   cout << "How many pounds do you weigh? ";
   cin >> weight;

   moon(weight);         // Call the moon() function and
                         //   pass it the weight.
   return 0;             // Return to the operating system.
}

moon(int weight)          // Declare the passed parameter.
{
   // Moon weights are 1/6th earth's weights
   weight /= 6;                      // Divide the weight by six.

   cout << "You weigh only " << weight <<
          " pounds on the moon!";
   return 0;                                // Return to main().
}
```

The output of this program follows:

```
How many pounds do you weigh? 120
You weigh only 20 pounds on the moon!
```

2. You can rename passed variables in the receiving function. They are distinct from the passing function's variable. The following is the same program as in Example 1, except the receiving function calls the passed variable earth_weight. A new variable, called moon_weight, is local to the called function and is used for the moon's equivalent weight.

Compute weight on moon

```
// Filename: C18PASS2.CPP
// Calculate the user's weight in a second function.
#include <iostream.h>
moon(int earth_weight);

main()
```

```
{
    int weight;                    // main()'s local weight.
    cout << "How many pounds do you weigh? ";
    cin >> weight;

    moon(weight);        // Call the moon() function and
                         // pass it the weight.
    return 0;            // Return to the operating system.
}


moon(int earth_weight)    // Declare the passed parameter.
{
    int moon_weight;                // Local to this function.

    // Moon's weights are 1/6th of earth's weights.
    moon_weight = earth_weight / 6;  // Divide weight by six.

    cout << "You only weigh " << moon_weight <<
            " pounds on the moon!";
    return 0;                              // Return to main().
}
```

The resulting output is identical to that of the previous program. Renaming the passed variable changes nothing.

3. The next example passes three variables—of three different types—to the called function. In the receiving function's parameter list, each of these variable types must be declared.

This program prompts users for three values in the main() function. The main() function then passes these variables to the receiving function, which calculates and prints values related to those passed variables. When the called function modifies a variable passed to the function, notice again that this does not affect the calling function's variable. When variables are passed by value, the value—not the variable—is passed.

```
// Filename: C18PASS3.CPP
// Get grade information for a student.
#include <iostream.h>
#include <iomanip.h>
check_grade(char lgrade, float average, int tests);
```

```
main()
{
   char lgrade;    // Letter grade.
   int  tests;     // Number of tests not yet taken.
   float average; // Student's average based on 4.0 scale.

   cout << "What letter grade do you want? ";
   cin >> lgrade;
   cout << "What is your current test average? ";
   cin >> average;
   cout << "How many tests do you have left? ";
   cin >> tests;

   check_grade(lgrade, average, tests);  // Calls function
                        //  and passes three variables by value.
   return 0;
}

check_grade(char lgrade, float average, int tests)
{
   switch (tests)
   {
     case (0): { cout << "You will get your current grade "
                         << "of " << lgrade;
                  break; }
     case (1): { cout << "You still have time to bring " <<
                            "up your average";
                  cout << "of " << setprecision(1) <<
                            average << "up. Study hard!";
                  break; }
     default:  { cout << "Relax. You still have plenty of "
                         <<  "time.";
                  break; }
   }
   return 0;
}
```

Passing by Address (by Reference)

When you pass by address, the address of the variable is passed to the receiving function.

The two phrases "by address" and "by reference" mean the same thing. The previous section described passing arguments by value (or by copy). This section teaches you how to pass arguments by address.

When you pass an argument (local variable) *by address,* the variable's address is sent to—and is assigned to—the receiving function's parameter. (If you pass more than one variable by address, each of their addresses is sent to—and is assigned to—the receiving function's parameters.)

Variable Addresses

All variables in memory (RAM) are stored at memory addresses—see Figure 18.2. If you want more information on the internal representation of memory, refer to Appendix A, "Memory Addressing, Binary, and Hexadecimal Review."

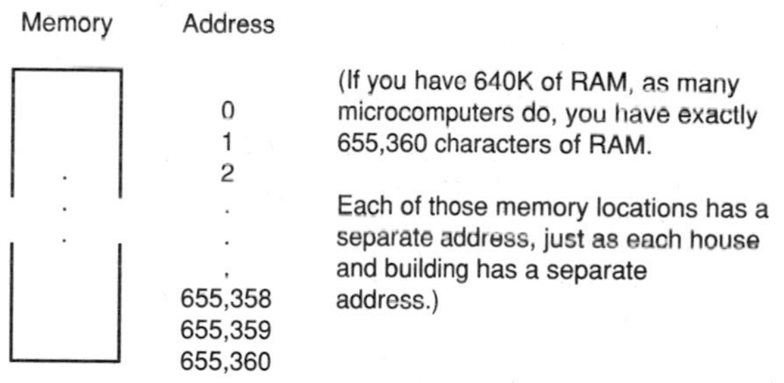

Figure 18.2. **Memory addresses.**

When you tell C++ to define a variable (such as `int i;`), you are requesting C++ to find an unused place in memory and assign that place (or memory address) to `i`. When your program uses the variable called `i`, C++ goes to `i`'s address and uses whatever is there.

If you define five variables as follows,

```
int i;
float x=9.8;
char ara[2] = {'A', 'B'};
int j=8, k=3;
```

C++ might arbitrarily place them in memory at the addresses shown in Figure 18.3.

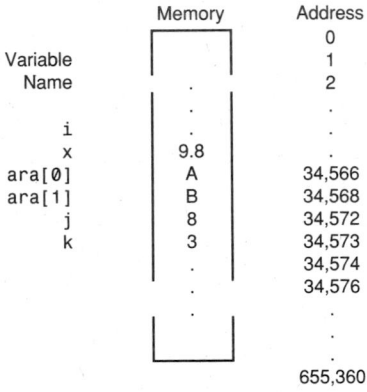

Figure 18.3. **Storing variables in memory.**

You don't know what is contained in the variable called i because you haven't put anything in it yet. Before you use i, you should initialize it with a value. (All variables—except character variables—usually use more than 1 byte of memory.)

Sample Program

All C++ arrays are passed by address.

The address of the variable, not its value, is copied to the receiving function when you pass a variable by address. In C++, *all arrays are automatically passed by address.* (Actually, a copy of their address is passed, but you will understand this better when you learn more about arrays and pointers.) The following important rule holds true for programs that pass by address:

Every time you pass a variable by address, if the receiving function changes the variable, it is changed also in the calling function.

Therefore, if you pass an array to a function and the function changes the array, those changes are still with the array when it returns to the calling function. Unlike passing by value, passing by address gives you the ability to change a variable in the *called* function and to keep those changes in effect in the *calling* function. The following sample program helps to illustrate this concept.

```cpp
// Filename: C18ADD1.CPP
// Passing by address example.
#include <iostream.h>
#include <string.h>
change_it(char c[4]);    // Prototype discussed later.
main()
{
   char name[4]="ABC";

   change_it(name);          // Passes by address because
                             // it is an array.
   cout << name << "\n";     // Called function can
                             // change array.

   return 0;
}


change_it(char c[4])         // You must tell the function
                             // that c is an array.
{
   cout << c << "\n";        // Print as it is passed.
   strcpy(c, "USA");         // Change the array, both
                             // here and in main().
   return 0;
}
```

Here is the output from this program:

```
ABC
USA
```

At this point, you should have no trouble understanding that the array is passed from `main()` to the function called `change_it()`. Even though `change_it()` calls the array `c`, it refers to the same array passed by the `main()` function (`name`).

Figure 18.4 shows how the array is passed. Although the address of the array—and not its value—is passed from `name` to `c`, both arrays are the same.

```
main()
{
    char ara[4] = "ABC";
    change_it(ara);
    printf("%s\n", ara);
    return 0
}
```

```
                                            ara

change_it(char c[4])

        printf("%s\n", c);
        strcpy(c, "USA");
        return 0
}
```

Figure 18.4. **Passing an array by address.**

Before going any further, a few additional comments are in order. Because the address of `name` is passed to the function—even though the array is called `c` in the receiving function—it is still the same array as `name`. Figure 18.5 shows how C++ accomplishes this task at the memory-address level.

```
                         Memory      Address

Variable
Name
                            .            .
                            .            .
                            .            .
name[0]--c[0]->             U         41,324      (Keep in mind that the
name[1]--c[1]->             S         41,325      actual address will depend
name[2]--c[2]->             A         41,326      on where your C++ compiler
                            .            .        puts the variables.)
                            .            .
                            .            .
```

Figure 18.5. **The array being passed is the same array in both functions.**

The variable array is referred to as `name` in `main()` and as `c` in `change_it()`. Because the address of `name` is copied to the receiving function, the variable is changed no matter what it is called in either function. Because `change_it()` changes the array, the array is changed also in `main()`.

Examples

1. You can now use a function to fill an array with user input. The following function asks users for their first name in the function called `get_name()`. As users type the name in the array, it is also entered in `main()`'s array. The `main()` function then passes the array to `pr_name()`, where it is printed. (If arrays were passed by value, this program would not work. Only the array value would be passed to the called functions.)

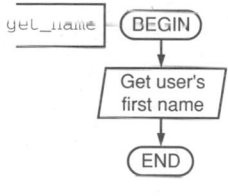

```cpp
// Filename: C18ADD2.CPP
// Get a name in an array, then print it using
// separate functions.
#include <iostream.h>
get_name(char name[25]);    // Prototypes discussed later.
print_name(char name[25]);

main()
{
    char name[25];
    get_name(name);              // Get the user's name.
    print_name(name);            // Print the user's name.
    return 0;
}

get_name(char name[25])      // Pass the array by address.
{
    cout << "What is your first name? ";
    cin >> name;
    return 0;
}

print_name(char name[25])
{
    cout << "\n\n Here you are, " << name;
    return 0;
}
```

When you pass an array, be sure to specify the array's type in the receiving function's parameter list. If the previous program declared the passed array with

```
get_name(char name)
```

the function `get_name()` would interpret this as a single character variable, *not* a character array. You never have to put the array size in brackets. The following statement also works as the first line of `get_name()`.

```
get_name(char name[])
```

Most C++ programmers put the array size in the brackets to clarify the array size, even though the size is not needed.

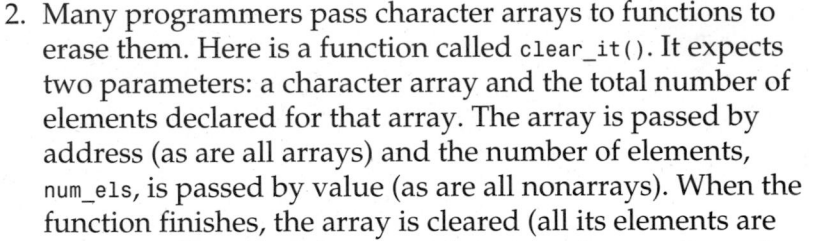

2. Many programmers pass character arrays to functions to erase them. Here is a function called `clear_it()`. It expects two parameters: a character array and the total number of elements declared for that array. The array is passed by address (as are all arrays) and the number of elements, `num_els`, is passed by value (as are all nonarrays). When the function finishes, the array is cleared (all its elements are reset to null zero). Subsequent functions that use it can then have an empty array.

```
clear_it(char ara[10], int num_els)
{
    int ctr;
    for (ctr=0; ctr<num_els; ctr++)
      { ara[ctr] = '\0'; }
    return 0;
}
```

The brackets after `ara` do not have to contain a number, as described in the previous example. The `10` in this example is simply a placeholder for the brackets. Any value (or no value) would work as well.

Passing Nonarrays by Address

You can pass nonarrays by address as well.

You now should see the difference between passing variables by address and by value. Arrays can be passed by address, and nonarrays can be passed by value. You can override the *by value* default for nonarrays. This is helpful sometimes, but it is not always recommended because the called function can damage values in the called function.

If you want a nonarray variable changed in a receiving function and also want the changes kept in the calling function, you must override the default and pass the variable by address. (You should understand this section better after you learn how arrays and pointers relate.) To pass a nonarray by address, you must precede the argument in the receiving function with an ampersand (&).

This might sound strange to you (and it is, at this point). Few C++ programmers override the default of passing by address. When you learn about pointers later, you should have little need to do so. Most C++ programmers don't like to clutter their code with these extra ampersands, but it's nice to know you can override the default if necessary.

The following examples demonstrate how to pass nonarray variables by address.

Examples

1. The following program passes a variable by address from main() to a function. The function changes it and returns to main(). Because the variable is passed by address, main() recognizes the new value.

```
// Filename: C18ADD3.CPP
// Demonstrate passing nonarrays by address.
#include <iostream.h>
do_fun(int &amt);    // Prototypes discussed later.

main()
{
    int amt;
```

```
amt = 100;                    // Assign a value in main().
cout << "In main(), amt is " << amt << "\n";

do_fun(amt);        // Pass amt by address
cout << "After return, amt is " << amt << " in main()\n";
return 0;
}

do_fun(int &amt)              // Inform function of
                             // passing by address.
{
amt = 85;                    // Assign new value to amt.
cout << "In do_fun(), amt is " << amt << "\n";
return 0;
}
```

The output from this program follows:

```
In main(), amt is 100
In do_fun(), amt is 85
After return, amt is 85 in main()
```

Notice that amt changed in the called function. Because it was passed by address, it is changed also in the calling function.

2. You can use a function to get the user's keyboard values. The main() function recognizes those values as long as you pass them by address. The following program calculates the cubic feet in a swimming pool. In one function, it requests the width, length, and depth. In another function, it calculates the cubic feet of water. Finally, in a third function, it prints the answer. The main() function is clearly a controlling function, passing variables between these functions by address.

Calculate
pool's cubic
feet

```
// Filename: C18POOL.CPP
// Calculates the cubic feet in a swimming pool.
#include <iostream.h>
get_values(int &length, int &width, int &depth);
calc_cubic(int &length, int &width, int &depth, int &cubic);
print_cubic(int &cubic);
```

```
main()
{
    int length, width, depth, cubic;

    get_values(length, width, depth);
    calc_cubic(length, width, depth, cubic);
    print_cubic(cubic);

    return 0;
}

get_values(int &length, int &width, int &depth)
{
    cout << "What is the pool's length? ";
    cin >> length;
    cout << "What is the pool's width? ";
    cin >> width;
    cout << "What is the pool's average depth? ";
    cin >> depth;
    return 0;
}

calc_cubic(int &length, int &width, int &depth, int &cubic)
{
    cubic = (length) * (width) * (depth);
    return 0;
}

print_cubic(int &cubic)
{
    cout << "\nThe pool has " << cubic << " cubic feet\n";
    return 0;
}
```

The output follows:

```
What is the pool's length? 16
What is the pool's width? 32
What is the pool's average depth? 6
The pool has 3072 cubic feet
```

All variables in a function must be preceded with an ampersand if they are to be passed by address.

Review Questions

The answers to the review questions are in Appendix B.

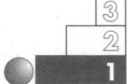

1. What type of variable is automatically passed by address?

2. What type of variable is automatically passed by value?

3. True or false: If a variable is passed by value, it is passed also by copy.

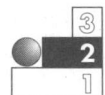

4. If a variable is passed to a function by value and the function changes the variable, is it changed in the calling function?

5. If a variable is passed to a function by address and the function changes the variable, is it changed in the calling function?

6. What is wrong with the following function?

```
do_fun(x, y, z)
{
    cout << "The variables are " << x << y << z;
    return 0;
}
```

7. Suppose you pass a nonarray variable and an array to a function at the same time. What is the default?

   a. Both are passed by address.

   b. Both are passed by value.

   c. One is passed by address and the other is passed by value.

Review Exercises

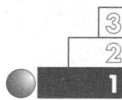

1. Write a main() function and a second function that main() calls. Ask users for their annual income in main(). Pass the income to the second function and print a congratulatory message if the user makes more than $50,000 or an encouragement message if the user makes less.

2. Write a three-function program, consisting of the following functions:

```
main()
fun1()
fun2()
```

Declare a 10-element character array in main(), fill it with the letters A through J in fun1(), then print that array backwards in fun2().

3. Write a program whose main() function passes a number to a function called print_aster(). The print_aster() function prints that many asterisks on a line, across the screen. If print_aster() is passed a number greater than 80, display an error because most screens cannot print more than 80 characters on the same line. When execution is finished, return control to main() and then return to the operating system.

4. Write a function that is passed two integer values by address. The function should declare a third local variable. Use the third variable as an intermediate variable and swap the values of both passed integers. For example, suppose the calling function passes your function old_pay and new_pay as in

```
swap_it(old_pay, new_pay);
```

The swap_it() function reverses the two values so, when control returns to the calling function, the values of old_pay and new_pay are swapped.

Summary

You now have a complete understanding of the various methods for passing data to functions. Because you will be using local variables as much as possible, you have to know how to pass local variables between functions but also keep the variables away from functions that don't need them.

You can pass data in two ways: by value and by address. When you pass data by value, which is the default method for nonarrays, only a copy of the variable's contents are passed. If the called function modifies its parameters, those variables are not modified in the calling function. When you pass data by address, as is done with arrays and nonarray variables preceded by an ampersand, the receiving function can change the data in both functions.

Whenever you pass values, you must ensure that they match in number and type. If you don't match them, you could have problems. For example, suppose you pass an array and a floating-point variable, but in the receiving function, you receive a floating-point variable followed by an array. The data does not reach the receiving function properly because the parameter data types do not match the variables being passed. Chapter 19, "Function Return Values and Prototypes," shows you how to protect against such disasters by prototyping all your functions.

Function Return Values and Prototypes

So far, you have passed variables to functions in only one direction—a calling function passed data to a receiving function. You have yet to see how data are passed back *from* the receiving function to the calling function. When you pass variables by address, the data are changed in both functions—but this is different from passing data back. This chapter focuses on writing function return values that improve your programming power.

After you learn to pass and return values, you have to *prototype* your own functions as well as C++'s built-in functions, such as cout and cin. By prototyping your functions, you ensure the accuracy of passed and returned values.

This chapter introduces you to the following:

- ◆ Returning values from functions

- ◆ Prototyping functions

- ◆ Understanding header files

By returning values from functions, you make your functions fully modular. They can now stand apart from the other functions.

They can receive and return values and act as building blocks that compose your complete application.

Function Return Values

Until now, all functions in this book have been *subroutines* or *subfunctions.* A C++ subroutine is a function that is called from another function, but it does not return any values. The difference between subroutines and functions is not as critical in C++ as it is in other languages. All functions, whether they are subroutines or functions that return values, are defined in the same way. You can pass variables to each of them, as you have seen throughout this section of the book.

Functions that return values offer you a new approach to programming. In addition to passing data one-way, from calling to receiving function, you can pass data back from a receiving function to its calling function. When you want to return a value from a function to its calling function, put the return value after the `return` statement. To clarify the return value even more, many programmers put parentheses around the return value, as shown in the following syntax:

Put the return value at the end of the `return` statement.

```
return (return value);
```

> **CAUTION:** Do not return global variables. There is no need to do so because their values are already known throughout the code.

The calling function must have a use for the return value. For example, suppose you wrote a function that calculated the average of any three integer variables passed to it. If you return the average, the calling function has to receive that return value. The following sample program helps to illustrate this principle.

Calculate average

```
// Filename: C19AVG.CPP
// Calculates the average of three input values.
#include <iostream.h>
int calc_av(int num1, int num2, int num3);    //Prototype
```

```
main()
{
   int num1, num2, num3;
   int avg;                    // Holds the return value.

   cout << "Please type three numbers (such as 23 54 85) ";
   cin >> num1 >> num2 >> num3;

   // Call the function, pass the numbers,
   // and accept the return value amount.
   avg = calc_av(num1, num2, num3);

   cout << "\n\nThe average is " << avg;      // Print the
                                              // return value.
   return 0;
}

int calc_av(int num1, int num2, int num3)
{
   int local_avg;  // Holds the average for these numbers.
   local_avg = (num1+num2+num3) / 3;

   return (local_avg);
}
```

Here is a sample output from the program:

```
Please type three numbers (such as 23 54 85) 30 40 50


The average is 40
```

Study this program carefully. It is similar to many you have seen, but a few additional points have to be considered now that the function returns a value. It might help to walk through this program a few lines at a time.

The first part of main() is similar to other programs you have seen. It declares its local variables: three for user input and one for the calculated average. The cout and cin are familiar to you. The function call to calc_av() is also familiar; it passes three variables (num1, num2, and num3) by value to `calc_av()`. (If it passed them by address, an ampersand (&) would have to precede each argument, as discussed in Chapter 18.)

The receiving function, `calc_av()`, seems similar to others you have seen. The only difference is that the first line, the function's definition line, has one addition—the `int` before its name. This is the *type* of the return value. You must always precede a function name with its return data type. If you do not specify a type, C++ assumes a type of `int`. Therefore, if this example had no return type, it would work just as well because an `int` return type would be assumed.

Because the variable being returned from `calc_av()` is an integer, the `int` return type is placed before `calc_av()`'s name.

You can see also that the return statement of `calc_av()` includes the return value, `local_avg`. This is the variable being sent back to the calling function, `main()`. You can return only a single variable to a calling function.

Even though a function can receive more than one parameter, it can return only a single value to the calling function. If a receiving function is modifying more than one value from the calling function, you must pass the parameters by address; you cannot return multiple values using a `return` statement.

After the receiving function, `calc_av()`, returns the value, `main()` must do something with that returned value. So far, you have seen function calls on lines by themselves. Notice in `main()` that the function call appears on the right side of the following assignment statement:

```
avg = calc_av(num1, num2, num3);
```

When the `calc_av()` function returns its value—the average of the three numbers—that value replaces the function call. If the average computed in `calc_av()` is 40, the C++ compiler interprets the following statement in place of the function call:

```
avg = 40;
```

You typed a function call to the right of the equal sign, but the program replaces a function call with its return value when the `return` takes place. In other words, a function that returns a value becomes that value. You must put such a function anywhere you put any variable or literal (usually to the right of an equal sign, in an expression, or in `cout`). The following is an *incorrect* way of calling `calc_av()`:

```
calc_av(num1, num2, num3);
```

If you did this, C++ would have nowhere to put the return value.

> **CAUTION:** Function calls that return values usually don't appear on lines by themselves. Because the function call is replaced by the return value, you should do something with that return value (such as assign it to a variable or use it in an expression). Return values can be ignored, but doing so usually defeats the purpose of creating them.

Examples

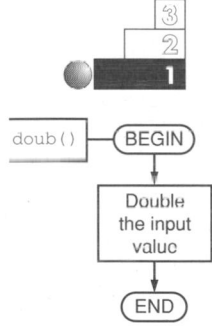

1. The following program passes a number to a function called `doub()`. The function doubles the number and returns the result.

```cpp
// Filename: C19DOUB.CPP
// Doubles the user's number.
#include <iostream.h>
int doub (int num);
main()
{
    int number;                        // Holds user's input.
    int d_number;       // Holds double the user's input.
    cout << "What number do you want doubled? ";
    cin >> number;

    d_number = doub(number);        // Assigns return value.
    cout << number << " doubled is " << d_number;
    return 0;
}
```

```
int doub(int num)
{
   int d_num;
   d_num = num * 2;              // Doubles the number.
   return (d_num);               // Returns the result.
}
```

The program produces output such as this:

```
What number do you want doubled? 5
5 doubled is 10
```

2. Function return values can be used *anywhere* literals, variables, and expressions are used. The following program is similar to the previous one. The difference is in main().

   The function call is performed not on a line by itself, but from a cout. This is a nested function call. You call the built-in function cout using the return value from one of the program's functions named doub(). Because the call to doub() is replaced by its return value, the cout has enough information to proceed as soon as doub() returns. This gives main() less overhead because it no longer needs a variable called d_number, although you must use your own judgment as to whether this program is easier to maintain. Sometimes it is wise to include function calls in other expressions; other times it is clearer to call the function and assign its return value to a variable before using it.

```
// Filename: C19DOUB2.CPP
// Doubles the user's number.
#include <iostream.h>
int doub(int num); // Prototype

main()
{
   int number;                        // Holds user's input.
   cout << "What number do you want doubled? ";
   cin >> number;
```

```
   // The third cout parameter is
   // replaced with a return value.
   cout << number << " doubled is " << doub(number);

   return 0;
}

int doub(int num)
{
   int d_num;
   d_num = num * 2;                 // Double the number.
   return (d_num);                  // Return the result.
}
```

3. The following program asks the user for a number. That number is then passed to a function called sum(), which adds the numbers from 1 to that number. In other words, if the user types a 6, the function returns the result of the following calculation:

```
1 + 2 + 3 + 4 + 5 + 6
```

This is known as the *sum of the digits* calculation, and it is sometimes used for depreciation in accounting.

```
// Filename: C10SUMD.CPP
// Compute the sum of the digits.
#include <iostream.h>
int sum(int num);  // Prototype

main()
{
   int num, sumd;

   cout << "Please type a number: ";
   cin >> num;

   sumd = sum(num);
   cout << "The sum of the digits is " << sumd;
   return 0;
}
```

```
int sum(int num)
{
   int ctr;                        // Local loop counter.
   int sumd=0;                     // Local to this function.
   if (num <= 0)   // Check whether parameter is too small.
     { sumd = num; }      // Returns parameter if too small.
   else
     { for (ctr=1; ctr<=num; ctr++)
          { sumd += ctr; }
     }
   return(sumd);
}
```

The following is a sample output from this program:

```
Please type a number: 6
The sum of the digits is 21
```

4. The following program contains two functions that return values. The first function, maximum(), returns the larger of two numbers entered by the user. The second one, minimum(), returns the smaller.

```
// Filename: C19MINMX.CPP
// Finds minimum and maximum values in functions.
#include <iostream.h>

int maximum(int num1, int num2);  // Prototypes
int minimum(int num1, int num2);

main()
{
   int num1, num2;                    // User's two numbers.
   int min, max;

   cout << "Please type two numbers (such as 46 75) ";
   cin >> num1 >> num2;

   max = maximum(num1, num2);     // Assign the return
   min = minimum(num1, num2);     // value of each
                                  // function to variables.
```

```
    cout << "The minimum number is " << min << "\n";
    cout << "The maximum number is " << max << "\n";
    return 0;
}

int maximum(int num1, int num2)
{
    int max;                     // Local to this function only.
    max = (num1 > num2) ? (num1) : (num2);
    return (max);
}

int minimum(int num1, int num2)
{
    int min;                     // Local to this function only.
    min = (num1 < num2) ? (num1) : (num2);
    return (min);
}
```

Here is a sample output from this program:

```
Please type two numbers (such as 46 75) 72 55
The minimum number is 55
The maximum number is 72
```

If the user types the same number, `minimum` and `maximum` are the same.

These two functions can be passed any two integer values. In such a simple example as this one, the user certainly already knows which number is lower or higher. The point of such an example is to show how to code return values. You might want to use similar functions in a more useful application, such as finding the highest paid employee from a payroll disk file.

Function Prototypes

The word *prototype* is sometimes defined as a model. In C++, a function prototype models the actual function. Before completing your study of functions, parameters, and return values, you must understand how to prototype each function in your program.

C++ requires that you prototype all functions in your program. When prototyping, you inform C++ of the function's parameter types and its return value, if any.

To prototype a function, copy the function's definition line to the top of your program (immediately before or after the `#include <iostream.h>` line). Place a semicolon at the end of the function definition line, and you have the prototype. The definition line (the function's first line) contains the return type, the function name, and the type of each argument, so the function prototype serves as a model of the function that follows.

If a function does not return a value, or if that function has no arguments passed to it, you should still prototype it. Place the keyword `void` in place of the return type or the parameters. `main()` is the only function that you do not have to prototype because it is *self-prototyping;* meaning `main()` is not called by another function. The first time `main()` appears in your program (assuming you follow the standard approach and make `main()` your program's first function), it is executed.

If a function returns nothing, `void` must be its return type. Put `void` in the argument parentheses of function prototypes with no arguments. All functions must match their prototypes.

All `main()` functions in this book have returned a `0`. Why? You now know enough to answer that question. Because `main()` is self-prototyping, and because the `void` keyword never appeared before `main()` in these programs, C++ assumed an `int` return type. All C++ functions prototyped as returning `int` or those without any return data type prototype assume `int`. If you wanted to not put `return 0;` at the end of `main()`'s functions, you must insert `void` before `main()` as in:

C++ assumes functions return `int` unless you put a different data return type, or use the `void` keyword.

```
void main()     // main() self-prototypes to return nothing.
```

You can look at a statement and tell whether it is a prototype or a function definition (the function's first line) by the semicolon on the end. All prototypes, unless you make `main()` self-prototype, end with a semicolon.

Prototype for Safety

Prototyping protects you from programming mistakes. Suppose you write a function that expects two arguments: an integer followed by a floating-point value. Here is the first line of such a function:

```
my_fun(int num, float amount)
```

What if you passed incorrect data types to `my_fun()`? If you were to call this function by passing it two literals, a floating-point followed by an integer, as in

```
my_fun(23.43, 5);        // Call the my_fun() function.
```

the function would not receive correct parameters. It is expecting an integer followed by a floating-point, but you did the opposite and sent it a floating-point followed by an integer.

In regular C programs, mismatched arguments such as these generate no error message even though the data are not passed correctly. C++ requires prototypes so you cannot send the wrong data types to a function (or expect the wrong data type to be returned). Prototyping the previous function results in this:

Prototyping protects your programs from function programming errors.

```
void my_fun(int num, float amount);        // Prototype
```

In doing so, you tell the compiler to check this function for accuracy. You inform the compiler to expect nothing after the `return` statement, not even 0, (due to the `void` keyword) and to expect an integer followed by a floating-point in the parentheses.

If you break any of the prototype's rules, the compiler informs you of the problem and you can correct it.

Prototype All Functions

You should prototype every function in your program. As just described, the prototype defines (for the rest of the program) which functions follow, their return types, and their parameter types. You should prototype C++'s built-in functions also, such as `printf()` and `scanf()` if you use them.

Think about how you prototype printf(). You don't always pass it the same types of parameters because you print different data with each printf(). Prototyping functions you write is easy: The prototype is basically the first line in the function. Prototyping functions you do not write might seem difficult, but it isn't—you have already done it with every program in this book!

The designers of C++ realized that all functions have to be prototyped. They realized also that you cannot prototype built-in functions, so they did it for you and placed the prototypes in header files on your disk. You have been including the printf() and scanf() prototypes in each program that used them in this book with the following statement:

```
#include <stdio.h>
```

Inside the stdio.h file is a prototype of many of C++'s input and output functions. By having prototypes of these functions, you ensure that they cannot be passed bad values. If someone attempts to pass incorrect values, C++ catches the problem.

Because printf() and scanf() are not used very often in C++, the cout and cin operators have their own header file called iostream.h that you have seen included in this book's programs as well. The iostream.h file does not actually include prototypes for cout and cin because they are operators and not functions, but iostream.h does include some needed definitions to make cout and cin work.

Remember too that iomanip.h has to be included if you use a setw or setprecision modifier in cout. Any time you use a new built-in C++ function or a manipulating operator, check your compiler's manual to find the name of the prototype file to include.

Prototyping is the primary reason why you should always include the matching header file when you use C++'s built-in functions. The strcpy() function you saw in previous chapters requires the following line:

```
#include <string.h>
```

This is the header file for the strcpy() function. Without it, the program does not work.

Examples

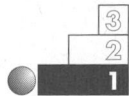

1. Prototype all functions in all programs except `main()`. Even `main()` must be prototyped if it returns nothing (not even `0`). The following program includes two prototypes: one for `main()` because it returns nothing, and one for the built-in `printf()` and `scanf()` functions.

```
// Filename: C19PRO1.CPP
// Calculates sales tax on a sale
#include <stdio.h>        // Prototype built-in functions.
void main(void);

void main(void)
{

   float total_sale;
   float tax_rate = .07;            // Assume seven percent
                                    // tax rate.

   printf("What is the sale amount? ");
   scanf(" %f", &total_sale);

   total_sale += (tax_rate * total_sale);
   printf("The total sale is %.2f", total_sale);
   return;       // No 0 required!
}
```

Notice that `main()`'s `return` statement needed only a semi-colon after it. As long as you prototype `main()` with a `void` return type, the last line in `main()` can be `return;` instead of having to type `return 0;` each time.

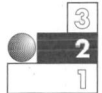

2. The following program asks the user for a number in `main()`, and passes that number to `ascii()`. The `ascii()` function returns the ASCII character that matches the user's number. This example illustrates a `character` return type. Functions can return any data type.

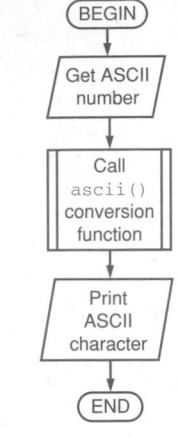

```
// Filename: C19ASC.CPP
// Prints the ASCII character of the user's number.
// Prototypes follow.
#include <iostream.h>
char ascii(int num);

void main()
{
    int num;
    char asc_char;

    cout << "Enter an ASCII number? ";
    cin >> num;

    asc_char = ascii(num);
    cout << "The ASCII character for " << num
         << " is " << asc_char;
    return;
}

char ascii(int num)
{
    char asc_char;
    asc_char = char(num);   // Type cast to a character.
    return (asc_char);
}
```

The output from this program follows:

```
Enter an ASCII number? 67
The ASCII character for 67 is C
```

3. Suppose you have to calculate net pay for a company. You find yourself multiplying the hours worked by the hourly pay, then deducting taxes to compute the net pay. The following program includes a function that does this for you. It requires three arguments: the hours worked, the hourly pay, and the tax rate (as a floating-point decimal, such as .30 for 30 percent). The function returns the net pay. The main() calling program tests the function by sending three different payroll values to the function and printing the three return values.

```
// Filename: C19NPAY.CPP
// Defines a function that computes net pay.
#include <iostream.h>   // Needed for cout and cin.
void main(void);
float netpayfun(float hours, float rate, float taxrate);

void main(void)
{
    float net_pay;

    net_pay = netpayfun(40.0, 3.50, .20);
    cout << "The pay for 40 hours at $3.50/hr., and a 20% "
        << "tax rate is $";
    cout << net_pay << "\n";

    net_pay = netpayfun(50.0, 10.00, .30);
    cout << "The pay for 50 hours at $10.00/hr., and a 30% "
        << "tax rate is $";
    cout << net_pay << "\n";

    net_pay = netpayfun(10.0, 5.00, .10);
    cout << "The pay for 10 hours at $5.00/hr., and a 10% "
        << " tax rate is $";
    cout << net_pay << "\n";

    return;
}

float netpayfun(float hours, float rate, float taxrate)
{
    float gross_pay, taxes, net_pay;
    gross_pay = (hours * rate);
    taxes = (taxrate * gross_pay);
    net_pay = (gross_pay - taxes);
    return (net_pay);
}
```

Review Questions

The answers to the review questions are in Appendix B.

1. How do you declare function return types?

2. What is the maximum number of return values a function can return?

3. What are header files for?

4. What is the default function return type?

5. True or false: a function that returns a value can be passed only a single parameter.

6. How do prototypes protect the programmer from bugs?

7. Why don't you have to return global variables?

8. What is the return type, given the following function prototype?

```
float my_fun(char a, int b, float c);
```

How many parameters are passed to `my_fun()`? What are their types?

Review Exercises

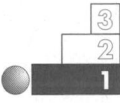

1. Write a program that contains two functions. The first function returns the square of the integer passed to it, and the second function returns the cube. Prototype `main()` so you do not have to return a value.

2. Write a function that returns the double-precision area of a circle, given that a double-precision radius is passed to it. The formula for calculating the area of a circle is

```
area = 3.14159 * (radius * radius)
```

3. Write a function that returns the value of a polynomial given this formula:

```
9x4 + 15x2 + x1
```

Assume x is passed from `main()` and it is supplied by the user.

Summary

You learned how to build your own collection of functions. When you write a function, you might want to use it in more than one program—there is no need to reinvent the wheel. Many programmers write useful functions and use them in more than one program.

You now understand the importance of prototyping functions. You should prototype all your own functions, and include the appropriate header file when you use one of C++'s built-in functions. Furthermore, when a function returns a value other than an integer, you must prototype so C++ recognizes the noninteger return value.

Default Arguments and Function Overloading

All functions that receive arguments do not have to be sent values. C++ enables you to specify default argument lists. You can write functions that assume argument values even if you do not pass them any arguments.

C++ also enables you to write more than one function with the same function name. This is called *overloading functions.* As long as their argument lists differ, the functions are differentiated by C++.

This chapter introduces you to the following:

♦ Default argument lists

♦ Overloaded functions

♦ Name-mangling

Default argument lists and overloaded functions are not available in regular C. C++ extends the power of your programs by providing these time-saving procedures.

Default Argument Lists

Suppose you were writing a program that has to print a message on-screen for a short period of time. For instance, you pass a function an error message stored in a character array and the function prints the error message for a certain period of time.

The prototype for such a function can be this:

```
void pr_msg(char note[]);
```

Therefore, to request that pr_msg() print the line "Turn printer on", you call it this way:

```
pr_msg("Turn printer on");    // Passes a message to be printed.
```

This command prints the message "Turn printer on" for a period of five seconds or so. To request that pr_msg() print the line "Press any key to continue...", you call it this way:

```
pr_msg("Press a key to continue...");    // Passes a message.
```

As you write more of the program, you begin to realize that you are printing one message, for instance the "Turn printer on" message, more often than any other message. It seems as if the pr_msg() function is receiving that message much more often than any other. This might be the case if you were writing a program that printed many reports to the printer. You still will use pr_msg() for other delayed messages, but the "Turn printer on" message is most frequently used.

Instead of calling the function over and over, typing the same message each time, you can set up the prototype for pr_msg() so it defaults to the "Turn printer on" in this way:

```
void pr_msg(char note[]="Turn printer on");// Prototype
```

List default argument values in the prototype.

After prototyping pr_msg() with the default argument list, C++ assumes you want to pass "Turn printer on" to the function unless you override the default by passing something else to it. For instance, in main(), you call pr_msg() this way:

```
pr_msg();    // C++ assumes you mean "Turn printer on".
```

This makes your programming job easier. Because most of the time you want pr_msg() to print "Turn printer on" the default argument list takes care of the message and you do not have to pass the message when you call the function. However, those few times when you want to pass something else, simply pass a different message. For example, to make `pr_msg()` print `"Incorrect value"` you type:

```
pr_msg("Incorrect value");    // Pass a new message.
```

> **TIP:** Any time you call a function several times and find yourself passing that function the same parameters most of the time, consider using a default argument list.

Multiple Default Arguments

You can specify more than one default argument in the prototype list. Here is a prototype for a function with three default arguments:

```
float funct1(int i=10, float x=7.5, char c='A');
```

There are several ways you can call this function. Here are some samples:

```
funct1();
```

All default values are assumed.

```
funct1(25);
```

A 25 is sent to the integer argument, and the default values are assumed for the rest.

```
funct1(25, 31.25);
```

A 25 is sent to the integer argument, 31.25 to the floating-point argument, and the default value of 'A' is assumed for the character argument.

NOTE: If only some of a function's arguments are default arguments, those default arguments must appear on the far *left* of the argument list. No default arguments can appear to the left of those not specified as default. This is an *invalid* default argument prototype:

```
float func2(int i=10, float x, char c, long n=10.232);
```

This is invalid because a default argument appears on the left of a nondefault argument. To fix this, you have to move the two default arguments to the far left (the start) of the argument list. Therefore, by rearranging the prototype (and the resulting function calls) as follows, C++ enables you to accomplish the same objective as you attempted with the previous line:

```
float func2(float x, char c, int i=10, long n=10.232);
```

Examples

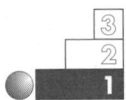

1. Here is a complete program that illustrates the message-printing function described earlier in this chapter. The `main()` function simply calls the delayed message-printing function three times, each time passing it a different set of argument lists.

```
// Filename: C20DEF1.CPP
// Illustrates default argument list.
#include <iostream.h>

void pr_msg(char note[]="Turn printer on"); // Prototype.

void main()
{
    pr_msg();                   // Prints default message.
    pr_msg("A new message");    // Prints another message.
    pr_msg();                   // Prints default message again.
    return;
}

void pr_msg(char note[])  // Only prototype contains defaults.
```

```
{
   long int delay;
   cout << note << "\n";
   for (delay=0; delay<500000; delay++)
      { ;   /* Do nothing while waiting */ }
   return;
}
```

The program produces the following output:

```
Turn printer on
A new message
Turn printer on
```

The delay loop causes each line to display for a couple of seconds or more, depending on the speed of your computer, until all three lines print.

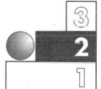

2. The following program illustrates the use of defaulting several arguments. main() calls the function de_fun() five times, sending de_fun() five sets of arguments. The de_fun() function prints five different things depending on main()'s argument list.

```
// Filename: C20DEF2.CPP
// Demonstrates default argument list with several parameters.
#include <iostream.h>
#include <iomanip.h>

void de_fun(int i=5, long j=40034, float x=10.25,
            char ch='Z', double d=4.3234); // Prototype

void main()
{
   de_fun();            // All defaults used.
   de_fun(2);           // First default overridden.
   de_fun(2, 75037);  // First and second default overridden.
   de_fun(2, 75037, 35.88);      // First, second, and third
   de_fun(2, 75037, 35.88, 'G'); // First, second, third,
                                 // and fourth
   de_fun(2, 75037, 35.88, 'G', .0023); // No defaulting.
```

```
      return;
   }

   void de_fun(int i, long j, float x, char ch, double d)
   {
      cout << setprecision(4) << "i: " << i << "    " << "j: " << j;
      cout << "    x: " << x << "    " << "ch: " << ch;
      cout << "    d: " << d << "\n";
      return;
   }
```

Here is the output from this program:

```
i: 5    j: 40034    x: 10.25    ch: Z    d: 4.3234
i: 2    j: 40034    x: 10.25    ch: Z    d: 4.3234
i: 2    j: 75037    x: 10.25    ch: Z    d: 4.3234
i: 2    j: 75037    x: 35.88    ch: Z    d: 4.3234
i: 2    j: 75037    x: 35.88    ch: G    d: 4.3234
i: 2    j: 75037    x: 35.88    ch: G    d: 0.0023
```

Notice that each call to de_fun() produces a different output because main() sends a different set of parameters each time main() calls de_fun().

Overloaded Functions

Unlike regular C, C++ enables you to have more than one function with the same name. In other words, you can have three functions called abs() in the same program. Functions with the same names are called overloaded functions. C++ requires that each overloaded function differ in its argument list. Overloaded functions enable you to have similar functions that work on different types of data.

For example, suppose you wrote a function that returned the absolute value of whatever number you passed to it. The absolute value of a number is its positive equivalent. For instance, the absolute value of 10.25 is 10.25 and the absolute value of –10.25 is 10.25.

Absolute values are used in distance, temperature, and weight calculations. The difference in the weights of two children is always positive. If Joe weighs 65 pounds and Mary weighs 55 pounds, their difference is a positive 10 pounds. You can subtract the 65 from 55 (−10) or 55 from 65 (+10) and the weight difference is always the absolute value of the result.

Suppose you had to write an absolute-value function for integers, and an absolute-value function for floating-point numbers. Without function overloading, you need these two functions:

```
int iabs(int i)    // Returns absolute value of an integer.
{
   if (i < 0)
   {  return (i * -1); }  // Makes positive.
   else
   {  return (i);  }      // Already positive.
}

float fabs(float x)  // Returns absolute value of a float.
{
   if (x < 0.0)
   {  return (x * -1.0); }  // Makes positive.
   else
   {  return (x);  }        // Already positive.
}
```

Without overloading, if you had a floating-point variable for which you needed the absolute value, you pass it to the fabs() function as in:

```
ans = fabs(weight);
```

If you needed the absolute value of an integer variable, you pass it to the iabs() function as in:

```
ians = iabs(age);
```

Because the code for these two functions differ only in their parameter lists, they are perfect candidates for overloaded functions. Call both functions abs(), prototype both of them, and code each of them separately in your program. After overloading the two functions (each of which works on two different types of parameters with the same name), you pass your floating-point or integer value to abs(). The C++ compiler determines which function you wanted to call.

CAUTION: If two or more functions differ only in their return types, C++ cannot overload them. Two or more functions that differ only in their return types must have different names and cannot be overloaded.

This process simplifies your programming considerably. Instead of having to remember several different function names, you only have to remember one function name. C++ passes the arguments to the proper function.

NOTE: C++ uses *name-mangling* to accomplish overloaded functions. Understanding name-mangling helps you as you become an advanced C++ programmer.

When C++ realizes that you are overloading two or more functions with the same name, each function differing only in its parameter list, C++ changes the name of the function and adds letters to the end of the function name that match the parameters. Different C++ compilers do this differently.

To understand what the compiler does, take the absolute value function described earlier. C++ might change the integer absolute value function to `absi()` and the floating-point absolute value function to `absf()`. When you call the function with this function call:

```
ians = abs(age);
```

C++ determines that you want the `absi()` function called. As far as you know, C++ is not mangling the names; you never see the name differences in your program's source code. However, the compiler performs the name-mangling so it can keep track of different functions that have the same name.

Examples

1. Here is the complete absolute value program described in the previous text. Notice that both functions are prototyped. (The two prototypes signal C++ that it must perform name-mangling to determine the correct function names to call.)

```cpp
// Filename: C20OVF1.CPP
// Overloads two absolute value functions.
#include <iostream.h>  // Prototype cout and cin.
#include <iomanip.h>   // Prototype setprecision(2).

int abs(int i);      // abs() is overloaded twice
float abs(float x);  // as shown by these prototypes.

void main()
{
   int ians;        // To hold return values.
   float fans;
   int i = -15;     // To pass to the two overloaded functions.
   float x = -64.53;

   ians = abs(i);    // C++ calls the integer abs().
   cout << "Integer absolute value of -15 is " << ians << "\n";

   fans = abs(x); // C++ calls the floating-point abs().
   cout << "Float absolute value of -64.53 is " <<
           setprecision(2) << fans << "\n";

   // Notice that you no longer have to keep track of two
   // different names. C++ calls the appropriate
   // function that matches the parameters.
   return;
}

int abs(int i)      // Integer absolute value function
{
   if (i < 0)
   { return (i * -1); }  // Makes positive.
   else
   { return (i); }       // Already positive.
}
```

```
float abs(float x)  // Floating-point absolute value function
{
   if (x < 0.0)
   {  return (x * -1.0); }  // Makes positive.
   else
   {  return (x);  }        // Already positive.
}
```

The output from this program follows:

```
Integer absolute value of -15 is 15
Float absolute value of -64.53 is 64.53
```

2. As you write more and more C++ programs, you will see many uses for overloaded functions. The following program is a demonstration program showing how you can build your own output functions to suit your needs. `main()` calls three functions named `output()`. Each time it's called, `main()` passes a different value to the function.

When `main()` passes `output()` a string, `output()` prints the string, formatted to a width (using the `setw()` manipulator described in Chapter 7, "Simple Input/Output") of 30 characters. When `main()` passes `output()` an integer, `output()` prints the integer with a width of five. When `main()` passes `output()` a floating-point value, `output()` prints the value to two decimal places and generalizes the output of different types of data. You do not have to format your own data. `output()` properly formats the data and you only have to remember one function name that outputs all three types of data.

```
// Filename: C20OVF2.CPP
// Outputs three different types of
// data with same function name.
#include <iostream.h>
#include <iomanip.h>
void output(char []);  // Prototypes for overloaded functions.
void output(int i);
void output(float x);
```

```
void main()
{
    char name[] = "C++ By Example makes C++ easy!";
    int ivalue = 2543;
    float fvalue = 39.4321;

    output(name);    // C++ chooses the appropriate function.
    output(ivalue);
    output(fvalue);

return;
}

void output(char name[])
{
    cout << setw(30) << name << "\n";
    // The width truncates string if it is longer than 30.
    return;
}

void output(int ivalue)
{
    cout << setw(5) << ivalue << "\n";
    // Just printed integer within a width of five spaces.
    return;
}

void output(float fvalue)
{
    cout << setprecision(2) << fvalue << "\n";
    // Limited the floating-point value to two decimal places.
    return;
}
```

Here is the output from this program:

```
C++ By Example makes C++ easy!
2543
39.43
```

Each of the three lines, containing three different lines of
information, was printed with the same function call.

Review Questions

The answers to the review questions are in Appendix B.

1. Where in the program do you specify the defaults for default argument lists?

2. What is the term for C++ functions that have the same name?

3. Does name-mangling help support default argument lists or overloaded functions?

4. True or false: You can specify only a single default argument.

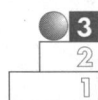

5. Fix the following prototype for a default argument list.

   ```
   void my_fun(int i=7, float x, char ch='A');
   ```

6. True or false: The following prototypes specify overloaded functions:

   ```
   int    sq_rt(int n);
   float sq_rt(int n);
   ```

Review Exercises

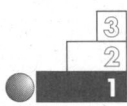

1. Write a program that contains two functions. The first function returns the square of the integer passed to it, and the second function returns the square of the float passed to it.

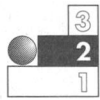

2. Write a program that computes net pay based on the values the user types. Ask the user for the hours worked, the rate per hour, and the tax rate. Because the majority of employees work 40 hours per week and earn $5.00 per hour, use these values as default values in the function that computes the net pay. If the user presses Enter in response to your questions, use the default values.

Summary

Default argument lists and overloaded functions speed up your programming time. You no longer have to specify values for common arguments. You do not have to remember several different names for those functions that perform similar routines and differ only in their data types.

The remainder of this book elaborates on earlier concepts so you can take advantage of separate, modular functions and local data. You are ready to learn more about how C++ performs input and output. Chapter 21, "Device and Character Input/Output," teaches you the theory behind I/O in C++, and introduces more built-in functions.

Part V

Character Input/Output and String Functions

Device and Character Input/Output

Unlike many programming languages, C++ contains no input or output commands. C++ is an extremely *portable* language; a C++ program that compiles and runs on one computer is able also to compile and run on another type of computer. Most incompatibilities between computers reside in their input/output mechanics. Each different device requires a different method of performing I/O (Input/Output).

By putting all I/O capabilities in common functions supplied with each computer's compiler, not in C++ statements, the designers of C++ ensured that programs were not tied to specific hardware for input and output. A compiler has to be modified for every computer for which it is written. This ensures the compiler works with the specific computer and its devices. The compiler writers write I/O functions for each machine; when your C++ program writes a character to the screen, it works the same whether you have a color PC screen or a UNIX X/Windows terminal.

This chapter shows you additional ways to perform input and output of data besides the cin and cout functions you have seen throughout the book. By providing character-based I/O functions, C++ gives you the basic I/O functions you need to write powerful data entry and printing routines.

This chapter introduces you to

♦ Stream input and output

♦ Redirecting I/O

♦ Printing to the printer

♦ Character I/O functions

♦ Buffered and nonbuffered I/O

By the time you finish this chapter, you will understand the fundamental built-in I/O functions available in C++. Performing character input and output, one character at a time, might sound like a slow method of I/O. You will soon realize that character I/O actually enables you to create more powerful I/O functions than `cin` and `cout`.

Stream and Character I/O

C++ views input and output from all devices as streams of characters.

C++ views all input and output as streams of characters. Whether your program receives input from the keyboard, a disk file, a modem, or a mouse, C++ only views a stream of characters. C++ does not have to know what type of device is supplying the input; the operating system handles the device specifics. The designers of C++ want your programs to operate on characters of data without regard to the physical method taking place.

This stream I/O means you can use the same functions to receive input from the keyboard as from the modem. You can use the same functions to write to a disk file, printer, or screen. Of course, you have to have some way of routing that stream input or output to the proper device, but each program's I/O functions works in a similar manner. Figure 21.1 illustrates this concept.

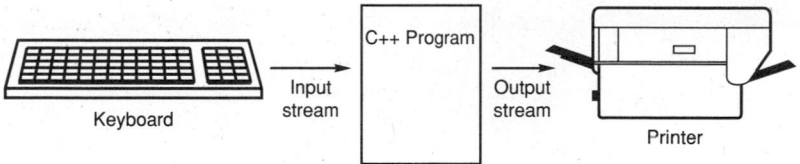

Figure 21.1. All I/O consists of streams of characters.

The Newline Special Character: /n

Portability is the key to C++'s success. Few companies have the resources to rewrite every program they use when they change computer equipment. They need a programming language that works on many platforms (hardware combinations). C++ achieves true portability better than almost any other programming language.

It is because of portability that C++ uses the generic newline character, \n, rather than the specific carriage return and line feed sequences other languages use. This is why C++ uses the \t for tab, as well as the other control characters used in I/O functions.

If C++ used ASCII code to represent these special characters, your programs would not be portable. You would write a C++ program on one computer and use a carriage return value such as 12, but 12 might not be the carriage return value on another type of computer.

By using newline and the other control characters available in C++, you ensure your program is compatible with any computer on which it is compiled. The specific compilers substitute their computer's actual codes for the control codes in your programs.

Standard Devices

Table 21.1 shows a listing of standard I/O devices. C++ always assumes input comes from *stdin*, meaning the *standard input device*. This is usually the keyboard, although you can reroute this default. C++ assumes all output goes to *stdout*, or the *standard output device*. There is nothing magic in the words stdin and stdout; however, many people learn their meanings for the first time in C++.

Table 21.1. Standard Devices in C++.

Description	C++ Name	MS-DOS Name
Screen	stdout	CON:
Keyboard	stdin	CON:
Printer	stdprn	PRN: or LPT1:
Serial Port	stdaux	AUX: or COM1:
Error Messages	stderr	CON:
Disk Files	none	Filename

Take a moment to study Table 21.1. You might think it is confusing that three devices are named CON:. MS-DOS differentiates between the screen device called CON: (which stands for *console*), and the keyboard device called CON: from the context of the data stream. If you send an output stream (a stream of characters) to CON:, MS-DOS routes it to the screen automatically. If you request input from CON:, MS-DOS retrieves the input from the keyboard. (These defaults hold true as long as you have not redirected these devices, as shown below.) MS-DOS sends all error messages to the screen (CON:) as well.

NOTE: If you want to route I/O to a second printer or serial port, see how to do so in Chapter 30, "Sequential Files."

Redirecting Devices from MS-DOS

The operating system gives you control over devices.

The reason cout goes to the screen is simply because stdout is routed to the screen, by default, on most computers. The reason cin inputs from the keyboard is because most computers consider the keyboard to be the standard input device, stdin. After compiling your program, C++ does not send data to the screen or retrieve it from the keyboard. Instead, the program sends output to stdout and receives input from stdin. The operating system routes the data to the appropriate device.

MS-DOS enables you to reroute I/O from their default locations to other devices through the use of the *output redirection symbol,* >, and the *input redirection symbol,* <. The goal of this book is not to delve deeply in operating-system redirection. To learn more about the handling of I/O, read a good book on MS-DOS, such as *Using MS-DOS 5.*

Basically, the output redirection symbol informs the operating system that you want standard output to go to a device other than the default (the screen). The input redirection symbol routes input away from the keyboard to another input device. The following example illustrates how this is done in MS-DOS.

Examples

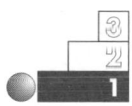

1. Suppose you write a program that uses only cin and cout for input and output. Instead of receiving input from the keyboard, you want the program to get the input from a file called MYDATA. Because cin receives input from stdin, you must redirect stdin. After compiling the program in a file called MYPGM.EXE, you can redirect its input away from the keyboard with the following DOS command:

```
C:>MYPGM < MYDATA
```

Of course, you can include a full pathname either before the program name or filename. There is a danger in redirecting all output such as this, however. All output, including screen prompts for keyboard input, goes to MYDATA. This is probably not acceptable to you in most cases; you still want prompts and some messages to go to the screen. In the next section, you learn how to separate I/O, and send some output to one device such as the screen and the rest to another device, such as a file or printer.

2. You can also route the program's output to the printer by typing this:

```
C:>MYPGM > PRN:
```

Route MYPGM output to the printer.

3. If the program required much input, and that input were stored in a file called ANSWERS, you could override the keyboard default device that `cin` uses, as in:

```
C:>MYPGM < ANSWERS
```

The program reads from the file called ANSWERS every time `cin` *required input.*

4. You can combine redirection symbols. If you want input from the ANSWERS disk file, and want to send the output to the printer, do the following:

```
C:>MYPGM < ANSWERS > PRN:
```

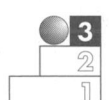

> **TIP**: You can route the output to a serial printer or a second parallel printer port by substituting COM1: or LPT2: for PRN:.

Printing Formatted Output to the Printer

ofstream allows your program to write to the printer.

It's easy to send program output to the printer using the `ofstream` function. The format of `ofstream` is

```
ofstream device(device_name);
```

ofstream uses
the fstream.h header
file.

The following examples show how you can combine cout and ofstream to write to both the screen and printer.

Example

The following program asks the user for his or her first and last name. It then prints the name, last name first, to the printer.

```
// Filename: C21FPR1.CPP
// Prints a name on the printer.

#include <fstream.h>

void main()
{
   char first[20];
   char last[20];

   cout << "What is your first name? ";
   cin >> first;
   cout << "What is your last name? ";
   cin >> last;

   // Send names to the printer.
   ofstream prn("PRN");
   prn << "In a phone book, your name looks like this: \n";
   prn << last << ", " << first << "\n";
   return;
}
```

Character I/O Functions

Because all I/O is actually character I/O, C++ provides many functions you can use that perform character input and output. The cout and cin functions are called *formatted I/O functions* because they give you formatting control over your input and output. The cout and cin functions are not character I/O functions.

There's nothing wrong with using cout for formatted output, but cin has many problems, as you have seen. You will now see how to write your own character input routines to replace cin, as well as use character output functions to prepare you for the upcoming section in this book on disk files.

The get() and put() Functions

get() and put() input and output characters from and to any standard devices.

The most fundamental character I/O functions are get() and put(). The put() function writes a single character to the standard output device (the screen if you don't redirect it from your operating system). The get() function inputs a single character from the standard input device (the keyboard by default).

The format for get() is

```
device.get(char_var);
```

The get() *device* can be any standard input device. If you were receiving character input from the keyboard, you use cin as the device. If you initialize your modem and want to receive characters from it, use ofstream to open the modem device and read from the device.

The format of put() is

```
device.put(char_val);
```

The char_val can be a character variable, expression, or constant. You output character data with put(). The device can be any standard output device. To write a character to your printer, you open PRN with ofstream.

Examples

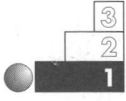

1. The following program asks the user for her or his initials a character at a time. Notice the program uses both cout and put(). The cout is still useful for formatted output such as messages to the user. Writing individual characters is best achieved with put().

   The program has to call two get() functions for each character typed. When you answer a get() prompt by typing a character followed by an Enter keypress, C++ interprets the input as a stream of two characters. The `get()` first receives the letter you typed, then it has to receive the `\n` (newline, supplied to C++ when you press Enter). There are examples that follow that fix this double `get()` problem.

```
// Filename: C21CH1.CPP
// Introduces get() and put().

#include <fstream.h>

void main()
{
   char  in_char;      // Holds incoming initial.
   char first, last;   // Holds converted first and last initial.

   cout << "What is your first name initial? ";
   cin.get(in_char);   // Waits for first initial.
   first = in_char;
   cin.get(in_char);   // Ignores newline.
   cout << "What is your last name initial? ";
   cin.get(in_char);   // Waits for last initial.
   last = in_char;
   cin.get(in_char);   // Ignores newline.
   cout << "\nHere they are: \n";
   cout.put(first);
   cout.put(last);
return;
}
```

Here is the output from this program:

```
What is your first name initial? G
What is your last name initial? P

Here they are:
GP
```

2. You can add carriage returns to space the output better. To print the two initials on two separate lines, use `put()` to put a newline character to `cout`, as the following program does:

```
// Filename: C21CH2.CPP
// Introduces get() and put() and uses put() to output
newline.

#include <fstream.h>

void main()
{
   char in_char;       // Holds incoming initial.
   char first, last;   // Holds converted first and last
                       // initial.

   cout << "What is your first name initial? ";
   cin.get(in_char);   // Waits for first initial.
   first = in_char;
   cin.get(in_char);   // Ignores newline.
   cout << "What is your last name initial? ";
   cin.get(in_char);   // Waits for last initial.
   last = in_char;
   cin.get(in_char);   // Ignores newline.
   cout << "\nHere they are: \n";
   cout.put(first);
   cout.put('\n');
   cout.put(last);
return;
}
```

3. It might have been clearer to define the newline character as a constant. At the top of the program, you have:

```
const char NEWLINE='\n'
```

The put() then reads:

```
cout.put(NEWLINE);
```

Some programmers prefer to define their character formatting constants and refer to them by name. It's up to you to decide whether you want to use this method, or whether you want to continue using the \n character constant in put().

The get() function is a *buffered* input function. As you type characters, the data does not immediately go to your program, rather, it goes to a buffer. The buffer is a section of memory (and has nothing to do with your PC's type-ahead buffers) managed by C++.

Figure 21.2 shows how this buffered function works. When your program approaches a `get()`, the program temporarily waits as you type the input. The program doesn't view the characters, as they're going to the buffer of memory. There is practically no limit to the size of the buffer; it fills with input until you press Enter. Your Enter keypress signals the computer to release the buffer to your program.

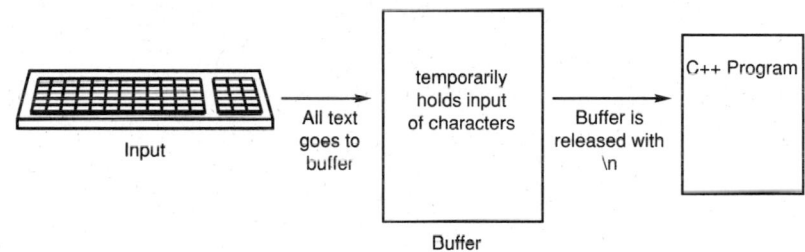

Figure 21.2. `get()` input goes to a buffer. The buffer is released when you press Enter.

Most PCs accept either buffered or nonbuffered input. The `getch()` function shown later in this chapter is nonbuffered. With `get()`, all input is buffered. Buffered text affects the timing of your program's input. Your program receives no characters from a `get()` until you press Enter. Therefore, if you ask a question such as

```
Do you want to see the report again (Y/N)?
```

and use `get()` for input, the user can press a Y, but the program does not receive the input until the user also presses Enter. The Y and Enter then are sent, one character at a time, to the program where it processes the input. If you want immediate response to a user's typing (such as the INKEY$ in BASIC allows), you have to use `getch()`.

> **TIP:** By using buffered input, the user can type a string of characters in response to a loop with `get()`, receive characters, and correct the input with Backspace before pressing Enter. If the input were nonbuffered, the Backspace would be another character of data.

Example

When receiving characters, you might have to discard the newline keypress.

C21CH2.CPP must discard the newline character. It did so by assigning the input character—from `get()`—to an extra variable. Obviously, the `get()` returns a value (the character typed). In this case, it's acceptable to ignore the return value by not using the character returned by `get()`. You know the user has to press Enter (to end the input) so it's acceptable to discard it with an unused `get()` function call.

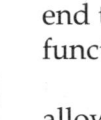

When inputting strings such as names and sentences, `cin` only allows one word to be entered at a time. The following string asks the user for his or her full name with these two lines:

```
cout << "What are your first and last names? ";
cin >> names;       // Receive name in character array names.
```

The array `names` only receives the first name; `cin` ignores all data to the right of the first space.

You can build your own input function using `get()` that doesn't have a single-word limitation. When you want to receive a string of characters from the user, such as his or her first and last name, you can call the `get_in_str()` function shown in the next program.

The `main()` function defines an array and prompts the user for a name. After the prompt, the program calls the `get_in_str()` function and builds the input array a character at a time using `get()`. The function keeps looping, using the `while` loop, until the user presses Enter (signaled by the newline character, `\n`, to C++) or until the maximum number of characters are typed. You might want to use this function in your own programs. Be sure to pass it a character array and an integer that holds the maximum array size (you don't want the input string to be longer than the character array that holds it). When control returns to main() (or whatever function called get_in_str()), the array has the user's full input, including the spaces.

```cpp
// Filename: C21IN.CPP
// Program that builds an input string array using get().

#include <fstream.h>
void get_in_str(char str[], int len);

const int MAX=25;  // Size of character array to be typed.

void main()
{
   char input_str[MAX];   // Keyboard input fills this.
   cout << "What is your full name? ";
   get_in_str(input_str, MAX);   // String from keyboard
   cout << "After return, your name is " << input_str << "\n";
   return;
}


//************************************************************
// The following function requires a string and the maximum
// length of the string be passed to it. It accepts input
// from the keyboard, and sends keyboard input in the string.
// On return, the calling routine has access to the string.
//************************************************************

void get_in_str(char str[ ], int len)
{
   int i = 0;   // index
   char input_char;   // character typed

   cin.get(input_char);   // Get next character in string.
   while (i < (len - 1) && (input_char != '\n'))
     {
       str[i] = input_char;  // Build string a character
```

```
      i++;                    // at a time.
      cin.get(input_char);  // Receive next character in string.
    }
  str[i] = '\0';   // Make the char array a string.
  return;
}
```

> **NOTE**: The loop checks for `len - 1` to save room for the null-terminating zero at the end of the input string.

The `getch()` and `putch()` Functions

The functions `getch()` and `putch()` are slightly different from the previous character I/O functions. Their format is similar to `get()` and `put()`; they read from the keyboard and write to the screen and cannot be redirected, even from the operating system. The formats of `getch()` and `putch()` are

`int_var = getch();`

and

`putch(int_var);`

getch() and putch() offer nonbuffered input and output that grab the user's characters immediately after the user types them.

`getch()` and `putch()` are not AT&T C++ standard functions, but they are usually available with most C++ compilers. `getch()` and `putch()` are nonbuffered functions. The `putch()` character output function is a mirror-image function to `getch()`; it is a nonbuffered output function. Because almost every output device made, except for the screen and modem, are inherently buffered, `putch()` effectively does the same thing as `put()`.

Another difference in `getch()` from the other character input functions is that `getch()` does not echo the input characters on the screen as it receives them. When you type characters in response to `get()`, you see the characters as you type them (as they are sent to the buffer). If you want to see characters received by `getch()`, you must follow `getch()` with a `putch()`. It is handy to echo the characters on the screen so the user can verify that she or he has typed correctly.

Characters input with getch() are not echoed to the screen as the user types them.

getch() and putch() use the conio.h header file.

Some programmers want to make the user press Enter after answering a prompt or selecting from a menu. They feel the extra time given with buffered input gives the user more time to decide if she or he wants to give that answer; the user can press Backspace and correct the input before pressing Enter.

Other programmers like to grab the user's response to a single-character answer, such as a menu response, and act on it immediately. They feel that pressing Enter is an added and unneeded burden for the user so they use getch(). The choice is yours. You should understand both buffered and nonbuffered input so you can use both.

> **TIP:** You can also use getche(). getche() is a nonbuffered input identical to getch(), except the input characters are echoed (displayed) to the screen as the user types them. Using getche() rather than getch() keeps you from having to call a putch() to echo the user's input to the screen.

Example

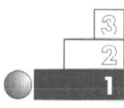

The following program shows the getch() and putch() functions. The user is asked to enter five letters. These five letters are added (by way of a for loop) to the character array named letters. As you run this program, notice that the characters are not echoed to the screen as you type them. Because getch() is unbuffered, the program actually receives each character, adds it to the array, and loops again, as you type them. (If this were buffered input, the program would not loop through the five iterations until you pressed Enter.)

A second loop prints the five letters using putch(). A third loop prints the five letters to the printer using put().

```
// Filename: C21GCH1.CPP
// Uses getch() and putch() for input and output.

#include <fstream.h>
```

```cpp
#include <conio.h>

void main()
{
   int ctr;    // for loop counter
   char letters[5];    // Holds five input characters. No
                       // room is needed for the null zero
                       // because this array never will be
                       // treated as a string.
   cout << "Please type five letters... \n";
   for (ctr = 0; ctr < 5; ctr++)
     {
        letters[ctr] = getch();      // Add input to array.
     }
   for (ctr = 0; ctr < 5; ctr++)    // Print them to screen.
   {
      putch(letters[ ctr ]);
   }
   ofstream prn("PRN");
   for (ctr = 0; ctr < 5; ctr++)    // Print them to printer.
   {
      prn.put(letters[ ctr ]);
   }
return;
}
```

When you run this program, do not press Enter after the five letters. The `getch()` function does not use the Enter. The loop automatically ends after the fifth letter because of the unbuffered input and the `for` loop.

Review Questions

The answers to the review questions are found in Appendix B.

1. Why are there no input or output commands in C++?

2. True or false: If you use the character I/O functions to send output to stdout, it always goes to the screen.

3. What is the difference between getch() and get()?

4. What function sends formatted output to devices other than the screen?

5. What are the MS-DOS redirection symbols?

6. What nonstandard function, most similar to getch(), echoes the input character to the screen as the user types it?

7. True or false: When using get(), the program receives your input as you type it.

8. Which keypress releases the buffered input to the program?

9. True or false: Using devices and functions described in this chapter, it is possible to write one program that sends some output to the screen, some to the printer, and some to the modem.

Review Exercises

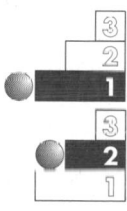

1. Write a program that asks the user for five letters and prints them in reverse order to the screen, and then to the printer.

2. Write a miniature typewriter program, using get() and put(). In a loop, get characters until the user presses Enter while he or she is getting a line of user input. Write the line of user input to the printer. Because get() is buffered, nothing goes to the printer until the user presses Enter at the end of each line of text. (Use the string-building input function shown in C21IN.CPP.)

3. Add a putch() inside the first loop of C21CH1.CPP (this chapter's first get() example program) so the characters are echoed to the screen as the user types them.

4. A *palindrome* is a word or phrase spelled the same forwards and backwards. Two example palindromes are

```
Madam, I'm Adam
Golf? No sir, prefer prison flog!
```

Write a C++ program that asks the user for a phrase. Build the input, a character at a time, using a character input function such as get(). Once you have the full string (store it in a character array), determine whether the phrase is a palindrome. You have to filter special characters (nonalphabetic), storing only alphabetic characters to a second character array. You also must convert the characters to uppercase as you store them. The first palindrome becomes:

```
MADAMIMADAM
```

Using one or more for or while loops, you can now test the phrase to determine whether it is a palindrome. Print the result of the test on the printer. Sample output should look like:

```
"Madam, I'm Adam" is a palindrome.
```

Summary

You now should understand the generic methods C++ programs use for input and output. By writing to standard I/O devices, C++ achieves portability. If you write a program for one computer, it works on another. If C++ were to write directly to specific hardware, programs would not work on every computer.

If you still want to use the formatted I/O functions, such as cout, you can do so. The ofstream() function enables you to write formatted output to any device, including the printer.

The methods of character I/O might seem primitive, and they are, but they give you the flexibility to build and create your own input functions. One of the most often-used C++ functions, a string-building character I/O function, was demonstrated in this chapter (the C21IN.CPP program).

The next two chapters (Chapter 22, "Character, String, and Numeric Functions," and Chapter 23, "Introducing Arrays") introduce many character and string functions, including string I/O functions. The string I/O functions build on the principles presented here. You will be surprised at the extensive character and string manipulation functions available in the language as well.

Character, String, and Numeric Functions

C++ provides many built-in functions in addition to the `cout`, `getch()`, and `strcpy()` functions you have seen so far. These built-in functions increase your productivity and save you programming time. You don't have to write as much code because the built in functions perform many useful tasks for you.

This chapter introduces you to

- ♦ Character conversion functions
- ♦ Character and string testing functions
- ♦ String manipulation functions
- ♦ String I/O functions
- ♦ Mathematical, trigonometric, and logarithmic functions
- ♦ Random-number processing

Character Functions

This section explores many of the character functions available in AT&T C++. Generally, you pass character arguments to the functions, and the functions return values that you can store or print. By using these functions, you off-load much of your work to C++ and allow it to perform the more tedious manipulations of character and string data.

Character Testing Functions

The character functions return True or False results based on the characters you pass to them.

Several functions test for certain characteristics of your character data. You can determine whether your character data is alphabetic, digital, uppercase, lowercase, and much more. You must pass a character variable or literal argument to the function (by placing the argument in the function parentheses) when you call it. These functions return a True or False result, so you can test their return values inside an `if` statement or a `while` loop.

> **NOTE:** All character functions presented in this section are prototyped in the ctype.h header file. Be sure to include ctype.h at the beginning of any programs that use them.

Alphabetic and Digital Testing

The following functions test for alphabetic conditions:

◆ `isalpha(c)`: Returns True (nonzero) if *c* is an uppercase or lowercase letter. Returns False (zero) if *c* is not a letter.

◆ `islower(c)`: Returns True (nonzero) if *c* is a lowercase letter. Returns False (zero) if *c* is not a lowercase letter.

◆ `isupper(c)`: Returns True (nonzero) if *c* is an uppercase letter. Returns False (zero) if *c* is not an uppercase letter.

Remember that any nonzero value is True in C++, and zero is always False. If you use the return values of these functions in a relational test, the True return value is not always 1 (it can be any nonzero value), but it is always considered True for the test.

The following functions test for digits:

♦ isdigit(c): Returns True (nonzero) if c is a digit 0 through 9. Returns False (zero) if c is not a digit.

♦ isxdigit(c): Returns True (nonzero) if c is any of the hexadecimal digits 0 through 9 or A, B, C, D, E, F, a, b, c, d, e, or f. Returns False (zero) if c is anything else. (See Appendix A, "Memory Addressing, Binary, and Hexadecimal Review," for more information on the hexadecimal numbering system.)

> **NOTE:** Although some character functions test for digits, the arguments are still character data and cannot be used in mathematical calculations, unless you calculate using the ASCII values of characters.

The following function tests for numeric or alphabetical arguments:

isalnum(c): Returns True (nonzero) if c is a digit 0 through 9 or an alphabetic character (either uppercase or lowercase). Returns False (zero) if c is not a digit or a letter.

> **CAUTION:** You can pass to these functions only a character value or an integer value holding the ASCII value of a character. You cannot pass an entire character array to character functions. If you want to test the elements of a character array, you must pass the array one element at a time.

Example

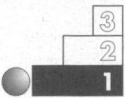

The following program asks users for their initials. If a user types anything but alphabetic characters, the program displays an error and asks again.

Identify the program and include the input/output header files. The program asks the user for his or her first initial, so declare the character variable initial *to hold the user's answer.*

1. *Ask the user for her or his first initial, and retrieve the user's answer.*

2. *If the answer was not an alphabetic character, tell the user this and repeat step one.*

Print a thank-you message on-screen.

```
// Filename: C22INI.CPP
// Asks for first initial and tests
// to ensure that response is correct.
#include <iostream.h>
#include <ctype.h>
void main()
{
   char initial;
   cout << "What is your first initial? ";
   cin >> initial;

   while (!isalpha(initial))
     {
       cout << "\nThat was not a valid initial! \n";
       cout << "\nWhat is your first initial? ";
       cin >> initial;
     }

   cout << "\nThanks!";
   return;
}
```

This use of the not operator (!) is quite clear. The program continues to loop as long as the entered character is not alphabetic.

Special Character-Testing Functions

A few character functions become useful when you have to read from a disk file, a modem, or another operating system device that you route input from. These functions are not used as much as the character functions you saw in the previous section, but they are useful for testing specific characters for readability.

The character-testing functions do not change characters.

The remaining character-testing functions follow:

- `iscntrl(c)`: Returns True (nonzero) if *c* is a *control character* (any character from the ASCII table numbered 0 through 31). Returns False (zero) if *c* is not a control character.

- `isgraph(c)`: Returns True (nonzero) if *c* is any printable character (a noncontrol character) except a space. Returns False (zero) if *c* is a space or anything other than a printable character.

- `isprint(c)`: Returns True (nonzero) if *c* is a printable character (a noncontrol character) from ASCII 32 to ASCII 127, including a space. Returns False (zero) if *c* is not a printable character.

- `ispunct(c)`: Returns True (nonzero) if *c* is any punctuation character (any printable character other than a space, a letter, or a digit). Returns False (zero) if *c* is not a punctuation character.

- `isspace(c)`: Returns True (nonzero) if *c* is a space, newline (\n), carriage return (\r), tab (\t), or vertical tab (\v) character. Returns False (zero) if *c* is anything else.

Character Conversion Functions

Both `tolower()` and `toupper()` return lowercase or uppercase arguments.

The two remaining character functions are handy. Rather than test characters, these functions change characters to their lower- or uppercase equivalents.

♦ `tolower(c)`: Converts *c* to lowercase. Nothing changes if you pass `tolower()` a lowercase letter or a nonalphabetic character.

♦ `toupper(c)`: Converts *c* to uppercase. Nothing changes if you pass `toupper()` an uppercase letter or a nonalphabetic character.

These functions return their changed character values. These functions are useful for user input. Suppose you are asking users a yes or no question, such as the following:

```
Do you want to print the checks (Y/N)?
```

Before `toupper()` and `tolower()` were developed, you had to check for both a *Y* and a *y* to print the checks. Instead of testing for both conditions, you can convert the character to uppercase, and test for a *Y*.

Example

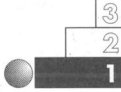

Here is a program that prints an appropriate message if the user is a girl or a boy. The program tests for *G* and *B* after converting the user's input to uppercase. No check for lowercase has to be done.

Identify the program and include the input/output header files. The program asks the user a question requiring an alphabetic answer, so declare the character variable ans *to hold the user's response.*

Ask whether the user is a girl or a boy, and store the user's answer in ans. *The user must press Enter, so incorporate and then discard the Enter keypress. Change the value of* ans *to uppercase. If the answer is G, print a message. If the answer is B, print a different message. If the answer is something else, print another message.*

```cpp
// Filename: C22GB.CPP
// Determines whether the user typed a G or a B.
#include <iostream.h>
#include <conio.h>
#include <ctype.h>
void main()
{
```

```
    char ans;                         // Holds user's response.
    cout << "Are you a girl or a boy (G/B)? ";
    ans=getch();                              // Get answer.
    getch();                            // Discard newline.

cout <<ans<<"\n";
    ans = toupper(ans);      // Convert answer to uppercase.
    switch (ans)
    {   case ('G'): { cout << "You look pretty today!\n";
                      break; }
        case ('B'): { cout << "You look handsome today!\n";
                      break; }
        default :   { cout << "Your answer makes no sense!\n";
                      break; }
    }
    return;
}
```

Here is the output from the program:

```
Are you a girl or a boy (G/B)? B
You look handsome today!
```

String Functions

Some of the most powerful built-in C++ functions are the string functions. They perform much of the tedious work for which you have been writing code so far, such as inputting strings from the keyboard and comparing strings.

As with the character functions, there is no need to "reinvent the wheel" by writing code when built-in functions do the same task. Use these functions as much as possible.

Now that you have a good grasp of the foundations of C++, you can master the string functions. They enable you to concentrate on your program's primary purpose, rather than spend time coding your own string functions.

Useful String Functions

You can use a handful of useful string functions for string testing and conversion. You have already seen (in earlier chapters) the strcpy() string function, which copies a string of characters to a character array.

> **NOTE:** All string functions in this section are prototyped in the string.h header file. Be sure to include string.h at the beginning of any program that uses the string functions.

The string functions work on string literals or on character arrays that contain strings.

String functions that test or manipulate strings follow:

◆ strcat(s1, s2): Concatenates (merges) the s2 string to the end of the s1 character array. The s1 array must have enough reserved elements to hold both strings.

◆ strcmp(s1, s2): Compares the s1 string with the s2 string on an alphabetical, element-by-element basis. If s1 alphabetizes before s2, strcmp() returns a negative value. If s1 and s2 are the same strings, strcmp() returns 0. If s1 alphabetizes after s2, strcmp() returns a positive value.

◆ strlen(s1): Returns the length of s1. Remember, the length of a string is the number of characters, not including the null zero. The number of characters defined for the character array has nothing to do with the length of the string.

> **TIP:** Before using strcat() to concatenate strings, use strlen() to ensure that the target string (the string being concatenated to) is large enough to hold both strings.

String I/O Functions

In the previous few chapters, you have used a character input function, cin.get(), to build input strings. Now you can begin to use the string input and output functions. Although the goal of the string-building functions has been to teach you the specifics of the language, these string I/O functions are much easier to use than writing a character input function.

The string input and output functions are listed as follows:

♦ `gets(s)`: Stores input from `stdin` (usually directed to the keyboard) to the string named `s`.

♦ `puts(s)`: Outputs the `s` string to `stdout` (usually directed to the screen by the operating system).

♦ `fgets(s, len, dev)`: Stores input from the standard device specified by `dev` (such as `stdin` or `stdaux`) in the `s` string. If more than `len` characters are input, `fgets()` discards them.

♦ `fputs(s, dev)`: Outputs the `s` string to the standard device specified by `dev`.

Both `gets()` and `puts()` input and output strings.

These four functions make the input and output of strings easy. They work in pairs. That is, strings input with `gets()` are usually output with `puts()`. Strings input with `fgets()` are usually output with `fputs()`.

> **TIP:** `gets()` replaces the string-building input function you saw in earlier chapters.

Terminate `gets()` or `fgets()` input by pressing Enter. Each of these functions handles string-terminating characters in a slightly different manner, as follows:

`gets()`   A newline input becomes a null zero (\0).

`puts()`   A null at the end of the string becomes a newline character (\n).

`fgets()`   A newline input stays, and a null zero is added after it.

`fputs()`   The null zero is dropped, and a newline character is not added.

Therefore, when you enter strings with `gets()`, C++ places a string-terminating character in the string at the point where you press Enter. This creates the input string. (Without the null zero, the input would not be a string.) When you output a string, the null zero at the end of the string becomes a newline character. This is preferred because a newline is at the end of a line of output and the cursor begins automatically on the next line.

Because `fgets()` and `fputs()` can input and output strings from devices such as disk files and telephone modems, it can be critical that the incoming newline characters are retained for the data's integrity. When outputting strings to these devices, you do not want C++ inserting extra newline characters.

> **CAUTION:** Neither `gets()` nor `fgets()` ensures that its input strings are large enough to hold the incoming data. It is up to you to make sure enough space is reserved in the character array to hold the complete input.

One final function is worth noting, although it is not a string function. It is the `fflush()` function, which flushes (empties) whatever standard device is listed in its parentheses. To flush the keyboard of all its input, you would code as follows:

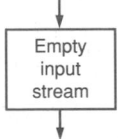

Empty input stream

```
fflush(stdin);
```

When you are doing string input and output, sometimes an extra newline character appears in the keyboard buffer. A previous answer to `gets()` or `getc()` might have an extra newline you forgot to discard. When a program seems to ignore `gets()`, you might have to insert `fflush(stdin)` before `gets()`.

Flushing the standard input device causes no harm, and using it can clear the input stream so your next `gets()` works properly. You can also flush standard output devices with `fflush()` to clear the output stream of any characters you sent to it.

> **NOTE:** The header file for `fflush()` is in stdio.h.

Example

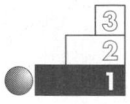

The following program shows you how easy it is to use `gets()` and `puts()`. The program requests the name of a book from the user using a single `gets()` function call, then prints the book title with `puts()`.

Identify the program and include the input/output header files. The program asks the user for the name of a book. Declare the character array book *with 30 elements to hold the user's answer.*

Ask the user for the book's title, and store the user's response in the book *array. Display the string stored in* book *to an output device, probably your screen. Print a thank-you message.*

```cpp
// C22GPS1.CPP
// Inputs and outputs strings.
#include <iostream.h>
#include <stdio.h>
#include <string.h>

void main()
{
   char book[30];

   cout << "What is the book title? ";
   gets(book);                        // Get an input string.
   puts(book);                        // Display the string.
   cout << "Thanks for the book!\n";
   return;
}
```

The output of the program follows:

```
What is the book title? Mary and Her Lambs
Mary and Her Lambs
Thanks for the book!
```

Converting Strings to Numbers

Sometimes you have to convert numbers stored in character strings to a numeric data type. AT&T C++ provides three functions that enable you to do this:

◆ `atoi(s)`: Converts *s* to an integer. The name stands for *a*lpha-betic *to i*nteger.

◆ `atol(s)`: Converts *s* to a long integer. The name stands for *a*lphabetic *to l*ong integer.

◆ `atof(s)`: Converts *s* to a floating-point number. The name stands for *a*lphabetic *to f*loating-point.

> **NOTE:** These three `ato()` functions are prototyped in the stdlib.h header file. Be sure to include stdlib.h at the beginning of any program that uses the `ato()` functions.

The string must contain a valid number. Here is a string that can be converted to an integer:

`"1232"`

The string must hold a string of digits short enough to fit in the target numeric data type. The following string could not be converted to an integer with the `atoi()` function:

`"-1232495.654"`

However, it could be converted to a floating-point number with the `atof()` function.

C++ cannot perform any mathematical calculation with such strings, even if the strings contain digits that represent numbers. Therefore, you must convert any string to its numeric equivalent before performing arithmetic with it.

> **NOTE:** If you pass a string to an `ato()` function and the string does not contain a valid representation of a number, the `ato()` function returns 0.

These functions become more useful to you after you learn about disk files and pointers.

Numeric Functions

This section presents many of the built-in C++ numeric functions. As with the string functions, these functions save you time by converting and calculating numbers instead of your having to write functions that do the same thing. Many of these are trigonometric and advanced mathematical functions. You might use some of these numeric functions only rarely, but they are there if you need them.

This section concludes the discussion of C++'s standard built-in functions. After mastering the concepts in this chapter, you are ready to learn more about arrays and pointers. As you develop more skills in C++, you might find yourself relying on these numeric, string, and character functions when you write more powerful programs.

Useful Mathematical Functions

Several built-in numeric functions return results based on numeric variables and literals passed to them. Even if you write only a few science and engineering programs, some of these functions are useful.

> **NOTE:** All mathematical and trigonometric functions are prototyped in the math.h header file. Be sure to include math.h at the beginning of any program that uses the numeric functions.

These numeric functions return double-precision values.

Here are the functions listed with their descriptions:

◆ `ceil(x)`: The `ceil()`, or *ceiling,* function rounds numbers up to the nearest integer.

◆ `fabs(x)`: Returns the absolute value of *x*. The absolute value of a number is its positive equivalent.

> **TIP:** Absolute value is used for distances (which are always positive), accuracy measurements, age differences, and other calculations that require a positive result.

◆ `floor(x)`: The `floor()` function rounds numbers down to the nearest integer.

◆ `fmod(x, y)`: The `fmod()` function returns the floating-point remainder of (x/y) with the same sign as x, and y cannot be zero. Because the modulus operator (`%`) works only with integers, this function is used to find the remainder of floating-point number divisions.

◆ `pow(x, y)`: Returns x raised to the y power, or x^y. If x is less than or equal to zero, y must be an integer. If x equals zero, y cannot be negative.

◆ `sqrt(x)`: Returns the square root of x; x must be greater than or equal to zero.

The *n*th Root

No function returns the *n*th root of a number, only the square root. In other words, you cannot call a function that gives you the 4th root of 65,536. (By the way, 16 is the 4th root of 65,536, because 16 times 16 times 16 times 16 = 65,536.)

You can use a mathematical trick to simulate the *n*th root, however. Because C++ enables you to raise a number to a fractional power—with the `pow()` function—you can raise a number to the *n*th root by raising it to the ($1/n$) power. For example, to find the 4th root of 65,536, you could type this:

```
root = pow(65536.0, (1.0/4.0));
```

Note that the decimal point keeps the numbers in floating-point format. If you leave them as integers, such as

```
root = pow(65536, (1/4));
```

C++ produces incorrect results. The `pow()` function and most other mathematical functions require floating-point values as arguments.

To store the 7th root of 78,125 in a variable called `root`, for example, you would type

```
root = pow(78125.0, (1.0/7.0));
```

This stores 5.0 in `root` because 5^7 equals 78,125.

Knowing how to compute the nth root is handy in scientific programs and also in financial applications, such as time-value-of-money problems.

Example

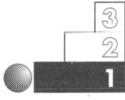

The following program uses the `fabs()` function to compute the difference between two ages.

```cpp
// Filename: C22ABS.CPP
// Computes the difference between two ages.
#include <iostream.h>
#include <math.h>
void main()
{
    float age1, age2, diff;
    cout << "\nWhat is the first child's age? ";
    cin >> age1;
    cout << "What is the second child's age? ";
    cin >> age2;

    // Calculates the positive difference.
    diff = age1 - age2;
    diff = fabs(diff);    // Determines the absolute value.

    cout << "\nThey are " << diff << " years apart.";
    return;
}
```

The output from this program follows. Due to `fabs()`, the order of the ages doesn't matter. Without absolute value, this program would produce a negative age difference if the first age was less than the second. Because the ages are relatively small, floating-point variables are used in this example. C++ automatically converts floating-point arguments to double precision when passing them to `fabs()`.

```
What is the first child's age? 10
What is the second child's age? 12

They are 2 years apart.
```

Trigonometric Functions

The following functions are available for trigonometric applications:

◆ `cos(x)`: Returns the cosine of the angle *x*, expressed in radians.

◆ `sin(x)`: Returns the sine of the angle *x*, expressed in radians.

◆ `tan(x)`: Returns the tangent of the angle *x*, expressed in radians.

These are probably the least-used functions. This is not to belittle the work of scientific and mathematical programmers who need them, however. Certainly, they are grateful that C++ supplies these functions! Otherwise, programmers would have to write their own functions to perform these three basic trigonometric calculations.

Most C++ compilers supply additional trigonometric functions, including hyperbolic equivalents of these three functions.

TIP: If you have to pass an angle that is expressed in degrees to these functions, convert the angle's degrees to radians by multiplying the degrees by π/180.0 (π equals approximately 3.14159).

Logarithmic Functions

Three highly mathematical functions are sometimes used in business and mathematics. They are listed as follows:

♦ `exp(x)`: Returns the base of natural logarithm (*e*) raised to a power specified by *x* (e^x); *e* is the mathematical expression for the approximate value of 2.718282.

♦ `log(x)`: Returns the natural logarithm of the argument *x*, mathematically written as `ln(x)`. *x* must be positive.

♦ `log10(x)`: Returns the base-10 logarithm of argument *x*, mathematically written as `log10(x)`. *x* must be positive.

Random-Number Processing

Random events happen every day. You wake up and it is sunny or rainy. You have a good day or a bad day. You get a phone call from an old friend or you don't. Your stock portfolio might go up or down in value.

Random events are especially important in games. Part of the fun in games is your luck with rolling dice or drawing cards, combined with your playing skills.

Simulating random events is an important task for computers. Computers, however, are finite machines; given the same input, they always produce the same output. This fact can create some boring games!

The `rand()` function produces random integer numbers.

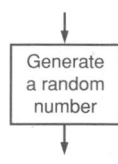

Generate a random number

The designers of C++ knew this computer setback and found a way to overcome it. They wrote a random-number generating function called `rand()`. You can use `rand()` to compute a dice roll or draw a card, for example.

To call the `rand()` function and assign the returned random number to test, use the following syntax:

```
test = rand();
```

The `rand()` function returns an integer from 0 to 32,767. Never use an argument in the `rand()` parentheses.

Every time you call `rand()` in the same program, you receive a different number. If you run the same program over and over, however, `rand()` returns the same set of random numbers. One way to receive a different set of random numbers is to call the `srand()` function. The format of `srand()` follows:

`srand(seed);`

where *seed* is an integer variable or literal. If you don't call `srand()`, C++ assumes a seed value of 1.

> **NOTE:** The `rand()` and `srand()` functions are prototyped in the stdlib.h header file. Be sure to include stdlib.h at the beginning of any program that uses `rand()` or `srand()`.

The *seed* value reseeds, or resets, the random-number generator, so the next random number is based on the new *seed* value. If you call `srand()` with a different *seed* value at the top of a program, `rand()` returns a different random number each time you run the program.

Why Do You Have To Do This?

There is considerable debate among C++ programmers concerning the random-number generator. Many think that the random numbers should be truly random, and that they should not have to seed the generator themselves. They think that C++ should do its own internal seeding when you ask for a random number.

However, many applications would no longer work if the random-number generator were randomized for you. Computers are used in business, engineering, and research to simulate the pattern of real-world events. Researchers have to be able to duplicate these simulations, over and over. Even though the events inside the simulations might be random from each other, the running of the simulations cannot be random if researchers are to study several different effects.

Mathematicians and statisticians also have to repeat random-number patterns for their analyses, especially when they work with risk, probability, and gaming theories.

Because so many computer users have to repeat their random-number patterns, the designers of C++ have wisely chosen to give you, the programmer, the option of keeping the same random patterns or changing them. The advantages far outweigh the disadvantage of including an extra `srand()` function call.

If you want to produce a different set of random numbers every time your program runs, you must determine how your C++ compiler reads the computer's system clock. You can use the seconds count from the clock to seed the random-number generator so it seems truly random.

Review Questions

The answers to the review questions are in Appendix B.

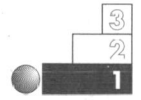

1. How do the character testing functions differ from the character conversion functions?

2. What are the two string input functions?

3. What is the difference between `floor()` and `ceil()`?

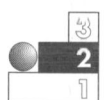

4. What does the following nested function return?

   ```
   isalpha(islower('s'));
   ```

5. If the character array `str1` contains the string `Peter` and the character array `str2` contains `Parker`, what does `str2` contain after the following line of code executes?

   ```
   strcat(str1, str2);
   ```

6. What is the output of the following `cout`?

   ```
   cout << floor(8.5) << " " << ceil(8.5);
   ```

7. True or false: The `isxdigit()` and `isgraph()` functions could return the same value, depending on the character passed to them.

8. Assume you declare a character array with the following statement:

```
char ara[5];
```

Now suppose the user types `Programming` in response to the following statement:

```
fgets(ara, 5, stdin);
```

Would `ara` contain `Prog`, `Progr`, or `Programming`?

9. True or false: The following statements print the same results.

```
cout << pow(64.0, (1.0/2.0)) ;
cout << sqrt(64.0);
```

Review Exercises

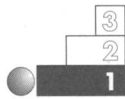

1. Write a program that asks users for their ages. If a user types anything other than two digits, display an error message.

2. Write a program that stores a password in a character array called `pass`. Ask users for the password. Use `strcmp()` to inform users whether they typed the proper password. Use the string I/O functions for all the program's input and output.

3. Write a program that rounds up and rounds down the numbers −10.5, −5.75, and 2.75.

4. Ask users for their names. Print every name in *reverse* case; print the first letter of each name in lowercase and the rest of the name in uppercase.

5. Write a program that asks users for five movie titles. Print the longest title. Use only the string I/O and manipulation functions presented in this chapter.

6. Write a program that computes the square root, cube root, and fourth root of the numbers from 10 to 25, inclusive.

7. Ask users for the titles of their favorite songs. Discard all the special characters in each title. Print the words in the title, one per line. For example, if they enter `My True Love Is Mine, Oh, Mine!`, you should output the following:

```
My
True
Love
Is
Mine
Oh
Mine
```

8. Ask users for the first names of 10 children. Using `strcmp()` on each name, write a program to print the name that comes first in the alphabet.

Summary

You have learned the character, string, and numeric functions that C++ provides. By including the ctype.h header file, you can test and convert characters that a user types. These functions have many useful purposes, such as converting a user's response to uppercase. This makes it easier for you to test user input.

The string I/O functions give you more control over both string and numeric input. You can receive a string of digits from the keyboard and convert them to a number with the ato() functions. The string comparison and concatenation functions enable you to test and change the contents of more than one string.

Functions save you programming time because they take over some of your computing tasks, leaving you free to concentrate on your programs. C++'s numeric functions round and manipulate numbers, produce trigonometric and logarithmic results, and produce random numbers.

Now that you have learned most of C++'s built-in functions, you are ready to improve your ability to work with arrays. Chapter 23, "Introducing Arrays," extends your knowledge of character arrays and shows you how to produce arrays of any data type.

Part VI

Arrays and Pointers

23

Introducing Arrays

This chapter discusses different types of arrays. You are already familiar with character arrays, which are the only method for storing character strings in the C++ language. A character array isn't the only kind of array you can use, however. There is an array for every data type in C++. By learning how to process arrays, you greatly improve the power and efficiency of your programs.

This chapter introduces

- ◆ Array basics of names, data types, and subscripts

- ◆ Initializing an array at declaration time

- ◆ Initializing an array during program execution

- ◆ Selecting elements from arrays

The sample programs in these next few chapters are the most advanced that you have seen in this book. Arrays are not difficult to use, but their power makes them well-suited to more advanced programming.

Array Basics

An array is a list of more than one variable having the same name.

Although you have seen arrays used as character strings, you still must have a review of arrays in general. An array is a *list* of more than one variable having the same name. Not all lists of variables are arrays. The following list of four variables, for example, does not qualify as an array.

```
sales      bonus_92      first_initial      ctr
```

This is a list of variables (four of them), but it isn't an array because each variable has a different name. You might wonder how more than one variable can have the same name; this seems to violate the rules for variables. If two variables have the same name, how can C++ determine which you are referring to when you use that name?

Array variables, or array elements, are differentiated by a *subscript*, which is a number inside brackets. Suppose you want to store a person's name in a character array called name. You can do this with

```
char name[] = "Ray Krebbs";
```

or

```
char name[11] = "Ray Krebbs";
```

Because C++ reserves an extra element for the null zero at the end of every string, you don't have to specify the 11 as long as you initialize the array with a value. The variable name is an array because brackets follow its name. The array has a single name, name, and it contains 11 elements. The array is stored in memory, as shown in Figure 23.1. Each element is a character.

> **NOTE:** All array subscripts begin with 0.

You can manipulate individual elements in the array by referencing their subscripts. For instance, the following cout prints Ray's initials.

Print the first and fifth elements of the array called name.

```
cout << name[0] << " " << name[4];
```

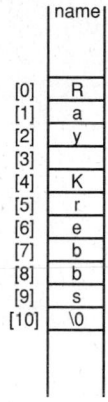

Figure 23.1. **Storing the name character array in memory.**

You can define an array as any data type in C++. You can have integer arrays, long integer arrays, double floating-point arrays, short integer arrays, and so on. C++ recognizes that the brackets [ ] following the array name signify that you are defining an array, and not a single nonarray variable.

The following line defines an array called ages, consisting of five integers:

```
int ages[5];
```

The first element in the ages array is ages[0]. The second element is ages[1], and the last one is ages[4]. This declaration of ages does not assign values to the elements, so you don't know what is in ages and your program does not automatically zero ages for you.

Here are some more array definitions:

```
int weights[25], sizes[100]; // Declare two integer arrays.
float salaries[8];      // Declare a floating-point array.
double temps[50];       // Declare a double floating-point
                        // array.
char letters[15];       // Declare an array of characters.
```

When you declare an array, you instruct C++ to reserve a specific number of memory locations for that array. C++ protects those elements. In the previous lines of code, if you assign a value to `letters[2]` you don't overwrite any data in `weights`, `sizes`, `salaries`, or `temps`. Also, if you assign a value to `sizes[94]`, you don't overwrite data stored in `weights`, `salaries`, `temps`, or `letters`.

Each element in an array occupies the same amount of storage as a nonarray variable of the same data type. In other words, each element in a character array occupies one byte. Each element in an integer array occupies two or more bytes of memory—depending on the computer's internal architecture. The same is true for every other data type.

Your program can reference elements by using formulas for subscripts. As long as the subscript can evaluate to an integer, you can use a literal, a variable, or an expression for the subscript. All the following are references to individual array elements:

```
ara[4]
sales[ctr+1]
bonus[month]
salary[month[i]*2]
```

All array elements are stored in a contiguous, back-to-back fashion. This is important to remember, especially as you write more advanced programs. You can always count on an array's first element preceding the second. The second element is always placed immediately before the third, and so on. Memory is not "padded"; meaning that C++ guarantees there is no extra space between array elements. This is true for character arrays, integer arrays, floating-point arrays, and every other type of array. If a floating-point value occupies four bytes of memory on your computer, the next element in a floating-point array always begins exactly four bytes after the previous element.

Array elements follow each other in memory, with nothing between them.

> ### The Size of Arrays
>
> The `sizeof()` function returns the number of bytes needed to hold its argument. If you request the size of an array name, `sizeof()` returns the number of bytes *reserved* for the entire array.

For example, suppose you declare an integer array of 100 elements called `scores`. If you were to find the size of the array, as in the following,

```
n = sizeof(scores);
```

`n` holds either 200 or 400 bytes, depending on the integer size of your computer. The `sizeof()` function always returns the reserved amount of storage, no matter what data are in the array. Therefore, a character array's contents—even if it holds a very short string—do not affect the size of the array that was originally reserved in memory. If you request the size of an individual array element, however, as in the following,

```
n = sizeof(scores[6]);
```

`n` holds either 2 or 4 bytes, depending on the integer size of your computer.

You must never go out-of-bounds of any array. For example, suppose you want to keep track of the exemptions and salary codes of five employees. You can reserve two arrays to hold such data, like this:

```
int  exemptions[5];   // Holds up to five employee exemptions.
char sal_codes[5];    // Holds up to five employee codes.
```

Figure 23.2 shows how C++ reserves memory for these arrays. The figure assumes a two-byte integer size, although this might differ on some computers. Notice that C++ reserves five elements for `exemptions` from the array declaration. C++ starts reserving memory for `sal_codes` after it reserves all five elements for `exemptions`. If you declare several more variables—either locally or globally—after these two lines, C++ always protects these reserved five elements for `exemptions` and `sal_codes`.

C++ protects only as many array elements as you specify.

Because C++ does its part to protect data in the array, so must you. If you reserve five elements for `exemptions`, you have five integer array elements referred to as `exemptions[0]`, `exemptions[1]`, `exemptions[2]`, `exemptions[3]`, and `exemptions[4]`. C++ does not protect more than five elements for `exemptions`! Suppose you put a value in an `exemptions` element you did not reserve:

```
exemptions[6] = 4;                      // Assign a value to an
                                        // out-of-range element.
```

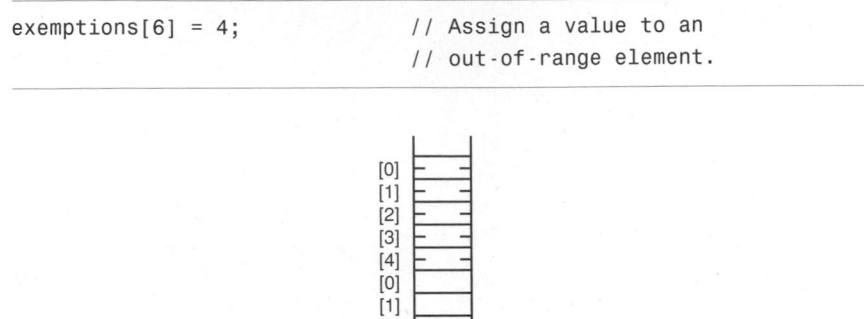

Figure 23.2. Locating two arrays in memory.

C++ enables you to do this—but the results are damaging! C++ overwrites other data (in this case, `sal_codes[2]` and `sal_codes[3]` because they are reserved in the location of the seventh element of `exemptions`). Figure 23.3 shows the damaging results of assigning a value to an out-of-range element.

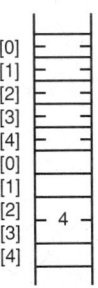

Figure 23.3. The arrays in memory after overwriting part of `sal_codes`.

Although you can define an array of any data type, you cannot declare an array of strings. A *string* is not a C++ variable data type. You learn how to hold multiple strings in an array-like structure in Chapter 27, "Pointers and Arrays."

> **CAUTION:** Unlike most programming languages, AT&T C++ enables you to assign values to out-of-range (nonreserved) subscripts. You must be careful not to do this; otherwise, you start overwriting your other data or code.

Initializing Arrays

You must assign values to array elements before using them. Here are the two ways to initialize elements in an array:

♦ Initialize the elements at declaration time

♦ Initialize the elements in the program

> **NOTE:** C++ automatically initializes global arrays to null zeros. Therefore, global character array elements are null, and all numeric array elements contain zero. You should limit your use of global arrays. If you use global arrays, explicitly initialize them to zero, even though C++ does this for you, to clarify your intentions.

Initializing Elements at Declaration Time

You already know how to initialize character arrays that hold strings when you define the arrays: You simply assign them a string. For example, the following declaration reserves six elements in a character array called `city`:

```
char city[6];                    // Reserve space for city.
```

If you want also to initialize `city` with a value, you can do it like this:

```
char city[6] = "Tulsa";          // Reserve space and
                                 //   initialize city.
```

Initialize arrays

The 6 is optional because C++ counts the elements needed to hold Tulsa, plus an extra element for the null zero at the end of the quoted string.

You also can reserve a character array and initialize it—a single character at a time—by placing braces around the character data. The following line of code declares an array called initials and initializes it with eight characters:

```
char initials[8] = {'Q', 'K', 'P', 'G', 'V', 'M', 'U', 'S'};
```

The array initials is not a string! Its data does not end in a null zero. There is nothing wrong with defining an array of characters such as this one, but you must remember that you cannot treat the array as if it were a string. Do not use string functions with it, or attempt to print the array with cout.

By using brackets, you can initialize any type of array. For example, if you want to initialize an integer array that holds your five children's ages, you can do it with the following declaration:

```
int child_ages[5] = {2, 5, 6, 8, 12};    // Declare and
                                          // initialize array.
```

In another example, if you want to keep track of the previous three years' total sales, you can declare an array and initialize it at the same time with the following:

```
double sales[] = {454323.43, 122355.32, 343324.96};
```

As with character arrays, you do not have to state explicitly the array size when you declare and initialize an array of any type. C++ determines, in this case, to reserve three double floating-point array elements for sales. Figure 23.4 shows the representation of child_ages and sales in memory.

> **NOTE:** You cannot initialize an array, using the assignment operator and braces, *after* you declare it. You can initialize arrays in this manner only when you declare them. If you want to fill an array with data after you declare the array, you must do so element-by-element or by using functions as described in the next section.

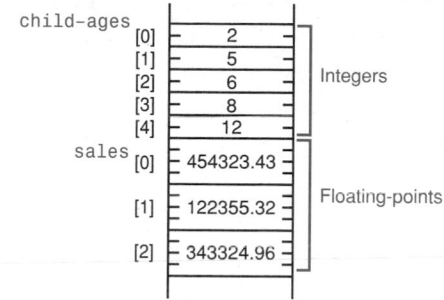

Figure 23.4. In-memory representation of two different types of arrays.

C++ assigns zero
nulls to all array
values that you do
not define explicitly
at declaration time.

Although C++ does not automatically initialize the array elements, if you initialize some but not all the elements when you declare the array, C++ finishes the job for you by assigning the remainder to zero.

> **TIP:** To initialize every element of a large array to zero at the same time, declare the entire array and initialize only its first value to zero. C++ fills the rest of the array to zero.

For instance, suppose you have to reserve array storage for profit figures of the three previous months as well as the three months to follow. You must reserve six elements of storage, but you know values for only the first three. You can initialize the array as follows:

```
double profit[6] = {67654.43, 46472.34, 63451.93};
```

Because you explicitly initialized three of the elements, C++ initializes the rest to zero. If you use cout to print the entire array, one element per line, you receive:

```
67654.43
46472.34
63451.93
00000.00
00000.00
00000.00
```

> **CAUTION:** Always declare an array with the maximum number of subscripts, unless you initialize the array at the same time. The following array declaration is illegal:
>
> ```
> int count[];               // Bad array declaration!
> ```
>
> C++ does not know how many elements to reserve for `count`, so it reserves none. If you then assign values to `count`'s nonreserved elements, you can (and probably will) overwrite other data.
>
> The only time you can leave the brackets empty is if you also assign values to the array, such as the following:
>
> ```
> int count[] = {15, 9, 22, -8, 12}; // Good definition.
> ```
>
> C++ can determine, from the list of values, how many elements to reserve. In this case, C++ reserves five elements for `count`.

Examples

1. Suppose you want to track the stock market averages for the previous 90 days. Instead of storing them in 90 different variables, it is much easier to store them in an array. You can declare the array like this:

   ```
   float stock[90];
   ```

   The remainder of the program can assign values to the averages.

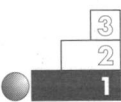

2. Suppose you just finished taking classes at a local university and want to average your six class scores. The following program initializes one array for the school name and another for the six classes. The body of the program averages the six scores.

   ```
   // Filename: C23ARA1.CPP
   // Averages six test scores.
   #include <iostream.h>
   #include <iomanip.h>
   void main()
   ```

```
{
    char s_name[] = "Tri Star University";
    float scores[6] = {88.7, 90.4, 76.0, 97.0, 100.0, 86.7};
    float average=0.0;
    int ctr;

    // Computes total of scores.
    for (ctr=0; ctr<6; ctr++)
        { average += scores[ctr]; }

    // Computes the average.
    average /= float(6);

    cout << "At " << s_name << ", your class average is "
        << setprecision(2) << average << "\n";
    return;
}
```

The output follows:

```
At Tri Star University, your class average is 89.8.
```

Notice that using arrays makes processing lists of information much easier. Instead of averaging six differently named variables, you can use a for loop to step through each array element. If you had to average 1000 numbers, you can still do so with a simple for loop, as in this example. If the 1000 variables were not in an array, but were individually named, you would have to write a considerable amount of code just to add them.

3. The following program is an expanded version of the previous one. It prints the six scores before computing the average. Notice that you must print array elements individually; you cannot print an entire array in a single cout. (You can print an entire character array with cout, but only if it holds a null-terminated string of characters.)

```
// Filename: C23ARA2.CPP
// Prints and averages six test scores.
#include <iostream.h>
#include <iomanip.h>
void pr_scores(float scores[]);  // Prototype
```

```
void main()
{
   char s_name[] = "Tri Star University";
   float scores[6] = {88.7, 90.4, 76.0, 97.0, 100.0, 86.7};
   float average=0.0;
   int ctr;

   // Call function to print scores.
   pr_scores(scores);

   // Computes total of scores.
   for (ctr=0; ctr<6; ctr++)
      { average += scores[ctr]; }

   // Computes the average.
   average /= float(6);

   cout << "At " << s_name << ", your class average is "
        << setprecision(2) << average;
   return;
}

void pr_scores(float scores[6])
{
   // Prints the six scores.
   int ctr;

   cout << "Here are your scores:\n";          // Title
   for (ctr=0; ctr<6; ctr++)
      cout << setprecision(2) << scores[ctr] << "\n";
   return;
}
```

To pass an array to a function, you must specify its name only. In the receiving function's parameter list, you must state the array type and include its brackets, which tell the function that it is an array. (You do not explicitly have to state the array size in the receiving parameter list, as shown in the prototype.)

4. To improve the maintainability of your programs, define all array sizes with the `const` instruction. What if you took four classes next semester but still wanted to use the same program? You can modify it by changing all the 6s to 4s, but if you had defined the array size with a constant, you have to change only one line to change the program's subscript limits. Notice how the following program uses a constant for the number of classes.

```cpp
// Filename: C23ARA3.CPP
// Prints and averages six test scores.
#include <iostream.h>
#include <iomanip.h>
void pr_scores(float scores[]);
const int CLASS_NUM = 6;   // Constant holds array size.

void main()
{
    char s_name[] = "Tri Star University";
    float scores[CLASS_NUM] = {88.7, 90.4, 76.0, 97.0,
                                  100.0, 86.7};
    float average=0.0;
    int ctr;

    // Calls function to print scores.
    pr_scores(scores);

    // Computes total of scores.
    for (ctr=0; ctr<CLASS_NUM; ctr++)
        { average += scores[ctr]; }

    // Computes the average.
    average /= float(CLASS_NUM);

    cout << "At " << s_name << ", your class average is "
         << setprecision(2) << average;
    return;
}

void pr_scores(float scores[CLASS_NUM])
```

```
{
  // Prints the six scores.
  int ctr;

  cout << "Here are your scores:\n";          // Title
  for (ctr=0; ctr<CLASS_NUM; ctr++)
    cout << setprecision(2) << scores[ctr] << "\n";
  return;
}
```

For such a simple example, using a constant for the maximum subscript might not seem like a big advantage. If you were writing a larger program that processed several arrays, however, changing the constant at the top of the program would be much easier than searching the program for each occurrence of that array reference.

Using constants for array sizes has the added advantage of protecting you from going out of the subscript bounds. You do not have to remember the subscript when looping through arrays; you can use the constant instead.

Initializing Elements in the Program

Rarely do you know the contents of arrays when you declare them. Usually, you fill an array with user input or a disk file's data. The for loop is a perfect tool for looping through arrays when you fill them with values.

> **CAUTION:** An array name cannot appear on the left side of an assignment statement.

You cannot assign one array to another. Suppose you want to copy an array called total_sales to a second array called saved_sales. You cannot do so with the following assignment statement:

```
saved_sales = total_sales;                    // Invalid!
```

Rather, you have to copy the arrays one element at a time, using a loop, such as the following section of code does:

You want to copy one array to another. You have to do so one element at a time, so you need a counter. Initialize a variable called ctr *to* 0; *the value of* ctr *represents a position in the array.*

1. *Assign the element that occupies the position in the first array represented by the value of* ctr *to the same position in the second array.*

2. *If the counter is less than the size of the array, add one to the counter. Repeat step one.*

```
for (ctr=0; ctr<ARRAY_SIZE; ctr++)
   { saved_sales[ctr] = total_sales[ctr]; }
```

The following examples illustrate methods for initializing arrays in a program. After learning about disk processing later in the book, you learn to read array values from a disk file.

Examples

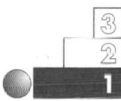

1. The following program uses the assignment operator to assign 10 temperatures to an array.

```
// Filename: C23ARA4.CPP
// Fills an array with 10 temperature values.
#include <iostream.h>
#include <iomanip.h>
const int NUM_TEMPS = 10;
void main()
{
   float temps[NUM_TEMPS];
   int ctr;

   temps[0] = 78.6;       // Subscripts always begin at 0.
   temps[1] = 82.1;
   temps[2] = 79.5;
   temps[3] = 75.0;
   temps[4] = 75.4;
```

```
temps[5] = 71.8;
temps[6] = 73.3;
temps[7] = 69.5;
temps[8] = 74.1;
temps[9] = 75.7;

// Print the temps.
cout << "Daily temperatures for the last " <<
        NUM_TEMPS << " days:\n";
for (ctr=0; ctr<NUM_TEMPS; ctr++)
   { cout << setprecision(1) << temps[ctr] << "\n"; }

return;
}
```

2. The following program uses a for loop and cin to assign eight integers entered individually by the user. The program then prints a total of the numbers.

```
// Filename: C23TOT.CPP
// Totals eight input values from the user.
#include <iostream.h>
const int NUM = 8;
void main()
{
   int nums[NUM];
   int total = 0;        // Holds total of user's eight numbers.
   int ctr;

   for (ctr=0; ctr<NUM; ctr++)
     { cout << "Please enter the next number...";
       cin >> nums[ctr];
       total += nums[ctr]; }

   cout << "The total of the numbers is " << total << "\n";
   return;
}
```

3. You don't have to access an array in the same order as you initialized it. Chapter 24, "Array Processing," shows you how to change the order of an array. You also can use the subscript to select items from an array of values.

The following program requests sales data for the preceding 12 months. Users can then type a month they want to see. That month's sales figure is then printed, without figures from other months getting in the way. This is how you begin to build a search program to find requested data: You store the data in an array (or in a disk file that can be read into an array, as you learn later), then wait for a user's request to see specific pieces of the data.

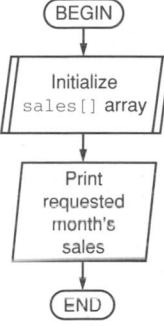

```cpp
// Filename: C23SAL.CPP
// Stores twelve months of sales and
// prints selected ones.
#include <iostream.h>
#include <ctype.h>
#include <conio.h>
#include <iomanip.h>
const int NUM = 12;
void main()
{
    float sales[NUM];
    int ctr, ans;
    int req_month;                  // Holds user's request.

    // Fill the array.
    cout << "Please enter the twelve monthly sales values\n";
    for (ctr=0; ctr<NUM; ctr++)
      { cout << "What are sales for month number "
            << ctr+1 << "? \n";
        cin >> sales[ctr]; }

    // Wait for a requested month.
    for (ctr=0; ctr<25; ctr++)
      { cout << "\n"; }                     // Clears the screen.

    cout << "*** Sales Printing Program ***\n";
    cout << "Prints any sales from the last " << NUM
        << " months\n\n";
    do
      { cout << "For what month (1-" << NUM << ") do you want "
            << "to see a sales value? ";
        cin >> req_month;
```

```
      // Adjust for zero-based subscript.
      cout << "\nMonth " << req_month <<
              "'s sales are " << setprecision(2) <<
              sales[req_month-1];
      cout << "\nDo you want to see another (Y/N)? ";
      ans=getch();
      ans=toupper(ans);
   } while (ans == 'Y');
 return;

}
```

Notice the helpful screen-clearing routine that prints 23 newline characters. This routine scrolls the screen until it is blank. (Most compilers come with a better built-in screen-clearing function, but the AT&T C++ standard does not offer one because the compiler is too closely linked with specific hardware.)

The following is the second screen from this program. After the 12 sales values are entered in the array, any or all can be requested, one at a time, simply by supplying the month's number (the number of the subscript).

```
*** Sales Printing Program ***
Prints any sales from the last 12 months


For what month (1-12) do you want to see a sales value? 2

Month 2's sales are 433.22
Do you want to see another (Y/N)?
For what month (1-12) do you want to see a sales value? 5

Month 5's sales are 123.45
Do you want to see another (Y/N)?
```

Review Questions

Answers to the review questions are in Appendix B.

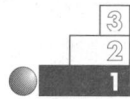

1. True or false: A single array can hold several values of different data types.

2. How do C++ programs tell one array element from another if all elements have identical names?

3. Why must you initialize an array before using it?

4. Given the following definition of an array, called `weights`, what is the value of `weights[5]`?

   ```
   int weights[10] = {5, 2, 4};
   ```

5. If you pass an integer array to a function and change it, does the array change also in the calling function? (*Hint:* Remember how character arrays are passed to functions.)

6. How does C++ initialize global array elements?

Review Exercises

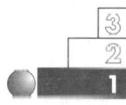

1. Write a program to store the ages of six of your friends in a single array. Store each of the six ages using the assignment operator. Print the ages on-screen.

2. Modify the program in Exercise 1 to print the ages in reverse order.

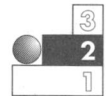

3. Write a simple data program to track a radio station's ratings (1, 2, 3, 4, or 5) for the previous 18 months. Use `cin` to initialize the array with the ratings. Print the ratings on-screen with an appropriate title.

4. Write a program to store the numbers from 1 to 100 in an array of 100 integer elements. (*Hint:* The subscripts should begin at 0 and end at 99.)

5. Write a program a small business owner can use to track customers. Assign each customer a number (starting at 0). Whenever a customer purchases something, record the sale in the element that matches the customer's number (that is, the next unused array element). When the store owner signals the end of the day, print a report consisting of each customer number with its matching sales, a total sales figure, and an average sales figure per customer.

Summary

You now know how to declare and initialize arrays consisting of various data types. You can initialize an array either when you declare it or in the body of your program. Array elements are much easier to process than other variables because each has a different name.

C++ has powerful sorting and searching techniques that make your programs even more serviceable. The next chapter introduces these techniques and shows you still other ways to access array elements.

Array Processing

C++ provides many ways to access arrays. If you have programmed in other computer languages, you will find that some of C++'s array indexing techniques are unique. Arrays in the C++ language are closely linked with *pointers*. Chapter 26, "Pointers," describes the many ways pointers and arrays interact. Because pointers are so powerful, and because learning about arrays provides a good foundation for learning about pointers, this chapter attempts to describe in detail how to reference arrays.

This chapter discusses the different types of array processing. You learn how to search an array for one or more values, find the highest and lowest values in an array, and sort an array into numerical or alphabetical order.

This chapter introduces the following concepts:

♦ Searching arrays

♦ Finding the highest and lowest values in arrays

♦ Sorting arrays

♦ Advanced subscripting with arrays

Many programmers see arrays as a turning point. Gaining an understanding of array processing makes your programs more accurate and allows for more powerful programming.

Searching Arrays

Arrays are one of the primary means by which data is stored in C++ programs. Many types of programs lend themselves to processing lists (arrays) of data, such as an employee payroll program, a scientific research of several chemicals, or customer account processing. As mentioned in the previous chapter, array data usually is read from a disk file. Later chapters describe disk file processing. For now, you should understand how to manipulate arrays so you see the data exactly the way you want to see it.

Chapter 23, "Introducing Arrays," showed how to print arrays in the same order that you entered the data. This is sometimes done, but it is not always the most appropriate method of looking at data.

For instance, suppose a high school used C++ programs for its grade reports. Suppose also that the school wanted to see a list of the top 10 grade-point averages. You could not print the first 10 grade-point averages in the list of student averages because the top 10 GPAs might not (and probably will not) appear as the first 10 array elements. Because the GPAs would not be in any sequence, the program would have to sort the array into numeric order, from high GPAs to low, or else search the array for the 10 highest GPAs.

You need a method for putting arrays in a specific order. This is called *sorting* an array. When you sort an array, you put that array in a specific order, such as in alphabetical or numerical order. A dictionary is in sorted order, and so is a phone book.

When you reverse the order of a sort, it is called a *descending sort*. For instance, if you wanted to look at a list of all employees in descending salary order, the highest-paid employees would be printed first.

Figure 24.1 shows a list of eight numbers in an array called unsorted. The middle list of numbers is an ascending sorted version of unsorted. The third list of numbers is a descending version of unsorted.

Array elements do not always appear in the order in which they are needed.

Unsorted	Ascending order	Descending order
6	1	8
1	2	7
2	3	6
4	4	5
7	5	4
8	6	3
3	7	2
5	8	1

Figure 24.1. A list of unsorted numbers sorted into an ascending and a descending order.

Before you learn to sort, it would be helpful to learn how to search an array for a value. This is a preliminary step in learning to sort. What if one of those students received a grade change? The computer must be able to access that specific student's grade to change it (without affecting the others). As the next section shows, programs can search for specific array elements.

NOTE: C++ provides a method for sorting and searching lists of strings, but you will not understand how to do this until you learn about pointers, starting in Chapter 26, "Pointers." The sorting and searching examples and algorithms presented in this chapter demonstrate sorting and searching arrays of numbers. The same concepts will apply (and will actually be much more usable for "real-world" applications) when you learn how to store lists of names in C++.

Searching for Values

You do not have to know any new commands to search an array for a value. Basically, the `if` and `for` loop statements are all you need. To search an array for a specific value, look at each element in that array, and compare it to the `if` statement to see whether they match. If they do not, you keep searching down the array. If you run out of array elements before finding the value, it is not in the array.

You do not have to sort an array to find its extreme values.

You can perform several different kinds of searches. You might have to find the highest or the lowest value in a list of numbers. This is informative when you have much data and want to know the extremes of the data (such as the highest and lowest sales region in your division). You also can search an array to see whether it contains a matching value. For example, you can see whether an item is already in an inventory by searching a part number array for a match.

The following programs illustrate some of these array-searching techniques.

Examples

1. To find the highest number in an array, compare each element with the first one. If you find a higher value, it becomes the basis for the rest of the array. Continue until you reach the end of the array and you will have the highest value, as the following program shows.

Identify the program and include the I/O header file. You want to find the highest value in an array, so define the array size as a constant, then initialize the array.

Loop through the array, comparing each element to the highest value. If an element is higher than the highest value saved, store the element as the new high value. Print the highest value found in the array.

```
// Filename: C24HIGH.CPP
// Finds the highest value in the array.
#include <iostream.h>
const int SIZE = 15;
void main()
```

```
{
   // Puts some numbers in the array.
   int ara[SIZE]={5,2,7,8,36,4,2,86,11,43,22,12,45,6,85};
   int high_val, ctr;

   high_val = ara[0];            // Initializes with first
                                 // array element.
   for (ctr=1; ctr<SIZE; ctr++)
     {                        // Stores current value if it is
                              // the higher than the highest.
       if (ara[ctr] > high_val)
         { high_val = ara[ctr]; }
     }

   cout << "The highest number in the list is "
        << high_val << "\n";
   return;
}
```

The output of the program is the following:

```
The highest number in the list is 86.
```

You have to save the element if and only if it is higher than the one you are comparing. Finding the smallest number in an array is just as easy, except that you determine whether each succeeding array element is less than the lowest value found so far.

2. The following example expands on the previous one by finding the highest and the lowest value. First, store the first array element in *both* the highest and the lowest variable to begin the search. This ensures that each element after that one is tested to see whether it is higher or lower than the first.

This example also uses the rand() function from Chapter 22, "Character, String, and Numeric Functions," to fill the array with random values from 0 to 99 by applying the modulus operator (%) and 100 against whatever value rand() produces. The program prints the entire array before starting the search for the highest and the lowest.

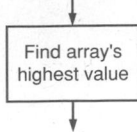

Find array's
highest value

```cpp
// Filename: C24HILO.CPP
// Finds the highest and the lowest value in the array.
#include <iostream.h>
#include <stdlib.h>
const int SIZE = 15;
void main()
{
   int ara[SIZE];
   int high_val, low_val, ctr;

   // Fills array with random numbers from 0 to 99.
   for (ctr=0; ctr<SIZE; ctr++)
     { ara[ctr] = rand() % 100; }

   // Prints the array to the screen.
   cout << "Here are the " << SIZE << " random numbers:\n";
   for (ctr=0; ctr<SIZE; ctr++)
     {  cout << ara[ctr] << "\n"; }

   cout << "\n\n";        // Prints a blank line.
   high_val = ara[0];     // Initializes first element to
                          // both high and low.
   low_val  = ara[0];

   for (ctr=1; ctr<SIZE; ctr++)
     {                       // Stores current value if it is
                             // higher than the highest.
       if (ara[ctr] > high_val)
         { high_val = ara[ctr]; }
       if (ara[ctr] < low_val)
         { low_val = ara[ctr]; }
     }

   cout << "The highest number in the list is " <<
           high_val << "\n";
   cout << "The lowest number in the list is " <<
           low_val << "\n";
   return;
}
```

Here is the output from this program:

```
Here are the 15 random numbers:
46
30
82
90
56
17
95
15
48
26
4
58
71
79
92
The highest number in the list is 95
The lowest number in the list is 4
```

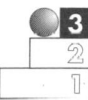

3. The next program fills an array with part numbers from an inventory. You must use your imagination, because the inventory array normally would fill more of the array, be initialized from a disk file, and be part of a larger set of arrays that hold descriptions, quantities, costs, selling prices, and so on. For this example, assignment statements initialize the array. The important idea from this program is not the array initialization, but the method for searching the array.

NOTE: If the newly entered part number is already on file, the program tells the user. Otherwise, the part number is added to the end of the array.

```
// Filename: C24SERCH.CPP
// Searches a part number array for the input value. If
```

```
// the entered part number is not in the array, it is
// added. If the part number is in the array, a message
// is printed.
#include <iostream.h>
const int MAX = 100;
void fill_parts(long int parts[MAX]);

void main()
{
   long int search_part;              // Holds user request.
   long int parts[MAX];
   int ctr;
   int num_parts=5;              // Beginning inventory count.

   fill_parts(parts);     // Fills the first five elements.
   do
   {
     cout << "\n\nPlease type a part number...";
     cout << "(-9999 ends program) ";
     cin >> search_part;
     if (search_part == -9999)
       { break; }                // Exits loop if user wants.
     // Scans array to see whether part is in inventory.
     for (ctr=0; ctr<num_parts; ctr++) // Checks each item.
     { if (search_part == parts[ctr])        // If it is in
                                              // inventory...
           { cout << "\nPart " << search_part <<
                      " is already in inventory";
             break;
           }
       else
        { if (ctr == (num_parts-1) )      // If not there,
                                          // adds it.
           { parts[num_parts] = search_part;   // Adds to
                                               // end of array.
            num_parts++;
            cout << search_part <<
                    " was added to inventory\n";
```

```
            break;
             }
         }
         }
    } while (search_part != -9999);      // Loops until user
                                         // signals end.
    return;
}


void fill_parts(long int parts[MAX])
{
    // Assigns five part numbers to array for testing.
    parts[0] = 12345;
    parts[1] = 24724;
    parts[2] = 54154;
    parts[3] = 73490;
    parts[4] = 83925;
    return;
}
```

Here is the output from this program:

```
Please type a part number...(-9999 ends program) 34234
34234 was added to inventory

Please type a part number...(-9999 ends program) 83925

Part 83925 is already in inventory

Please type a part number...(-9999 ends program) 52786
52786 was added to inventory

Please type a part number...(-9999 ends program) -9999
```

Sorting Arrays

There are many times when you must sort one or more arrays. Suppose you were to take a list of numbers, write each number on a separate piece of paper, and throw all the pieces of paper into the air. The steps you take—shuffling and changing the order of the pieces of paper and trying to put them in order—are similar to what your computer goes through to sort numbers or character data.

Because sorting arrays requires exchanging values of elements back and forth, it helps if you first learn the technique for swapping variables. Suppose you had two variables named score1 and score2. What if you wanted to reverse their values (putting score2 into the score1 variable, and vice versa)? You could not do this:

```
score1 = score2;     // Does not swap the two values.
score2 = score1;
```

Why doesn't this work? In the first line, the value of score1 is replaced with score2's value. When the first line finishes, both score1 and score2 contain the same value. Therefore, the second line cannot work as desired.

To swap two variables, you have to use a third variable to hold the intermediate result. (This is the only function of this third variable.) For instance, to swap score1 and score2, use a third variable (called hold_score in this code), as in

```
hold_score = score1;    // These three lines properly
score1 = score2;        // swap score1 and score2.
score2 = hold_score;
```

This exchanges the values in the two variables.

There are several different ways to sort arrays. These methods include the *bubble sort*, the *quicksort*, and the *shell sort*. The basic goal of each method is to compare each array element to another array element and swap them if the higher value is less than the other.

The lowest values in a list "float" to the top with the bubble sort algorithm.

The theory behind these sorts is beyond the scope of this book, however, the bubble sort is one of the easiest to understand. Values in the array are compared to each other, a pair at a time, and swapped if they are not in back-to-back order. The lowest value eventually "floats" to the top of the array, like a bubble in a glass of soda.

Figure 24.2 shows a list of numbers before, during, and after a bubble sort. The bubble sort steps through the array and compares pairs of numbers to determine whether they have to be swapped. Several passes might have to be made through the array before it is finally sorted (no more passes are needed). Other types of sorts improve on the bubble sort. The bubble sort procedure is easy to program, but it is slower compared to many of the other methods.

First Pass

3	2	2	2
2	3	3	3
5	5	1	1
1	1	5	4
4	4	4	5

Second Pass

2	2
3	1
1	3
4	4
5	5

Third Pass

2	1
1	2
3	3
4	4
5	5

Fourth Pass

1
2
3
4
5

Figure 24.2. Sorting a list of numbers using the bubble sort.

The following programs show the bubble sort in action.

Examples

1. The following program assigns 10 random numbers between 0 and 99 to an array, then sorts the array. A nested `for` loop is perfect for sorting numbers in the array (as shown in the `sort_array()` function). Nested `for` loops provide a nice mechanism for working on pairs of values, swapping them if needed. As the outside loop counts down the list, referencing each element, the inside loop compares each of the remaining values to those array elements.

```cpp
// Filename: C24SORT1.CPP
// Sorts and prints a list of numbers.
const int MAX = 10;
#include <iostream.h>
#include <stdlib.h>
void fill_array(int ara[MAX]);
void print_array(int ara[MAX]);
void sort_array(int ara[MAX]);

void main()
{
    int ara[MAX];

    fill_array(ara);    // Puts random numbers in the array.

    cout << "Here are the unsorted numbers:\n";
    print_array(ara);   // Prints the unsorted array.

    sort_array(ara);    // Sorts the array.

    cout << "\n\nHere are the sorted numbers:\n";
    print_array(ara);   // Prints the newly sorted array.
    return;
}

void fill_array(int ara[MAX])
{
```

```
   // Puts random numbers in the array.
   int ctr;
   for (ctr=0; ctr<MAX; ctr++)
      { ara[ctr] = (rand() % 100); }    // Forces number to
                                        // 0-99 range.
   return;
}

void print_array(int ara[MAX])
{
   // Prints the array.
   int ctr;
   for (ctr=0; ctr<MAX; ctr++)
      { cout << ara[ctr] << "\n"; }
   return;
}

void sort_array(int ara[MAX])
{
   // Sorts the array.
   int temp;              // Temporary variable to swap with
   int ctr1, ctr2;              // Need two loop counters to
                                //    swap pairs of numbers.
   for (ctr1=0; ctr1<(MAX 1); ctr1++)
      { for (ctr2=(ctr1+1); ctr2<MAX; ctr2++) // Test pairs.
           { if (ara[ctr1] > ara[ctr2])     // Swap if this
                { temp = ara[ctr1]; // pair is not in order.
                   ara[ctr1] = ara[ctr2];
                   ara[ctr2] = temp;   // "Float" the lowest
                                       // to the highest.

                }
           }
      }
   return;
}
```

The output from this program appears next. If any two randomly generated numbers were the same, the bubble sort would work properly, placing them next to each other in the list.

```
Here are the unsorted numbers:
46
30
82
90
56
17
95
15
48
26


Here are the sorted numbers:
15
17
26
30
46
48
56
82
90
95
```

To produce a descending sort, use the less-than (<) logical operator when swapping array elements.

2. The following program is just like the previous one, except it prints the list of numbers in descending order.

A descending sort is as easy to write as an ascending sort. With the ascending sort (from low to high values), you compare pairs of values, testing to see whether the first is greater than the second. With a descending sort, you test to see whether the first is less than the second one.

```cpp
// Filename: C24SORT2.CPP
// Sorts and prints a list of numbers in reverse
// and descending order.
const int MAX = 10;
#include <iostream.h>
#include <stdlib.h>
void fill_array(int ara[MAX]);
```

```cpp
void print_array(int ara[MAX]);
void sort_array(int ara[MAX]);

void main()
{
   int ara[MAX];

   fill_array(ara);      // Puts random numbers in the array.

   cout << "Here are the unsorted numbers:\n";
   print_array(ara);           // Prints the unsorted array.

   sort_array(ara);                       // Sorts the array.

   cout << "\n\nHere are the sorted numbers:\n";
   print_array(ara);       // Prints the newly sorted array.
   return;
}

void fill_array(int ara[MAX])
{
   // Puts random numbers in the array.
   int ctr;
   for (ctr=0; ctr<MAX; ctr++)
      { ara[ctr] = (rand() % 100); }        // Forces number
                                            // to 0-99 range.
   return;
}

void print_array(int ara[MAX])
{
   // Prints the array
   int ctr;
   for (ctr=0; ctr<MAX; ctr++)
      { cout << ara[ctr] << "\n"; }
   return;
}

void sort_array(int ara[MAX])
{
   // Sorts the array.
   int temp;              // Temporary variable to swap with.
```

```
    int ctr1, ctr2;              // Need two loop counters
                                 //   to swap pairs of numbers.
    for (ctr1=0; ctr1<(MAX-1); ctr1++)
       { for (ctr2=(ctr1+1); ctr2<MAX; ctr2++) // Test pairs
            // Notice the difference in descending (here)
            // and ascending.
            { if (ara[ctr1] < ara[ctr2]) // Swap if this
                 { temp = ara[ctr1]; // pair is not in order.
                   ara[ctr1] = ara[ctr2];
                   ara[ctr2] = temp;  // "Float" the lowest
                                      //    to the highest.
                 }
            }
       }
    return;
}
```

TIP: You can save the previous programs' sort functions in two separate files named `sort_ascend` and `sort_descend`. When you must sort two different arrays, `#include` these files inside your own programs. Even better, compile each of these routines separately and link the one you need to your program. (You must check your compiler's manual to learn how to do this.)

You can sort character arrays just as easily as you sort numeric arrays. C++ uses the ASCII character set for its sorting comparisons. If you look at the ASCII table in Appendix C, you will see that numbers sort before letters and that uppercase letters sort before lowercase letters.

Advanced Referencing of Arrays

The array notation you have seen so far is common in computer programming languages. Most languages use subscripts inside brackets (or parentheses) to refer to individual array elements. For instance, you know the following array references describe the first and fifth element of the array called `sales` (remember that the starting subscript is always `0`):

```
sales[0]
sales[4]
```

C++ provides another approach to referencing arrays. Even though the title of this section includes the word "advanced," this array-referencing method is not difficult. It is very different, however, especially if you are familiar with another programming language's approach.

There is nothing wrong with referring to array elements in the manner you have seen so far, however, the second approach, unique to C and C++, will be helpful when you learn about pointers in upcoming chapters. Actually, C++ programmers who have programmed for several years rarely use the subscript notation you have seen.

An array name is the address of the starting element of the array.

In C++, an array's name is not just a label for you to use in programs. To C++, the array name is the actual address where the first element begins in memory. Suppose you define an array called `amounts` with the following statement:

```
int amounts[6] = {4, 1, 3, 7, 9, 2};
```

Figure 24.3 shows how this array is stored in memory. The figure shows the array beginning at address 405,332. (The actual addresses of variables are determined by the computer when you load and run your compiled program.) Notice that the name of the array, `amounts`, is located somewhere in memory and contains the address of `amounts[0]`, or 405,332.

You can refer to an array by its regular subscript notation, or by modifying the address of the array. The following refer to the third element of `amounts`:

```
amounts[3] and (amounts + 3)[0]
```

Because C++ considers the array name to be an address in memory that contains the location of the first array element, nothing keeps you from using a different address as the starting address and referencing from there. Taking this one step further, each of the following also refers to the third element of `amounts`:

(amounts+0)[3] and (amounts+2)[1] and (amounts-2)[5]
(1+amounts)[2] and (3+amounts)[0] and (amounts+1)[2]

You can print any of these array elements with cout.

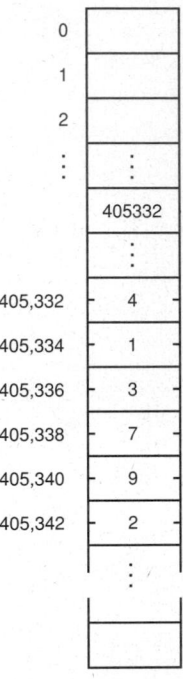

Figure 24.3. The array name amounts holds the address of amounts[0].

When you print strings inside character arrays, referencing the arrays by their modified addresses is more useful than with integers. Suppose you stored three strings in a single character array. You could initialize this array with the following statement:

```
char names[]={'T','e','d','\0','E','v','a','\0','S','a','m','\0'};
```

Figure 24.4 shows how this array might look in memory. The array name, names, contains the address of the first element, names[0] (the letter *T*).

CAUTION: The hierarchy table in Appendix D, "C++ Precedence Table," shows that array subscripts have precedence over addition and subtraction. Therefore, you must enclose array names in parentheses if you want to modify the name as shown in these examples. The following are not equivalent:

`(2+amounts)[1]` and `2+amounts[1]`

The first example refers to `amounts[3]` (which is 7). The second example takes the value of `amounts[1]` (which is 1 in this example array) and adds 2 to it (resulting in a value of 3).

This second method of array referencing might seem like more trouble than it is worth, but learning to reference arrays in this fashion will make your transition to pointers much easier. An array name is actually a pointer, because the array contains the address of the first array element (it "points" to the start of the array).

[0]	T
[1]	e
[2]	d
[3]	\0
[4]	E
[5]	v
[6]	a
[7]	\0
[8]	S
[9]	a
[10]	m
[11]	\0

Figure 24.4. Storing more than one string in a single character array.

You have yet to see a character array that holds more than one string, but C++ allows it. The problem with such an array is how you reference, and especially how you print, the second and third strings. If you were to print this array using cout:

```
cout << names;
```

C++ would print the following:

```
Ted
```

cout prints strings in arrays starting at the array's address and continuing until it reaches the null zero.

Because cout requires a starting address, you can print the three strings with the following couts:

```
cout << names;        // Prints Ted
cout << (names+4);    // Prints Eva
cout << (names+8);    // Prints Sam
```

To test your understanding, what do the following couts print?

```
cout << (names+1);
cout << (names+6);
```

The first cout prints ed. The characters ed begin at (names+1) and the cout stops printing when it reaches the null zero. The second cout prints a. Adding six to the address at names produces the address where the a is located. The "string" is only one character long because the null zero appears in the array immediately after the a.

To sum up character arrays, the following refer to individual array elements (single characters):

```
names[2] and (names+1)[1]
```

The following refer to addresses only, and as such, you can print the full strings with cout:

```
names and (names+4)
```

CAUTION: Never use the printf()'s %c control code to print an address reference, even if that address contains a character. Print strings by specifying an address with %s, and single characters by specifying the character element with %c.

The following examples are a little different from most you have seen. They do not perform "real-world" work, but were designed as study examples for you to familiarize yourself with this new method of array referencing. The next few chapters expand on these methods.

Examples

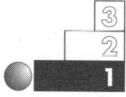

1. The following program stores the numbers from 100 to 600 in an array, then prints elements using the new method of array subscripting.

```cpp
// Filename: C24REF1.CPP
// Print elements of an integer array in different ways.
#include <iostream.h>
void main()
{
   int num[6] = {100, 200, 300, 400, 500, 600};

   cout << "num[0] is \t" << num[0] << "\n";
   cout << "(num+0)[0] is \t" << (num+0)[0] << "\n";
   cout << "(num-2)[2] is \t" << (num-2)[2] << "\n\n";

   cout << "num[1] is \t" << num[1] << "\n";
   cout << "(num+1)[0] is \t" << (num+1)[0] << "\n\n";

   cout << "num[5] is \t" << num[5] << "\n";
   cout << "(num+5)[0] is \t" << (num+5)[0] << "\n";
   cout << "(num+2)[3] is \t" << (num+2)[3] << "\n\n";

   cout << "(3+num)[1] is \t" << (3+num)[1] << "\n";
   cout << "3+num[1] is \t" << 3+num[1] << "\n";
   return;
}
```

Here is the output of this program:

```
num[0] is        100
(num+0)[0] is    100
(num-2)[2] is    100
```

```
num[1] is        200
(num+1)[0] is    200

num[5] is        600
(num+5)[0] is    600
(num+2)[3] is    600

(3+num)[1] is    500
3+num[1] is      203
```

2. The following program prints strings and characters from a character array. The couts all print properly.

```cpp
// Filename: C24REF2.CPP
// Prints elements and strings from an array.
#include <iostream.h>
void main()
{
   char names[]={'T','e','d','\0','E','v','a','\0',
                 'S', 'a','m','\0'};

   // Must use extra percent (%) to print %s and %c.
   cout << "names " << names << "\n";
   cout << "names+0 " << names+0 << "\n";
   cout << "names+1 " << names+1 << "\n";
   cout << "names+2 " << names+2 << "\n";
   cout << "names+3 " << names+3 << "\n";
   cout << "names+5 " << names+5 << "\n";
   cout << "names+8 " << names+8 << "\n\n";

   cout << "(names+0)[0] " << (names+0)[0] << "\n";
   cout << "(names+0)[1] " << (names+0)[1] << "\n";
   cout << "(names+0)[2] " << (names+0)[2] << "\n";
   cout << "(names+0)[3] " << (names+0)[3] << "\n";
   cout << "(names+0)[4] " << (names+0)[4] << "\n";
   cout << "(names+0)[5] " << (names+0)[5] << "\n\n";

   cout << "(names+2)[0] " << (names+2)[0] << "\n";
   cout << "(names+2)[1] " << (names+2)[1] << "\n";
   cout << "(names+1)[4] " << (names+1)[4] << "\n\n";

   return;
}
```

Study the output shown below by comparing it to the program. You will learn more about strings, characters, and character array referencing from studying this one example than from 20 pages of textual description.

```
names Ted
names+0 Ted
names+1 ed
names+2 d
names+3
names+5 va
names+8 Sam

(names+0)[0] T
(names+0)[1] e
(names+0)[2] d
(names+0)[3]
(names+0)[4] E
(names+0)[5] v

(names+2)[0] d
(names+2)[1]
(names+1)[4] v
```

Review Questions

The answers to the review questions are in Appendix B.

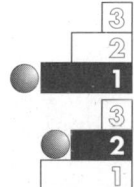

1. True or false: You must access an array in the same order you initialized it.

2. Where did the bubble sort get its name?

3. Are the following values sorted in ascending or descending order?

33	55	78	78	90	102	435	859
976	4092						

4. How does C++ use the name of an array?

5. Given the following array definition:

```
char teams[] = {'E','a','g','l','e','s','\0',
                'R', 'a','m','s','\0'};
```

What is printed with each of these statements? (Answer "invalid" if the cout is illegal.)

a. cout << teams;

b. cout << teams+7;

c. cout << (teams+3);

d. cout << teams[0];

e. cout << (teams+0)[0];

f. cout << (teams+5);

Review Exercises

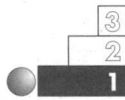

1. Write a program to store six of your friends' ages in a single array. Assign the ages in random order. Print the ages, from low to high, on-screen.

2. Modify the program in Exercise 1 to print the ages in descending order.

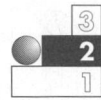

3. Using the new approach of subscripting arrays, rewrite the programs in Exercises 1 and 2. Always put a 0 in the subscript brackets, modifying the address instead (use (ages+3)[0] rather than ages[3]).

4. Sometimes *parallel arrays* are used in programs that must track more than one list of values that are related. For instance, suppose you had to maintain an inventory, tracking the integer part numbers, prices, and quantities of each item. This would require three arrays: an integer part number array, a floating-point price array, and an integer quantity array. Each array would have the same number of elements (the total number of parts in the inventory). Write a program to maintain such an inventory, and reserve enough elements

for 100 parts in the inventory. Present the user with an input screen. When the user enters a part number, search the part number array. When you locate the position of the part, print the corresponding price and quantity. If the part does not exist, enable the user to add it to the inventory, along with the matching price and quantity.

Summary

You are beginning to see the true power of programming languages. Arrays give you the ability to search and sort lists of values. Sorting and searching are what computers do best; computers can quickly scan through hundreds and even thousands of values, looking for a match. Scanning through files of paper by hand, looking for just the right number, takes much more time. By stepping through arrays, your program can quickly scan, print, sort, and calculate a list of values. You now have the tools to sort lists of numbers, as well as search for values in a list.

You will use the concepts learned here for sorting and searching lists of character string data as well, when you learn a little more about the way C++ manipulates strings and pointers. To help build a solid foundation for this and more advanced material, you now know how to reference array elements without using conventional subscripts.

Now that you have mastered this chapter, the next one will be easy. Chapter 25, "Multidimensional Arrays," shows you how you can keep track of arrays in a different format called a *matrix*. Not all lists of data lend themselves to matrices, but you should be prepared for when you need them.

25

Multidimensional Arrays

Some data fits in lists, such as the data discussed in the previous two chapters, and other data is better suited for tables of information. This chapter takes arrays one step further. The previous chapters introduced single-dimensional arrays; arrays that have only one subscript and represent lists of values.

This chapter introduces arrays of more than one dimension, called *multidimensional arrays*. Multidimensional arrays, sometimes called *tables* or *matrices*, have at least two dimensions (rows and columns). Many times they have more than two.

This chapter introduces the following concepts:

- ◆ Multidimensional arrays

- ◆ Reserving storage for multidimensional arrays

- ◆ Putting data in multidimensional arrays

- ◆ Using nested `for` loops to process multidimensional arrays

If you understand single-dimensional arrays, you should have no trouble understanding arrays that have more than one dimension.

Multidimensional Array Basics

A multidimensional array has more than one subscript.

A multidimensional array is an array with more than one subscript. Whereas a single-dimensional array is a list of values, a multidimensional array simulates a table of values, or multiple tables of values. The most commonly used table is a two-dimensional table (an array with two subscripts).

Suppose a softball team wanted to keep track of its players' batting records. The team played 10 games, and there are 15 players on the team. Table 25.1 shows the team's batting record.

Table 25.1. A softball team's batting record.

Player Name	Game 1	2	3	4	5	6	7	8	9	10
Adams	2	1	0	0	2	3	3	1	1	2
Berryhill	1	0	3	2	5	1	2	2	1	0
Downing	1	0	2	1	0	0	0	0	2	0
Edwards	0	3	6	4	6	4	5	3	6	3
Franks	2	2	3	2	1	0	2	3	1	0
Grady	1	3	2	0	1	5	2	1	2	1
Howard	3	1	1	1	2	0	1	0	4	3
Jones	2	2	1	2	4	1	0	7	1	0
Martin	5	4	5	1	1	0	2	4	1	5
Powers	2	2	3	1	0	2	1	3	1	2
Smith	1	1	2	1	3	4	1	0	3	2
Smithtown	1	0	1	2	1	0	3	4	1	2
Townsend	0	0	0	0	0	0	1	0	0	0
Ulmer	2	2	2	2	2	1	1	3	1	3
Williams	2	3	1	0	1	2	1	2	0	3

Do you see that the softball table is a two-dimensional table? It has rows (the first dimension) and columns (the second dimension). Therefore, this is called a two-dimensional table with 15 rows and 10 columns. (Generally, the number of rows is specified first.)

Each row has a player's name, and each column has a game number associated with it, but these are not part of the actual data. The data consists of only 150 values (15 rows by 10 columns). The data in a two-dimensional table always is the same type of data; in this case, every value is an integer. If it were a table of salaries, every element would be a floating-point decimal.

The number of dimensions, in this case two, corresponds to the dimensions in the physical world. The single-dimensioned array is a line, or list of values. Two dimensions represent both length and width. You write on a piece of paper in two dimensions; two dimensions represent a flat surface. Three dimensions represent width, length, and depth. You have seen 3-D movies. Not only do the images have width and height, but they also seem to have depth. Figure 25.1 shows what a three-dimensional array looks like if it has a depth of four, six rows, and three columns. Notice that a three-dimensional table resembles a cube.

A three-dimensional table has three dimensions: depth, rows, and columns.

It is difficult to visualize more than three dimensions. However, you can think of each dimension after three as another occurrence. In other words, a list of one player's season batting record can be stored in an array. The team's batting record (as shown in Table 25.1) is two-dimensional. The league, made of up several teams' batting records, represents a three-dimensional table. Each team (the depth of the table) has rows and columns of batting data. If there is more than one league, it is another dimension (another set of data).

C++ enables you to store several dimensions, although "real-world" data rarely requires more than two or three.

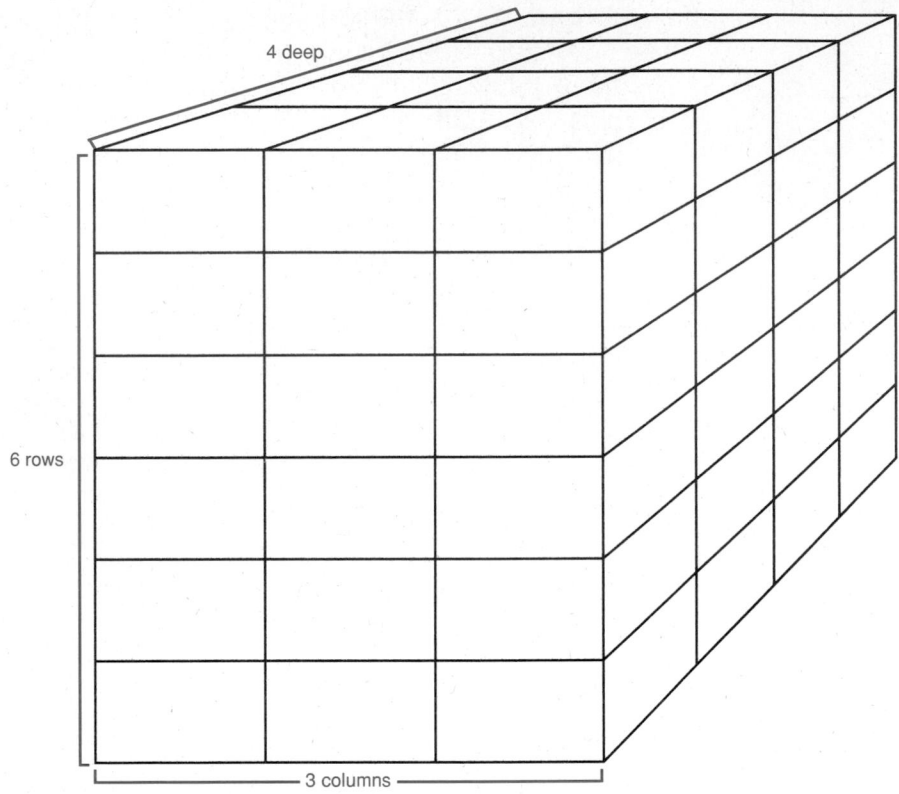

4 deep

6 rows

3 columns

Figure 25.1. Representing a three-dimensional table (a cube).

Reserving Multidimensional Arrays

When you reserve a multidimensional array, you must inform C++ that the array has more than one dimension by putting more than one subscript in brackets after the array name. You must put a separate number, in brackets, for each dimension in the table. For example, to reserve the team data from Table 25.1, you use the following multidimensional array declaration.

Declare an integer array called teams *with 15 rows and 10 columns.*

```
int teams[15][10];  // Reserves a two-dimensional table.
```

> **CAUTION:** Unlike other programming languages, C++ requires you to enclose each dimension in brackets. Do not reserve multidimensional array storage like this:
>
> ```
> int teams[15,10];   // Invalid table declaration.
> ```

Properly reserving the teams table produces a table with 150 elements. Figure 25.2 shows what each element's subscript looks like.

columns

[0] [0]	[0] [1]	[0] [2]	[0] [3]	[0] [4]	[0] [5]	[0] [6]	[0] [7]	[0] [8]	[0] [9]
[1] [0]	[1] [1]	[1] [2]	[1] [3]	[1] [4]	[1] [5]	[1] [6]	[1] [7]	[1] [8]	[1] [9]
[2] [0]	[2] [1]	[2] [2]	[2] [3]	[2] [4]	[2] [5]	[2] [6]	[2] [7]	[2] [8]	[2] [9]
[3] [0]	[3] [1]	[3] [2]	[3] [3]	[3] [4]	[3] [5]	[3] [6]	[3] [7]	[3] [8]	[3] [9]
[4] [0]	[4] [1]	[4] [2]	[4] [3]	[4] [4]	[4] [5]	[4] [6]	[4] [7]	[4] [8]	[4] [9]
[5] [0]	[5] [1]	[5] [2]	[5] [3]	[5] [4]	[5] [5]	[5] [6]	[5] [7]	[5] [8]	[5] [9]
[0] [0]	[0] [1]	[0] [2]	[0] [3]	[0] [4]	[6] [5]	[6] [6]	[6] [7]	[6] [8]	[6] [9]
[7] [0]	[7] [1]	[7] [2]	[7] [3]	[7] [4]	[7] [5]	[7] [6]	[7] [7]	[7] [8]	[7] [9]
[8] [0]	[8] [1]	[8] [2]	[8] [3]	[8] [4]	[8] [5]	[8] [6]	[8] [7]	[8] [8]	[8] [9]
[9] [0]	[9] [1]	[9] [2]	[9] [3]	[9] [4]	[9] [5]	[9] [6]	[9] [7]	[9] [8]	[9] [9]
[10] [0]	[10] [1]	[10] [2]	[10] [3]	[10] [4]	[10] [5]	[10] [6]	[10] [7]	[10] [8]	[10] [9]
[11] [0]	[11] [1]	[11] [2]	[11] [3]	[11] [4]	[11] [5]	[11] [6]	[11] [7]	[11] [8]	[11] [9]
[12] [0]	[12] [1]	[12] [2]	[12] [3]	[12] [4]	[12] [5]	[12] [6]	[12] [7]	[12] [8]	[12] [9]
[13] [0]	[13] [1]	[13] [2]	[13] [3]	[13] [4]	[13] [5]	[13] [6]	[13] [7]	[13] [8]	[13] [9]
[14] [0]	[14] [1]	[14] [2]	[14] [3]	[14] [4]	[14] [5]	[14] [6]	[14] [7]	[14] [8]	[14] [9]

rows

Figure 25.2. Subscripts for the softball team table.

If you had to track three teams, each with 15 players and 10 games, the three-dimensional table would be created as follows:

```
int teams[3][15][10]; // Reserves a three-dimensional table.
```

The far-right dimension always represents columns, the next represents rows, and so on.

When creating a two-dimensional table, always put the maximum number of rows first, and the maximum number of columns second. C++ always uses 0 as the starting subscript of each dimension. The last element, the lower-right element of the teams table, is teams[2][14][9].

Examples

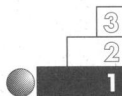

1. Suppose you wanted to keep track of utility bills for the year. You can store 12 months of four utilities in a two-dimensional table of floating-point amounts, as the following array declaration demonstrates:

```
float utilities[12][4];        // Reserves 48 elements.
```

You can compute the total number of elements in a multi-dimensional array by multiplying the subscripts. Because 12 times 4 is 48, there are 48 elements in this array (12 rows, 4 columns). Each of these elements is a floating-point data type.

2. If you were keeping track of five years' worth of utilities, you have to add an extra dimension. The first dimension is the years, the second is the months, and the last is the individual utilities. Here is how you reserve storage:

```
float utilities[5][12][4];     // Reserves 240 elements.
```

Mapping Arrays to Memory

C++ approaches multidimensional arrays a little differently than most programming languages do. When you use subscripts, you do not have to understand the internal representation of multidimensional arrays. However, most C++ programmers think a deeper understanding of these arrays is important, especially when programming advanced applications.

A two-dimensional array is actually an *array of arrays*. You program multidimensional arrays as though they were tables with rows and columns. A two-dimensional array is actually a single-dimensional array, but each of its elements is not an integer, floating-point, or character, but another array.

Knowing that a multidimensional array is an array of other arrays is critical when passing and receiving such arrays. C++ passes all arrays, including multidimensional arrays, by address. Suppose you were using an integer array called scores, reserved as a 5-by-6 table. You can pass scores to a function called print_it(), as follows:

```
print_it(scores);            // Passes table to a function.
```

The function print_it() has to identify the type of parameter being passed to it. The print_it() function also must recognize that the parameter is an array. If scores were one-dimensional, you could receive it as

```
print_it(int scores[])       // Works only if scores
                             // is one-dimensional.
```

or

```
print_it(int scores[10])     // Assuming scores
                             // has 10 elements.
```

If scores were a multidimensional table, you would have to designate each pair of brackets and put the maximum number of subscripts in its brackets, as in

```
print_it(int scores[5][6])   // Inform print_it() of
                             // the array's dimensions.
```

or

```
print_it(int scores[][6])    // Inform print_it() of
                             // the array's dimensions.
```

Notice you do not have to explicitly state the maximum subscript on the first dimension when receiving multidimensional arrays, but you must designate the second. If scores were a three-dimensional table, dimensioned as 10 by 5 by 6, you would receive it with print_it() as

```
print_it(int scores[][5][6])    // Only first dimension
                                // is optional.
```

or

```
print_it(int scores[10][5][6])    // Inform print_it() of
                                  // array's dimensions.
```

You should not have to worry too much about the way tables are physically stored. Even though a two-dimensional table is actually an array of arrays (and each of those arrays contains another array if it is a three-dimensional table), you can use subscripts to program multidimensional arrays as if they were stored in row-and-column order.

Multidimensional arrays are stored in *row order*. Suppose you want to keep track of a 3-by-4 table. The top of Figure 25.3 shows how that table (and its subscripts) are visualized. Despite the two-dimensional table organization, your memory is still sequential storage. C++ has to map multidimensional arrays to single-dimensional memory, and it does so in row order.

Each row fills memory before the next row is stored. Figure 25.3 shows how a 3-by-4 table is mapped to memory.

The entire first row (table[0][0] through table[0][3]) is stored first in memory before any of the second row. A table is actually an array of arrays, and, as you learned in previous chapters, array elements are always stored sequentially in memory. Therefore, the first row (array) completely fills memory before the second row. Figure 25.3 shows how two-dimensional arrays map to memory.

C++ stores multidimensional arrays in row order.

Defining Multidimensional Arrays

C++ is not picky about the way you define a multidimensional array when you initialize it at declaration time. As with single-dimensional arrays, you initialize multidimensional arrays with braces that designate dimensions. Because a multidimensional array is an array of arrays, you can nest braces when you initialize them.

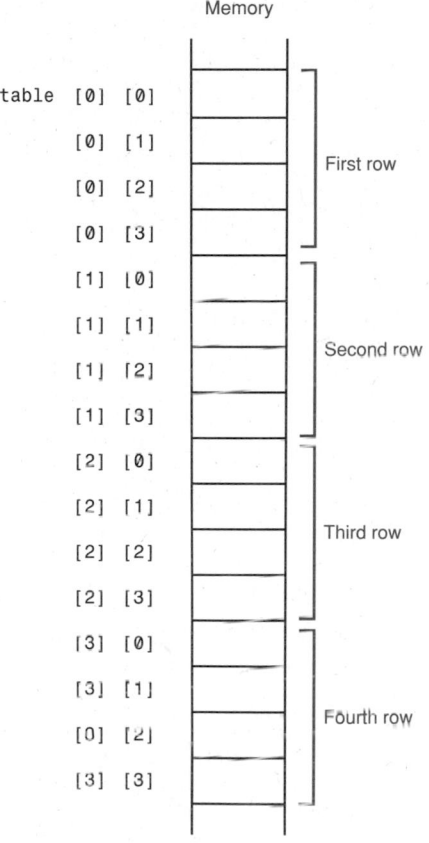

Figure 25.3. Mapping a two-dimensional table to memory.

The following three array definitions fill the three arrays ara1, ara2, and ara3, as shown in Figure 25.4:

```
int ara1[5] = {8, 5, 3, 25, 41};  // One-dimensional array.
int ara2[2][4]={{4, 3, 2, 1},{1, 2, 3, 4}};
int ara3[3][4]={{1, 2, 3, 4},{5, 6, 7, 8},{9, 10, 11, 12}};
```

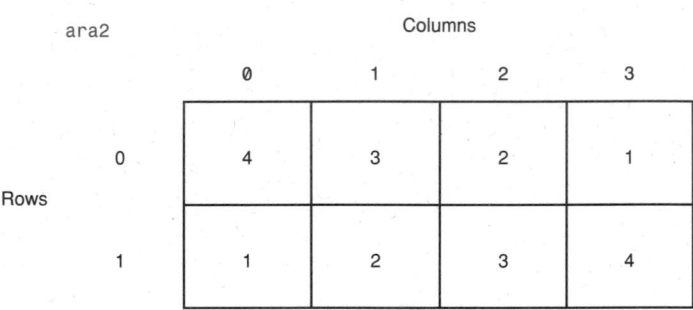

Figure 25.4. After initializing a table.

Notice that the multidimensional arrays are stored in row order. In ara3, the first row receives the first four elements of the definition (1, 2, 3, and 4).

> **TIP:** To make a multidimensional array initialization match the array's subscripts, some programmers like to show how arrays are filled. Because C++ programs are free-form, you can initialize ara2 and ara3 as
>
> ```
> int ara2[2][4]={{4, 3, 2, 1},   // Does exactly the same
>                 {1, 2, 3, 4}}; // thing as before.
>
>
> int ara3[3][4]={{1, 2, 3, 4},
>                 {5, 6, 7, 8},
>                 {9, 10, 11, 12}; // Visually more
>                                  // obvious.
> ```

You can initialize a multidimensional array as if it were single-dimensional in C++. You must keep track of the row order if you do this. For instance, the following two definitions also reserve storage for and initialize ara2 and ara3:

```
int ara2[2][4]={4, 3, 2, 1, 1, 2, 3, 4};
int ara3[3][4]={1, 2, 3, 4, 5, 6, 7, 8, 9, 10, 11, 12, 13};
```

There is no difference between initializing ara2 and ara3 with or without the nested braces. The nested braces seem to show the dimensions and how C++ fills them a little better, but the choice of using nested braces is yours.

> **TIP:** Multidimensional arrays (unless they are global) are not initialized to specific values unless you assign them values at declaration time or in the program. As with single-dimensional arrays, if you initialize one or more of the elements, but not all of them, C++ fills the rest with zeros. If you want to fill an entire multidimensional array with zeros, you can do so with the following:
>
> ```
> float sales[3][4][7][2] = {0};   // Fills all sales
>                                  // with zeros.
> ```

One last point to consider is how multidimensional arrays are viewed by your compiler. Many people program in C++ for years, but never understand how tables are stored internally. As long as you use subscripts, a table's internal representation should not matter. When you learn about pointer variables, however, you might want to know how C++ stores your tables in case you want to reference them with pointers (as shown in the next few chapters).

Figure 25.5 shows the way C++ stores a 3-by-4 table in memory. Unlike single-dimensional arrays, each element is stored contiguously, but notice how C++ views the data. Because a table is an array of arrays, the array name contains the address of the start of the primary array. Each of those elements points to the arrays it contains (the data in each row). This coverage of table storage is for your information only, at this point. As you become more proficient in C++, and write more powerful programs that manipulate internal memory, you might want to review this table storage method.

Tables and for Loops

As the following examples show, nested for loops are useful when you want to loop through every element of a multidimensional table.

For instance, the section of code,

```
for (row=0; row<2; row++)
   { for (col=0; col<3; col++)
       { cout << row << " " << col "\n"; }
   }
```

produces the following output:

```
0    0
0    1
0    2
1    0
1    1
1    2
```

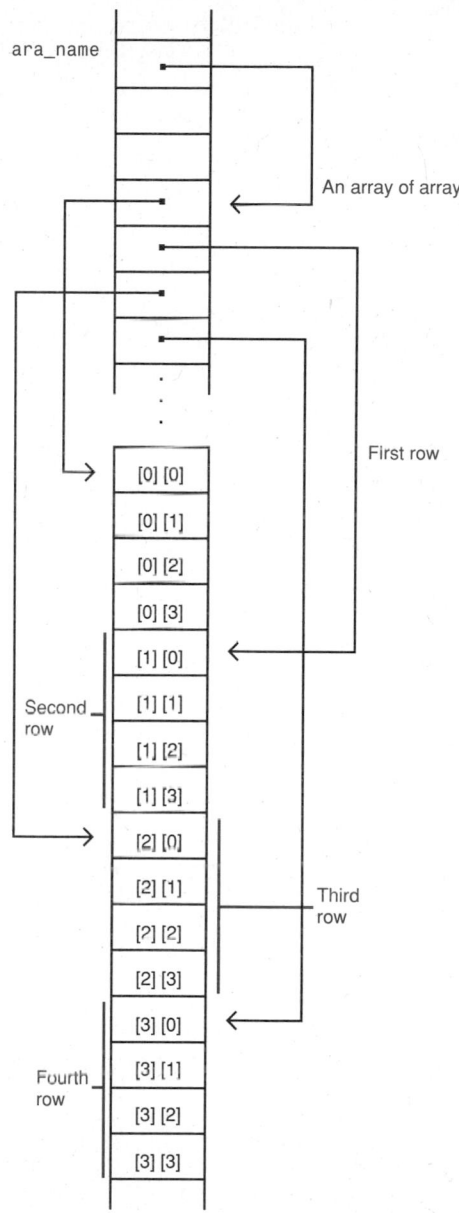

Figure 25.5. Internal representation of a two-dimensional table.

These numbers are the subscripts, in row order, for a two-row by three-column table dimensioned with

```
int table[2][3];
```

Nested loops work well with multi-dimensional arrays.

Notice there are as many `for` loops as there are subscripts in the array (two). The outside loop represents the first subscript (the rows), and the inside loop represents the second subscript (the columns). The nested `for` loop steps through each element of the table.

You can use `cin`, `gets()`, `get`, and other input functions to fill a table, and you also can assign values to the elements when declaring the table. More often, the data comes from data files on the disk. Regardless of what method stores the values in multidimensional arrays, nested `for` loops are excellent control statements to step through the subscripts. The following examples demonstrate how nested `for` loops work with multidimensional arrays.

Examples

1. The following statements reserve enough memory elements for a television station's ratings (*A* through *D*) for one week:

   ```
   char ratings[7][48];
   ```

   These statements reserve enough elements to hold seven days (the rows) of ratings for each 30-minute time slot (48 of them in a day).

   Every element in a table is always the same type. In this case, each element is a character variable. Some are initialized with the following assignment statements:

   ```
   shows[3][12] = 'B';      // Stores B in 4th row, 13th column.
   shows[1][5] = 'A' ;      // Stores C in 2nd row, 6th column.
   shows[6][20] = getch();  // Stores the letter the user types.
   ```

2. A computer company sells two sizes of disks: 3 1/2-inch and 5 1/4-inch. Each disk comes in one of four capacities: single-sided double-density, double-sided double-density, single-sided high-density, and double-sided high-density.

The disk inventory is well-suited for a two-dimensional table. The company determined that the disks have the following retail prices:

| | Double Density | | High Density | |
	Single	Double	Single	Double
3 1/2-*inch*	2.30	2.75	3.20	3.50
5 1/4-*inch*	1.75	2.10	2.60	2.95

The company wants to store the price of each disk in a table for easy access. The following program stores the prices with assignment statements.

```
// Filename: C25DISK1.CPP
// Assigns disk prices to a table.
#include <iostream.h>
#include <iomanip.h>
void main()
{
   float disks[2][4];  // Table of disk prices.
   int row, col;       // Subscript variables.

   disks[0][0] = 2.39;     // Row 1, column 1
   disks[0][1] = 2.75;     // Row 1, column 2
   disks[0][2] = 3.29;     // Row 1, column 3
   disks[0][3] = 3.59;     // Row 1, column 4
   disks[1][0] = 1.75;     // Row 2, column 1
   disks[1][1] = 2.19;     // Row 2, column 2
   disks[1][2] = 2.69;     // Row 2, column 3
   disks[1][3] = 2.95;     // Row 2, column 4

   // Print the prices.
   for (row=0; row<2; row++)
      { for (col=0; col<4; col++)
        { cout << "$" << setprecision(2) <<
                  disks[row][col] << "\n"; }
      }

   return;
}
```

BEGIN

Fill disk inventory table

Print table to screen

END

This program displays the prices as follows:

```
$2.39
$2.75
$3.29
$3.59
$1.75
$2.19
$2.69
$2.95
```

It prints them one line at a time, without any descriptive titles. Although the output is not labeled, it illustrates how you can use assignment statements to initialize a table, and how nested for loops can print the elements.

3. The preceding disk inventory would be displayed better if the output had descriptive titles. Before you add titles, it is helpful for you to see how to print a table in its native row and column format.

Typically, you use a nested for loop, such as the one in the previous example, to print rows and columns. You should not output a newline character with every cout, however. If you do, you see one value per line, as in the previous program's output, which is not the row and column format of the table.

You do not want to see every disk price on one line, but you want each row of the table printed on a separate line. You must insert a cout << "\n"; to send the cursor to the next line each time the row number changes. Printing newlines after each row prints the table in its row and column format, as this program shows:

```
// Filename: C25DISK2.CPP
// Assigns disk prices to a table
// and prints them in a table format.
#include <iostream.h>
#include <iomanip.h>
void main()
{
```

```
float disks[2][4];   // Table of disk prices.
int row, col;

disks[0][0] = 2.39;      // Row 1, column 1
disks[0][1] = 2.75;      // Row 1, column 2
disks[0][2] = 3.29;      // Row 1, column 3
disks[0][3] = 3.59;      // Row 1, column 4
disks[1][0] = 1.75;      // Row 2, column 1
disks[1][1] = 2.19;      // Row 2, column 2
disks[1][2] = 2.69;      // Row 2, column 3
disks[1][3] = 2.95;      // Row 2, column 4

// Print the prices
for (row=0; row<2; row++)
   { for (col=0; col<4; col++)
     { cout << "$" << setprecision(2) <<
              disks[row][col] << "\t";
     }

     cout << "\n";   // Prints a new line after each row.
   }

   return;
}
```

Here is the output of the disk prices in their native table order:

$2.39	$2.75	$3.29	$3.59
$1.75	$2.19	$2.69	$2.95

4. To add the titles, simply print a row of titles before the first row of values, then print a new column title before each column, as shown in the following program:

```
// Filename: C25DISK3.CPP
// Assigns disk prices to a table
// and prints them in a table format with titles.
#include <iostream.h>
#include <iomanip.h>
```

```
void main()
{
   float disks[2][4];   // Table of disk prices.
   int row, col;

   disks[0][0] = 2.39;       // Row 1, column 1
   disks[0][1] = 2.75;       // Row 1, column 2
   disks[0][2] = 3.29;       // Row 1, column 3
   disks[0][3] = 3.59;       // Row 1, column 4
   disks[1][0] = 1.75;       // Row 2, column 1
   disks[1][1] = 2.19;       // Row 2, column 2
   disks[1][2] = 2.69;       // Row 2, column 3
   disks[1][3] = 2.95;       // Row 2, column 4

   // Print the column titles.
   cout << "\tSingle-sided\tDouble-sided\tSingle-sided\t" <<
           "Double-sided\n";
   cout << "\tDouble-density\tDouble-density\tHigh-density" <<
           "\tHigh-density\n";

   // Print the prices
   for (row=0; row<2; row++)
      { if (row == 0)
        { cout << "3-1/2\"\t"; }            // Need \" to
                                            // print quotation.

      else
        { cout << "5-1/4\"\t"; }
        for (col=0; col<4; col++)     // Print the current row.
        { cout << setprecision(2) << "$" << disks[row][col]
             << "\t\t";
          }
        cout << "\n";     // Print a newline after each row.
      }

   return;
}
```

Here is the output from this program:

	Single-sided Double-density	Double-sided Double-density	Single-sided High-density	Double-sided High-density
3-1/2"	$2.39	$2.75	$3.29	$3.59
5-1/4"	$1.75	$2.19	$2.69	$2.95

Review Questions

The answers to the review questions are in Appendix B.

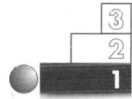

1. What statement reserves a two-dimensional table of integers called `scores` with five rows and six columns?

2. What statement reserves a three-dimensional table of four character arrays called `initials` with 10 rows and 20 columns?

3. In the following statement, which subscript (first or second) represents rows and which represents columns?

   ```
   int weights[5][10];
   ```

4. How many elements are reserved with the following statement?

   ```
   int ara[5][6];
   ```

5. The following table of integers is called `ara`:

4	1	3	5	9
10	2	12	1	6
25	42	2	91	8

What values do the following elements contain?

a. `ara[2][2]`

b. `ara[0][1]`

c. `ara[2][3]`

d. `ara[2][4]`

6. What control statement is best for stepping through multidimensional arrays?

7. Notice the following section of a program:

```
int grades[3][5] = {80,90,96,73,65,67,90,68,92,84,70,
                    55,95,78,100};
```

What are the values of the following:

a. `grades[2][3]`

b. `grades[2][4]`

c. `grades[0][1]`

Review Exercises

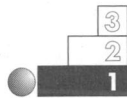

1. Write a program that stores and prints the numbers from 1 to 21 in a 3-by-7 table. (*Hint:* Remember C++ begins subscripts at 0.)

2. Write a program that reserves storage for three years' worth of sales data for five salespeople. Use assignment statements to fill the table with data, then print it, one value per line.

3. Instead of using assignment statements, use the `cin` function to fill the salespeople data from Exercise 2.

4. Write a program that tracks the grades for five classes, each having 10 students. Input the data using the `cin` function. Print the table in its native row and column format.

Summary

You now know how to create, initialize, and process multidimensional arrays. Although not all data fits in the compact format of tables, much does. Using nested `for` loops makes stepping through a multidimensional array straightforward.

One of the limitations of a multidimensional array is that each element must be the same data type. This keeps you from being able to store several kinds of data in tables. Chapter 28, "Structures," shows you how to store data in different ways to overcome this limitation.

Pointers

C++ reveals its true power through pointer variables. Pointer variables (or *pointers*, as they generally are called) are variables that contain addresses of other variables. All variables you have seen so far have held data values. You understand that variables hold various data types: character, integer, floating-point, and so on. Pointer variables contain the location of regular data variables; they in effect point to the data because they hold the address of the data.

When first learning C++, students of the language tend to shy away from pointers, thinking that pointers will be difficult. Pointers do not have to be difficult. In fact, after you work with them for a while, you will find they are easier to use than arrays (and much more flexible).

This chapter introduces the following concepts:

♦ Pointers

♦ Pointers of different data types

♦ The "address of" (&) operator

♦ The dereferencing (*) operator

♦ Arrays of pointers

Pointers offer a highly efficient means of accessing and changing data. Because pointers contain the actual address of your data, your compiler has less work to do when finding that data in memory. Pointers do not have to link data to specific variable names. A pointer can point to an unnamed data value. With pointers, you gain a "different view" of your data.

Introduction to Pointer Variables

Pointers contain addresses of other variables.

Pointers are variables. They follow all the normal naming rules of regular, nonpointer variables. As with regular variables, you must declare pointer variables before using them. There is a type of pointer for every data type in C++; there are integer pointers, character pointers, floating-point pointers, and so on. You can declare global pointers or local pointers, depending on where you declare them.

About the only difference between pointer variables and regular variables is the data they hold. Pointers do not contain data in the usual sense of the word. Pointers contain addresses of data. If you need a quick review of addresses and memory, see Appendix A, "Memory Addressing, Binary, and Hexadecimal Review."

There are two pointer operators in C++:

&   The "address of" operator

*   The dereferencing operator

Don't let these operators throw you; you might have seen them before! The & is the bitwise AND operator (from Chapter 11, "Additional C++ Operators") and the * means, of course, multiplication. These are called *overloaded* operators. They perform more than one function, depending on how you use them in your programs. C++ does not confuse * for multiplication when you use it as a dereferencing operator with pointers.

Any time you see the & used with pointers, think of the words "address of." The & operator always produces the memory address of whatever it precedes. The * operator, when used with pointers, either declares a pointer or dereferences the pointer's value. The next section explains each of these operators.

Declaring Pointers

Because you must declare all pointers before using them, the best way to begin learning about pointers is to understand how to declare and define them. Actually, declaring pointers is almost as easy as declaring regular variables. After all, pointers are variables.

If you must declare a variable that holds your age, you could do so with the following variable declaration:

```
int age=30;        // Declare a variable to hold my age.
```

Declaring age like this does several things. It enables C++ to identify a variable called age, and to reserve storage for that variable. Using this format also enables C++ to recognize that you will store only integers in age, not floating-point or double floating-point data. The declaration also requests that C++ store the value of 30 in age after it reserves storage for age.

Where did C++ store age in memory? As the programmer, you should not really care where C++ stores age. You do not have to know the variable's address because you will never refer to age by its address. If you want to calculate with or print age, you call it by its name, age.

> **TIP:** Make your pointer variable names meaningful. The name file_ptr makes more sense than x13 for a file-pointing variable, although either name is allowed.

Suppose you want to declare a pointer variable. This pointer variable will not hold your age, but it will point to age, the variable that holds your age. (Why you would want to do this is explained in this and the next few chapters.) p_age might be a good name for the pointer variable. Figure 26.1 illustrates what you want to do. The figure assumes C++ stored age at the address 350,606. Your C++ compiler, however, arbitrarily determines the address of age, so it could be anything.

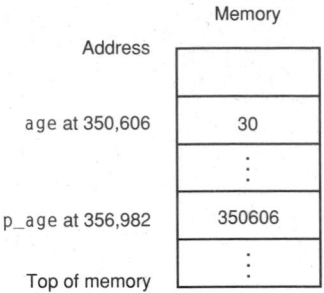

Figure 26.1. p_age contains the address of age; p_age points to the age variable.

The name p_age has nothing to do with pointers, except that it is the name you made up for the pointer to age. Just as you can name variables anything (as long as the name follows the legal naming rules of variables), p_age could just as easily have been named house, x43344, space_trek, or whatever else you wanted to call it. This reinforces the idea that a pointer is just a variable you reserve in your program. Create meaningful variable names, even for pointer variables. p_age is a good name for a variable that points to age (as would be ptr_age and ptr_to_age).

To declare the p_age pointer variable, you must program the following:

```
int * p_age;          // Declares an integer pointer.
```

Similar to the declaration for age, this declaration reserves a variable called p_age. The p_age variable is not a normal integer variable, however. Because of the dereferencing operator, *, C++ knows this is to be a pointer variable. Some C++ programmers prefer to declare such a variable without a space after the *, as follows:

```
int *p_age;           // Declares an integer pointer.
```

Either method is okay, but you must remember the * is *not* part of the name. When you later use p_age, you will not prefix the name with the *, unless you are dereferencing it at the time (as later examples show).

> **TIP:** Whenever the dereferencing operator, *, appears in a variable definition, the variable being declared is *always* a pointer variable.

Consider the declaration for p_age if the asterisk were not there: C++ would think you were declaring a regular integer variable. The * is important, because it tells C++ to interpret p_age as a pointer variable, not as a normal, data variable.

Assigning Values to Pointers

Pointers can point only to data of their own type.

p_age is an integer pointer. This is very important. p_age can point only to integer values, never to floating-point, double floating-point, or even character variables. If you needed to point to a floating-point variable, you might do so with a pointer declared as

```
float *point;     // Declares a floating-point pointer.
```

As with any automatic variable, C++ does not initialize pointers when you declare them. If you declared p_age as previously described, and you wanted p_age to point to age, you would have to explicitly assign p_age to the address of age. The following statement does this:

```
p_age = &age;     // Assign the address of age to p_age.
```

What value is now in p_age? You do not know exactly, but you know it is the address of age, wherever that is. Rather than assign the address of age to p_age with an assignment operator, you can declare and initialize pointers at the same time. These lines declare and initialize both age and p_age:

```
int age=30;       // Declares a regular integer
                  // variable, putting 30 in it.
```

```
int *p_age=&age;     // Declares an integer pointer,
                     // initializing it with the address
                     // of p_age.
```

These two lines produce the variables described in Figure 26.1.

If you wanted to print the value of age, you could do so with the following cout:

```
cout << age;          // Prints the value of age.
```

You also can print the value of age like this:

Print value that pointer points to

```
cout << *p_age;       // Dereferences p_age.
```

The dereference operator produces a value that tells the pointer where to point. Without the *, the last cout would print an address (the address of age). With the *, the cout prints the value at that address.

You can assign a different value to age with the following statement:

```
age=41;               // Assigns a new value to age.
```

You also can assign a value to age like this:

```
*p_age=41;
```

This declaration assigns 41 to the value to which p_age points.

> **TIP:** The * appears before a pointer variable in only two places—when you declare a pointer variable, and when you dereference a pointer variable (to find the data it points to).

Pointers and Parameters

Now that you understand the pointer's * and & operators, you can finally see why scanf()'s requirements were not as strict as they first seemed. While passing a regular variable to scanf(), you had to prefix the variable with the & operator. For instance, the following scanf() gets three integer values from the user:

```
scanf(" %d %d %d", &num1, &num2, &num3);
```

This scanf() does not pass the three variables, but passes the addresses of the three variables. Because scanf() knows the exact locations of these parameters in memory (because their addresses were passed), it goes to those addresses and puts the keyboard input values into those addresses.

This is the only way scanf() could work. If you passed these variables by copy, without putting the "address of" operator (&) before them, scanf() would get the keyboard input and fill a *copy* of the variables, but not the actual variables num1, num2, and num3. When scanf() then returned control to your program, you would not have the input values. Of course, the cin operator does not have the ampersand (&) requirement and is easier to use for most C++ programs.

You might recall from Chapter 18, "Passing Values," that you can override C++'s normal default of passing by copy (or "by value"). To pass by address, receive the variable preceded by an & in the receiving function. The following function receives tries by address:

```
pr_it(int &tries);   // Receive integer tries in pr_it() by
                     // address (pr_it would normally receive
                     // tries by copy).
```

Now that you understand the & and * operators, you can understand completely the passing of nonarray parameters by address to functions. (Arrays default to passing by address without requiring that you use &.)

Examples

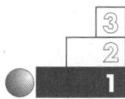

1. The following section of code declares three regular variables of three different data types, and three corresponding pointer variables:

```
char initial= 'Q';    // Declares three regular variables
int num=40;           // of three different types.
float sales=2321.59;
```

```
char *p_initial=&initial;   // Declares three pointers.
int * ptr_num=&num;         // Pointer names and spacing
float * sales_add = &sales; // after * are not critical.
```

2. Just like regular variables, you can initialize pointers with assignment statements. You do not have to initialize them when you declare them. The next few lines of code are equivalent to the code in Example 1:

```
char initial;      // Declares three regular variables
int num;           // of three different types.
float sales;

char *p_initial;   // Declares three pointers but does
int * ptr_num;     // not initialize them yet.
float * sales_add;

initial='Q';       // Initializes the regular variables
num=40;            // with values.
sales=2321.59;

p_initial=&initial;    // Initializes the pointers with
ptr_num=&num;          // the addresses of their
sales_add=&sales;      // corresponding variables.
```

Notice that you do not put the * operator before the pointer variable names when assigning them values. You would prefix a pointer variable with the * only if you were dereferencing it.

> **NOTE:** In this example, the pointer variables could have been assigned the addresses of the regular variables before the regular variables were assigned values. There would be no difference in the operation. The pointers are assigned the addresses of the regular variables no matter what the data in the regular variables are.

Keep the data type of each pointer consistent with its corresponding variable. Do not assign a floating-point variable to an integer's address. For instance, you cannot make the following assignment statement:

```
p_initial = &sales;        // Invalid pointer assignment.
```

because p_initial can point only to character data, not to floating-point data.

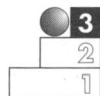

3. The following program is an example you should study closely. It shows more about pointers and the pointer operators, & and *, than several pages of text can do.

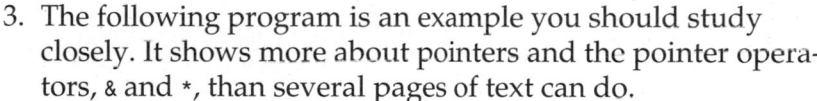

```cpp
// Filename: C26POINT.CPP
// Demonstrates the use of pointer declarations
// and operators.
#include <iostream.h>

void main()
{
    int num=123;            // A regular integer variable.
    int *p_num;             // Declares an integer pointer.

    cout << "num is " << num << "\n";  // Prints value of num.
    cout << "The address of num is " << &num << "\n";
                            // Prints num's location.
    p_num = &num,           // Puts address of num in p_num,
                            // in effect making p_num point
                            // to num.
                            // No * in front of p_num.
    cout << "*p_num is " << *p_num << "\n"; // Prints value
                                            // of num.
    cout << "p_num is " << p_num << "\n";   // Prints location
                                            // of num.

    return;
}
```

Here is the output from this program:

```
num is 123
The address of num is 0x8fbd0ffe
*p_num is 123
p_num is 0x8fbd0ffe
```

If you run this program, you probably will get different results for the value of p_num because your compiler will place num at a different location, depending on your memory setup. The value of p_num prints in hexadecimal because it is an address of memory. The actual address does not matter, however. Because the pointer p_num always contains the address of num, and because you can dereference p_num to get num's value, the actual address is not critical.

4. The following program includes a function that swaps the values of any two integers passed to it. You might recall that a function can return only a single value. Therefore, before now, you could not write a function that changed two different values and returned both values to the calling function.

To swap two variables (reversing their values for sorting, as you saw in Chapter 24, "Array Processing"), you need the ability to pass both variables by address. Then, when the function reverses the variables, the calling function's variables also are swapped.

Notice the function's use of dereferencing operators before each occurrence of num1 and num2. It does not matter at which address num1 and num2 are stored, but you must make sure that you dereference whatever addresses were passed to the function.

Be sure to receive arguments with the prefix & in functions that receive by address, as done here.

Identify the program and include the I/O header file. This program swaps two integers, so initialize two integer variables in main()*. Pass the variables to the swapping function, called* swap_them*, then switch their values. Print the results of the swap in* main()*.*

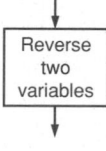

Reverse
two
variables

```cpp
// Filename: C26SWAP.CPP
// Program that includes a function that swaps
// any two integers passed to it
#include <iostream.h>
void swap_them(int &num1, int &num2);

void main()
{
    int i-10, j=20;
    cout << "\n\nBefore swap, i is " << i <<
            " and j is " << j << "\n\n";
    swap_them(i, j);
    cout << "\n\nAfter swap, i is " << i <<
            " and j is " << j << "\n\n";
    return;
}
void swap_them(int &num1, int &num2)
{
    int temp;            // Variable that holds
                         // in-between swapped value.
    temp = num1;         // The calling function's variables
    num1 - num2;         // (and not copies of them) are
    num2 = temp;         // changed in this function.
    return;
}
```

Arrays of Pointers

If you have to reserve many pointers for many different values, you might want to declare an array of pointers. You know that you can reserve an array of characters, integers, long integers, and floating-point values, as well as an array of every other data type available. You also can reserve an array of pointers, with each pointer being a pointer to a specific data type.

The following reserves an array of 10 integer pointer variables:

```
int *iptr[10]; // Reserves an array of 10 integer pointers
```

Figure 26.2 shows how C++ views this array. Each element holds an address (after being assigned values) that points to other values in memory. Each value pointed to must be an integer. You can assign an element from `iptr` an address just as you would for nonarray pointer variables. You can make `iptr[4]` point to the address of an integer variable named `age` by assigning it like this:

```
iptr[4] = &age;    // Make iptr[4] point to address of age.
```

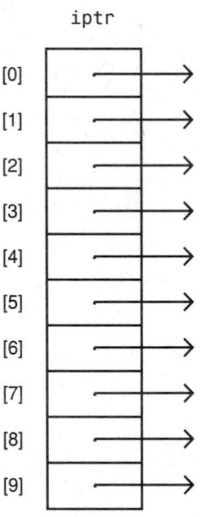

Figure 26.2. **An array of 10 integer pointers.**

The following reserves an array of 20 character pointer variables:

```
char *cpoint[20];      // Array of 20 character pointers.
```

Again, the asterisk is not part of the array name. The asterisk lets C++ know that this is an array of integer pointers and not just an array of integers.

Some beginning C++ students get confused when they see such a declaration. Pointers are one thing, but reserving storage for arrays of pointers tends to bog novices down. However, reserving storage for arrays of pointers is easy to understand. Remove the asterisk from the previous declaration as follows,

```
char cpoint[20];
```

and what do you have? You have just reserved a simple array of 20 characters. Adding the asterisk tells C++ to go one step further: rather than an array of character variables, you want an array of character pointing variables. Rather than having each element be a character variable, you have each element hold an address that points to characters.

Reserving arrays of pointers will be much more meaningful after you learn about structures in the next few chapters. As with regular, nonpointing variables, an array makes processing several pointer variables much easier. You can use a subscript to reference each variable (element) without having to use a different variable name for each value.

Review Questions

Answers to review questions are in Appendix B.

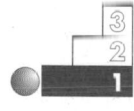

1. What type of variable is reserved in each of the following?

   a. `int *a;`

   b. `char * cp;`

   c. `float * dp;`

2. What words should come to mind when you see the `&` operator?

3. What is the dereferencing operator?

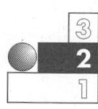

4. How would you assign the address of the floating-point variable `salary` to a pointer called `pt_sal`?

5. True or false: You must define a pointer with an initial value when declaring it.

6. In both of the following sections of code:

```
int i;
int * pti;
i=56;
pti = &i;
```

and

```
int i;
int * pti;
pti = &i;        // These two lines are reversed
i=56;            // from the preceding example.
```

is the value of `pti` the same after the fourth line of each section?

7. In the following section of code:

```
float pay;
float *ptr_pay;
pay=2313.54;
ptr_pay = &pay;
```

What is the value of each of the following (answer "invalid" if it cannot be determined):

a. `pay`

b. `*ptr_pay`

c. `*pay`

d. `&pay`

8. What does the following declare?

```
double *ara[4][6];
```

a. An array of double floating-point values

b. An array of double floating-point pointer variables

c. An invalid declaration statement

> **NOTE:** Because this is a theory-oriented chapter, review exercises are saved until you master Chapter 27, "Pointers and Arrays."

Summary

Declaring and using pointers might seem troublesome at this point. Why assign *p_num a value when it is easier (and clearer) to assign a value directly to num? If you are asking yourself that question, you probably understand everything you should from this chapter and are ready to begin learning the true power of pointers: combining pointers and array processing.

Pointers and Arrays

Arrays and pointers are closely related in the C++ programming language. You can address arrays as if they were pointers and address pointers as if they were arrays. Being able to store and access pointers and arrays gives you the ability to store strings of data in array elements. Without pointers, you could not store strings of data in arrays because there is no fundamental string data type in C++ (no string variables, only string literals).

This chapter introduces the following concepts:

♦ Array names and pointers

♦ Character pointers

♦ Pointer arithmetic

♦ Ragged-edge arrays of string data

This chapter introduces concepts you will use for much of your future programming in C++. Pointer manipulation is important to the C++ programming language.

Array Names as Pointers

An array name is just a pointer, nothing more. To prove this, suppose you have the following array declaration:

```
int ara[5] = {10, 20, 30, 40, 50};
```

If you printed ara[0], you would see 10. Because you now fully understand arrays, this is the value you would expect.

An array name is a pointer.

But what if you were to print *ara? Would *ara print anything? If so, what? If you thought an error message would print because ara is not a pointer but an array, you would be wrong. An array name is a pointer. If you print *ara, you also would see 10.

Recall how arrays are stored in memory. Figure 27.1 shows how ara would be mapped in memory. The array name, ara, is nothing more than a pointer pointing to the first element of the array. Therefore, if you dereference that pointer, you dereference the value stored in the first element of the array, which is 10. Dereferencing ara is exactly the same thing as referencing to ara[0], because they both produce the same value.

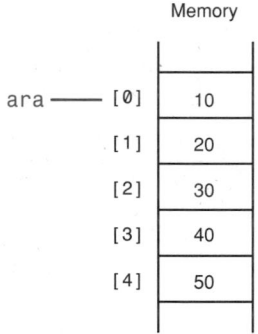

Figure 27.1. Storing the array called ara in memory.

You now see that you can reference an array with subscripts or with pointer dereferencing. Can you use pointer notation to print the third element of ara? Yes, and you already have the tools to do so. The following cout prints ara[2] (the third element of ara) without using a subscript:

```
cout << *(ara+2) ;              // Prints ara[2].
```

The expression `*(ara+2)` is not vague at all, if you remember that an array name is just a pointer that always points to the array's first element. `*(ara+2)` takes the address stored in `ara`, adds two to the address, and dereferences that location. The following holds true:

ara+0 points to ara[0]

ara+1 points to ara[1]

ara+2 points to ara[2]

ara+3 points to ara[3]

ara+4 points to ara[4]

Therefore, to print, store, or calculate with an array element, you can use either the subscript notation or the pointer notation. Because an array name contains the address of the array's first element, you must dereference the pointer to get the element's value.

Internal Locations

C++ knows the internal data size requirements of characters, integers, floating-points, and the other data types on your computer. Therefore, because `ara` is an integer array, and because each element in an integer array consumes two to four bytes of storage, depending on the computer, C++ adds two or four bytes to the address if you reference arrays as just shown.

If you write `*(ara+3)` to refer to `ara[3]`, C++ would add six or twelve bytes to the address of `ara` to get the third element. C++ does not add an actual three. You do not have to worry about this, because C++ handles these internals. When you write `*(ara+3)`, you are actually requesting that C++ add three integer addresses to the address of `ara`. If `ara` were a floating-point array, C++ would add three floating-point addresses to `ara`.

559

Pointer Advantages

An array name is a pointer constant.

Although arrays are actually pointers in disguise, they are special types of pointers. An array name is a *pointer constant*, not a pointer variable. You cannot change the value of an array name, because you cannot change constants. This explains why you cannot assign an array new values during a program's execution. For instance, even if cname is a character array, the following is not valid in C++:

```
cname = "Christine Chambers";  // Invalid array assignment.
```

The array name, cname, cannot be changed because it is a constant. You would not attempt the following

```
5 = 4 + 8 * 21;                // Invalid assignment
```

because you cannot change the constant 5 to any other value. C++ knows that you cannot assign anything to 5, and C++ prints an error message if you attempt to change 5. C++ also knows an array name is a constant and you cannot change an array to another value. (You can assign values to an array only at declaration time, one element at a time during execution, or by using functions such as strcpy().)

This brings you to the most important reason to learn pointers: pointers (except arrays referenced as pointers) are variables. You can change a pointer variable, and being able to do so makes processing virtually any data, including arrays, much more powerful and flexible.

Examples

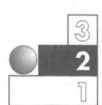

1. By changing pointers, you make them point to different values in memory. The following program demonstrates how to change pointers. The program first defines two floating-point values. A floating-point pointer points to the first variable, v1, and is used in the cout. The pointer is then changed so it points to the second floating-point variable, v2.

```
// Filename: C27PTRCH.CPP
// Changes the value of a pointer variable.
#include <iostream.h>
```

```
#include <iomanip.h>
void main()
{
   float v1=676.54;                                // Defines two
   float v2=900.18;               // floating-point variables.
   float * p_v;             / Defines a floating-point pointer.

   p_v = &v1;                      // Makes pointer point to v1.
   cout << "The first value is " << setprecision(2) <<
           *p_v << "\n";                    // Prints 676.54.

   p_v = &v2;                      // Changes the pointer so it
                                   // points to v2.
   cout << "The second value is " << setprecision(2) <<
           *p_v << "\n";                    // Prints 900.18.
   return;
}
```

Because they can change pointers, most C++ programmers use pointers rather than arrays. Because arrays are easy to declare, C++ programmers sometimes declare arrays and then use pointers to reference those arrays. If the array data changes, the pointer helps to change it.

2. You can use pointer notation and reference pointers as arrays with array notation. The following program declares an integer array and an integer pointer that points to the start of the array. The array and pointer values are printed using subscript notation. Afterwards, the program uses array notation to print the array and pointer values.

Study this program carefully. You see the inner workings of arrays and pointer notation.

```
// Filename: C27ARPTR.CPP
// References arrays like pointers and
// pointers like arrays.
#include <iostream.h>
void main()
{
   int ctr;
   int iara[5] = {10, 20, 30, 40, 50};
```

```
    int *iptr;

    iptr = iara;        // Make iptr point to array's first
                        // element. This would work also:
                        // iptr = &iara[0];

cout << "Using array subscripts:\n";
cout << "iara\tiptr\n";
for (ctr=0; ctr<5; ctr++)
   { cout << iara[ctr] << "\t" << iptr[ctr] << "\n";  }

cout << "\nUsing pointer notation:\n";
cout << "iara\tiptr\n";
 for (ctr=0; ctr<5; ctr++)
    { cout << *(iara+ctr) << "\t" << *(iptr+ctr) << "\n";  }

 return;
}
```

Here is the program's output:

```
Using array subscripts:
iara    iptr
10      10
20      20
30      30
40      40
50      50

Using pointer notation:
iara    iptr
10      10
20      20
30      30
40      40
50      50
```

Using Character Pointers

The ability to change pointers is best seen when working with character strings in memory. You can store strings in character arrays, or point to them with character pointers. Consider the following two string definitions:

```
char cara[] = "C++ is fun";      // An array holding a string

char *cptr = "C++ By Example";   // A pointer to the string
```

Character pointers can point to the first character of a string.

Figure 27.2 shows how C++ stores these two strings in memory. C++ stores both in basically the same way. You are familiar with the array definition. When assigning a string to a character pointer, C++ finds enough free memory to hold the string and assign the address of the first character to the pointer. The previous two string definition statements do almost exactly the same thing; the only difference between them is that the two pointers can easily be exchanged (the array name and the character pointers).

Because cout prints strings starting at the array or pointer name until the null zero is reached, you can print each of these strings with the following cout statements:

```
cout << "String 1: " << cara << "\n";

oout << "Otring 2: " << cptr << "\n";
```

You print strings in arrays and pointed-to strings the same way. You might wonder what advantage one method of storing strings has over the other. The seemingly minor difference between these stored strings makes a big difference when you change them.

Suppose you want to store the string Hello in the two strings. You cannot assign the string to the array like this:

```
cara = "Hello";                          // Invalid
```

Because you cannot change the array name, you cannot assign it a new value. The only way to change the contents of the array is by assigning the array characters from the string an element at a time, or by using a built-in function such as strcpy(). You can, however, make the character array point to the new string like this:

```
cptr = "Hello";              // Change the pointer so
                             // it points to the new string.
```

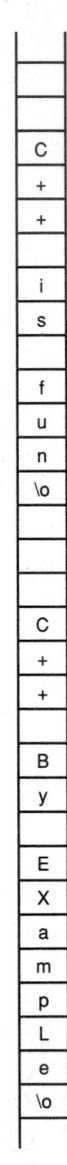

Figure 27.2. **Storing two strings: One in an array and one pointed to by a pointer variable.**

TIP: If you want to store user input in a string pointed to by a pointer, first you must reserve enough storage for that input string. The easiest way to do this is to reserve a character array, then assign a character pointer to the beginning element of that array like this:

```
char input[81];          // Holds a string as long as
                         // 80 characters.
char *iptr=input;        // Also could have done this:
                         // char *iptr=&input[0];
```

Now you can input a string by using the pointer:

```
gets(iptr);              // Make sure iptr points to
                         // the string typed by the user.
```

You can use pointer manipulation, arithmetic, and modification on the input string.

Examples

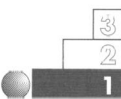

1. Suppose you want to store your sister's full name and print it. Rather than using arrays, you can use a character pointer. The following program does just that.

```
// Filename: C27CP1.CPP
// Stores a name in a character pointer.
#include <iostream.h>
void main()
{
   char *c="Bettye Lou Horn";

   cout << "My sister's name is " << c << "\n";
   return;
}
```

This prints the following:

```
My sister's name is Bettye Lou Horn
```

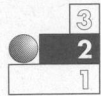

2. Suppose you must change a string pointed to by a character pointer. If your sister changed her last name to Henderson, your program can show both strings in the following manner:

Identify the program and include the I/O header file. This program uses a character pointer, c, to point to a string literal in memory. Point to the string literal, and print the string. Make the character-pointer point to a new string literal, then print the new string.

```
// Filename: C27CP2.CPP
// Illustrates changing a character string.
#include <iostream.h>
void main()
{
    char *c="Bettye Lou Horn";

    cout << "My sister's maiden name was " << c << "\n";

    c = "Bettye Lou Henderson";  // Assigns new string to c.

    cout << "My sister's married name is " << c << "\n";
    return;
}
```

The output is as follows:

```
My sister's maiden name was Bettye Lou Horn
My sister's married name is Bettye Lou Henderson
```

3. Do not use character pointers to change string constants. Doing so can confuse the compiler, and you probably will not get the results you expect. The following program is similar to those you just saw. Rather than making the character pointer point to a new string, this example attempts to change the contents of the original string.

```
// Filename: C27CP3.CPP
// Illustrates changing a character string improperly.
#include <iostream.h>
void main()
```

```
{
    char *c="Bettye Lou Horn";

    cout << "My sister's maiden name was " << c << "\n";

    c += 11;              // Makes c point to the last name
                         //   (the twelfth character).
    c = "Henderson";      // Assigns a new string to c.

    cout << "My sister's married name is " << c << "\n";
    return;
}
```

The program seems to change the last name from Horn to Henderson, but it does not. Here is the output of this program:

```
My sister's maiden name was Bettye Lou Horn
My sister's married name is Henderson
```

Why didn't the full string print? Because the address pointed to by c was incremented by 11, c still points to Henderson, so that was all that printed.

4. You might guess at a way to fix the previous program. Rather than printing the string stored at c after assigning it to Henderson, you might want to decrement it by 11 so it points to its original location, the start of the name. The code to do this follows, but it does not work as expected. Study the program before reading the explanation.

```
// Filename: C27CP4.C
// Illustrates changing a character string improperly.
#include <iostream.h>
void main()
{
    char *c="Bettye Lou Horn";

    cout << "My sister's maiden name was " << c << "\n";

    c += 11;                  // Makes c point to the last
                             // name (the twelfth character).
```

```
    c = "Henderson";            // Assigns a new string to c.
    c -= 11;                        // Makes c point to its
                                // original location (???).

    cout << "My sister's married name is " << c << "\n";
    return;
}
```

This program produces garbage at the second `cout`. There are actually two string literals in this program. When you first assign c to `Bettye Lou Horn`, C++ reserves space in memory for the constant string and puts the starting address of the string in `c`.

When the program then assigns c to `Henderson`, C++ finds room for *another* character constant, as shown in Figure 27.3. If you subtract 11 from the location of `c`, after it points to the new string `Henderson`, c points to an area of memory your program is not using. There is no guarantee that printable data appears before the string constant `Henderson`. If you want to manipulate parts of the string, you must do so an element at a time, just as you must with arrays.

Pointer Arithmetic

You saw an example of pointer arithmetic when you accessed array elements with pointer notation. By now you should be comfortable with the fact that both of these array or pointer references are identical:

```
ara[sub] and *(ara + sub)
```

You can increment or decrement a pointer. If you increment a pointer, the address inside the pointer variable increments. The pointer does not always increment by one, however.

Suppose `f_ptr` is a floating-point pointer indexing the first element of an array of floating-point numbers. You could initialize `f_ptr` as follows:

```
float fara[] = {100.5, 201.45, 321.54, 389.76, 691.34};
f_ptr = fara;
```

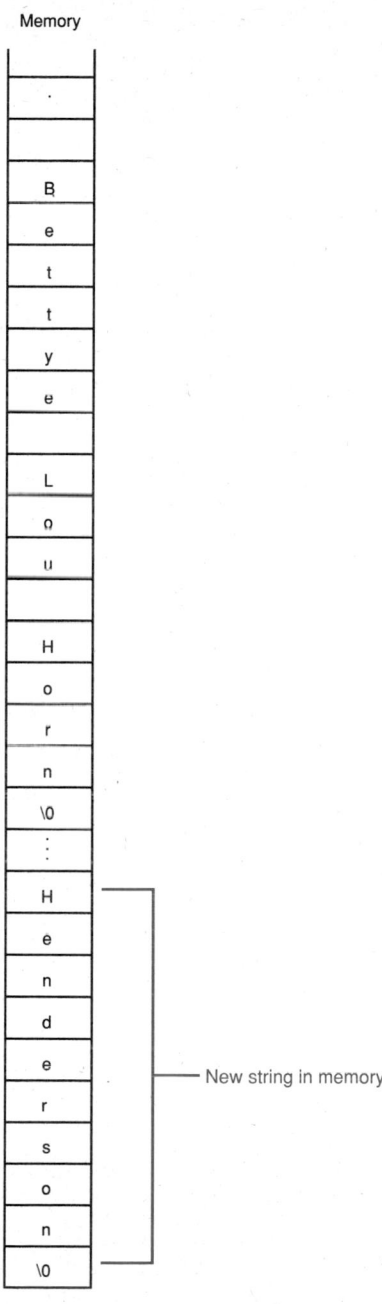

Figure 27.3. Two string constants appear in memory because two string constants are used in the program.

Figure 27.4 shows what these variables look like in memory. Each floating-point value in this example takes four bytes of memory.

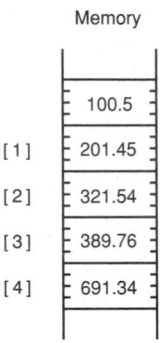

Memory

[1] 201.45

[2] 321.54

[3] 389.76

[4] 691.34

100.5

Figure 27.4. **A floating-point array and a pointer.**

Incrementing a pointer can add more than one byte to the pointer.

If you print the value of *f_ptr, you see 100.5. Suppose you increment f_ptr by one with the following statement:

```
f_ptr++;
```

C++ does not add one to the address in f_ptr, even though it seems as though one should be added. In this case, because floating-point values take four bytes each on this machine, C++ adds four to f_ptr. How does C++ know how many bytes to add to f_ptr? C++ knows from the pointer's declaration how many bytes of memory pointers take. This is why you have to declare the pointer with the correct data type.

After incrementing f_ptr, if you were to print *f_ptr, you would see 201.45, the second element in the array. If C++ added only one to the address in f_ptr, f_ptr would point only to the second byte, 100.5. This would output garbage to the screen.

> **NOTE:** When you increment a pointer, C++ adds one full data-type size (in bytes) to the pointer, not one byte. When you decrement a pointer, C++ subtracts one full data type size (in bytes) from the pointer.

Examples

1. The following program defines an array with five values. An integer pointer is then initialized to point to the first element in the array. The rest of the program prints the dereferenced value of the pointer, then increments the pointer so it points to the next integer in the array.

   Just to show you what is going on, the size of integer values is printed at the bottom of the program. Because (in this case) integers take two bytes, C++ increments the pointer by two so it points to the next integer. (The integers are two bytes apart from each other.)

```cpp
// Filename: C27PTI.CPP
// Increments a pointer through an integer array.
#include <iostream.h>
void main()
{
    int iara[] = {10,20,30,40,50};
    int *ip = iara;                 // The pointer points to
                                    // The start of the array.
    cout << *ip << "\n";
    ip++;                           // Two are actually added.
    cout << *ip << "\n";
    ip++;                           // Two are actually added.
    cout << *ip << "\n";
    ip++;                           // Two are actually added.
    cout << *ip << "\n";
    ip++;                           // Two are actually added.
    cout << *ip << "\n\n";
    cout << "The integer size is " << sizeof(int);
    cout << " bytes on this machine \n\n";
    return;
}
```

Here is the output from the program:

```
10
20
30
40
50

The integer size is two bytes on this machine
```

2. Here is the same program using a character array and a
   character pointer. Because a character takes only one byte of
   storage, incrementing a character pointer actually adds just
   one to the pointer; only one is needed because the characters
   are only one byte apart.

```cpp
// Filename: C27PTC.CPP
// Increments a pointer through a character array.
#include <iostream.h>
void main()
{
   char cara[] = {'a', 'b', 'c', 'd', 'e'};
   char *cp = cara;                // The pointers point to
                                   // the start of the array.
   cout << *cp << "\n";
   cp++;                                     // One is actually added.
   cout << *cp << "\n";
   cp++;                                     // One is actually added.
   cout << *cp << "\n";
   cp++;                                     // One is actually added.
   cout << *cp << "\n";
   cp++;                                     // One is actually added.
   cout << *cp << "\n\n";
   cout << "The character size is " << sizeof(char);
   cout << " byte on this machine\n";
   return;
}
```

3. The next program shows the many ways you can add to,
   subtract from, and reference arrays and pointers. The program defines a floating-point array and a floating-point
   pointer. The body of the program prints the values from the
   array using array and pointer notation.

```
// Filename: C27ARPT2.CPP
// Comprehensive reference of arrays and pointers.
#include <iostream.h>
void main()
{
    float ara[] = {100.0, 200.0, 300.0, 400.0, 500.0};
    float *fptr;                    // Floating-point pointer.

    // Make pointer point to array's first value.
    fptr = &ara[0];                 // Also could have been this:
                                    // fptr = ara;

    cout << *fptr << "\n";              // Prints 100.0
    fptr++;         // Points to next floating-point value.
    cout << *fptr << "\n";              // Prints 200.0
    fptr++;         // Points to next floating-point value.
    cout << *fptr << "\n";              // Prints 300.0
    fptr++;         // Points to next floating-point value.
    cout << *fptr << "\n";              // Prints 400.0
    fptr++;         // Points to next floating-point value.
    cout << *fptr << "\n";              // Prints 500.0

    fptr = ara;             // Points to first element again.
    cout << *(fptr+2) << "\n";         // Prints 300.00 but
                                    // does not change fptr.

    // References both array and pointer using subscripts.
    cout << (fptr+0)[0] << " " << (ara+0)[0] << "\n";
    // 100.0   100.0
    cout << (fptr+1)[0] << " " << (ara+1)[0] << "\n";
    // 200.0   200.0
    cout << (fptr+4)[0] << " " << (ara+4)[0] << "\n";
    // 500.0   500.0
    return;
}
```

The following is the output from this program:

```
100.0
200.0
300.0
400.0
```

```
500.0
300.0
100.0   100.0
200.0   200.0
500.0   500.0
```

Arrays of Strings

You now are ready for one of the most useful applications of character pointers: storing arrays of strings. Actually, you cannot store an array of strings, but you can store an array of character pointers, and each character pointer can point to a string in memory.

An array that a character pointer defines is a ragged-edge array.

By defining an array of character pointers, you define a *ragged-edge array.* A ragged-edge array is similar to a two-dimensional table, except each row contains a different number of characters (instead of being the same length).

The word *ragged-edge* derives from the use of word processors. A word processor typically can print text fully justified or with a ragged-right margin. The columns of this paragraph are fully justified, because both the left and the right columns align evenly. Letters you write by hand and type on typewriters (remember what a typewriter is?) generally have ragged-right margins. It is difficult to type so each line ends in exactly the same right column.

All two-dimensional tables you have seen so far have been fully justified. For example, if you declared a character table with five rows and 20 columns, each row would contain the same number of characters. You could define the table with the following statement:

```
char names[5][20]={ {"George"},
                    {"Michelle"},
                    {"Joe"},
                    {"Marcus"},
                    {"Stephanie"} };
```

This table is shown in Figure 27.5. Notice that much of the table is wasted space. Each row takes 20 characters, even though the data in each row takes far fewer characters. The unfilled elements contain null zeros because C++ nullifies all elements you do not initialize in arrays. This type of table uses too much memory.

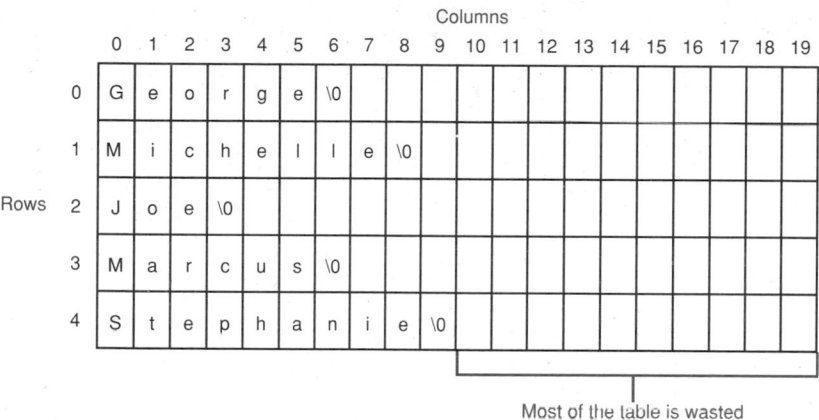

Figure 27.5. A fully justified table.

To fix the memory-wasting problem of fully justified tables, you should declare a single-dimensional array of character pointers. Each pointer points to a string in memory, and the strings do not have to be the same length.

Here is the definition for such an array:

```
char *names[5]={ {"George"},
                 {"Michelle"},
                 {"Joe"},
                 {"Marcus"},
                 {"Stephanie"} };
```

This array is single-dimensional. The definition should not confuse you, although it is something you have not seen. The asterisk before names makes this an array of pointers. The data type of the pointers is character. The strings are not being assigned to the array elements, but they are being pointed to by the array elements. Figure 27.6 shows this array of pointers. The strings are stored elsewhere in memory. Their actual locations are not critical because each pointer points to the starting character. The strings waste no data. Each string takes only as much memory as needed by the string and its terminating zero. This gives the data its ragged-right appearance.

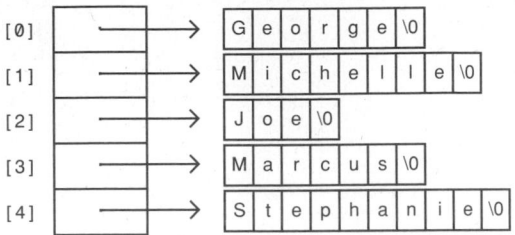

Figure 27.6. The array that points to each of the five strings.

To print the first string, you would use this `cout`:

```
cout << *names;            // Prints George
```

To print the second string, you would use this `cout`:

```
cout << *(names+1);        // Prints Michelle
```

Whenever you dereference any pointer element with the `*` dereferencing operator, you access one of the strings in the array. You can use a dereferenced element any place you use a string constant or character array (with `strcpy()`, `strcmp()`, and so on).

> **TIP:** Working with pointers to strings is much more efficient than working directly with the strings. For instance, sorting a list of strings takes much time if they are stored as a fully justified table. Sorting strings pointed to by a pointer array is much faster. You swap only pointers during the sort, not entire strings.

Examples

1. Here is a full program that uses the pointer array with five names. The `for` loop controls the `cout` function, printing each name in the string data. Now you can see why learning about pointer notation for arrays pays off!

```
// Filename: C27PTST1.CPP
// Prints strings pointed to by an array.
#include <iostream.h>
```

```
void main()
{
    char *name[5]={ {"George"},      // Defines a ragged-edge
                    {"Michelle"},  // array of pointers to
                    {"Joe"},       // strings.
                    {"Marcus"},
                    {"Stephanie"} };
    int ctr;

    for (ctr=0; ctr<5; ctr++)
      { cout << "String #" << (ctr+1) <<
              " is " << *(name+ctr) << "\n"; }

    return;
}
```

The following is the output from this program:

```
String #1 is George
String #2 is Michelle
String #3 is Joe
String #4 is Marcus
String #5 is Stephanie
```

2. The following program stores the days of the week in an array. When the user types a number from 1 to 7, the day of the week that matches that number (with Sunday being 1) displays by dereferencing the pointer referencing that string.

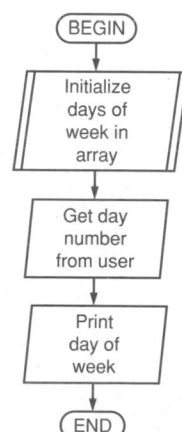

BEGIN

Initialize days of week in array

Get day number from user

Print day of week

END

```
// Filename: C27PTST2.CPP
// Prints the day of the week based on an input value.
#include <iostream.h>
void main()
{
    char *days[] = {"Sunday",    // The seven separate sets
            "Monday",            // of braces are optional.
            "Tuesday",
            "Wednesday",
            "Thursday",
            "Friday",
            "Saturday"};
    int day_num;
```

```
      do
        { cout << "What is a day number (from 1 to 7)? ";
          cin >> day_num;
        } while ((day_num<1) || (day_num>7));      // Ensures
                                         // an accurate number.


      day_num--;                         // Adjusts for subscript.
      cout << "The day is " << *(days+day_num) << "\n";
      return;
    }
```

Review Questions

The answers to the review questions are in Appendix B.

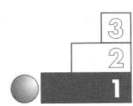

1. What is the difference between an array name and a pointer?

2. If you performed the following statement (assume `ipointer` points to integers that take four bytes of memory),

    ```
    ipointer += 2;
    ```

    how many bytes are added to `ipointer`?

3. Which of the following are equivalent, assuming `iary` is an integer array and `iptr` is an integer pointer pointing to the start of the array?

    a. `iary` and `iptr`

    b. `iary[1]` and `iptr+1`

    c. `iary[3]` and `*(iptr + 3)`

    d. `*iary` and `iary[0]`

    e. `iary[4]` and `*iptr+4`

4. Why is it more efficient to sort a ragged-edge character array than a fully justified string array?

5. Given the following array and pointer definition

```
int ara[] = {1, 2, 3, 4, 5, 6, 7, 8, 9, 10};
int *ip1, *ip2;
```

which of the following is allowed?

a. `ip1 = ara;`

b. `ip2 = ip1 = &ara[3];`

c. `ara = 15;`

d. `*(ip2 + 2) = 15;   // Assuming ip2 and ara are equal.`

Review Exercises

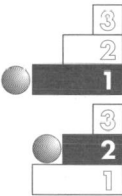

1. Write a program to store your family members' names in a character array of pointers. Print the names.

2. Write a program that asks the user for 15 daily stock market averages and stores those averages in a floating-point array. Using only pointer notation, print the array forward and backward. Again using only pointer notation, print the highest and lowest stock market quotes in the list.

3. Modify the bubble sort shown in Chapter 24, "Array Processing," so that it sorts using pointer notation. Add this bubble sort to the program in Exercise 2 to print the stock market averages in ascending order

4. Write a program that requests 10 song titles from the user. Store the titles in an array of character pointers (a ragged-edge array). Print the original titles, print the alphabetized titles, and print the titles in reverse alphabetical order (from Z to A).

Summary

You deserve a break! You now understand the foundation of C++'s pointers and array notation. When you have mastered this section, you are on your way to thinking in C++ as you design your programs. C++ programmers know that C++'s arrays are pointers in disguise, and they program them accordingly.

Being able to use ragged-edge arrays offers two advantages: You can hold arrays of string data without wasting extra space, and you can quickly change the pointers without having to move the string data around in memory.

As you progress into advanced C++ concepts, you will appreciate the time you spend mastering pointer notation. The next chapter introduces a new topic called *structures*. Structures enable you to store data in a more unified manner than simple variables have allowed.

Part VII

Structures and File Input/Output

28

Structures

Using structures, you have the ability to group data and work with the grouped data as a whole. Business data processing uses the concept of structures in almost every program. Being able to manipulate several variables as a single group makes your programs easier to manage.

This chapter introduces the following concepts:

♦ Structure definitions

♦ Initializing structures

♦ The dot operator (.)

♦ Structure assignment

♦ Nested structures

This chapter is one of the last in the book to present new concepts. The remainder of the book builds on the structure concepts you learn in this chapter.

Introduction to Structures

A *structure* is a collection of one or more variable types. As you know, each element in an array must be the same data type, and you must refer to the entire array by its name. Each element (called a *member*) in a structure can be a different data type.

Suppose you wanted to keep track of your CD music collection. You might want to track the following pieces of information about each CD:

Title
Artist
Number of songs
Cost
Date purchased

There would be five members in this CD structure.

TIP: If you have programmed in other computer languages, or if you have ever used a database program, C++ structures are analogous to file records, and members are analogous to fields in those records.

After deciding on the members, you must decide what data type each member is. The title and artist are character arrays, the number of songs is an integer, the cost is floating-point, and the date is another character array. This information is represented like this:

Member Name	Data Type
Title	Character array of 25 characters
Artist	Character array of 20 characters
Number of songs	Integer
Cost	Floating-point
Date purchased	Character array of eight characters

Each structure you define can have an associated structure name called a *structure tag*. Structure tags are not required in most cases, but it is generally best to define one for each structure in your program. The structure tag is not a variable name. Unlike array names, which reference the array as variables, a structure tag is simply a label for the structure's format.

You name structure tags yourself, using the same naming rules for variables. If you give the CD structure a structure tag named `cd_collection`, you are informing C++ that the tag called `cd_collection` looks like two character arrays, followed by an integer, a floating-point value, and a final character array.

A structure tag is a label for the structure's format.

A structure tag is actually a newly defined data type that you, the programmer, define. When you want to store an integer, you do not have to define to C++ what an integer is. C++ already recognizes an integer. When you want to store a CD collection's data, however, C++ is not capable of recognizing what format your CD collection takes. You have to tell C++ (using the example being described here) that you need a new data type. That data type will be your structure tag, called `cd_collection` in this example, and it looks like the structure previously described (two character arrays, integer, floating-point, and character array).

> **NOTE:** No memory is reserved for structure tags. A structure tag is your own data type. C++ does not reserve memory for the integer data type until you declare an integer variable. C++ does not reserve memory for a structure until you declare a structure variable.

Figure 28.1 shows the CD structure, graphically representing the data types in the structure. Notice that there are five members and each member is a different data type. The entire structure is called `cd_collection` because that is the structure tag.

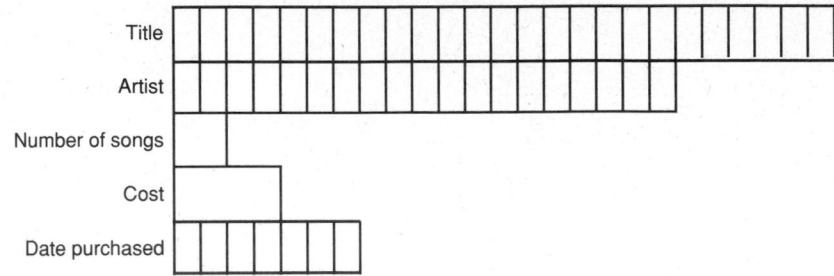

Figure 28.1. The layout of the `cd_collection` structure.

> **NOTE:** The mailing-list application in Appendix F uses a structure to hold people's names, addresses, cities, states, and ZIP codes.

Examples

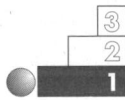

1. Suppose you were asked to write a program for a company's inventory system. The company had been using a card-file inventory system to track the following items:

   Item name
   Quantity in stock
   Quantity on order
   Retail price
   Wholesale price

   This would be a perfect use for a structure containing five members. Before defining the structure, you have to determine the data types of each member. After asking questions about the range of data (you must know the largest item name, and the highest possible quantity that would appear on order to ensure your data types can hold the data), you decide to use the following structure tag and data types:

Member	Data Type
Item name	Character array of 20 characters
Quantity in stock	`long int`
Quantity on order	`long int`
Retail price	`double`
Wholesale price	`double`

2. Suppose the same company also wanted you to write a program to keep track of their monthly and annual salaries and to print a report at the end of the year that showed each month's individual salary and the total salary at the end of the year.

What would the structure look like? Be careful! This type of data probably does not need a structure. Because all the monthly salaries must be the same data type, a floating-point or a double floating-point array holds the monthly salaries nicely without the complexity of a structure.

Structures are useful for keeping track of data that must be grouped, such as inventory data, a customer's name and address data, or an employee data file.

Defining Structures

To define a structure, you must use the `struct` statement. The `struct` statement defines a new data type, with more than one member, for your program. The format of the `struct` statement is

```
struct [structure tag]
   {
     member definition;
     member definition;
        :
     member definition;
   } [one or more structure variables];
```

As mentioned earlier, *structure tag* is optional (hence the brackets in the format). Each *member definition* is a normal variable definition, such as `int i;` or `float sales[20];` or any other valid variable definition, including variable pointers if the structure requires a pointer as a member. At the end of the structure's definition, before the final semicolon, you can specify one or more structure variables.

If you specify a structure variable, you request C++ to reserve space for that variable. This enables C++ to recognize that the variable is not integer, character, or any other internal data type. C++ also recognizes that the variable must be a type that looks like the structure. It might seem strange that the members do not reserve storage, but they don't. The structure variables do. This becomes clear in the examples that follow.

Here is the way you declare the CD structure:

```
struct cd_collection
    {
    char title[25];
    char artist[20];
    int num_songs;
    float price;
    char date_purch[9];
    } cd1, cd2, cd3;
```

Before going any further, you should be able to answer the following questions about this structure:

◆ What is the structure tag?

◆ How many members are there?

◆ What are the member data types?

◆ What are the member names?

◆ How many structure variables are there?

◆ What are their names?

The structure tag is called `cd_collection`. There are five members, two character arrays, an integer, a floating-point, and a character array. The member names are `title`, `artist`, `num_songs`, `price`, and `date_purch`. There are three structure variables—`cd1`, `cd2`, and `cd3`.

> **TIP:** Often, you can visualize structure variables as a card-file inventory system. Figure 28.2 shows how you might keep your CD collection in a 3-by-5 card file. Each CD takes one card (represented by its structure variable), which contains the information about that CD (the structure members).

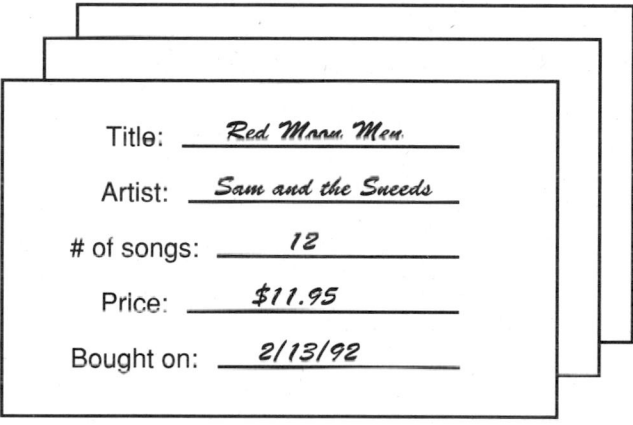

Figure 28.2. Using a card-file CD inventory system.

If you had 1000 CDs, you would have to declare 1000 structure variables. Obviously, you would not want to list that many structure variables at the end of a structure definition. To help define structures for a large number of occurrences, you must define an *array of structures*. Chapter 29, "Arrays of Structures," shows you how to do that. For now, concentrate on familiarizing yourself with structure definitions.

Examples

1. Here is a structure definition of the inventory application described earlier in this chapter.

```
struct inventory
{
   char item_name[20];
   long int in_stock;
   long int order_qty;
   float retail;
   float wholesale;
} item1, item2, item3, item4;
```

Four inventory structure variables are defined. Each structure variable—item1, item2, item3, and item4—looks like the structure.

2. Suppose a company wanted to track its customers and personnel. The following two structure definitions would create five structure variables for each structure. This example, having five employees and five customers, is very limited, but it shows how structures can be defined.

```
struct employees
{
   char emp_name[25];               // Employee's full name.
   char address[30];                 // Employee's address.
   char city[10];
   char state[2];
   long int zip;
   double salary;                         // Annual salary.
} emp1, emp2, emp3, emp4, emp5;

struct customers
{
   char cust_name[25];               // Customer's full name.
   char address[30];                  // Customer's address.
   char city[10];
   char state[2];
   long int zip;
   double balance;              // Balance owed to company.
} cust1, cust2, cust3, cust4, cust5;
```

Each structure has similar data. Later in this chapter, you learn how to consolidate similar member definitions by creating nested structures.

TIP: Put comments to the right of members in order to document the purpose of the members.

Initializing Structure Data

You can define a structure's data when you declare the structure.

There are two ways to initialize members of a structure. You can initialize members when you declare a structure, and you can initialize a structure in the body of the program. Most programs lend themselves to the latter method, because you do not always know structure data when you write your program.

Here is an example of a structure declared and initialized at the same time:

```
struct cd_collection
   {
   char titlc[25];
   char artist[20];
   int num_songs;
   float pricc;
   char date_purch[9];
   } cd1 = {"Red Moon Men", "Sam and the Sneeds",
           12, 11.95, "02/13/92"};
```

When first learning about structures, you might be tempted to initialize members individually inside the structure, such as

```
char artist[20]="Sam and the Sneeds";        // Invalid
```

You cannot initialize individual members because they are not variables. You can assign only values to variables. The only structure variable in this structure is cd1. The braces must enclose the data you initialize in the structure variables, just as they enclose data when you initialize arrays.

This method of initializing structure variables becomes tedious when there are several structure variables (as there usually are). Putting the data in several variables, each set of data enclosed in braces, becomes messy and takes too much space in your code.

More importantly, you usually do not even know the contents of the structure variables. Generally, the user enters data to be stored in structures, or you read them from a disk file.

Use the dot operator to initialize members of structures.

A better approach to initializing structures is to use the *dot operator* (.). The dot operator is one way to initialize individual members of a structure variable in the body of your program. With the dot operator, you can treat each structure member almost as if it were a regular nonstructure variable.

The format of the dot operator is

```
structure_variable_name.member_name
```

A structure variable name must always precede the dot operator, and a member name must always appear after the dot operator. Using the dot operator is easy, as the following examples show.

Examples

1. Here is a simple program using the CD collection structure and the dot operator to initialize the structure. Notice the program treats members as if they were regular variables when combined with the dot operator.

Identify the program and include the necessary header file. Define a CD structure variable with five members. Fill the CD structure variable with data, then print it.

```cpp
// Filename: C28ST1.CPP
// Structure initialization with the CD collection.
#include <iostream.h>
#include <string.h>
void main()
{
   struct cd_collection
   {
     char title[25];
     char artist[20];
     int num_songs;
     float price;
     char date_purch[9];
   } cd1;
```

```
// Initialize members here.
strcpy(cd1.title, "Red Moon Men");
strcpy(cd1.artist, "Sam and the Sneeds");
cd1.num_songs=12;
cd1.price=11.95;
strcpy(cd1.date_purch, "02/13/92");

// Print the data to the screen.
cout << "Here is the CD information:\n\n";
cout << "Title: " << cd1.title << "\n";
cout << "Artist: " << cd1.artist << "\n";
cout << "Songs: " << cd1.num_songs << "\n";
cout << "Price: " << cd1.price << "\n";
cout << "Date purchased: " << cd1.date_purch << "\n";

return;
}
```

Here is the output from this program:

```
Here is the CD information:

Title: Red Moon Men
Artist: Sam and the Sneeds
Songs: 12
Price: 11.95
Date purchased: 02/13/92
```

2. By using the dot operator, you can receive structure data from the keyboard with any of the data-input functions you know, such as cin, gets(), and get.

The following program asks the user for student information. To keep the example reasonably short, only two students are defined in the program.

```
// Filename: C28ST2.CPP
// Structure input with student data.
#include <iostream.h>
#include <string.h>
#include <iomanip.h>
#include <stdio.h>
```

```
void main()
{
   struct students
   {
     char name[25];
     int age;
     float average;
   } student1, student2;

   // Get data for two students.
   cout << "What is first student's name? ";
   gets(student1.name);
   cout << "What is the first student's age? ";
   cin >> student1.age;
   cout << "What is the first student's average? ";
   cin >> student1.average;

   fflush(stdin);     // Clear input buffer for next input.

   cout << "\nWhat is second student's name? ";
   gets(student2.name);
   cout << "What is the second student's age? ";
   cin >> student2.age;
   cout << "What is the second student's average? ";
   cin >> student2.average;

   // Print the data.
   cout << "\n\nHere is the student information you " <<
           "entered:\n\n";
   cout << "Student #1:\n";
   cout << "Name:    " << student1.name << "\n";
   cout << "Age:     " << student1.age << "\n";
   cout << "Average: " << setprecision(2) << student1.average
                       << "\n";

   cout << "\nStudent #2:\n";
   cout << "Name:    " << student2.name << "\n";
   cout << "Age:     " << student2.age << "\n";
   cout << "Average: " << student2.average << "\n";

   return;
}
```

Here is the output from this program:

```
What is first student's name? Larry
What is the first student's age? 14
What is the first student's average? 87.67

What is second student's name? Judy
What is the second student's age? 15
What is the second student's average? 95.38


Here is the student information you entered:

Student #1:
Name:    Larry
Age:     14
Average: 87.67

Student #2:
Name:    Judy
Age:     15
Average: 95.38
```

3. Structure variables are passed by copy, not by address as arrays are. Therefore, if you fill a structure in a function, you must return it to the calling function in order for the calling function to recognize the structure, or use global structure variables, which is generally not recommended.

> **TIP:** A good solution to the local/global structure problem is this: Define your structures globally without any structure variables. Define all your structure variables locally to the functions that need them. As long as your structure definition is global, you can declare local structure variables from that structure. All subsequent examples in this book use this method.

Define structures globally and structure variables locally.

The structure tag plays an important role in the local/global problem. Use the structure tag to define local structure variables. The following program is similar to the previous one. Notice the student structure is defined globally with no structure variables. In each function, local structure variables are declared by referring to the structure tag. The structure tag keeps you from having to redefine the structure members every time you define a new structure variable.

```cpp
// Filename: C28ST3.CPP
// Structure input with student data passed to functions.
#include <iostream.h>
#include <string.h>
#include <stdio.h>
#include <iomanip.h>
struct students fill_structs(struct students student_var);
void pr_students(struct students student_var);

struct students                        // A global structure.
   {
     char name[25];
     int age;
     float average;
   };                                  // No memory reserved.

void main()
{
   students student1, student2;     // Defines two
                                    // local variables.

   // Call function to fill structure variables.
   student1 = fill_structs(student1);        // student1
                    // is passed by copy, so it must be
                    // returned for main() to recognize it.
   student2 = fill_structs(student2);

   // Print the data.
   cout << "\n\nHere is the student information you";
   cout << " entered:\n\n";
   pr_students(student1);   // Prints first student's data.
   pr_students(student2);   // Prints second student's data.

   return;
}
```

```
struct students fill_structs(struct students student_var)
{
    // Get student's data
    fflush(stdin);     // Clears input buffer for next input.
    cout << "What is student's name? ";
    gets(student_var.name);
    cout << "What is the student's age? ";
    cin >> student_var.age;
    cout << "What is the student's average? ";
    cin >> student_var.average;

    return (student_var);
}

void pr_students(struct students student_var)
{
    cout << "Name:    " << student_var.name << "\n";
    cout << "Age:     " << student_var.age << "\n";
    cout << "Average: " << setprecision(2) <<
                            student_var.average << "\n";
    return;
}
```

The prototype and definition of the `fill_structs()` function might seem complicated, but it follows the same pattern you have seen throughout this book. Before a function name, you must declare `void` or put the return data type if the function returns a value. `fill_structs()` does return a value, and the type of value it returns is `struct students`.

4. Because structure data is nothing more than regular variables grouped together, feel free to calculate using structure members. As long as you use the dot operator, you can treat structure members just as you would other variables.

The following example asks for a customer's balance and uses a discount rate, included in the customer's structure, to calculate a new balance. To keep the example short, the structure's data is initialized at variable declaration time.

This program does not actually require structures because only one customer is used. Individual variables could have been used, but they don't illustrate the concept of calculating with structures.

```
// Filename: C28CUST.CPP
// Updates a customer balance in a structure.
#include <iostream.h>
#include <iomanip.h>

struct customer_rec
   {
      char cust_name[25];
      double balance;
      float dis_rate;
   } ;

void main()
{
   struct customer_rec customer = {"Steve Thompson",
                                    431.23, .25};

   cout << "Before the update, " << customer.cust_name;
   cout << " has a balance of $" << setprecision(2) <<
            customer.balance << "\n";

   // Update the balance
   customer.balance *= (1.0-customer.dis_rate);

   cout << "After the update, " << customer.cust_name;
   cout << " has a balance of $" << customer.balance << "\n";
   return;
}
```

5. You can copy the members of one structure variable to the members of another as long as both structures have the same format. Some older versions of C++ require you to copy each member individually when you want to copy one structure variable to another, but AT&T C++ makes duplicating structure variables easy.

Being able to copy one structure variable to another will seem more meaningful when you read Chapter 29, "Arrays of Structures."

The following program declares three structure variables, but initializes only the first one with data. The other two are then initialized by assigning the first structure variable to them.

Copy members of one structure to another

```cpp
// Filename: C28STCPY.CPP
// Demonstrates assigning one structure to another.
#include <iostream.h>
#include <iomanip.h>

struct student
{
   char st_name[25];
   char grade;
   int age;
   float average;
};

void main()
{
   student std1 = {"Joe Brown", 'A', 13, 91.4};
   struct student std2, std3;            // Not initialized

   std2 = std1;             // Copies each member of std1
   std3 = std1;             // to std2 and std3.


   cout << "The contents of std2:\n";
   cout << std2.st_name << " " << std2.grade << " ";
   cout << std2.age << " " << setprecision(1) << std2.average
        << "\n\n";

   cout << "The contents of std3:\n";
   cout << std3.st_name << " " << std3.grade << " ";
   cout << std3.age << " " << std3.average << "\n";
   return;
}
```

Here is the output from the program:

```
The contents of std2
Joe Brown, A, 13, 91.4

The contents of std3
Joe Brown, A, 13, 91.4
```

Notice each member of std1 was assigned to std2 and std3 with two single assignments.

Nested Structures

C++ gives you the ability to nest one structure definition in another. This saves time when you are writing programs that use similar structures. You have to define the common members only once in their own structure and then use that structure as a member in another structure.

The following two structure definitions illustrate this point:

```
struct employees
{
   char emp_name[25];        // Employee's full name.
   char address[30];         // Employee's address.
   char city[10];
   char state[2];
   long int zip;
   double salary;            // Annual salary.
};

struct customers
{
   char cust_name[25];       // Customer's full name.
   char address[30];         // Customer's address.
   char city[10];
   char state[2];
   long int zip;
   double balance;           // Balance owed to company.
};
```

These structures hold different data. One structure is for employee data and the other holds customer data. Even though the data should be kept separate (you don't want to send a customer a paycheck!), the structure definitions have much overlap and can be consolidated by creating a third structure.

Suppose you created the following structure:

```
struct address_info
{
   char address[30];        // Common address information.
   char city[10];
   char state[2];
   long int zip;
};
```

This structure could then be used as a member in the other structures like this:

```
struct employees
{
   char emp_name[25];        // Employee's full name.
   address_info e_address;   // Employee's address.
   double salary;            // Annual salary.
};
```

```
struct customers
{
   char cust_name[25];       // Customer's full name.
   address_info c_address;   // Customer's address.
   double balance;           // Balance owed to company.
};
```

It is important to realize there are a total of three structures, and that they have the tags address_info, employees, and customers. How many members does the employees structure have? If you answered three, you are correct. There are three members in both employees and customers. The employees structure has the structure of a character array, followed by the address_info structure, followed by the double floating-point member, salary.

Figure 28.3 shows how these structures look.

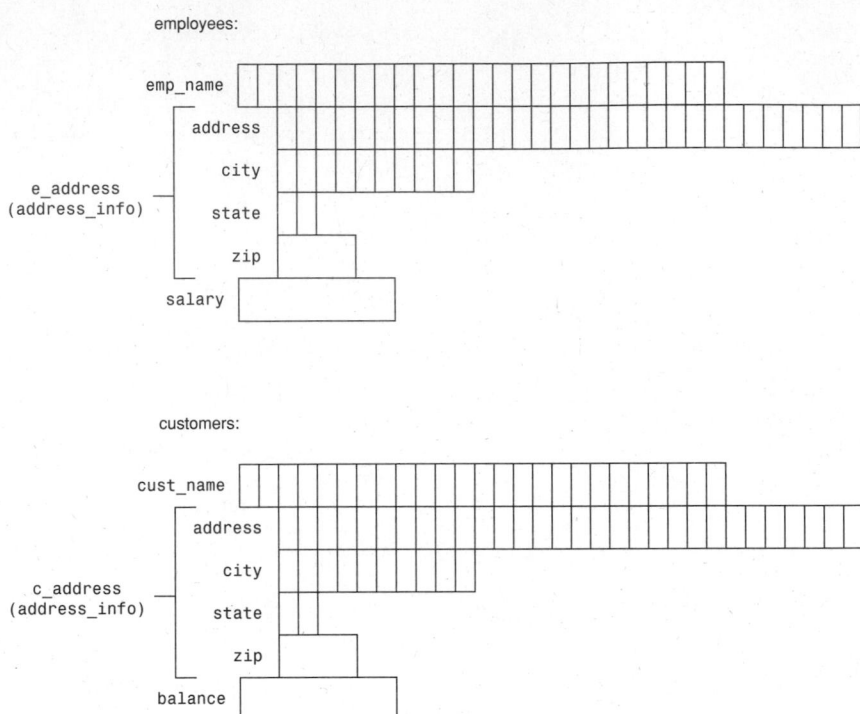

Figure 28.3. Defining a nested structure.

When you define a structure, that structure becomes a new data type in the program and can be used anywhere a data type (such as int, float, and so on) can appear.

You can assign members values using the dot operator. To assign the customer balance a number, type something like this:

```
customer.balance = 5643.24;
```

The nested structure might seem to pose a problem. How can you assign a value to one of the nested members? By using the dot operator, you must nest the dot operator just as you nest the structure definitions. You would assign a value to the customer's ZIP code like this:

```
customer.c_address.zip = 34312;
```

To assign a value to the employee's ZIP code, you would do this:

```
employee.e_address.zip = 59823;
```

Review Questions

The answers to the review questions are in Appendix B.

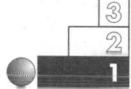

1. What is the difference between structures and arrays?

2. What are the individual elements of a structure called?

3. What are the two ways to initialize members of a structure?

4. Do you pass structures by copy or by address?

5. True or false: The following structure definition reserves storage in memory:

```
struct crec
   { char name[25];
     int age;
     float sales[5];
     long int num;
   }
```

6. Should you declare a structure globally or locally?

7. Should you declare a structure variable globally or locally?

8. How many members does the following structure declaration contain?

```
struct item
   {
     int quantity;
     part_rec item_desc;
     float price;
     char date_purch[8];
   };
```

Review Exercises

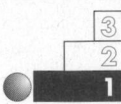

1. Write a structure in a program that tracks a video store's tape inventory. Be sure the structure includes the tape title, the length of the tape (in minutes), the initial purchase price of the tape, the rental price of the tape, and the date of the movie's release.

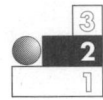

2. Write a program using the structure you declared in Exercise 1. Define three structure variables and initialize them when you declare the variables with data. Print the data to the screen.

3. Write a teacher's program to keep track of 10 students' names, ages, letter grades, and IQs. Use 10 different structure variable names and retrieve the data for the students in a for loop from the keyboard. Print the data on the printer when the teacher finishes entering the information for all the students.

Summary

With structures, you have the ability to group data in more flexible ways than with arrays. Your structures can contain members of different data types. You can initialize the structures either at declaration time or during the program with the dot operator.

Structures become even more powerful when you declare arrays of structure variables. Chapter 29, "Arrays of Structures," shows you how to declare several structure variables without giving them each a different name. This enables you to step through structures much quicker with loop constructs.

Arrays of Structures

This chapter builds on the previous one by showing you how to create many structures for your data. After creating an array of structures, you can store many occurrences of your data values.

Arrays of structures are good for storing a complete employee file, inventory file, or any other set of data that fits in the structure format. Whereas arrays provide a handy way to store several values that are the same type, arrays of structures store several values of different types together, grouped as structures.

This chapter introduces the following concepts:

♦ Creating arrays of structures

♦ Initializing arrays of structures

♦ Referencing elements from a structure array

♦ Arrays as members

Many C++ programmers use arrays of structures as a prelude to storing their data in a disk file. You can input and calculate your disk data in arrays of structures, and then store those structures in memory. Arrays of structures also provide a means of holding data you read from the disk.

Declaring Arrays of Structures

It is easy to declare an array of structures. Specify the number of reserved structures inside array brackets when you declare the structure variable. Consider the following structure definition:

```
struct stores
    { int employees;
        int registers;
        double sales;
    } store1, store2, store3, store4, store5;
```

This structure should not be difficult for you to understand because there are no new commands used in the structure declaration. This structure declaration creates five structure variables. Figure 29.1 shows how C++ stores these five structures in memory. Each of the structure variables has three members—two integers followed by a double floating-point value.

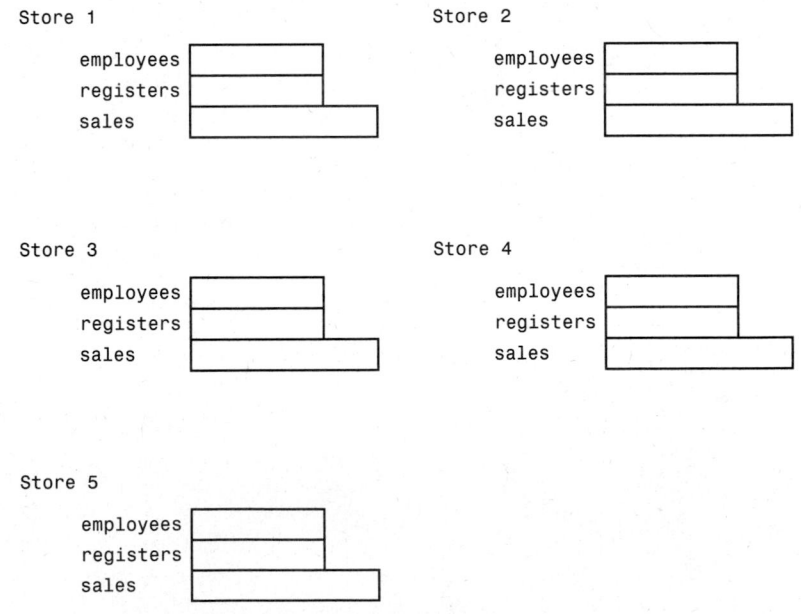

Figure 29.1. The structure of Store 1, Store 2, Store 3, Store 4, and Store 5.

If the fourth store increased its employee count by three, you could update the store's employee number with the following assignment statement:

```
store4.employees += 3;        // Add three to this store's
                              // employee count.
```

Suppose the fifth store just opened and you want to initialize its members with data. If the stores are a chain and the new store is similar to one of the others, you can begin initializing the store's data by assigning each of its members the same data as another store's, like this:

```
store5 = store2;              // Define initial values for
                              // the members of store5.
```

Arrays of structures make working with large numbers of structure variables manageable.

Such structure declarations are fine for a small number of structures, but if the stores were a national chain, five structure variables would not be enough. Suppose there were 1000 stores. You would not want to create 1000 different store variables and work with each one individually. It would be much easier to create an array of store structures.

Consider the following structure declaration:

```
struct stores
    { int employees;
        int registers;
        double sales;
    } store[1000];
```

In one quick declaration, this code creates 1000 store structures, each one containing three members. Figure 29.2 shows how these structure variables appear in memory. Notice the name of each individual structure variable: `store[0]`, `store[1]`, `store[2]`, and so on.

> **CAUTION:** Be careful that your computer does not run out of memory when you create a large number of structures. Arrays of structures quickly consume valuable memory. You might have to create fewer structures, storing more data in disk files and less data in memory.

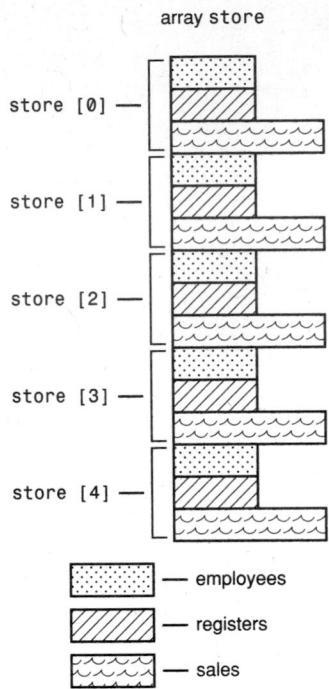

array store

store [0] —

store [1] —

store [2] —

store [3] —

store [4] —

— employees

— registers

— sales

Figure 29.2. **An array of the store structures.**

The element store[2] is an array element. This array element, unlike the others you have seen, is a structure variable. Therefore, it contains three members, each of which you can reference with the dot operator.

The dot operator works the same way for structure array elements as it does for regular structure variables. If the number of employees for the fifth store (store[4]) increased by three, you could update the structure variable like this:

```
store[4].employees += 3;        // Add three to this store's
                                // employee count.
```

You can assign complete structures to one another also by using array notation. To assign all the members of the 20th store to the 45th store, you would do this:

```
store[44] = store[19];      // Copy all members from the
                            // 20th store to the 45th.
```

The rules of arrays are still in force here. Each element of the array called store is the same data type. The data type of store is the structure stores. As with any array, each element must be the same data type; you cannot mix data types in the same array. This array's data type happens to be a structure you created containing three members. The data type for store[316] is the same for store[981] and store[74].

The name of the array, store, is a pointer constant to the starting element of the array, store[0]. Therefore, you can use pointer notation to reference the stores. To assign store[60] the same value as store[23], you can reference the two elements like this:

```
*(store+60) = *(store+23);
```

You also can mix array and pointer notation, such as

```
store[60] = *(store+23);
```

and receive the same results.

You can increase the sales of store[8] by 40 percent using pointer or subscript notation as well, as in

Increase sales by 40 percent

```
store[8].sales = (*(store+8)).sales * 1.40;
```

The extra pair of parentheses are required because the dot operator has precedence over the dereferencing symbol in C++'s hierarchy of operators (see Appendix D, "C++ Precedence Table"). Of course, in this case, the code is not helped by the pointer notation. The following is a much clearer way to increase the sales by 40 percent:

```
store[8].sales *= 1.40;
```

The following examples build an inventory data-entry system for a mail-order firm using an array of structures. There is very little new you have to know when working with arrays of structures. To become comfortable with the arrays of structure notation, concentrate on the notation used when accessing arrays of structures and their members.

Keep Your Array Notation Straight

You would never access the member `sales` like this:

```
store.sales[8] = 3234.54;          // Invalid
```

Array subscripts follow only array elements. `sales` is not an array; it was declared as being a double floating-point number. `store` can never be used without a subscript (unless you are using pointer notation).

Here is a corrected version of the previous assignment statement:

```
store[8].sales=3234.54;            // Correctly assigns
                                   // the value.
```

Examples

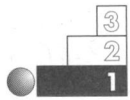

1. Suppose you work for a mail-order company that sells disk drives. You are given the task of writing a tracking program for the 125 different drives you sell. You must keep track of the following information:

> Storage capacity in megabytes
> Access time in milliseconds
> Vendor code (A, B, C, or D)
> Cost
> Price

Because there are 125 different disk drives in the inventory, the data fits nicely into an array of structures. Each array element is a structure containing the five members described in the list.

The following structure definition defines the inventory:

```
struct inventory
{
```

```
        long int storage;
        int access_time;
        char vendor_code;
        double code;
        double price;
} drive[125];  // Defines 125 occurrences of the structure.
```

2. When working with a large array of structures, your first concern should be how the data inputs into the array elements. The best method of data-entry depends on the application.

   For example, if you are converting from an older computerized inventory system, you have to write a conversion program that reads the inventory file in its native format and saves it to a new file in the format required by your C++ programs. This is no easy task. It demands that you have extensive knowledge of the system from which you are converting.

   If you are writing a computerized inventory system for the first time, your job is a little easier because you do not have to convert the old files. You still must realize that someone has to type the data into the computer. You must write a data-entry program that receives each inventory item from the keyboard and saves it to a disk file. You should give the user a chance to edit inventory data to correct any data he or she originally might have typed incorrectly.

   One of the reasons disk files are introduced in the last half of the book is that disk-file formats and structures share a common bond. When you store data in a structure, or more often, in an array of structures, you can easily write that data to a disk file using straightforward disk I/O commands.

   The following program takes the array of disk drive structures shown in the previous example and adds a data-entry function so the user can enter data into the array of structures. The program is menu-driven. The user has a choice, when starting the program, to add data, print data on-screen, or exit the program. Because you have yet to see disk I/O commands, the data in the array of structures goes away when the program ends. As mentioned earlier, saving those structures to disk is an easy task after you learn C++'s disk I/O commands. For now, concentrate on the manipulation of the structures.

This program is longer than many you previously have seen in this book, but if you have followed the discussions of structures and the dot operator, you should have little trouble following the code.

Identify the program and include the necessary header files. Define a structure that describes the format of each inventory item. Create an array of structures called disk.

Display a menu that gives the user the choice of entering new inventory data, displaying the data on-screen, or quitting the program. If the user wants to enter new inventory items, prompt the user for each item and store the data into the array of structures. If the user wants to see the inventory, loop through each inventory item in the array, displaying each one on-screen.

```
// Filename: C29DSINV.CPP
// Data-entry program for a disk drive company.
#include <iostream.h>
#include <stdlib.h>
#include <iomanip.h>
#include <stdio.h>

struct inventory            // Global structure definition.
{
   long int storage;
   int access_time;
   char vendor_code;
   float cost;
   float price;
};               // No structure variables defined globally.

void disp_menu(void);
struct inventory enter_data();
void see_data(inventory disk[125], int num_items);

void main()
```

```
    {
        inventory disk[125];    // Local array of structures.
        int ans;
        int num_items=0;                    // Number of total items
                                            // in the inventory.

        do
          {
            do
             { disp_menu();     // Display menu of user choices.
               cin >> ans;                  // Get user's request.
             } while ((ans<1) || (ans>3));

             switch (ans)
           { case (1): { disk[num_items] = enter_data(); // Enter
                                                     // disk data.
                         num_items++;   // Increment number of items.
                         break; }
             case (2): { see_data(disk, num_items);  // Display
                                                     // disk data.
                         break; }
             default : { break; }
           }
          } while (ans!=3);                 // Quit program
                                            // when user is done.

        return;
    }

void disp_menu(void)
{

    cout << "\n\n*** Disk Drive Inventory System ***\n\n";
    cout << "Do you want to:\n\n";
    cout << "\t1. Enter new item in inventory\n\n";
    cout << "\t2. See inventory data\n\n";
    cout << "\t3. Exit the program\n\n";
    cout << "What is your choice? ";
    return;
}

inventory enter_data()
```

```
{
    inventory disk_item;    // Local variable to fill
                            // with input.

    cout << "\n\nWhat is the next drive's storage in bytes? ";
    cin >> disk_item.storage;
    cout << "What is the drive's access time in ms? ";
    cin >> disk_item.access_time;
    cout << "What is the drive's vendor code (A, B, C, or D)? ";
    fflush(stdin);  // Discard input buffer
                    // before accepting character.
    disk_item.vendor_code = getchar();
    getchar();  // Discard carriage return
    cout << "What is the drive's cost? ";
    cin >> disk_item.cost;
    cout << "What is the drive's price? ";
    cin >> disk_item.price;

    return (disk_item);
}

void see_data(inventory disk[125], int num_items)
{
    int ctr;
    cout << "\n\nHere is the inventory listing:\n\n";
    for (ctr=0;ctr<num_items;ctr++)
        {
        cout << "Storage: " << disk[ctr].storage << "\t";
        cout << "Access time: " << disk[ctr].access_time << "\n";
        cout << "Vendor code: " << disk[ctr].vendor_code << "\t";
        cout << setprecision(2);
        cout << "Cost: $" << disk[ctr].cost << "\t";
        cout << "Price: $" << disk[ctr].price << "\n";
        }
    return;

}
```

Figure 29.3 shows an item being entered into the inventory file. Figure 29.4 shows the inventory listing being displayed to the screen. There are many features and error-checking functions you can add, but this program is the foundation of a more comprehensive inventory system. You can easily adapt it to a different type of inventory, a video tape collection, a coin collection, or any other tracking system by changing the structure definition and the member names throughout the program.

```
*** Disk Drive Inventory System ***

Do you want to:

         1. Enter new item in inventory

         2. See inventory data

         3. Exit the program

What is your choice? 1


What is the next drive's storage in bytes? 120000
What is the drive's access time in ms? 17
What is the drive's vendor code (A, B, C, or D)? A
What is the drive's cost? 121.56
What is the drive's price? 240.00
```

Figure 29.3. Entering inventory information.

Arrays as Members

Members of structures can be arrays. Array members pose no new problems, but you have to be careful when you access individual array elements. Keeping track of arrays of structures that contain array members might seem like a great deal of work on your part, but there is nothing to it.

Consider the following structure definition. This statement declares an array of 100 structures, each structure holding payroll information for a company. Two of the members, name and department, are arrays.

```
struct payroll
  { char name[25];                    // Employee name array.
```

```
    int dependents;
    char department[10];          // Department name array.
    float salary;
} employee[100];                  // An array of 100 employees.
```

```
What is your choice? 2


Here is the inventory listing:

Storage: 120000 Access time: 17
Vendor code: A  Cost: $121.56    Price: $240.00
Storage: 320000 Access time: 21
Vendor code: D  Cost: $230.85    Price: $409.57
Storage: 280000 Access time: 19
Vendor code: C  Cost: $210.84    Price: $398.67


*** Disk Drive Inventory System ***

Do you want to:

        1. Enter new item in inventory

        2. See inventory data

        3. Exit the program

What is your choice? 3
```

Figure 29.4. **Displaying the inventory data.**

Figure 29.5 shows what these structures look like. The first and third members are arrays. name is an array of 25 characters, and department is an array of 10 characters.

Suppose you must save the 25th employee's initial in a character variable. Assuming initial is already declared as a character variable, the following statement assigns the employee's initial to the varible initial:

```
initial = employee[24].name[0];
```

The double subscripts might look confusing, but the dot operator requires a structure variable on its left (employee[24]) and a member on its right (name's first array element). Being able to refer to member arrays makes the processing of character data in structures simple.

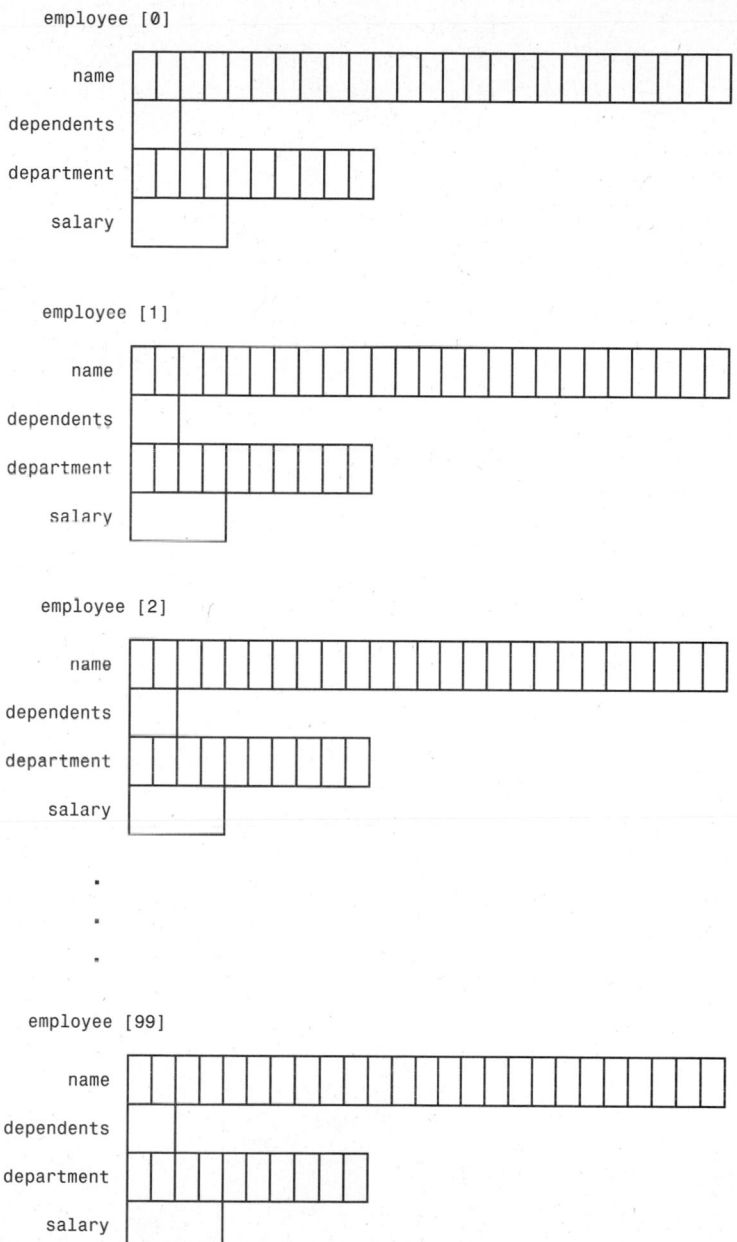

Figure 29.5. The payroll data.

Examples

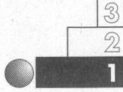

1. Suppose an employee got married and wanted her name changed in the payroll file. (She happens to be the 45th employee in the array of structures.) Given the payroll structure described in the previous section, this would assign a new name to her structure:

```
strcpy(employee[44].name, "Mary Larson");    // Assign
                                             // a new name.
```

When you refer to a structure variable using the dot operator, you can use regular commands and functions to process the data in the structure members.

2. A bookstore wants to catalog its inventory of books. The following program creates an array of 100 structures. Each structure contains several types of variables, including arrays. This program is the data-entry portion of a larger inventory system. Study the references to the members to see how member-arrays are used.

```cpp
// Filename: C29BOOK.CPP
// Bookstore data-entry program.
#include <iostream.h>
#include <stdio.h>
#include <ctype.h>

struct inventory
  { char title[25];                // Book's title.
    char pub_date[19];             // Publication date.
    char author[20];               // Author's name.
    int num;                       // Number in stock.
    int on_order;                  // Number on order.
    float retail;                  // Retail price.
  };

void main()
{
   inventory book[100];
   int total=0;                    // Total books in inventory.
   int ans;
```

```
do       // This program enters data into the structures.
  { cout << "Book #" << (total+1) << ":\n", (total+1);
  cout << "What is the title? ";
  gets(book[total].title);
  cout << "What is the publication date? ";
  gets(book[total].pub_date);
  cout << "Who is the author? ";
  gets(book[total].author);
  cout << "How many books of this title are there? ";
  cin >> book[total].num;
  cout << "How many are on order? ";
  cin >> book[total].on_order;
  cout << "What is the retail price? ";
  cin >> book[total].retail;
  fflush(stdin);
  cout << "\nAre there more books? (Y/N) ";
  ans=getchar();
  fflush(stdin);             // Discard carriage return.
  ans=toupper(ans);          // Convert to uppercase.
  if (ans=='Y')
    { total++;
      continue; }
  } while (ans=='Y');
return;
}
```

You need much more to make this a usable inventory program. An exercise at the end of this chapter recommends ways you can improve on this program by adding a printing routine and a title and author search. One of the first things you should do is put the data-entry routine in a separate function to make the code more modular. Because this example is so short, and because the program performs only one task (data-entry), there was no advantage to putting the data-entry task in a separate function.

3. Here is a comprehensive example of the steps you might go through to write a C++ program. You should begin to understand the C++ language enough to start writing some advanced programs.

Assume you have been hired by a local bookstore to write a magazine inventory system. You have to track the following:

Magazine title (at most, 25 characters)
Publisher (at most, 20 characters)
Month (1, 2, 3,...12)
Publication year
Number of copies in stock
Number of copies on order
Price of magazine (dollars and cents)

Suppose there is a projected maximum of 1000 magazine titles the store will ever carry. This means you need 1000 occurrences of the structure, not 1000 magazines total. Here is a good structure definition for such an inventory:

```
struct mag_info
   { char title[25];
     char pub[25];
     int month;
     int year;
     int stock_copies;
     int order_copies;
     float price;
   } mags[1000];                    // Define 1000 occurrences.
```

Because this program consists of more than one function, it is best to declare the structure globally, and the structure variables locally in the functions that need them.

This program needs three basic functions: a `main()` controlling function, a data-entry function, and a data printing function. You can add much more, but this is a good start for an inventory system. To keep the length of this example reasonable, assume the user wants to enter several magazines, then print them. (To make the program more "usable," you should add a menu so the user can control when she or he adds and prints the information, and should add more error-checking and editing capabilities.)

Here is an example of the complete data-entry and printing
program with prototypes. The arrays of structures are
passed between the functions from `main()`.

Print every
member of
every structure
in the array

```cpp
// Filename: C29MAG.CPP
// Magazine inventory program for adding and displaying
// a bookstore's magazines.
#include <iostream.h>
#include <ctype.h>
#include <stdio.h>

struct mag_info
   { char title[25];
     char pub[25];
     int month;
     int year;
     int stock_copies;
     int order_copies;
     float price;
   };

mag_info fill_mags(struct mag_info mag);
void print_mags(struct mag_info mags[], int mag_ctr);

void main()
{
   mag_info mags[1000];
   int mag_ctr=0;              // Number of magazine titles.
   char ans;

   do
   {                          // Assumes there is
                              // at least one magazine filled.
      mags[mag_ctr] = fill_mags(mags[mag_ctr]);
      cout << "Do you want to enter another magazine? ";
      fflush(stdin);
      ans = getchar();
      fflush(stdin);          // Discards carriage return.
      if (toupper(ans) == 'Y')
        { mag_ctr++; }
        } while (toupper(ans) == 'Y');
  print_mags(mags, mag_ctr);
```

```
            return;                   // Returns to operating system.
       }

   void print_mags(mag_info mags[], int mag_ctr)
   {
      int i;
      for (i=0; i<=mag_ctr; i++)
        { cout << "\n\nMagazine " << i+1 << ":\n";// Adjusts for
                                                  // subscript.
          cout << "\nTitle: " << mags[i].title << "\n";
          cout << "\tPublisher: " << mags[i].pub << "\n";
          cout << "\tPub. Month: " << mags[i].month << "\n";
          cout << "\tPub. Year: " << mags[i].year << "\n";
          cout << "\tIn-stock: " << mags[i].stock_copies << "\n";
          cout << "\tOn order: " << mags[i].order_copies << "\n";
          cout << "\tPrice: " << mags[i].price << "\n";
        }
      return;
   }


   mag_info fill_mags(mag_info mag)
   {
      puts("\n\nWhat is the title? ");
      gets(mag.title);
      puts("Who is the publisher? ");
      gets(mag.pub);
      puts("What is the month (1, 2, ..., 12)? ");
      cin >> mag.month;
      puts("What is the year? ");
      cin >> mag.year;
      puts("How many copies in stock? ");
      cin >> mag.stock_copies;
      puts("How many copies on order? ");
      cin >> mag.order_copies;
      puts("How much is the magazine? ");
      cin >> mag.price;
      return (mag);
   }
```

Review Questions

The answers to the review questions are in Appendix B.

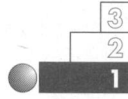

1. True or false: Each element in an array of structures must be the same type.

2. What is the advantage of creating an array of structures rather than using individual variable names for each structure variable?

3. Given the following structure declaration:

```
struct item
  { char part_no[8];
    char descr[20];
    float price;
    int in_stock;
  } inventory[100];
```

   a. How would you assign a price of 12.33 to the 33rd item's in-stock quantity?

   b. How would you assign the first character of the 12th item's part number the value of X?

   c. How would you assign the 97th inventory item the same values as the 63rd?

4. Given the following structure declaration:

```
struct item
  { char desc[20];
    int num;
    float cost;
  } inventory[25];
```

   a. What is wrong with the following statement?

   ```
   item[1].cost = 92.32;
   ```

   b. What is wrong with the following statement?

   ```
   strcpy(inventory.desc, "Widgets");
   ```

c. What is wrong with the following statement?

```
inventory.cost[10] = 32.12;
```

Review Exercises

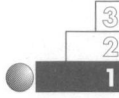

1. Write a program that stores an array of friends' names, phone numbers, and addresses and prints them two ways: with their name, address, and phone number, or with only their name and phone number for a phone listing.

2. Add a sort function to the program in Exercise 1 so you can print your friends' names in alphabetical order. (*Hint:* You have to make the member holding the names a character pointer.)

3. Expand on the book data-entry program, C29BOOK.CPP, by adding features to make it more usable (such as search book by author, by title, and print an inventory of books on order).

Summary

You have mastered structures and arrays of structures. Many useful inventory and tracking programs can be written using structures. By being able to create arrays of structures, you can now create several occurrences of data.

The next step in the process of learning C++ is to save these structures and other data to disk files. The next two chapters explore the concepts of disk file processing.

30

Sequential Files

So far, every example in this book has processed data that resided inside the program listing or came from the keyboard. You assigned constants and variables to other variables and created new data values from expressions. The programs also received input with cin, gets(), and the character input functions.

The data created by the user and assigned to variables with assignment statements is sufficient for some applications. With the large volumes of data most real-world applications must process, however, you need a better way of storing that data. For all but the smallest computer programs, disk files offer the solution.

After storing data on the disk, the computer helps you enter, find, change, and delete the data. The computer and C++ are simply tools to help you manage and process data. This chapter focuses on disk- and file-processing concepts and teaches you the first of two methods of disk access, *sequential file access*.

This chapter introduces you to the following concepts:

♦ An overview of disk files

♦ The types of files

♦ Processing data on the disk

♦ Sequential file access

♦ File I/O functions

After this chapter, you will be ready to tackle the more advanced random-file-access methods covered in the next chapter. If you have programmed computerized data files with another programming language, you might be surprised at how C++ borrows from other programming languages, especially BASIC, when working with disk files. If you are new to disk-file processing, disk files are simple to create and to read.

Why Use a Disk?

The typical computer system has much less memory storage than hard disk storage. Your disk drive holds much more data than can fit in your computer's RAM. This is the primary reason for using the disk for storing your data. The disk memory, because it is nonvolatile, also lasts longer; when you turn your computer off, the disk memory is not erased, whereas RAM is erased. Also, when your data changes, you (or more important, your users) do not have to edit the program and look for a set of assignment statements. Instead, the users run previously written programs that make changes to the disk data.

Disks hold more data than computer memory.

This makes programming more difficult at first because programs have to be written to change the data on the disk. Nonprogrammers, however, can then use the programs and modify the data without knowing C++.

The capacity of your disk makes it a perfect place to store your data as well as your programs. Think about what would happen if all data had to be stored with a program's assignment statements. What if the Social Security Office in Washington, D.C., asked you to write a C++ program to compute, average, filter, sort, and print each person's name and address in his or her files? Would you want your program to include millions of assignment statements? Not only would you not want the program to hold that much data, but it could not do so because only relatively small amounts of data fit in a program before you run out of RAM.

By storing data on your disk, you are much less limited because you have more storage. Your disk can hold as much data as you have disk capacity. Also, if your program requirements grow, you can usually increase your disk space, whereas you cannot always add more RAM to your computer.

> **NOTE:** C++ cannot access the special extended or expanded memory some computers have.

When working with disk files, C++ does not have to access much RAM because C++ reads data from your disk drive and processes the data only parts at a time. Not all your disk data has to reside in RAM for C++ to process it. C++ reads some data, processes it, and then reads some more. If C++ requires disk data a second time, it rereads that place on the disk.

Types of Disk File Access

Your programs can access files two ways: through sequential access or random access. Your application determines the method you should choose. The access mode of a file determines how you read, write, change, and delete data from the file. Some of your files can be accessed in both ways, sequentially and randomly as long as your programs are written properly and the data lends itself to both types of file access.

A sequential file has to be accessed in the same order the file was written. This is analogous to cassette tapes: You play music in the same order it was recorded. (You can quickly fast-forward or rewind over songs you do not want to listen to, but the order of the songs dictates what you do to play the song you want.) It is difficult, and sometimes impossible, to insert data in the middle of a sequential file. How easy is it to insert a new song in the middle of two other songs on a tape? The only way to truly add or delete records from the middle of a sequential file is to create a completely new file that combines both old and new records.

It might seem that sequential files are limiting, but it turns out that many applications lend themselves to sequential-file processing.

Unlike sequential files, you can access random-access files in any order you want. Think of data in a random-access file as you would songs on a compact disc or record; you can go directly to any song you want without having to play or fast-forward over the other songs. If you want to play the first song, the sixth song, and then the fourth song, you can do so. The order of play has nothing to do with the order in which the songs were originally recorded. Random-file access sometimes takes more programming but rewards your effort with a more flexible file-access method. Chapter 31 discusses how to program for random-access files.

Sequential File Concepts

There are three operations you can perform on sequential disk files. You can

◆ Create disk files

◆ Add to disk files

◆ Read from disk files

Your application determines what you must do. If you are creating a disk file for the first time, you must create the file and write the initial data to it. Suppose you wanted to create a customer data file. You would create a new file and write your current customers to that file. The customer data might originally be in arrays, arrays of structures, pointed to with pointers, or placed in regular variables by the user.

Over time, as your customer base grows, you can add new customers to the file (called *appending* to the file). When you add to the end of a file, you append to that file. As your customers enter your store, you would read their information from the customer data file.

Customer disk processing is an example of one disadvantage of sequential files, however. Suppose a customer moves and wants you to change his or her address in your files. Sequential-access files do not lend themselves well to changing data stored in them. It is also difficult to remove information from sequential files. Random files, described in the next chapter, provide a much easier approach to changing and removing data. The primary approach to changing or removing data from a sequential-access file is to create a new one, from the old one, with the updated data. Because of the updating ease provided with random-access files, this chapter concentrates on creating, reading, and adding to sequential files.

Opening and Closing Files

Before you can create, write to, or read from a disk file, you must open the file. This is analogous to opening a filing cabinet before working with a file stored in the cabinet. Once you are done with a cabinet's file, you close the file drawer. You also must close a disk file when you finish with it.

When you open a disk file, you only have to inform C++ of the filename and what you want to do (write to, add to, or read from). C++ and your operating system work together to make sure the disk is ready and to create an entry in your file directory (if you are creating a file) for the filename. When you close a file, C++ writes any remaining data to the file, releases the file from the program, and updates the file directory to reflect the file's new size.

> **CAUTION:** You must ensure that the FILES= statement in your CONFIG.SYS file is large enough to hold the maximum number of disk files you have open, with one left for your C++ program. If you are unsure how to do this, check your DOS reference manual or a beginner's book about DOS.

To open a file, you must call the open() function. To close a file, call the close() function. Here is the format of these two function calls:

```
file_ptr.open(file_name, access);
```

and

```
file_ptr.close();
```

file_ptr is a special type of pointer that only points to files, not data variables.

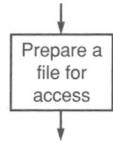

Prepare a file for access

Your operating system handles the exact location of your data in the disk file. You don't want to worry about the exact track and sector number of your data on the disk. Therefore, you let *file_ptr* point to the data you are reading and writing. Your program only has to generically manage *file_ptr*, whereas C++ and your operating system take care of locating the actual physical data.

file_name is a string (or a character pointer that points to a string) containing a valid filename for your computer. *file_name* can contain a complete disk and directory pathname. You can specify the filename in uppercase or lowercase letters.

access must be one of the values from Table 30.1.

Table 30.1. Possible access modes.

Mode	Description
app	Open the file for appending (adding to it).
ate	Seek to end of file on opening it.
in	Open the file for reading.
out	Open the file for writing.
binary	Open the file in binary mode.
trunc	Discard contents if file exists
nocreate	If file doesn't exist, open fails.
noreplace	If file exists, open fails unless appending or seeking to end of file on opening.

The default access mode for file access is a *text mode.* A text file is an ASCII file, compatible with most other programming languages and applications. Text files do not always contain text, in the word-processing sense of the word. Any data you have to store can go in a text file. Programs that read ASCII files can read data you create as C++ text files. For a discussion of binary file access, see the box that follows.

Binary Modes

If you specify binary access, C++ creates or reads the file in a binary format. Binary data files are "squeezed"—they take less space than text files. The disadvantage of using binary files is that other programs cannot always read the data files. Only C++ programs written to access binary files can read and write to them. The advantage of binary files is that you save disk space because your data files are more compact. Other than the access mode in the open() function, you use no additional commands to access binary files with your C++ programs.

The binary format is a system-specific file format. In other words, not all computers can read a binary file created on another computer.

If you open a file for writing, C++ creates the file. If a file by that name already exists, C++ overwrites the old file with no warning. You must be careful when opening files so you do not overwrite existing data that you want to save.

If an error occurs during the opening of a file, C++ does not create a valid file pointer. Instead, C++ creates a file pointer equal to zero. For example, if you open a file for output, but use a disk name that is invalid, C++ cannot open the file and makes the file pointer equal to zero. Always check the file pointer when writing disk file programs to ensure the file opened properly.

TIP: Beginning programmers like to open all files at the beginning of their programs and close them at the end. This is not always the best method. Open files immediately before you access them and close them immediately when you are done with them. This habit protects the files because they are closed immediately after you are done with them. A closed file is more likely to be protected in the unfortunate (but possible) event of a power failure or computer breakdown.

This section contains much information on file-access theories. The following examples help illustrate these concepts.

Examples

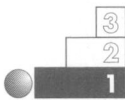

1. Suppose you want to create a file for storing your house payment records for the previous year. Here are the first few lines in the program which creates a file called HOUSE.DAT on your disk:

```
#include <fstream.h>

main()
{
   ofstream file_ptr;   // Declares a file pointer for writing
   file_ptr.open("house.dat", ios::out);  // Creates the file
```

The remainder of the program writes data to the file. The program never has to refer to the filename again. The program uses the `file_ptr` variable to refer to the file. Examples in the next few sections illustrate how. There is nothing special about `file_ptr`, other than its name (although the name is meaningful in this case). You can name file pointer variables xyz or a908973 if you like, but these names would not be meaningful.

You must include the fstream.h header file because it contains the definition for the `ofstream` and `ifstream` declarations. You don't have to worry about the physical specifics. The `file_ptr` "points" to data in the file as you write it. Put the declarations in your programs where you declare other variables and arrays.

> **TIP:** Because files are not part of your program, you might find it useful to declare file pointers globally. Unlike data in variables, there is rarely a reason to keep file pointers local.

Before finishing with the program, you should close the file. The following `close()` function closes the house file:

```
file_ptr.close();      // Close the house payment file.
```

2. If you want, you can put the complete pathname in the file's name. The following opens the household payment file in a subdirectory on the D: disk drive:

```
file_ptr.open("d:\mydata\house.dat", ios::out);
```

3. If you want, you can store a filename in a character array or point to it with a character pointer. Each of the following sections of code is equivalent:

```
char    fn[ ] = "house.dat";   // Filename in character array.
file_ptr.open(fn, ios::out);    // Creates the file.

char    *myfile = "house.dat";    // Filename pointed to.
file_ptr.open(myfile, ios::out);    // Creates the file.

// Let the user enter the filename.
cout << "What is the name of the household file? ";
gets(filename); // Filename must be an array or
                // character pointer.
file_ptr.open(filename, ios::out);    // Creates the file.
```

No matter how you specify the filename when opening the file, close the file with the file pointer. This `close()` function closes the open file, no matter which method you used to open the file:

```
file_ptr.close();     // Close the house payment file.
```

4. You should check the return value from `open()` to ensure the file opened properly. Here is code after `open()` that checks for an error:

Check
whether an
error
occurred

```
#include <fstream.h>

main()
{
    ofstream file_ptr;    // Declares a file pointer.
```

```
file_ptr.open("house.dat", ios::out); // Creates the file.
if (!file_ptr)
{   cout << "Error opening file.\n"; }
else
{
    // Rest of output commands go here.
```

5. You can open and write to several files in the same program. Suppose you wanted to read data from a payroll file and create a backup payroll data file. You have to open the current payroll file using the in reading mode, and the backup file in the output out mode.

For each open file in your program, you must declare a different file pointer. The file pointers used by your input and output statement determine on which file they operate. If you have to open many files, you can declare an array of file pointers.

Here is a way you can open the two payroll files:

```
#include <fstream.h>

ifstream        file_in;       // Input file
ofstream        file_out;      // Output file

main()
{
    file_in.open("payroll.dat", ios::in);    // Existing file
    file_out.open("payroll.BAK", ios::out); // New file
```

When you finish with these files, be sure to close them with these two close() function calls:

```
file_in.close();
file_out.close();
```

Writing to a File

Any input or output function that requires a device performs input and output with files. You have seen most of these already. The most common file I/O functions are

```
get() and put()
gets() and puts()
```

You also can use *file_ptr* as you do with cout or cin.

The following function call reads three integers from a file pointed to by *file ptr*:

```
file_ptr >> num1 >> num2 >> num3;    // Reads three variables.
```

There is always more than one way to write data to a disk file. Most the time, more than one function will work. For example, if you write many names to a file, both puts() and file_ptr << work. You also can write the names using put(). You should use whichever function you are most comfortable with. If you want a newline character (\n) at the end of each line in your file, the file_ptr << and puts() are probably easier than put(), but all three will do the job.

> **TIP:** Each line in a file is called a *record*. By putting a newline character at the end of file records, you make the input of those records easier.

Examples

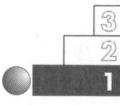

1. The following program creates a file called NAMES.DAT. The program writes five names to a disk file using file_ptr <<.

```
// Filename: C30WR1.CPP
// Writes five names to a disk file.
#include <fstream.h>

ofstream fp;
```

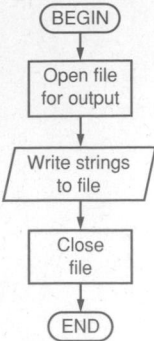

```
void main()
{
    fp.open("NAMES.DAT", ios::out);  // Creates a new file.

    fp << "Michael Langston\n";
    fp << "Sally Redding\n";
    fp << "Jane Kirk\n";
    fp << "Stacy Wikert\n";
    fp << "Joe Hiquet\n";
    fp.close();   // Release the file.
    return;
}
```

To keep this first example simple, error checking was not done on the `open()` function. The next few examples check for the error.

NAMES.TXT is a text data file. If you want, you can read this file into your word processor (use your word processor's command for reading ASCII files) or use the MS-DOS TYPE command (or your operating system's equivalent command) to display this file on-screen. If you were to display NAMES.TXT, you would see:

```
Michael Langston
Sally Redding
Jane Kirk
Stacy Wikert
Joe Hiquet
```

2. The following file writes the numbers from 1 to 100 to a file called NUMS.1.

```
// Filename: C30WR2.CPP
// Writes 1 to 100 to a disk file.

#include <fstream.h>

ofstream        fp;

void main()
```

```
{
    int ctr;

    fp.open("NUMS.1", ios::out);    // Creates a new file.
    if (!fp)
      {  cout << "Error opening file.\n"; }
    else
      {
         for (ctr = 1; ctr < 101; ctr++)
            {  fp << ctr << " "; }
      }
    fp.close();
    return;
}
```

The numbers are not written one per line, but with a space between each of them. The format of the file_ptr << determines the format of the output data. When writing data to disk files, keep in mind that you have to read the data later. You have to use "mirror-image" input functions to read data you output to files.

Writing to a Printer

Functions such as open() and others were not designed to write only to files. They were designed to write to any device, including files, the screen, and the printer. If you must write data to a printer, you can treat the printer as if it were a file. The following program opens a file pointer using the MS-DOS name for a printer located at LPT1 (the MS-DOS name for the first parallel printer port):

```
// Filename: C30PRNT.CPP
// Prints to the printer device

#include <fstream.h>

ofstream prnt;    // Points to the printer.

void main()
```

```
{
   prnt.open("LPT1", ios::out);
   prnt << "Printer line 1\n";      // 1st line printed.
   prnt << "Printer line 2\n";      // 2nd line printed.
   prnt << "Printer line 3\n";      // 3rd line printed.
   prnt.close();
return;
}
```

Make sure your printer is on and has paper before you run this program. When you run the program, you see this printed on the printer:

```
Printer line 1
Printer line 2
Printer line 3
```

Adding to a File

You can easily add data to an existing file or create new files, by opening the file in append access mode. Data files on the disk are rarely static; they grow almost daily due to (hopefully!) increased business. Being able to add to data already on the disk is very useful, indeed.

Files you open for append access (using ios::app) do not have to exist. If the file exists, C++ appends data to the end of the file when you write the data. If the file does not exist, C++ creates the file (as is done when you open a file for write access).

Example

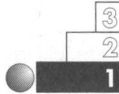

The following program adds three more names to the NAMES.DAT file created in an earlier example.

```
// Filename: C30AP1.CPP
// Adds three names to a disk file.

#include <fstream.h>
```

```
ofstream    fp;

void main()
{
   fp.open("NAMES.DAT", ios::app);   // Adds to file.
   fp << "Johnny Smith\n";
   fp << "Laura Hull\n";
   fp << "Mark Brown\n";
   fp.close();                       // Release the file.
   return;
}
```

Here is what the file now looks like:

```
Michael Langston
Sally Redding
Jane Kirk
Stacy Wikert
Joe Hiquet
Johnny Smith
Laura Hull
Mark Brown
```

> **NOTE:** If the file does not exist, C++ creates it and stores the three names to the file.

Basically, you only have to change the open() function's access mode to turn a file-creation program into a file-appending program.

Reading from a File

Files must exist prior to opening them for read access.

Once the data is in a file, you must be able to read that data. You must open the file in a read access mode. There are several ways to read data. You can read character data one character at a time or one string at a time. The choice depends on the format of the data.

Files you open for read access (using ios::in) must exist already, or C++ gives you an error. You cannot read a file that does not exist. open() returns zero if the file does not exist when you open it for read access.

Another event happens when reading files. Eventually, you read all the data. Subsequent reading produces errors because there is no more data to read. C++ provides a solution to the end-of-file occurrence. If you attempt to read from a file that you have completely read the data from, C++ returns the value of zero. To find the end-of-file condition, be sure to check for zero when reading information from files.

Examples

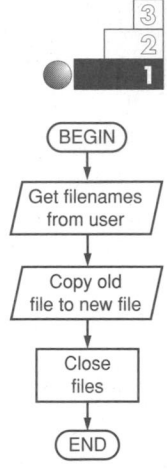

1. This program asks the user for a filename and prints the contents of the file to the screen. If the file does not exist, the program displays an error message.

```cpp
// Filename: C30RE1.CPP
// Reads and displays a file.

#include <fstream.h>
#include <stdlib.h>

ifstream fp;

void main()
{
    char filename[12]; // Holds user's filename.
    char in_char;      // Input character.

    cout << "What is the name of the file you want to see? ";
    cin >> filename;
    fp.open(filename, ios::in);
    if (!fp)
    {
      cout << "\n\n*** That file does not exist ***\n";
      exit(0);    // Exit program.
    }
    while (fp.get(in_char))
      {  cout << in_char;  }
    fp.close();
    return;
}
```

Here is the resulting output when the NAMES.DAT file is requested:

```
What is the name of the file you want to see? NAMES.DAT
Michael Langston
Sally Redding
Jane Kirk
Stacy Wikert
Joe Hiquet
Johnny Smith
Laura Hull
Mark Brown
```

Because newline characters are in the file at the end of each name, the names appear on-screen, one per line. If you attempt to read a file that does not exist, the program displays the following message:

```
*** That file does not exist ***
```

2. This program reads one file and copies it to another. You might want to use such a program to back up important data in case the original file is damaged.

The program must open two files, the first for reading, and the second for writing. The file pointer determines which of the two files is being accessed.

```cpp
// Filename: C30RE2.CPP
// Makes a copy of a file.

#include <fstream.h>
#include <stdlib.h>

ifstream in_fp;
ofstream out_fp;

void main()
{
    char in_filename[12];    // Holds original filename.
    char out_filename[12];   // Holds backup filename.
    char in_char;            // Input character.
```

```
   cout << "What is the name of the file you want to back up?
";
   cin >> in_filename;
   cout << "What is the name of the file ";
   cout << "you want to copy " << in_filename << " to? ";
   cin >> out_filename;
   in_fp.open(in_filename, ios::in);
   if (!in_fp)
   {
     cout << "\n\n*** " << in_filename << " does not exist
***\n";
     exit(0);    // Exit program
   }
   out_fp.open(out_filename, ios::out);
   if (!out_fp)
   {
     cout << "\n\n*** Error opening " << in_filename << "
***\n";
     exit(0);    // Exit program
   }
   cout << "\nCopying...\n";    // Waiting message.
   while (in_fp.get(in_char))
     { out_fp.put(in_char); }
   cout << "\nThe file is copied.\n";
   in_fp.close();
   out_fp.close();
   return;
}
```

Review Questions

Answers to the review questions are in Appendix B.

1. What are the three ways to access sequential files?

2. What advantage do disk files have over holding data in memory?

3. How do sequential files differ from random-access files?

4. What happens if you open a file for read access and the file does not exist?

5. What happens if you open a file for write access and the file already exists?

6. What happens if you open a file for append access and the file does not exist?

7. How does C++ inform you that you have reached the end-of-file condition?

Review Exercises

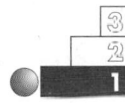

1. Write a program that creates a file containing the following data:

   Your name
   Your address
   Your phone number
   Your age

2. Write a second program that reads and prints the data file you created in Exercise 1.

3. Write a program that takes your data created in Exercise 1 and writes it to the screen one word per line.

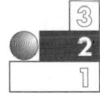

4. Write a program for PCs that backs up two important files: the AUTOEXEC.BAT and CONFIG.SYS. Call the backup files AUTOEXEC.SAV and CONFIG.SAV.

5. Write a program that reads a file and creates a new file with the same data, except reverse the case on the second file. Everywhere uppercase letters appear in the first file, write lowercase letters to the new file, and everywhere lowercase letters appear in the first file, write uppercase letters to the new file.

Summary

You can now perform one of the most important requirements of data processing: writing and reading to and from disk files. Before this chapter, you could only store data in variables. The short life of variables (they only last as long as your program is running) made long-term storage of data impossible. You can now save large amounts of data in disk files to process later.

Reading and writing sequential files involves learning more concepts than actual commands or functions. The `open()` and `close()` functions are the most important functions you learned in this chapter. You are now familiar with most of the I/O functions needed to retrieve data to and from disk files.

The next chapter concludes the discussion of disk files in this book. You will learn how to create and use random-access files. By programming with random file access, you can read selected data from a file, as well as change data without having to rewrite the entire file.

Random-Access Files

This chapter introduces the concept of random file access. Random file access enables you to read or write any data in your disk file without having to read or write every piece of data before it. You can quickly search for, add, retrieve, change, and delete information in a random-access file. Although you need a few new functions to access files randomly, you find that the extra effort pays off in flexibility, power, and speed of disk access.

This chapter introduces

♦ Random-access files

♦ File records

♦ The seekg() function

♦ Special-purpose file I/O functions

With C++'s sequential and random-access files, you can do everything you would ever want to do with disk data.

Random File Records

Random files exemplify the power of data processing with C++. Sequential file processing is slow unless you read the entire file into arrays and process them in memory. As explained in Chapter 30, however, you have much more disk space than RAM, and most disk files do not even fit in your RAM at one time. Therefore, you need a way to quickly read individual pieces of data from a file in any order and process them one at a time.

Generally, you read and write file *records*. A record to a file is analogous to a C++ structure. A record is a collection of one or more data values (called *fields*) you read and write to disk. Generally, you store data in structures and write the structures to disk where they are called records. When you read a record from disk, you generally read that record into a structure variable and process it with your program.

Unlike most programming languages, not all disk data for C++ programs has to be stored in record format. Typically, you write a stream of characters to a disk file and access that data either sequentially or randomly by reading it into variables and structures.

The process of randomly accessing data in a file is simple. Think about the data files of a large credit card organization. When you make a purchase, the store calls the credit card company to receive authorization. Millions of names are in the credit card company's files. There is no quick way the credit card company could read every record sequentially from the disk that comes before yours. Sequential files do not lend themselves to quick access. It is not feasible, in many situations, to look up individual records in a data file with sequential access.

The credit card companies must use a random file access so their computers can go directly to your record, just as you go directly to a song on a compact disk or record album. The functions you use are different from the sequential functions, but the power that results from learning the added functions is worth the effort.

When your program reads and writes files randomly, it treats the file like a big array. With arrays, you know you can add, print, or remove values in any order. You do not have to start at the first

A record to a file is like a structure to variables.

You do not have to rewrite an entire file to change random-access file data.

array element, sequentially looking at the next one, until you get the element you need. You can view your random-access file in the same way, accessing the data in any order.

Most random file records are *fixed-length* records. Each record (usually a row in the file) takes the same amount of disk space. Most of the sequential files you read and wrote in the previous chapters were variable-length records. When you are reading or writing sequentially, there is no need for fixed-length records because you input each value one character, word, string, or number at a time, and look for the data you want. With fixed-length records, your computer can better calculate where on the disk the desired record is located.

Although you waste some disk space with fixed-length records (because of the spaces that pad some of the fields), the advantages of random file access compensate for the "wasted" disk space (when the data do not actually fill the structure size).

TIP: With random-access files, you can read or write records in any order. Therefore, even if you want to perform sequential reading or writing of the file, you can use random-access processing and "randomly" read or write the file in sequential record number order.

Opening Random-Access Files

Just as with sequential files, you must open random-access files before reading or writing to them. You can use any of the read access modes mentioned in Chapter 30 (such as `ios::in`) only to read a file randomly. However, to modify data in a file, you must open the file in one of the update modes, repeated for you in Table 31.1.

Table 31.1. Random-access update modes.

Mode	Description
app	Open the file for appending (adding to it)
ate	Seek to end of file on opening it
in	Open file for reading
out	Open file for writing
binary	Open file in binary mode
trunc	Discard contents if file exists
nocreate	If file doesn't exist, open fails
noreplace	If file exists, open fails unless appending or seeking to end of file on opening

There is really no difference between sequential files and random files in C++. The difference between the files is not physical, but lies in the method you use to access them and update them.

Examples

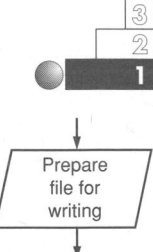

Prepare file for writing

1. Suppose you want to write a program to create a file of your friends' names. The following open() function call suffices, assuming fp is declared as a file pointer:

```
fp.open("NAMES.DAT", ios::out);
if (!fp)
  { cout << "\n*** Cannot open file ***\n"; }
```

No update open() access mode is needed if you are only creating the file. However, what if you wanted to create the file, write names to it, and give the user a chance to change any of the names before closing the file? You then have to open the file like this:

```
fp.open("NAMES.DAT", ios::in ¦ ios::out);
if (!fp)
    cout << "\n*** Cannot open file ***\n";
```

This code enables you to create the file, then change data you wrote to the file.

2. As with sequential files, the only difference between using a binary open() access mode and a text mode is that the file you create is more compact and saves disk space. You cannot, however, read that file from other programs as an ASCII text file. The previous open() function can be rewritten to create and allow updating of a binary file. All other file-related commands and functions work for binary files just as they do for text files.

```
fp.open("NAMES.DAT", ios::in | ios::out | ios::binary);
if (!fp)
   cout << "\n*** Cannot open file ***\n";
```

The seekg() Function

C++ provides a function that enables you to read to a specific point in a random-access data file. This is the seekg() function. The format of seekg() is

file_ptr.seekg(*long_num*, *origin*);

file ptr is the pointer to the file that you want to access, initialized with an open() statement. *long_num* is the number of bytes in the file you want to skip. C++ does not read this many bytes, but literally skips the data by the number of bytes specified in *long_num*. Skipping the bytes on the disk is much faster than reading them. If *long_num* is negative, C++ skips backwards in the file (this allows for rereading of data several times). Because data files can be large, you must declare *long_num* as a long integer to hold a large amount of bytes.

origin is a value that tells C++ where to begin the skipping of bytes specified by *long_num*. *origin* can be any of the three values shown in Table 31.2.

You can read forwards or backwards from any point in the file with seekg().

Table 31.2. Possible origin values.

Description	origin	Equivalent
Beginning of file	SEEK_SET	ios::beg
Current file position	SEEK_CUR	ios::cur
End of file	SEEK_END	ios::end

The origins SEEK_SET, SEEK_CUR, and SEEK_END are defined in stdio.h. The equivalents ios::beg, ios::cur, and ios::end are defined in fstream.h.

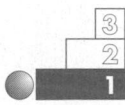

> **NOTE:** Actually, the file pointer plays a much more important role than simply "pointing to the file" on the disk. The file pointer continually points to the exact location of the *next byte to read or write.* In other words, as you read data from either a sequential or random-access file, the file pointer increments with each byte read. By using seekg(), you can move the file pointer forward or backward in the file.

Examples

1. No matter how far into a file you have read, the following seekg() function positions the file pointer back to the beginning of a file:

```
fp.seekg(0L, SEEK_SET); // Position file pointer at beginning.
```

The constant 0L passes a long integer 0 to the seekg() function. Without the L, C++ passes a regular integer and this does not match the prototype for seekg() that is located in fstream.h. Chapter 4, "Variables and Literals," explained the use of data type suffixes on numeric constants, but the suffixes have not been used until now.

This seekg() function literally reads "move the file pointer 0 bytes from the beginning of the file."

2. The following example reads a file named MYFILE.TXT twice, once to send the file to the screen and once to send the file to the printer. Three file pointers are used, one for each device (the file, the screen, and the printer).

```cpp
// Filename: C31TWIC.CPP
// Writes a file to the printer, rereads it,
// and sends it to the screen.

#include <fstream.h>
#include <stdlib.h>
#include <stdio.h>

ifstream in_file;    // Input file pointer.
ofstream scrn;       // Screen pointer.
ofstream prnt;       // Printer pointer.

void main()
{
    char in_char;

    in_file.open("MYFILE.TXT", ios::in);
    if (!in_file)
    {
        cout << "\n*** Error opening MYFILE.TXT ***\n";
        exit(0);
    }
    scrn.open("CON", ios::out);    // Open screen device.
    while (in_file.get(in_char))
    { scrn << in_char; } // Output characters to the screen.
    scrn.close();  // Close screen because it is no
                   // longer needed.
    in_file.seekg(0L, SEEK_SET);   // Reposition file pointer.
    prnt.open("LPT1", ios::out);   // Open printer device.
    while (in_file.get(in_char))
      { prnt << in_char; }   // Output characters to the
                             // printer.
    prnt.close();            // Always close all open files.
    in_file.close();
    return;
}
```

You also can close then reopen a file to position the file pointer at the beginning, but using seekg() is a more efficient method.

Of course, you could have used regular I/O functions to write to the screen, rather than having to open the screen as a separate device.

3. The following seekg() function positions the file pointer at the 30th byte in the file. (The next byte read is the 31st byte.)

```
file_ptr.seekg(30L, SEEK_SET);   // Position file pointer
                                 // at the 30th byte.
```

This seekg() function literally reads "move the file pointer 30 bytes from the beginning of the file."

If you write structures to a file, you can quickly seek any structure in the file using the sizeof() function. Suppose you want the 123rd occurrence of the structure tagged with inventory. You would search using the following seekg() function:

```
file_ptr.seekg((123L * sizeof(struct inventory)), SEEK_SET);
```

4. The following program writes the letters of the alphabet to a file called ALPH.TXT. The seekg() function is then used to read and display the ninth and 17th letters (*I* and *Q*).

```
// Filename: C31ALPH.CPP
// Stores the alphabet in a file, then reads
// two letters from it.

#include <fstream.h>
#include <stdlib.h>
#include <stdio.h>

fstream fp;

void main()
{
    char ch;     // Holds A through Z.
```

```
// Open in update mode so you can read file after writing to it.
fp.open("alph.txt", ios::in | ios::out);
if (!fp)
{
  cout << "\n*** Error opening file ***\n";
  exit(0);
}
for (ch = 'A'; ch <= 'Z'; ch++)
{ fp << ch;  }  // Write letters.
fp.seekg(8L, ios::beg);    // Skip eight letters, point to I.
fp >> ch;
cout << "The first character is " << ch << "\n";
fp.seekg(16L, ios::beg);   // Skip 16 letters, point to Q.
fp >> ch;
cout << "The second character is " << ch << "\n";
fp.close();
return;
}
```

5. To point to the end of a data file, you can use the `seekg()` function to position the file pointer at the last byte. Subsequent `seekg()`s should then use a negative `long_num` value to skip backwards in the file. The following `seekg()` function makes the file pointer point to the end of the file:

```
file_ptr.seekg(0L, SEEK_END); // Position file
                              // pointer at the end.
```

This `seekg()` function literally reads "move the file pointer 0 bytes from the end of the file." The file pointer now points to the end-of-file marker, but you can `seekg()` backwards to find other data in the file.

6. The following program reads the ALPH.TXT file (created in Exercise 4) backwards, printing each character as it skips back in the file.

```
// Filename: C31BACK.CPP
// Reads and prints a file backwards.
```

```
#include <fstream.h>
#include <stdlib.h>
#include <stdio.h>

ifstream fp;

void main()
{
   int ctr;    // Steps through the 26 letters in the file.
   char in_char;

   fp.open("ALPH.TXT", ios::in);
   if (!fp)
   {
     cout << "\n*** Error opening file ***\n";
     exit(0);
   }
   fp.seekg(-1L, SEEK_END);    // Point to last byte in
                               // the file.
   for (ctr = 0; ctr < 26; ctr++)
   {
      fp >> in_char;
      fp.seekg(-2L, SEEK_CUR);
      cout << in_char;
   }
   fp.close();
   return;
}
```

This program also uses the SEEK_CUR *origin* value. The last seekg() in the program seeks two bytes backwards from the *current position,* not the beginning or end as the previous examples have. The for loop towards the end of the program performs a "skip-two-bytes-back, read-one-byte-forward" method to skip through the file backwards.

7. The following program performs the same actions as Example 4 (C31ALPH.CPP), with one addition. When the letters *I* and *Q* are found, the letter *x* is written over the *I* and *Q.* The seekg() must be used to back up one byte in the file to overwrite the letter just read.

```
// Filename: C31CHANG.CPP
// Stores the alphabet in a file, reads two letters from it,
// and changes those letters to xs.

#include <fstream.h>
#include <stdlib.h>
#include <stdio.h>

fstream fp;

void main()
{
   char ch;    // Holds A through Z.

// Open in update mode so you can read file after writing to it.
   fp.open("alph.txt", ios::in | ios::out);
   if (!fp)
   {
     cout << "\n*** Error opening file ***\n";
     exit(0);
   }
   for (ch = 'A'; ch <= 'Z'; ch++)
      { fp << ch; }    // Write letters
   fp.seekg(8L, SEEK_SET);  // Skip eight letters, point to I.
   fp >> ch;
   // Change the Q to an x.
   fp.seekg(-1L, SEEK_CUR);
   fp << 'x';
   cout << "The first character is " << ch << "\n";
   fp.seekg(16L, SEEK_SET);    // Skip 16 letters, point to Q.
   fp >> ch;
   cout << "The second character is " << ch << "\n";
   // Change the Q to an x.
   fp.seekg(-1L, SEEK_CUR);
   fp << 'x';
   fp.close();
   return;
}
```

The file named ALPH.TXT now looks like this:

ABCDEFGHxJKLMNOPxRSTUVWXYZ

This program forms the basis of a more complete data file management program. After you master the `seekg()` functions and become more familiar with disk data files, you will begin to write programs that store more advanced data structures and access them.

The mailing list application in Appendix F is a good example of what you can do with random file access. The user is given a chance to change names and addresses already in the file. The program, using random access, seeks for and changes selected data without rewriting the entire disk file.

Other Helpful I/O Functions

There are several more disk I/O functions available that you might find useful. They are mentioned here for completeness. As you perform more powerful disk I/O, you might find a use for many of these functions. Each of these functions is prototyped in the fstream.h header file.

◆ `read(array, count)`: Reads the data specified by `count` into the array or pointer specified by `array`. `read()` is called a *buffered I/O* function. `read()` enables you to read much data with a single function call.

◆ `write(array, count)`: Writes `count array` bytes to the specified file. `write()` is a buffered I/O function. `write()` enables you to write much data in a single function call.

◆ `remove(filename)`: Erases the file named by `filename`. `remove()` returns a `0` if the file was erased successfully and `-1` if an error occurred.

Many of these (and other built-in I/O functions that you learn in your C++ programming career) are helpful functions that you could duplicate using what you already know.

The buffered I/O file functions enable you to read and write entire arrays (including arrays of structures) to the disk in a single function call.

Examples

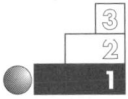

1. The following program requests a filename from the user and erases the file from the disk using the `remove()` function.

```
// Filename: C31ERAS.CPP
// Erases the file specified by the user.

#include <stdio.h>
#include <iostream.h>

void main()
{
   char filename[12];

   cout << "What is the filename you want me to erase? ";
   cin >> filename;
   if (remove(filename) == -1)
   {  cout << "\n*** I could not remove the file ***\n"; }
   else
   {  cout << "\nThe file " << filename << " is now romoved\n",}
   return;
}
```

2. The following function is part of a larger program that receives inventory data, in an array of structures, from the user. This function is passed the array name and the number of elements (structure variables) in the array. The `write()` function then writes the complete array of structures to the disk file pointed to by `fp`.

```
void write_str(inventory items[ ], int inv_cnt)
{
   fp.write(items, inv_cnt * sizeof(inventory));
   return;
}
```

If the inventory array had 1,000 elements, this one-line function would still write the entire array to the disk file. You could use the `read()` function to read the entire array of structures from the disk in a single function call.

Review Questions

The answers to the review questions are in Appendix B.

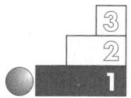

1. What is the difference between records and structures?

2. True or false: You have to create a random-access file before reading from it randomly.

3. What happens to the file pointer as you read from a file?

4. What are the two buffered file I/O functions?

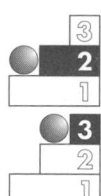

5. What is wrong with this program?

```
#include <fstream.h>
ifstream  fp;
void main()
{
   char in_char;
   fp.open(ios::in | ios::binary);
   if (fp.get(in_char))
   {  cout << in_char;  }   // Write to the screen
   fp.close();
   return;
}
```

Review Exercises

1. Write a program that asks the user for a list of five names, then writes the names to a file. Rewind the file and display its contents on-screen using the `seekg()` and `get()` functions.

2. Rewrite the program in Exercise 1 so it displays every other character in the file of names.

3. Write a program that reads characters from a file. If the input character is a lowercase letter, change it to uppercase. If the input character is an uppercase letter, change it to lowercase. Do not change other characters in the file.

4. Write a program that displays the number of nonalphabetic characters in a file.

5. Write a grade-keeping program for a teacher. Allow the teacher to enter up to 10 students' grades. Each student has three grades for the semester. Store the students' names and their three grades in an array of structures and store the data on the disk. Make the program menu-driven. Include options of adding more students, viewing the file's data, or printing the grades to the printer with a calculated class average.

Summary

C++ supports random-access files with several functions. These functions include error checking, file pointer positioning, and the opening and closing of files. You now have the tools you need to save your C++ program data to disk for storage and retrieval.

The mailing-list application in Appendix F offers a complete example of random-access file manipulation. The program enables the user to enter names and addresses, store them to disk, edit them, change them, and print them from the disk file. The mailing-list program combines almost every topic from this book into a complete application that "puts it all together."

Introduction to Object-Oriented Programming

The most widely used object-oriented programming language today is C++. C++ provides *classes*—which are its objects. Classes really distinguish C++ from C. In fact, before the name C++ was coined, the C++ language was called "C with classes."

This chapter attempts to expose you to the world of object-oriented programming, often called *OOP.* You will probably not become a master of OOP in these few short pages, however, you are ready to begin expanding your C++ knowledge.

This chapter introduces the following concepts:

♦ C++ classes

♦ Member functions

♦ Constructors

♦ Destructors

This chapter concludes your introduction to the C++ language. After mastering the techniques taught in this book, you will be ready to modify the mailing list program in Appendix F to suit your own needs.

What Is a Class?

A *class* is a user-defined data type that resembles a structure. A class can have data members, but unlike the structures you have seen thus far, classes can also have *member functions*. The data members can be of any type, whether defined by the language or by you. The member functions can manipulate the data, create and destroy class variables, and even redefine C++'s operators to act on the class objects.

Classes have several types of members, but they all fall into two categories: data members and member functions.

Data Members

Data members can be of any type. Here is a simple class:

```
// A sphere class.
class Sphere
{
public:
   float r;          // Radius of sphere
   float x, y, z;    // Coordinates of sphere
};
```

Notice how this class resembles structures you have already seen, with the exception of the public keyword. The Sphere class has four data members: r, x, y, and z. In this case, the public keyword plays an important role; it identifies the class Sphere as a structure. As a matter of fact, in C++, a *public class* is physically identical to a structure. For now, ignore the public keyword; it is explained later in this chapter.

Member Functions

A class can also have *member functions* (members of a class that manipulate data members). This is one of the primary features that distinguishes a class from a structure. Here is the Sphere class again, with member functions added:

```
#include  <math.h>

const float PI = 3.14159;
// A sphere class.
class Sphere
{
public:
   float r;         // Radius of sphere
   float x, y, z;   // Coordinates of sphere
   Sphere(float xcoord, float ycoord, float zcoord, float radius)
     { x = xcoord; y = ycoord; z = zcoord; r = radius; }
   ~Sphere() { }
   float volume()
   {
      return (r * r * r * 4 * PI / 3);
   }
   float surface_area()
   {
      return (r * r * 4 * PI);
   }
};
```

This Sphere class has four member functions: Sphere(), ~Sphere(), volume(), and surface_area(). The class is losing its similarity to a structure. These member functions are very short. (The one with the strange name of ~Sphere() has no code in it.) If the codes of the member functions were much longer, only the prototypes would appear in the class, and the code for the member functions would follow later in the program.

C++ programmers call class data *objects* because classes do more than simply hold data. Classes act on data; in effect, a class is an object that manipulates itself. All the data you have seen so far in this book is *passive* data (data that has been manipulated by code in the program). Classes' member functions actually manipulate class data.

Constructors create and initialize class data.

In this example, the class member Sphere() is a special function. It is a *constructor* function, and its name must always be the same as its class. Its primary use is declaring a new instance of the class.

Examples

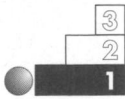

1. The following program uses the Sphere() class to initialize a class variable (called a class *instance*) and print it.

```cpp
// Filename: C32CON.CPP
// Demonstrates use of a class constructor function.

#include  <iostream.h>
const float PI = 3.14159;  // Approximate value of pi.

// A sphere class.
class Sphere
{
public:
   float r;           // Radius of sphere
   float x, y, z;   // Coordinates of sphere
   Sphere(float xcoord, float ycoord,
          float zcoord, float radius)
       { x = xcoord; y = ycoord; z = zcoord; r = radius; }
   ~Sphere() { }
   float volume()
   {
     return (r * r * r * 4 * PI / 3);
   }
   float surface_area()
   {
      return (r * r * 4 * PI);
   }
};

void main()
{
  Sphere s(1.0, 2.0, 3.0, 4.0);

  cout << "X = " << s.x << ", Y = " << s.y
       << ", Z = " << s.z << ", R = " << s.r << "\n";
  return;
}
```

> **Note:** In OOP, the `main()` function (and all it calls) becomes smaller because member functions contain the code that manipulates all class data.

Indeed, this program looks different from those you have seen so far. This example is your first true exposure to OOP programming. Here is the output of this program:

```
X = 1, Y = 2, Z = 3, R = 4
```

This program illustrates the `Sphere()` constructor function. The constructor function is the only member function called by the program. Notice the `~Sphere()` member function constructed s, and initialized its data members as well.

Destructors erase
class data.

The other special function is the *destructor* function, `~Sphere()`. Notice that it also has the same name as the class, but with a *tilde* (-) as a prefix. The destructor function never takes arguments, and never returns values. Also notice that this destructor doesn't do anything. Most destructors do very little. If a destructor has no real purpose, you do not have to specify it. When the class variable goes out of scope, the memory allocated for that class variable is returned to the system (in other words, an automatic destruction occurs). Programmers use destructor functions to free memory occupied by class data in advanced C++ applications.

Similarly, if a constructor doesn't serve any specific function, you aren't required to declare one. C++ allocates memory for a class variable when you define the class variable, just as it does for all other variables. As you learn more about C++ programming, especially when you begin using the advanced concept of *dynamic memory allocation*, constructors and destructors become more useful.

2. To illustrate that the `~Sphere()` destructor does get called (it just doesn't do anything), you can put a `cout` statement in the constructor as seen in the next program:

```
// Filename: C32DES.CPP
// Demonstrates use of a class destructor function.
```

```
#include  <iostream.h>
#include  <math.h>
const float PI = 3.14159;   // Approximate value of pi.

// A sphere class
class Sphere
{
public:
   float  r;         // Radius of sphere
   float  x, y, z;   // Coordinates of sphere
   Sphere(float xcoord, float ycoord,
          float zcoord, float radius)
   { x = xcoord; y = ycoord; z = zcoord; r = radius; }
   ~Sphere()
   {
    cout << "Sphere (" << x << ", " << y
        << ", " << z << ", " << r << ") destroyed\n";
   }
   float volume()
   {
      return (r * r * r * 4 * PI / 3);
   }
   float surface_area()
   {
      return (r * r * 4 * PI);
   }
};

void main(void)
{
   Sphere s(1.0, 2.0, 3.0, 4.0);
   // Construct a class instance.
   cout << "X = " << s.x << ", Y = "
        << s.y << ", Z = " << s.z << ", R = " << s.r << "\n";
   return;
}
```

Here is the output of this program:

```
X = 1, Y = 2, Z = 3, R = 4
Sphere (1, 2, 3, 4) destroyed
```

Notice that `main()` did not explicitly call the destructor function, but `~Sphere()` was called automatically when the class instance went out of scope.

3. The other member functions have been waiting to be used. The following program uses the `volume()` and `surface_area()` functions:

```cpp
// Filename: C32MEM.CPP
// Demonstrates use of class member functions.

#include  <iostream.h>
#include  <math.h>
const float PI = 3.14159;   // Approximate value of pi.

// A sphere class.
class Sphere
{
public:
    float r;          // Radius of sphere
    float x, y, z;    // Coordinates of sphere
    Sphere(float xcoord, float ycoord,
           float zcoord, float radius)
    { x = xcoord; y = ycoord; z = zcoord; r = radius; }
    ~Sphere()
    {
        cout << "Sphere (" << x << ", " << y
             << ", " << z << ", " << r << ") destroyed\n";
    }
    float volume()
    {
        return (r * r * r * 4 * PI / 3);
    }
    float surface_area()
    {
        return (r * r * 4 * PI);
    }
};   // End of class.

void main()
{
    Sphere s(1.0, 2.0, 3.0, 4.0);
    cout << "X = " << s.x << ", Y = " << s.y
         << ", Z = " << s.z << ", R = " << s.r << "\n";
```

```
        cout << "The volume is " << s.volume() << "\n";
        cout << "The surface area is "
            << s.surface_area() << "\n";
    }
```

The `volume()` and `surface_area()` functions could have been
made *in-line*. This means that the compiler embeds the
functions in the code, rather than calling them as functions.
In C32MEM.CPP, there is essentially a separate function that
is called using the data in `Sphere()`. By making it in-line,
`Sphere()` essentially becomes a macro and is expanded in the
code.

4. In the following program, `volume()` has been changed to an
   in-line function, creating a more efficient program:

```
// Filename: C32MEM1.CPP
// Demonstrates use of in-line class member functions.

#include  <iostream.h>
#include  <math.h>
const float PI = 3.14159;   // Approximate value of pi.

// A sphere class.
class Sphere
{
public:
    float r;        // Radius of sphere
    float x, y, z;  // Coordinates of sphere
    Sphere(float xcoord, float ycoord, float zcoord, float radius)
    { x = xcoord; y = ycoord; z = zcoord; r = radius; }
    ~Sphere()
    {
      cout << "Sphere (" << x << ", " << y
          << ", " << z << ", " << r << ") destroyed\n";
    }
    inline float volume()
    {
      return (r * r * r * 4 * PI / 3);
    }
    float surface_area()
    {
        return (r * r * 4 * PI);
```

```
   }
};

void main()
{
   Sphere s(1.0, 2.0, 3.0, 4.0);
   cout << "X = " << s.x << ", Y = " << s.y
        << ", Z = " << s.z << ", R = " << s.r << "\n";
   cout << "The volume is " << s.volume() << "\n";
   cout << "The surface area is " << s.surface_area() << "\n";
}
```

The inline functions expand to look like this to the compiler:

```
// C32MEM1A.CPP
// Demonstrates use of in-line class member functions.

#include <iostream.h>
#include <math.h>
const float PI = 3.14159;  // Approximate value of pi.

// A sphere class
class Sphere
{
public:
   float r;         // Radius of sphere
   float x, y, z;   // Coordinates of sphere
   Sphere(float xcoord, float ycoord, float zcoord, float radius)
   { x = xcoord; y = ycoord; z = zcoord; r = radius; }
   ~Sphere()
   {
      cout << "Sphere (" << x << ", " << y
           << ", " << z << ", " << r << ") destroyed\n";
   }
   inline float volume()
   {
      return (r * r * r * 4 * PI / 3);
   }
   float surface_area()
   {
      return (r * r * 4 * PI);
   }
};
```

```
void main()
{
    Sphere s(1.0, 2.0, 3.0, 4.0);
    cout << "X = " << s.x << ", Y = " << s.y
        << ", Z = " << s.z << ", R = " << s.r << "\n";
    cout << "The volume is " << (s.r * s.r * s.r * 4 * PI / 3)
        << "\n";
    cout << "The surface area is " << s.surface_area() << "\n";
}
```

The advantage of using in-line functions is that they execute faster—there's no function-call overhead involved because no function is actually called. The disadvantage is that if your functions are used frequently, your programs become larger and larger as functions are expanded.

Default Member Arguments

You can also give member functions arguments by default. Assume by default that the *y* coordinate of a sphere will be 2.0, the *z* coordinate will be 2.5, and the radius will be 1.0. Rewriting the previous example's constructor function to do this results in this code:

```
Sphere(float xcoord, float ycoord = 2.0, float zcoord = 2.5,
       float radius = 1.0)
  { x = xcoord; y = ycoord; z = zcoord; r = radius; }
```

You can create a sphere with the following instructions:

```
Sphere s(1.0);                   // Use all default

Sphere t(1.0, 1.1);              // Override y coord

Sphere u(1.0, 1.1, 1.2);         // Override y and z

Sphere v(1.0, 1.1, 1.2, 1.3);    // Override all defaults
```

Examples

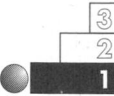

1. Default arguments are used in the following code.

```cpp
// Filename: C32DEF.CPP
// Demonstrates use of default arguments in
// class member functions.

#include <iostream.h>
#include <math.h>
const float PI = 3.14159;   // Approximate value of pi.

// A sphere class.
class Sphere
{
public:
    float r;        // Radius of sphere
    float x, y, z;  // Coordinates of sphere
    Sphere(float xcoord, float ycoord = 2.0,
           float zcoord = 2.5, float radius = 1.0)
     { x = xcoord; y = ycoord; z = zcoord; r = radius; }
    ~Sphere()
     {
       cout << "Sphere (" << x << ", " << y
            << ", " << z << ", " << r << ") destroyed\n";
     }
    inline float volume()
    {
      return (r * r * r * 4 * PI / 3);
    }
    float surface_area()
    {
     return (r * r * 4 * PI);
    }
};

void main()
{
    Sphere s(1.0);               // use all default
    Sphere t(1.0, 1.1);          // override y coord
    Sphere u(1.0, 1.1, 1.2);     // override y and z
    Sphere v(1.0, 1.1, 1.2, 1.3); // override all defaults
    cout << "s: X = " << s.x << ", Y = " << s.y
         << ", Z = " << s.z << ", R = " << s.r << "\n";
```

```
    cout << "The volume of s is " << s.volume() << "\n";
    cout << "The surface area of s is " << s.surface_area() << "\n";
    cout << "t: X = " << t.x << ", Y = " << t.y
         << ", Z = " << t.z << ", R = " << t.r << "\n";
    cout << "The volume of t is " << t.volume() << "\n";
    cout << "The surface area of t is " << t.surface_area() << "\n";
    cout << "u: X = " << u.x << ", Y = " << u.y
         << ", Z = " << u.z << ", R = " << u.r << "\n";
    cout << "The volume of u is " << u.volume() << "\n";
    cout << "The surface area of u is " << u.surface_area() << "\n";
    cout << "v: X = " << v.x << ", Y = " << v.y
         << ", Z = " << v.z << ", R = " << v.r << "\n";
    cout << "The volume of v is " << v.volume() << "\n";
    cout << "The surface area of v is " << v.surface_area() << "\n";
    return;

}
```

Here is the output from this program:

```
s: X = 1, Y = 2, Z = 2.5, R = 1
The volume of s is 4.188787
The surface area of s is 12.56636
t: X = 1, Y = 1.1, Z = 2.5, R = 1
The volume of t is 4.188787
The surface area of t is 12.56636
u: X = 1, Y = 1.1, Z = 1.2, R = 1
The volume of u is 4.188787
The surface area of u is 12.56636
v: X = 1, Y = 1.1, Z = 1.2, R = 1.3
The volume of v is 9.202764
The surface area of v is 21.237148
Sphere (1, 1.1, 1.2, 1.3) destroyed
Sphere (1, 1.1, 1.2, 1) destroyed
Sphere (1, 1.1, 2.5, 1) destroyed
Sphere (1, 2, 2.5, 1) destroyed
```

Notice that when you use a default value, you must also use the other default values to its right. Similarly, once you define a function's parameter as having a default value, every parameter to its right must have a default value as well.

2. You also can call more than one constructor; this is called *overloading* the constructor. When having more than one constructor, all with the same name of the class, you must give them each a different parameter list so the compiler can determine which one you intend to use. A common use of overloaded constructors is to create an uninitialized object on the receiving end of an assignment, as you see done here:

```cpp
// C32OVCON.CPP
// Demonstrates use of overloaded constructors.

#include  <iostream.h>
#include  <math.h>
const float PI  = 3.14159;   // Approximate value of pi.

// A sphere class.
class Sphere
{
public:
   float r;         // Radius of sphere
   float x, y, z;   // Coordinates of sphere
   Sphere() { /* doesn't do anything... */ }
   Sphere(float xcoord, float ycoord,
          float zcoord, float radius)
   { x = xcoord; y = ycoord; z = zcoord; r = radius; }
   ~Sphere()
   {
      cout << "Sphere (" << x << ", " << y
           << ", " << z << ", " << r << ") destroyed\n";
   }
   inline float volume()
   {
      return (r * r * r * 4 * PI / 3);
   }
   float surface_area()
   {
      return (r * r * 4 * PI);
   }
};

void main()
{
   Sphere s(1.0, 2.0, 3.0, 4.0);
```

```
   Sphere t;     // No parameters (an uninitialized sphere).

   cout << "X = " << s.x << ", Y = " << s.y
        << ", Z = " << s.z << ", R = " << s.r << "\n";
   t = s;
   cout << "The volume of t is " << t.volume() << "\n";
   cout << "The surface area of t is " << t.surface_area()
        << "\n";
   return;
}
```

Class Member Visibility

Recall that the Sphere() class had the label public. Declaring the public label is necessary because, by default, all members of a class are *private*. Private members cannot be accessed by anything but a member function. In order for data or member functions to be used by other programs, they must be explicitly declared public. In the case of the Sphere() class, you probably want to hide the actual data from other classes. This protects the data's integrity. The next program adds a cube() and square() function to do some of the work of the volume() and surface_area() functions. There is no need for other functions to use those member functions.

```
// Filename: C32VISIB.CPP
// Demonstrates use of class visibility labels.

#include   <iostream.h>
#include   <math.h>
const float PI = 3.14159;   // Approximate value of pi.

// A sphere class.
class Sphere
{
private:
   float r;        // Radius of sphere
   float x, y, z;  // Coordinates of sphere
   float cube() { return (r * r * r); }
   float square() { return (r * r); }
```

```
public:
   Sphere(float xcoord, float ycoord, float zcoord, float radius)
   { x = xcoord; y = ycoord; z = zcoord; r = radius; }
   ~Sphere()
   {
     cout << "Sphere (" << x << ", " << y
          << ", " << z << ", " << r << ") destroyed\n";
   }
   float volume()
   {
     return (cube() * 4 * PI / 3);
   }
   float surface_area()
   {
      return (square() * 4 * PI);
   }
};

void main()
{
   Sphere s(1.0, 2.0, 3.0, 4.0);
   cout << "The volume is " << s.volume() << "\n";
   cout << "The surface area is " << s.surface_area() << "\n";
   return;
}
```

Notice that the line showing the data members had to be removed from main(). The data members are no longer directly accessible except by a member function of class Sphere. In other words, main() can never directly manipulate data members such as r and z, even though it calls the constructor function that created them. The private member data is only visible in the member functions. This is the true power of *data hiding;* even your own code cannot get to the data! The advantage is that you define specific data-retrieval, data-display, and data-changing member functions that main() must call to manipulate member data. Through these member functions, you set up a buffer between your program and the program's data structures. If you change the way the data is stored, you do not have to change main() or any functions that main() calls. You only have to change the member functions of that class.

Review Questions

The answers to the review questions are in Appendix B.

1. What are the two types of class members called?

2. Is a constructor always necessary?

3. Is a destructor always necessary?

4. What is the default visibility of a class data member?

5. How do you make a class member visible outside its class?

Review Exercise

Construct a class to hold personnel records. Use the following data members, and keep them private:

```
char      name[25];
float     salary;
char      date_of_birth[9];
```

Create two constructors, one to initialize the record with its necessary values and another to create an uninitialized record. Create member functions to alter the individual's name, salary, and date of birth.

Summary

You have now been introduced to classes, the data type that distinguishes C++ from its predecessor, C. This was only a cursory glimpse of object-oriented programming. However, you saw that OOP offers an advanced view of your data, combining the data with the member functions that manipulate that data. If you desire to learn more about C++ and become a "guru" of sorts, try *Using Microsoft C/C++ 7* (Que, 0-88022-809-1).

Part VIII

References

Memory Addressing, Binary, and Hexadecimal Review

You do not have to understand the concepts in this appendix to become well-versed in C++. You can master C++, however, only if you spend some time learning about the behind-the-scenes roles played by binary numbers. The material presented here is not difficult, but many programmers do not take the time to study it; hence, there are a handful of C++ masters who learn this material and understand how C++ works "under the hood," and there are those who will never master the language as they could.

You should take the time to learn about addressing, binary numbers, and hexadecimal numbers. These fundamental principles are presented here for you to learn, and although a working knowledge of C++ is possible without knowing them, they greatly enhance your C++ skills (and your skills in every other programming language).

After reading this appendix, you will better understand why different C++ data types hold different ranges of numbers. You also will see the importance of being able to represent hexadecimal numbers in C++, and you will better understand C++ array and pointer addressing.

Computer Memory

Each memory location inside your computer holds a single character called a *byte*. A byte is any character, whether it is a letter of the alphabet, a numeric digit, or a special character such as a period, question mark, or even a space (a *blank* character). If your computer contains 640K of memory, it can hold a total of approximately 640,000 bytes of memory. This means that as soon as you fill your computer's memory with 640K, there is no room for an additional character unless you overwrite something.

Before describing the physical layout of your computer's memory, it is best to take a detour and explain exactly what 640K means.

Memory and Disk Measurements

K means approximately 1000 bytes and exactly 1024 bytes.

By appending the *K* (from the metric word *kilo*) to memory measurements, the manufacturers of computers do not have to attach as many zeros to the end of numbers for disk and memory storage. The *K* stands for approximately 1000 bytes. As you will see, almost everything inside your computer is based on a power of 2. Therefore, the *K* of computer memory measurements actually equals the power of 2 closest to 1000, which is 2 to the 10th power, or 1024. Because 1024 is very close to 1000, computer-users often think of *K* as meaning 1000, even though they know it only approximately equals 1000.

Think for a moment about what 640K exactly equals. Practically speaking, 640K is about 640,000 bytes. To be exact, however, 640K equals 640 times 1024, or 655,360. This explains why the PC DOS command CHKDSK returns 655,360 as your total memory (assuming that you have 640K of RAM) rather than 640,000.

M means approximately 1,000,000 bytes and exactly 1,048,576 bytes.

Because extended memory and many disk drives can hold such a large amount of data, typically several million characters, there is an additional memory measurement shortcut called *M*, which stands for *meg*, or *megabytes*. The *M* is a shortcut for approximately one million bytes. Therefore, 20M is approximately 20,000,000 characters, or bytes, of storage. As with *K*, the *M* literally stands for 1,048,576 because that is the closest power of 2 (2 to the 20th power) to one million.

How many bytes of storage is 60 megabytes? It is approximately 60 million characters, or 62,914,560 characters to be exact.

Memory Addresses

Each memory location in your computer, just as with each house in your town, has a unique *address*. A memory address is simply a sequential number, starting at 0, that labels each memory location. Figure A.1 shows how your computer memory addresses are numbered if you have 640K of RAM.

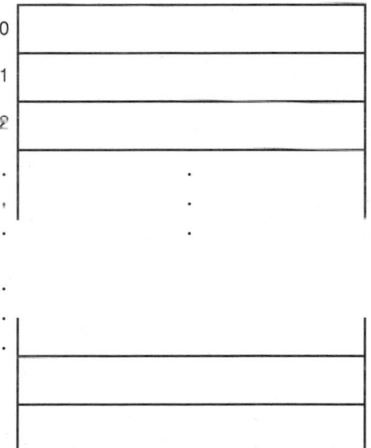

Figure A.1. Memory addresses for a 640K computer.

By using unique addresses, your computer can track memory. When the computer stores a result of a calculation in memory, it finds an empty address, or one matching the data area where the result is to go, and stores the result at that address.

Your C++ programs and data share computer memory with DOS. DOS must always reside in memory while you operate your computer. Otherwise, your programs would have no way to access disks, printers, the screen, or the keyboard. Figure A.2 shows computer memory being shared by DOS and a C++ program. The exact amount of memory taken by DOS and a C++ program is determined by the version of DOS you use, how many DOS extras (such as device drivers and buffers) your computer uses, and the size and needs of your C++ programs and data.

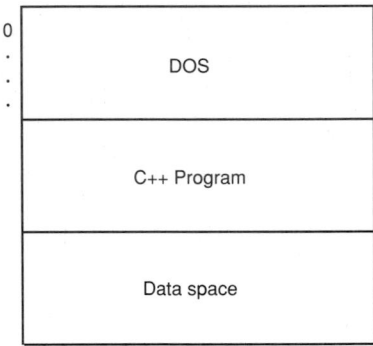

Figure A.2. DOS, your C++ program, and your program's data share the same memory.

Bits and Bytes

You now know that a single address of memory might contain any character, called a byte. You know that your computer holds many bytes of information, but it does not store those characters in the same way that humans think of characters. For example, if you type a letter *W* on your keyboard while working in your C++ editor, you see the *W* on-screen, and you also know that the *W* is stored in a memory location at some unique address. Actually, your computer does not store the letter *W*; it stores electrical impulses that stand for the letter *W*.

The binary digits 1
and 0 (called *bits*)
represent on and off
states of electricity.

Electricity, which runs through the components of your computer and makes it understand and execute your programs, can exist in only two states—on or off. As with a light bulb, electricity is either flowing (it is on) or it is not flowing (it is off). Even though you can dim some lights, the electricity is still either on or off.

Today's modern digital computers employ this on-or-off concept. Your computer is nothing more than millions of on and off switches. You might have heard about integrated circuits, transistors, and even vacuum tubes that computers have contained over the years. These electrical components are nothing more than switches that rapidly turn electrical impulses on and off.

This two-state on and off mode of electricity is called a *binary* state of electricity. Computer people use a 1 to represent an on state (a switch in the computer that is on) and a 0 to represent an off state (a switch that is off). These numbers, 1 and 0, are called *binary digits.* The term binary digits is usually shortened to *bits.* A bit is either a 1 or a 0 representing an on or an off state of electricity. Different combinations of bits represent different characters.

Several years ago, someone listed every single character that might be represented on a computer, including all uppercase letters, all lowercase letters, the digits 0 through 9, the many other characters (such as %, *, {, and +), and some special control characters. When you add the total number of characters that a PC can represent, you get 256 of them. The 256 ASCII characters are listed in Appendix C's ASCII (pronounced *ask-ee*) table.

The order of the ASCII table's 256 characters is basically arbitrary, just as the telegraph's Morse code table is arbitrary. With Morse code, a different set of long and short beeps represent different letters of the alphabet. In the ASCII table, a different combination of bits (1s and 0s strung together) represent each of the 256 ASCII characters. The ASCII table is a standard table used by almost every PC in the world. ASCII stands for *American Standard Code for Information Interchange.* (Some minicomputers and mainframes use a similar table called the EBCDIC table.)

It turns out that if you take every different combination of eight 0s strung together, to eight 1s strung together (that is, from 00000000, 00000001, 00000010, and so on until you get to 11111110, and finally, 11111111), you have a total of 256 of them. (256 is 2 to the 8th power.)

Each memory location in your computer holds eight bits each. These bits can be any combination of eight 1s and 0s. This brings us to the following fundamental rule of computers.

> **NOTE:** Because it takes a combination of eight 1s and 0s to represent a character, and because each byte of computer memory can hold exactly one character, eight bits equals one byte.

To bring this into better perspective, consider that the bit pattern needed for the uppercase letter *A* is 01000001. No other character in the ASCII table "looks" like this to the computer because each of the 256 characters is assigned a unique bit pattern.

Suppose that you press the *A* key on your keyboard. Your keyboard does *not* send a letter *A* to the computer; rather, it looks in its ASCII table for the on and off states of electricity that represent the letter *A*. As Figure A.3 shows, when you press the *A* key, the keyboard actually sends 01000001 (as on and off impulses) to the computer. Your computer simply stores this bit pattern for *A* in a memory location. Even though you can think of the memory location as holding an *A*, it really holds the byte 01000001.

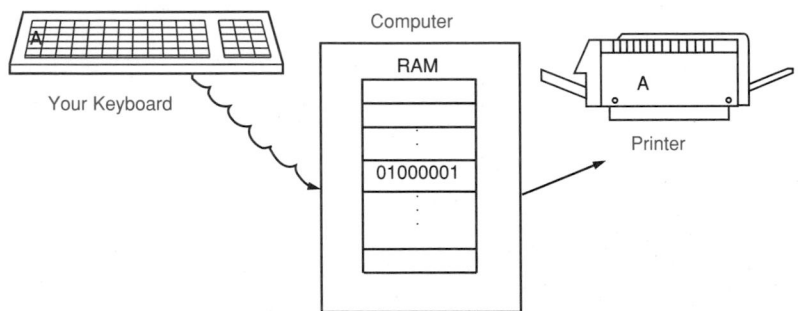

Figure A.3. Your computer keeps track of characters by their bit patterns.

If you were to print that *A*, your computer would not send an *A* to the printer; it would send the 01000001 bit pattern for an *A* to the printer. The printer receives that bit pattern, looks up the correct letter in the ASCII table, and prints an *A*.

From the time you press the *A* until the time you see it on the printer, it is not a letter *A!* It is the ASCII pattern of bits that the computer uses to represent an *A*. Because a computer is electrical, and because electricity is easily turned on and off, this is a nice way for the computer to manipulate and move characters, and it can do so very quickly. Actually, if it were up to the computer, you would enter everything by its bit pattern, and look at all results in their bit patterns. Of course, it would be much more difficult for us to learn to program and use a computer, so devices such as the keyboard, screen, and printer are created to work part of the time with letters as we know them. That is why the ASCII table is such an integral part of a computer.

There are times when your computer treats two bytes as a single value. Even though memory locations are typically eight bits wide, many CPUs access memory two bytes at a time. If this is the case, the two bytes are called a *word* of memory. On other computers (commonly mainframes), the word size might be four bytes (32 bits) or even eight bytes (64 bits).

Summarizing Bits and Bytes

A bit is a 1 or a 0 representing an on or an off state of electricity.

Eight bits represents a byte.

A byte, or eight bits, represents one character.

Each memory location of your computer is eight bits (a single byte) wide. Therefore, each memory location can hold one character of data. Appendix C is an ASCII table listing all possible characters.

If the CPU accesses memory two bytes at a time, those two bytes are called a word of memory.

The Order of Bits

To further understand memory, you should understand how programmers refer to individual bits. Figure A.4 shows a byte and a two-byte word. Notice that the bit on the far right is called bit 0. From bit 0, keep counting by ones as you move left. For a byte, the bits are numbered 0 to 7, from right to left. For a double-byte (a 16-bit word), the bits are numbered from 0 to 15, from right to left.

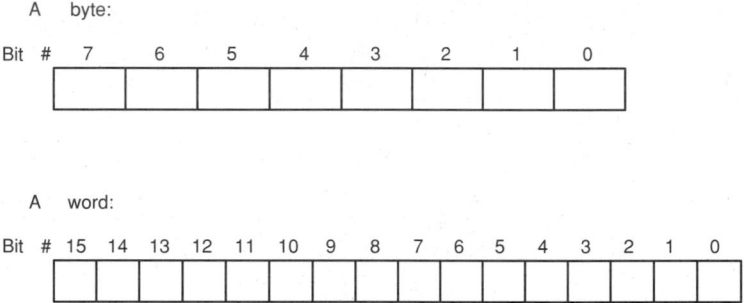

Figure A.4. The order of bits in a byte and a two-byte word.

Bit 0 is called the *least-significant bit,* or sometimes the *low-order bit.* Bit 7 (or bit 15 for a two-byte word) is called the *most-significant bit,* or sometimes the *high-order bit.*

Binary Numbers

Because a computer works best with 1s and 0s, its internal numbering method is limited to a *base-2* (binary) numbering system. People work in a *base-10* numbering system in the "real" world. The base-10 numbering system is sometimes called the decimal numbering system. There are always as many different digits as the base in a numbering system. For example, in the base-10 system, there are ten digits, 0 through 9. As soon as you count to 9 and run out of digits, you have to combine some that you already used. The number 10 is a representation of ten values, but it combines the digits 1 and 0.

The same is true of base-2. There are only two digits, 0 and 1. As soon as you run out of digits, after the second one, you have to reuse digits. The first seven binary numbers are 0, 1, 10, 11, 100, 101, and 110.

It is okay if you do not understand how these numbers were derived; you will see how in a moment. For the time being, you should realize that no more than two digits, 0 and 1, can be used to represent any base-2 number, just as no more than ten digits, 0 through 9, can be used to represent any base-10 number in the regular numbering system.

You should know that a base-10 number, such as 2981, does not really mean anything by itself. You must assume what base it is. You get very used to working with base-10 numbers because you use them every day. However, the number 2981 actually represents a quantity based on powers of 10. For example, Figure A.5 shows what the number 2981 actually represents. Notice that each digit in the number represents a certain number of a power of 10.

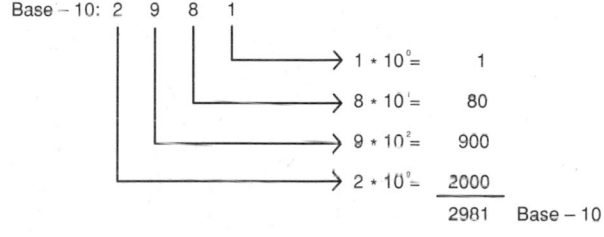

Figure A.5. The base-10 breakdown of the number 2981.

A binary number can contain only the digits 1 and 0.

This same concept applies when you work in a base-2 numbering system. Your computer does this because the power of 2 is just as common to your computer as the power of 10 is to you. The only difference is that the digits in a base-2 number represent powers of 2 and not powers of 10. Figure A.6 shows you what the binary numbers 10101 and 10011110 are in base-10. This is how you convert any binary number to its base-10 equivalent.

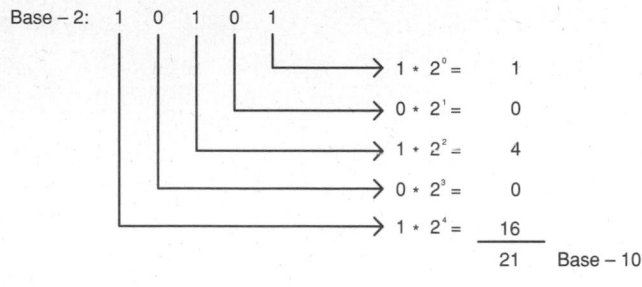

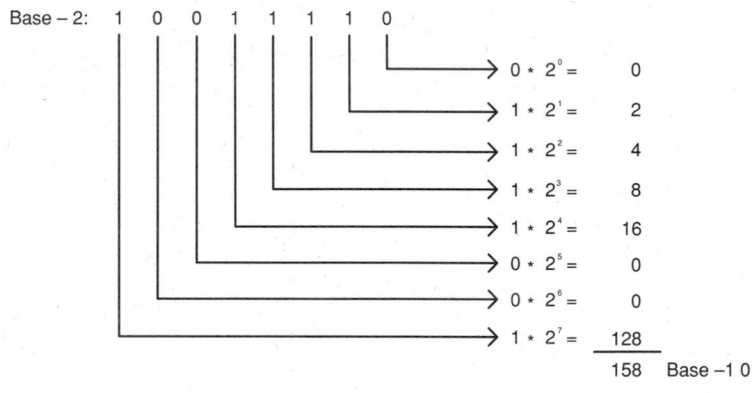

Figure A.6. The base-2 breakdown of the numbers 10101 and 10011110.

A base-2 number contains only 1s and 0s. To convert any base-2 number to base-10, add each power of 2 everywhere a 1 appears in the number. The base-2 number 101 represents the base-10 number 5. (There are two 1s in the number, one in the 2 to the 0 power, which equals 1, and one in the 2 to the second power, which equals 4.) Table A.1 shows the first 18 base-10 numbers and their matching base-2 numbers.

Table A.1. The first 17 base-10 and base-2 (binary) numbers.

Base-10	Base-2
0	0
1	1
2	10
3	11
4	100
5	101
6	110
7	111
8	1000
9	1001
10	1010
11	1011
12	1100
13	1101
14	1110
15	1111
16	10000
17	10001

You do not have to memorize this table; you should be able to figure the base-10 numbers from their matching binary numbers by adding the powers of two for each 1 (on) bit. Many programmers do memorize the first several binary numbers because it comes in handy in advanced programming techniques.

What is the largest binary number a byte can hold? The answer is all 1s, or 11111111. If you add the first eight powers of 2, you get 255.

A byte holds either a number or an ASCII character, depending on how it is accessed. For example, if you were to convert the base-2 number 01000001 to a base-10 number, you would get 65. However, this also happens to be the ASCII bit pattern for the uppercase letter A. If you check the ASCII table, you see that the A is ASCII code 65. Because the ASCII table is so closely linked with the bit patterns, the computer knows whether to work with a number 65 or a letter A—by the context of how the patterns are used.

A binary number is not limited to a byte, as an ASCII character is. Sixteen or 32 bits at a time can represent a binary number (and usually do). There are more powers of 2 to add when converting that number to a base-10 number, but the process is the same. By now you should be able to figure out that 1010101010101010 is 43,690 in base-10 decimal numbering system (although it might take a little time to calculate).

To convert from decimal to binary takes a little more effort. Luckily, you rarely need to convert in that direction. Converting from base-10 to base-2 is not covered in this appendix.

Binary Arithmetic

At their lowest level, computers can only add and convert binary numbers to their negative equivalents. Computers cannot truly subtract, multiply, or divide, although they simulate these operations through judicious use of the addition and negative-conversion techniques.

If a computer were to add the numbers 7 and 6, it could do so (at the binary level). The result is 13. If, however, the computer were instructed to subtract 7 from 13, it could not do so. It can, however, take the negative value of 7 and add that to 13. Because –7 plus 13 equals 6, the result is a *simulated* subtraction.

To multiply, computers perform repeated addition. To multiply 6 by 7, the computer adds seven 6s together and gets 42 as the answer. To divide 42 by 7, a computer keeps subtracting 7 from 42 repeatedly until it gets to a 0 answer (or less than 0 if there is a remainder), then counts the number of times it took to reach 0.

Because all math is done at the binary level, the following additions are possible in binary arithmetic:

$0 + 0 = 0$

$0 + 1 = 1$

$1 + 0 = 1$

$1 + 1 = 10$

Because these are binary numbers, the last result is not the number 10, but the binary number 2. (Just as the binary 10 means "no ones, and carry an additional power of 2," the decimal number 10 means "no ones, and carry a power of 10.") No binary digit represents a 2, so you have to combine the 1 and the 0 to form the new number.

Because binary addition is the foundation of all other math, you should learn how to add binary numbers. You will then understand how computers do the rest of their arithmetic.

Using the binary addition rules shown previously, look at the following binary calculations:

```
 01000001  (65 decimal)
+00101100  (44 decimal)
 01101101  (109 decimal)
```

The first number, 01000001, is 65 decimal. This also happens to be the bit pattern for the ASCII *A*, but if you add with it, the computer interprets it as the number 65 rather than the character *A*.

The following binary addition requires a carry into bit 4 and bit 6:

```
 00101011  (43 decimal)
+00100111  (39 decimal)
 01010010   (82 decimal)
```

Typically, you have to ignore bits that carry past bit 7, or bit 15 for double-byte arithmetic. For example, both of the following binary additions produce incorrect positive results:

10000000 (128 decimal)   1000000000000000
                                           (65536 decimal)

+10000000 (128 decimal)   +1000000000000000
  00000000 (0 decimal)   (65536 decimal)

                                           0000000000000000
                                           (0 decimal)

There is no 9th or 17th bit for the carry, so both of these seem to produce incorrect results. Because the byte and 16-bit word cannot hold the answers, the magnitude of both these additions is not possible. The computer must be programmed, at the bit level, to perform *multiword arithmetic*, which is beyond the scope of this book.

Binary Negative Numbers

Because subtracting requires understanding binary negative numbers, you need to learn how computers represent them. The computer uses *2's complement* to represent negative numbers in binary form. To convert a binary number to its 2's complement (to its negative) you must:

Negative binary numbers are stored in their 2's complement format.

1. Reverse the bits (the 1s to 0s and the 0s to 1s).

2. Add 1.

This might seem a little strange at first, but it works very well for binary numbers. To represent a binary –65, you have to take the binary 65 and convert it to its 2's complement, such as

01000001 (65 decimal)
10111110 (Reverse the bits)
+1 (Add 1)
10111111 (–65 binary)

By converting the 65 to its 2's complement, you produce –65 in binary. You might wonder what makes 10111111 mean –65, but by the 2's complement definition it means –65.

If you were told that 10111111 is a negative number, how would you know which binary number it is? You perform the 2's complement on it. Whatever number you produce is the positive of that negative number. For example:

10111111 (–65 decimal)
01000000 (Reverse the bits)
<u>   +1</u> (Add 1)
01000001 (65 decimal)

Something might seem wrong at this point. You just saw that 10111111 is the binary –65, but isn't 10111111 also 191 decimal (adding the powers of 2 marked by the 1s in the number, as explained earlier)? It depends whether the number is a *signed* or an *unsigned* number. If a number is signed, the computer looks at the most-significant bit (the bit on the far left), called the *sign bit*. If the most-significant bit is a 1, the number is negative. If it is 0, the number is positive.

Most numbers are 16 bits long. That is, two-byte words are used to store most integers. This is not always the case for all computers, but it is true for most PCs.

In the C++ programming language, you can designate numbers as either signed integers or unsigned integers (they are signed by default if you do not specify otherwise). If you designate a variable as a signed integer, the computer interprets the high-order bit as a sign bit. If the high-order bit is on (1), the number is negative. If the high-order bit is off (0), the number is positive. If, however, you designate a variable as an unsigned integer, the computer uses the high-order bit as just another power of 2. That is why the range of unsigned integer variables goes higher (generally from 0 to 65535, but it depends on the computer) than for signed integer variables (generally from –32768 to +32767).

After so much description, a little review is in order. Assume that the following 16-bit binary numbers are unsigned:

0011010110100101

1001100110101010

1000000000000000

These numbers are unsigned, so the bit 15 is not the sign bit, but simply another power of 2. You should practice converting these large 16-bit numbers to decimal. The decimal equivalents are

13733

39338

32768

If, on the other hand, these numbers are signed numbers, the high-order bit (bit 15) indicates the sign. If the sign bit is 0, the numbers are positive and you convert them to decimal in the usual manner. If the sign bit is 1, you must convert the numbers to their 2's complement to find what they equal. Their decimal equivalents are

+13733

−26198

−32768

To compute the last two binary numbers to their decimal equivalents, take their 2's complement and convert it to decimal. Put a minus sign in front of the result and you find what the original number represents.

> **TIP:** To make sure that you convert a number to its 2's complement correctly, you can add the 2's complement to its original positive value. If the answer is 0 (ignoring the extra carry to the left), you know that the 2's complement number is correct. This is similar to the concept that decimal opposites, such as −72 + 72, add up to zero.

Hexadecimal Numbers

Hexadecimal numbers use 16 unique digits, 0 through F.

All those 1s and 0s get confusing. If it were up to your computer, however, you would enter *everything* as 1s and 0s! This is unacceptable to people because we do not like to keep track of all those 1s and 0s. Therefore, a *hexadecimal* numbering system (sometimes called *hex*) was devised. The hexadecimal numbering system is based on base-16 numbers. As with other bases, there are 16 unique digits in the base-16 numbering system. Here are the first 19 hexadecimal numbers:

0 1 2 3 4 5 6 7 8 9 A B C D E F 10 11 12

Because there are only 10 unique digits (0 through 9), the letters *A* through *F* represent the remaining six digits. (Anything could have been used, but the designers of the hexadecimal numbering system decided to use the first six letters of the alphabet.)

To understand base-16 numbers, you should know how to convert them to base-10 so they represent numbers with which people are familiar. Perform the conversion to base-10 from base-16 the same way you did with base-2, but instead of using powers of 2, represent each hexadecimal digit with powers of 16. Figure A.7 shows how to convert the number 3C5 to decimal.

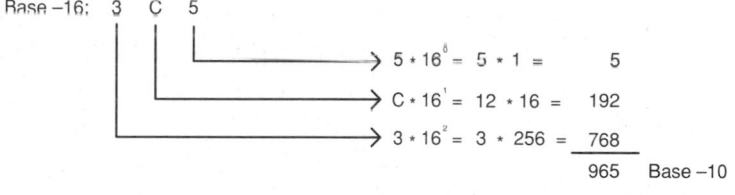

$$
\begin{aligned}
&\text{Base}-16\text{:} \quad 3 \quad C \quad 5 \\
&5 * 16^0 = 5 * 1 = \quad\quad 5 \\
&C * 16^1 = 12 * 16 = \quad 192 \\
&3 * 16^2 = 3 * 256 = \quad \underline{768} \\
& 965 \quad \text{Base}-10
\end{aligned}
$$

3 C 5

Figure A.7. Converting hexadecimal 3C5 to its decimal equivalent.

> **TIP:** There are calculators available that convert numbers between base-16, base-10, and base-2, and also perform 2's complement arithmetic.

You should be able to convert 2B to its decimal 43 equivalent, and E1 to decimal 225 in the same manner. Table A.2 shows the first 20 decimal, binary, and hexadecimal numbers.

Table A.2. The first 20 base-10, base-2 (binary), and base-16 (hexadecimal) numbers.

Base-10	Base-2	Base-16
1	1	1
2	10	2
3	11	3
4	100	4
5	101	5
6	110	6
7	111	7
8	1000	8
9	1001	9
10	1010	A
11	1011	B
12	1100	C
13	1101	D
14	1110	E
15	1111	F
16	10000	10
17	10001	11
18	10010	12
19	10011	13
20	10100	14

Why Learn Hexadecimal?

Because of its close association to the binary numbers your computer uses, hexadecimal notation is extremely efficient for describing memory locations and values. It is much easier for you (and more importantly at this level, for your computer) to convert from base-16 to base-2 than from base-10 to base-2. Therefore, you sometimes want to represent data at the bit level, but using hexadecimal notation is easier (and requires less typing) than using binary numbers.

To convert from hexadecimal to binary, convert each hex digit to its four-bit binary number. You can use Table A.2 as a guide for this. For example, the following hexadecimal number

5B75

can be converted to binary by taking each digit and converting it to four binary numbers. If you need leading zeroes to "pad" the four digits, use them. The number becomes

0101 1011 0111 0101

It turns out that the binary number 0101101101110101 is exactly equal to the hexadecimal number 5B75. This is much easier than converting them both to decimal first.

To convert from binary to hexadecimal, reverse this process. If you were given the following binary number

1101000011110111111010

you could convert it to hexadecimal by grouping the bits into groups of four, starting with the bit on the far right. Because there is not an even number of groups of four, pad the one on the far left with zeroes. You then have the following:

0011 0100 0011 1101 1111 1010

Now you only have to convert each group of four binary digits into their hexadecimal number equivalent. You can use Table A.2 to help. You then get the following base-16 number:

343DFA

The C++ programming language also supports the base-8 *octal* representation of numbers. Because octal numbers are rarely used with today's computers, they are not covered in this appendix.

How Binary and Addressing Relate to C++

The material presented here may seem foreign to many programmers. The binary and 2's complement arithmetic reside deep in your computer, shielded from most programmers (except assembly-language programmers). Understanding this level of your computer, however, makes everything else you learn seem more clear.

Many C++ programmers learn C++ before delving into binary and hexadecimal representation. For those programmers, much about the C++ language seems strange, but it could be explained very easily if they understood the basic concepts.

For example, a signed integer holds a different range of numbers than an unsigned integer. You now know that this is because the sign bit is used in two different ways, depending on whether the number is designated as signed or unsigned.

The ASCII table (see Appendix C) also should make more sense to you after this discussion. The ASCII table is an integral part of your computer. Characters are not actually stored in memory and variables; rather, their ASCII bit patterns are. That is why C++ can move easily between characters and integers. The following two C++ statements are allowed, whereas they probably would not be in another programming language:

```
char c = 65;   // Places the ASCII letter A in c.
int ci = 'A';  // Places the number 65 in ci.
```

The hexadecimal notation also makes much more sense if you truly understand base-16 numbers. For example, if you see the following line in a C++ program

```
char a = '\x041';
```

you could convert the hex 41 to decimal (65 decimal) if you want to know what is being assigned. Also, C++ systems programmers find that they can better interface with assembly-language programs when they understand the concepts presented in this appendix.

If you gain only a cursory knowledge of this material at this point, you will be very much ahead of the game when you program in C++!

Answers to Review Questions

Chapter 1

1. BCPL or Algol

2. True

3. 1980s

4. False. C++'s compact size makes it an excellent programming language for smaller computers.

5. The hard disk

6. A modem

7. b. Input. By moving the mouse, you give cursor-direction commands to the computer.

8. NumLock

9. UNIX

10. When you turn off the computer, the contents of RAM are destroyed.

11. True

12. 524,288 bytes (512 times 1,024)

13. *Mo*dulate, *dem*odulate

Chapter 2

1. A set of detailed instructions that tells the computer what to do.

2. Buy one or write it yourself.

3. False

4. The program produces the output.

5. A program editor

6. The .CPP extension

7. You must first plan the program by deciding which steps you will take to produce the final program.

8. To get the errors out of your program

9. So your programs work with various compilers and computer equipment

10. False. You must compile a program before linking it. Most compilers link the program automatically.

Chapter 3

1. Two comment markers (//)

2. A holding place for data that can be changed

3. A value that cannot be changed

4. The +, -, *, and / operators

5. The = assignment operator.

6. False. There are floating-point, double floating-point, short integers, long integers, and many more variable data types.

7. `cout`

8. `city` must be a variable name because it is not enclosed in quotation marks.

9. All C++ commands must be in lowercase.

Chapter 4

1. `my_name` and `sales_89`

2. Characters: `'X'` and `'0'`

   Strings: `"2.0"` and `"X"`

   Integers: `0` and `-708`

   Floating-point literals: `-12.0` and `65.4`

3. Seven variables are declared: three integers, three characters, and one floating-point variable.

4. A null zero, also called a binary zero or an ASCII zero.

5. True

6. 1

7. It is stored as a series of ASCII values, representing the characters and blanks in the string, ending in an ASCII `0`.

8. It is stored as a single ASCII `0`.

9. The constant value called `age` cannot be changed.

Chapter 5

1. `char my_name[] "This is C++";`

2. The string is 11 characters long.

3. It consumes 12 bytes.

4. All string literals end with a binary zero.

5. Two character arrays are declared, each with 25 elements.

6. False. The keyword `char` must precede the variable name.

7. True. The binary zero terminates the string.

8. False. The characters do not represent a string because there is no terminating zero.

Chapter 6

1. False. You can define only constants with the `#define` preprocessor directive.

2. The `#include` directive

3. The `#define` directive

4. True

5. The preprocessor changes your source code before the compiler reads the source code.

6. The `const` keyword

7. Use angled brackets when the `include` files reside in the compiler's `include` subdirectory. Use quotation marks when the `include` file resides in the same subdirectory as the source program.

8. Defined literals are easier to change because you have to change only the line with `#define` and not several other lines in the program.

9. iostream.h

10. False. You cannot define constants enclosed in quotation marks (as `"MESSAGE"` is in the `cout` statement).

11. `Amount is 4`

Chapter 7

1. `cout` sends output to the screen, and `cin` gets input from the keyboard.

2. The prompt tells the user what is expected.

3. The user enters four values.

4. `cin` assigns values to variables when the user types them, whereas the programmer must assign data when using the assignment operator (=).

5. True. When printing strings, you do not need %s.

6. Arrays

7. The backslash "\" character is special

8. The following value prints, with one leading space: `123.456`

Chapter 8

1. a. 5

   b. 6

   c. 5

2. a. 2

   b. 7

3. a. `a = (3+3) / (4+4);`

   b. `x = (a-b)*( (a-c) * (a-c));`

   c. `f = (a*a)/(b*b*b);`

   d. `d = ((8 - x*x)/(x - 9))-((4*2 - 1)/(x*x*x));`

4. The area of a circle:

```
#include stdio.h>
const float PI = 3.14159;
main()
```

```
{
    printf("%f", (PI*(4*4)));
    return;
}
```

5. Assignment and `printf()` statements:

```
r = 100%4;
cout <<  r;
```

Chapter 9

1. The `==` operator

2. a. True

   b. True

   c. True

   d. True

3. True

4. The `if` statement determines what code executes when the relational test is true. The `if-else` statement determines what happens for both the True and the False relational test.

5. No

6. a. False

   b. False

   c. False

Chapter 10

1. The `&&`, `¦¦`, and `!` operators are the three logical operators.

2. a. False

   b. False

   c. True

   d. True

3. a. True

   b. True

   c. True

4. `g is 25 and f got changed to 8`

5. a. True

   b. True

   c. False

   d. True

6. Yes

Chapter 11

1. The `if-else` statement

2. The conditional operator is the only C++ operator with three arguments.

3.
```
if (a == b)
    { ans = c + 2; }
else
    { ans = c + 3; }
```

4. True

5. The increment and decrement operators compile into single assembly instructions.

6. A comma operator (,), which forces a left-to-right execution of the statements on either side

7. The output cannot be determined reliably. Do not pass an increment operator as an argument.

8. `The size of name is 20`

9. a. True

   b. True

   c. False

   d. False

Chapter 12

1. The `while` loop tests for a true condition at the beginning of the loop. The `do-while` tests for the condition at the end of the loop.

2. A counter variable increments by one. A total variable increments by the addition to the total you are performing.

3. The `++` operator

4. If the body of the loop is a single statement, the braces are not required. However, braces are *always* recommended.

5. There are no braces. The second `cout` always executes, regardless of the result of the `while` loop's relational test.

6. The stdlib.h header file

7. One time

8. By returning a value inside the `exit()` function's parentheses

9. ```
   This is the outer loop
   This is the outer loop
   This is the outer loop
   This is the outer loop
   ```
   ```

Chapter 13

1. A loop is a sequence of one or more instructions executed repeatedly.

2. False

3. A nested loop is a loop within a loop.

4. Because the expressions might be initialized elsewhere, such as before the loop or in the body of the loop

5. The inner loop

6. 10

   7

   4

   1

7. True

8. The body of the `for` loop stops repeating.

9. False, due to the semicolon after the first `for` loop

10. There is no output. The value of `start` is already less than `end` when the loop begins; therefore, the `for` loop's test is immediately False.

Chapter 14

1. Timing loops force a program to pause.

2. Because some computers are faster than others.

3. If the `continue` and `break` statements were unconditional, there would be little use for them.

4. Because of the unconditional `continue` statement, there is no output.

5. *****

6. A single variable rarely can hold a large enough value for the timer's count.

Chapter 15

1. The program does not execute sequentially, as it would without `goto`.

2. The `switch` statement

3. A `break` statement

4. False because you should place the `case` most likely to execute at the beginning of the `case` options.

5.
```
switch (num)
{ case (1) : { cout << "Alpha";
                break; }
  case (2) : { cout << "Beta";
                break; }
  case (3) : { cout << "Gamma";
                break; }
  default :  { cout << "Other";
                break; }
}
```

6.
```
do
  { cout << "What is your first name? ";
    cin >> name;
  } while ((name[0] < 'A') || (name[0] > 'Z'));
```

Chapter 16

1. True

2. `main()`

3. Several smaller functions are better because each function can perform a single task.

4. Function names always end with a pair of parentheses.

5. By putting separating comments between functions.

6. The function sq_25() cannot be nested in calc_it().

7. A function definition (a prototype).

8. True

Chapter 17

1. True

2. Local variables are passed as arguments.

3. False

4. The variable data types

5. Static

6. You should never pass global variables—they do not need to be passed.

7. Two arguments (the string "The rain has fallen %d inches", and the variable, rainf)

Chapter 18

1. Arrays

2. Nonarray variables are always passed by value, unless you override the default with & before each variable name.

3. True

4. No

5. Yes

6. The data types of variables x, y, and z are not declared in the receiving parameter list.

7. c

Chapter 19

1. By putting the return type to the left of the function name.

2. One

3. To prototype built-in functions.

4. int

5. False

6. Prototypes ensure that the correct number of parameters is being passed.

7. Global variables are already known across functions.

8. The return type is float. Three parameters are passed: a character, an integer, and a floating-point variable.

Chapter 20

1. In the function prototypes.

2. Overloaded functions

3. Overloaded functions

4. False. You can specify multiple default arguments.

5. `void my_fun(float x, int i=7, char ch='A');`

6. False. Overloaded functions must differ in their argument lists, not only in their return values.

Chapter 21

1. For portability between different computers

2. False. The standard output can be redirected to any device through the operating system.

3. `getch()` assumes `stdin` for the input device.

4. `get`

5. `>` and `<`

6. `getche()`

7. False. The input from `get` goes to a buffer as you type it.

8. Enter

9. True

Chapter 22

1. The character-testing functions do not change the character passed to them.

2. `gets()` and `fgets()`

3. `floor()` rounds down and `ceil()` rounds up.

4. The function returns `0` (false) because `islower('s')` returns a `1` (true) and `isalpha(1)` is `0`.

5. `PeterParker`

6. `8 9`

7. True

8. `Prog` with a null zero at the end.

9. True

Chapter 23

1. False

2. The array subscripts differentiate array elements.

3. C does not initialize arrays for you.

4. `0`

5. Yes. All arrays are passed by address because an array name is nothing more than an address to that array.

6. C++ initializes all types of global variables (and every other static variable in your program) to zero or null zero.

Chapter 24

1. False

2. From the low numbers floating to the top of the array like bubbles.

3. Ascending order

4. The name of an array is an address to the starting element of that array.

5. a. `Eagles`

   b. `Rams`

   c. `les`

   d. `E`

   e. `E`

   f. The statement prints the character string, `s`.

   g. The third letter of "Eagles" (`g`) prints.

Chapter 25

1. `int scores[5][6];`

2. `char initials[4][10][20]`

3. The first subscript represents rows and the last represents columns.

4. 30 elements

5. a. 2

   b. 1

   c. 91

   d. 8

6. Nested `for` loops step through multidimensional tables very easily.

7. a. 78

   b. 100

   c. 90

Chapter 26

1. a. Integer pointer

   b. Character pointer

   c. Floating-point pointer

2. "Address of "

3. The * operator

4. `pt_sal = &salary;`

5. False

6. Yes

7. a. 2313.54

    b. 2313.54

    c. invalid

    d. invalid

8. b

Chapter 27

1. Array names are pointer constants, not pointer variables.

2. 8

3. *a*, *c*, and *d* are equivalent. Parentheses are needed around iptr+4 and iptr+1 to make *b* and *e* valid.

4. You have to move only pointers, not entire strings.

5. a and d

Chapter 28

1. Structures hold groups of more than one value, each of which can be a different data type.

2. Members

3. At declaration time and at runtime

4. Structures pass by copy.

5. False. Memory is reserved only when structure variables are declared.

6. Globally

7. Locally

8. 4

Chapter 29

1. True

2. Arrays are easier to manage.

3. a. `inventory[32].price = 12.33;`

   b. `inventory[11].part_no[0] = 'X';`

   c. `inventory[96] = inventory[62];`

4. a. `item` is not a structure variable.

   b. `inventory` is an array and must have a subscript.

   c. `inventory` is an array and must have a subscript.

Chapter 30

1. Write, append, and read.

2. Disks hold more data than memory.

3. You can access sequential files only in the same order that they were originally written.

4. An error condition occurs.

5. The old file is overwritten.

6. The file is created.

7. C++ returns an end-of-file condition.

Chapter 31

1. Records are stored in files and structures are stored in memory.

2. False

3. The file pointer continually updates to point to the next byte to read.

4. `read()` and `write()`

5. The `open()` function cannot be called without a filename.

Chapter 32

1. Data members and member functions

2. No

3. No

4. Private

5. Declare it with the `public` keyword.

ASCII Table
(Including IBM Extended Character Codes)

Dec X_{10}	Hex X_{16}	Binary X_2	ASCII Character
000	00	0000 0000	null
001	01	0000 0001	☺
002	02	0000 0010	☻
003	03	0000 0011	♥
004	04	0000 0100	♦
005	05	0000 0101	♣
006	06	0000 0110	♠
007	07	0000 0111	●
008	08	0000 1000	■
009	09	0000 1001	○
010	0A	0000 1010	■
011	0B	0000 1011	♂
012	0C	0000 1100	♀
013	0D	0000 1101	♪
014	0E	0000 1110	♪♪
015	0F	0000 1111	☼
016	10	0001 0000	►

Dec X_{10}	Hex X_{16}	Binary X_2	ASCII Character
017	11	0001 0001	◄
018	12	0001 0010	↕
019	13	0001 0011	‼
020	14	0001 0100	¶
021	15	0001 0101	§
022	16	0001 0110	−
023	17	0001 0111	↨
024	18	0001 1000	↑
025	19	0001 1001	↓
026	1A	0001 1010	→
027	1B	0001 1011	←
028	1C	0001 1100	FS
029	1D	0001 1101	GS
030	1E	0001 1110	RS
031	1F	0001 1111	US
032	20	0010 0000	SP
033	21	0010 0001	!
034	22	0010 0010	"
035	23	0010 0011	#
036	24	0010 0100	$
037	25	0010 0101	%
038	26	0010 0110	&
039	27	0010 0111	'
040	28	0010 1000	(
041	29	0010 1001	)
042	2A	0010 1010	*
043	2B	0010 1011	+
044	2C	0010 1100	'
045	2D	0010 1101	-
046	2E	0010 1110	.
047	2F	0010 1111	/

Dec X_{10}	Hex X_{16}	Binary X_2	ASCII Character
048	30	0011 0000	0
049	31	0011 0001	1
050	32	0011 0010	2
051	33	0011 0011	3
052	34	0011 0100	4
053	35	0011 0101	5
054	36	0011 0110	6
055	37	0011 0111	7
056	38	0011 1000	8
057	39	0011 1001	9
058	3A	0011 1010	:
059	3B	0011 1011	;
060	3C	0011 1100	<
061	3D	0011 1101	=
062	3E	0011 1110	>
063	3F	0011 1111	?
064	40	0100 0000	@
065	41	0100 0001	A
066	42	0100 0010	B
067	43	0100 0011	C
068	44	0100 0100	D
069	45	0100 0101	E
070	46	0100 0110	F
071	47	0100 0111	G
072	48	0100 1000	H
073	49	0100 1001	I
074	4A	0100 1010	J
075	4B	0100 1011	K
076	4C	0100 1100	L
077	4D	0100 1101	M
078	4E	0100 1110	N

Dec X_{10}	Hex X_{16}	Binary X_2	ASCII Character
079	4F	0100 1111	O
080	50	0101 0000	P
081	51	0101 0001	Q
082	52	0101 0010	R
083	53	0101 0011	S
084	54	0101 0100	T
085	55	0101 0101	U
086	56	0101 0110	V
087	57	0101 0111	W
088	58	0101 1000	X
089	59	0101 1001	Y
090	5A	0101 1010	Z
091	5B	0101 1011	[
092	5C	0101 1100	\
093	5D	0101 1101	]
094	5E	0101 1110	^
095	5F	0101 1111	–
096	60	0110 0000	`
097	61	0110 0001	a
098	62	0110 0010	b
099	63	0110 0011	c
100	64	0110 0100	d
101	65	0110 0101	e
102	66	0110 0110	f
103	67	0110 0111	g
104	68	0110 1000	h
105	69	0110 1001	i
106	6A	0110 1010	j
107	6B	0110 1011	k
108	6C	0110 1100	l
109	6D	0110 1101	m

Dec X_{10}	Hex X_{16}	Binary X_2	ASCII Character
110	6E	0110 1110	n
111	6F	0110 1111	o
112	70	0111 0000	p
113	71	0111 0001	q
114	72	0111 0010	r
115	73	0111 0011	s
116	74	0111 0100	t
117	75	0111 0101	u
118	76	0111 0110	v
119	77	0111 0111	w
120	78	0111 1000	x
121	79	0111 1001	y
122	7A	0111 1010	z
123	7B	0111 1011	{
124	7C	0111 1100	¦
125	7D	0111 1101	}
126	7E	0111 1110	~
127	7F	0111 1111	DEL
128	80	1000 0000	Ç
129	81	1000 0001	ü
130	82	1000 0010	é
131	83	1000 0011	å
132	84	1000 0100	ä
133	85	1000 0101	à
134	86	1000 0110	å
135	87	1000 0111	ç
136	88	1000 1000	ê
137	89	1000 1001	ë
138	8A	1000 1010	è
139	8B	1000 1011	ï
140	8C	1000 1100	î

Dec X_{10}	Hex X_{16}	Binary X_2	ASCII Character
141	8D	1000 1101	ì
142	8E	1000 1110	Ä
143	8F	1000 1111	Å
144	90	1001 0000	É
145	91	1001 0001	æ
146	92	1001 0010	Æ
147	93	1001 0011	ô
148	94	1001 0100	ö
149	95	1001 0101	ò
150	96	1001 0110	û
151	97	1001 0111	ù
152	98	1001 1000	ÿ
153	99	1001 1001	Ö
154	9A	1001 1010	Ü
155	9B	1001 1011	¢
156	9C	1001 1100	£
157	9D	1001 1101	¥
158	9E	1001 1110	P$_t$
159	9F	1001 1111	ƒ
160	A0	1010 0000	á
161	A1	1010 0001	í
162	A2	1010 0010	ó
163	A3	1010 0011	ú
164	A4	1010 0100	ñ
165	A5	1010 0101	Ñ
166	A6	1010 0110	a̲
167	A7	1010 0111	o̲
168	A8	1010 1000	¿
169	A9	1010 1001	⌐
170	AA	1010 1010	¬
171	AB	1010 1011	½

Dec X_{10}	Hex X_{16}	Binary X_2	ASCII Character
172	AC	1010 1100	¼
173	AD	1010 1101	¡
174	AE	1010 1110	«
175	AF	1010 1111	»
176	B0	1011 0000	▓
177	B1	1011 0001	▓
178	B2	1011 0010	▓
179	B3	1011 0011	│
180	B4	1011 0100	┤
181	B5	1011 0101	╡
182	B6	1011 0110	╢
183	B7	1011 0111	╖
184	B8	1011 1000	╕
185	B9	1011 1001	╣
186	BA	1011 1010	║
187	BB	1011 1011	╗
188	BC	1011 1100	╝
189	BD	1011 1101	╜
190	BE	1011 1110	╛
191	BF	1011 1111	┐
192	C0	1100 0000	└
193	C1	1100 0001	┴
194	C2	1100 0010	┬
195	C3	1100 0011	├
196	C4	1100 0100	─
197	C5	1100 0101	┼
198	C6	1100 0110	╞
199	C7	1100 0111	╟
200	C8	1100 1000	╚
201	C9	1100 1001	╔
202	CA	1100 1010	╩

Dec X_{10}	Hex X_{16}	Binary X_2	ASCII Character
203	CB	1100 1011	⊤⊤
204	CC	1100 1100	╠
205	CD	1100 1101	=
206	CE	1100 1110	╬
207	CF	1100 1111	╧
208	D0	1101 0000	╨
209	D1	1101 0001	╤
210	D2	1101 0010	╥
211	D3	1101 0011	╙
212	D4	1101 0100	╘
213	D5	1101 0101	╒
214	D6	1101 0110	╓
215	D7	1101 0111	╫
216	D8	1101 1000	╪
217	D9	1101 1001	┘
218	DA	1101 1010	┌
219	DB	1101 1011	█
220	DC	1101 1100	▄
221	DD	1101 1101	▌
222	DE	1101 1110	▐
223	DF	1101 1111	▀
224	E0	1110 0000	α
225	E1	1110 0001	β
226	E2	1110 0010	Γ
227	E3	1110 0011	π
228	E4	1110 0100	Σ
229	E5	1110 0101	σ
230	E6	1110 0110	μ
231	E7	1110 0111	τ
232	E8	1110 1000	Φ
233	E9	1110 1001	θ

Dec X_{10}	Hex X_{16}	Binary X_2	ASCII Character
234	EA	1110 1010	Ω
235	EB	1110 1011	δ
236	EC	1110 1100	∞
237	ED	1110 1101	ø
238	EE	1110 1110	∈
239	EF	1110 1111	∩
240	F0	1111 0000	≡
241	F1	1111 0001	±
242	F2	1111 0010	≥
243	F3	1111 0011	≤
244	F4	1111 0100	⌠
245	F5	1111 0101	⌡
246	F6	1111 0110	÷
247	F7	1111 0111	≈
248	F8	1111 1000	°
249	F9	1111 1001	•
250	FA	1111 1010	·
251	FB	1111 1011	
252	FC	1111 1100	η
253	FD	1111 1101	²
254	FE	1111 1110	■
255	FF	1111 1111	

C++ Precedence Table

Precedence Level	Symbol	Description	Associativity
1 Highest	( )	Function call	Left to right
	[ ]	Array subscript	
	→	C++ indirect component selector	
	::	C++ scope access/resolution	
	.	C++ direct component selector	
2 Unary	!	Logical negation	Right to left
	~	Bitwise (1's) complement	
	+	Unary plus	
	-	Unary minus	

Precedence Level	Symbol	Description	Associativity
	++	Preincrement or postincrement	
	--	Predecrement or postdecrement	
	&	Address of	
	*	Indirection	
	sizeof	(Returns size of operand, in bytes.)	
	new	(Dynamically allocates C++ storage.)	
	delete	(Dynamically deallocates C++ storage.)	
3 Member Access	.*	C++ dereference	Left to right
	→*	C++ dereference	
4 Multipli-cative	*	Multiply	Left to right
	/	Divide	
	%	Remainder (modulus)	
5 Additive	+	Binary plus	Left to right
	-	Binary minus	
6 Shift	<<	Shift left	Left to right
	>>	Shift right	

Precedence Level	Symbol	Description	Associativity
7 Relational	<	Less than	Left to right
	<=	Less than or equal to	
	>	Greater than	
	>=	Greater than or equal to	
8 Equality	==	Equal to	Left to right
	!-	Not equal to	
9	&	Bitwise AND	Left to right
10	^	Bitwise XOR	Left to right
11	¦	Bitwise OR	Left to right
12	&&	Logical AND	Left to right
13	¦¦	Logical OR	Left to right
14 Conditional	?:		Right to left
15 Assignment	=	Simple assignment	Right to left
	*=	Assign product	
	/=	Assign quotient	

Precedence Level	Symbol	Description	Associativity
	%=	Assign remainder	Right to left
	+=	Assign sum	
	-=	Assign difference	
	&=	Assign bitwise AND	
	^=	Assign bitwise XOR	
	¦=	Assign bitwise OR	
	<<=	Assign left shift	
	>>=	Assign right shift	
16 Comma	,	Evaluate	Left to right

E

Keyword and Function Reference

These are the 46 C++ standard keywords:

auto	double	new*	switch
asm*	else	operator*	template
break	enum	private*	this*
case	extern	protected	typedef
catch*	float	public*	union
char	for	register	unsigned
class*	friend*	return	virtual*
const	goto	short	void
continue	if	signed	volatile
default	inline*	sizeof	while
delete*	int	static	
do	long	struct	

* These keywords are specific to C++. All others exist in both C and C++.

The following are the built-in function prototypes, listed by their header files. The prototypes describe the parameter data types that each function requires.

stdio.h

```
int fclose(FILE *stream);
int feof(FILE *stream);
int ferror(FILE *stream);
int fflush(FILE *stream);
int fgetc(FILE *stream);
char *fgets(char *, int, FILE *stream);
FILE *fopen(const char *filename, const char *mode);
int fprintf(FILE *stream, const char *format, ...);
int fputc(int, FILE *stream);
int fputs(const char *, FILE *stream);
size_t fread(void *, size_t, size_t, FILE *stream);
int fscanf(FILE *stream, const char *format, ...);
int fseek(FILE *stream, long offset, int origin);
size_t fwrite(const void *, size_t, size_t, FILE *stream);
int getc(FILE *stream);
int getchar(void);
char *gets(char *);
void perror(const char *);
int putc(int, FILE *stream);
int putchar(int);
int puts(const char *);
int remove(const char *filename);
void rewind(FILE *stream);
int scanf(const char *format, ...);
```

ctype.h

```
int isalnum(unsigned char);
int asalpha(unsigned char);
int iscntrl(unsigned char);
int isdigit(unsigned char);
int isgraph(unsigned char);
int islower(unsigned char);
```

```
      int isprint(unsigned char);
      int ispunct(unsigned char);
      int isspace(unsigned char);
      int isupper(unsigned char);
      int isxdigit(unsigned char);
      int tolower(int);
      int toupper(int);
```

string.h

```
      char *strcat(char *, char *);
      int strcmp(char *, char *);
      int strcpy(char *, char *);
      size_t strlen(char *);
```

math.h

```
      double ceil(double);
      double cos(double);
      double exp(double);
      double fabs(double);
      double floor(double);
      double fmod(double, double);
      double log(double);
      double log10(double);
      double pow(double, double);
      double sin(double);
      double sqrt(double);
      double tan(double);
```

stdlib.h

```
      double atof(const char *);
      int atoi(const char *);
      long atol(const char *);
      void exit(int);
      int rand(void);
      void srand(unsigned int);
```

The Mailing List Application

This appendix shows a complete program that contains most the commands and functions you learned in this book. This program manages a mailing list for your personal or business needs.

When you run the program, you are presented with a menu of choices that guides you through the program's operation. Comments throughout the program offer improvements you might want to make. As your knowledge and practice of C++ improve, you might want to expand this mailing list application into a complete database of contacts and relatives.

Here is the listing of the complete program:

```
// Filename: MAILING.CPP
// * Mailing List Application *
//    -----------------------
//
//    This program enables the user to enter, edit, maintain, and
//    print a mailing list of names and addresses.
//
//    All commands and concepts included in this program are
//    explained throughout the text of C++ By Example.
```

```
//
//
//
// These are items you might want to add or change:
// 1. Find your compiler's clear screen function to
//     improve upon the screen-clearing function.
// 2. Add an entry for the 'code' member to track different
//     types of names and addresses (i.e., business codes,
//     personal codes, etc.)
// 3. Search for a partial name (i.e., typing "Sm" finds
//     "Smith" and "Smitty" and "Smythe" in the file).
// 4. When searching for name matches, ignore case (i.e.,
//     typing "smith" finds "Smith" in the file).
// 5. Print mailing labels on your printer.
// 6. Allow for sorting a listing of names and address by name
//     or ZIP code.


// Header files used by the program:

#include <conio.h>
#include <ctype.h>
#include <fstream.h>
#include <iostream.h>
#include <string.h>

const char FILENAME[] = "ADDRESS.DAT";

// Prototype all of this program's functions.

char get_answer(void);
void disp_menu (void);
void clear_sc (void);
void change_na (void);
void print_na (void);
void err_msg (char err_msg[ ]);
void pause_sc (void);

const int NAME_SIZE = 25;
const int ADDRESS_SIZE = 25;
const int CITY_SIZE = 12;
```

```cpp
const int STATE_SIZE = 3;
const int ZIPCODE_SIZE = 6;
const int CODE_SIZE = 7;

// Class of a name and address
class    Mail
{
private:
   char name[NAME_SIZE];  // Name stored here, should
                           // be Last, First order
   char address[ADDRESS_SIZE];
   char city[CITY_SIZE];
   char state[STATE_SIZE];    // Save room for null zero.
   char zipcode[ZIPCODE_SIZE];
   char code[CODE_SIZE];   // For additional expansion.  You
                           // might want to use this member
                           // for customer codes, vendor codes,
                           // or holiday card codes.
public:
   void pr_data(Mail *item)
   {
   // Prints the name and address sent to it.
      cout << "\nName    : " << (*item).name << "\n";
      cout << "Address: " << (*item).address << "\n";
      cout << "City    : " << (*item).city << "\tState: "
           << (*item).state << "  Zipcode: " << (*item).zipcode
           << "\n";
   }

   void get_new_item(Mail *item)
   {
      Mail temp_item;    // Holds temporary changed input.

      cout << "\nEnter new name and address information below\n(Press the ";
      cout << "Enter key without typing data to retain old "
              "information)\n\n";
      cout << "What is the new name? ";
      cin.getline(temp_item.name, NAME_SIZE);
      if (strlen(temp_item.name)) // Only save new data if user
      { strcpy((*item).name, temp_item.name); } // types something.
      cout << "What is the address? ";
      cin.getline(temp_item.address, ADDRESS_SIZE);
```

```
            if (strlen(temp_item.address))
            {  strcpy((*item).address, temp_item.address); }
            cout << "What is the city? ";
            cin.getline(temp_item.city, CITY_SIZE);
            if (strlen(temp_item.city))
            {  strcpy((*item).city, temp_item.city); }
            cout << "What is the state? (2 letter abbreviation only) ";
            cin.getline(temp_item.state, STATE_SIZE);
            if (strlen(temp_item.state))
            {  strcpy((*item).state, temp_item.state); }
            cout << "What is the ZIP code? ";
            cin.getline(temp_item.zipcode, ZIPCODE_SIZE);
            if (strlen(temp_item.zipcode))
            {  strcpy((*item).zipcode, temp_item.zipcode); }
            (*item).code[0] = 0;   // Null out the code member
                                   // (unused here).
        }

    void add_to_file(Mail *item);
    void change_na(void);
    void enter_na(Mail *item);
    void getzip(Mail *item);
};

void Mail::change_na(void)
{
// This search function can be improved by using the
// code member to assign a unique code to each person on the
// list.  Names are difficult to search for since there are
// so many variations (such as Mc and Mac and St. and Saint).

    Mail item;
    fstream file;
    int ans;
    int s;    // Holds size of structure.
    int change_yes = 0; // Will become TRUE if user finds
    char test_name[25]; // a name to change.

    cout << "\nWhat is the name of the person you want to change? ";
    cin.getline(test_name, NAME_SIZE);
    s = sizeof(Mail); // To ensure fread() reads properly.
```

```
        file.open(FILENAME, ios::in ¦ ios::out);
        if (!file)
        {
            err_msg("*** Read error - Ensure file exists before "
                    "reading it ***");
            return;
        }
        do
        {
            file.read((unsigned char *)&item, sizeof(Mail));
            if (file.gcount() != s)
            {
                if (file.eof())
                { break; }
            }
            if (strcmp(item.name, test_name) == 0)
            {
                item.pr_data(&item);     // Print name and address.
                cout << "\nIs this the name and address to " <<
                        "change? (Y/N) ";
                ans = get_answer();
                if (toupper(ans) == 'N')
                {  break;  } // Get another name.
                get_new_item(&item);  // Enable user to type new
                                      // information.
                file.seekg((long)-s, ios::cur);  // Back up a structure.
                file.write((const unsigned char *)(&item),
                        sizeof(Mail));   // Rewrite information.
                change_yes = 1;  // Changed flag.
                break; // Finished
            }
        }
    }
    while (!file.eof());
    if (!change_yes)
    { err_msg("*** End of file encountered before finding the name ***");}
}

void Mail::getzip(Mail *item) // Ensure that ZIP code
                              // is all digits.
{
    int ctr;
```

```cpp
   int bad_zip;

   do
   {
      bad_zip = 0;
      cout << "What is the ZIP code? ";
      cin.getline((*item).zipcode, ZIPCODE_SIZE);
      for (ctr = 0; ctr < 5; ctr++)
      {
         if (isdigit((*item).zipcode[ ctr ]))
         { continue; }
         else
         {
            err_msg("*** The ZIP code must consist of digits only ***");
         bad_zip = 1;
         break;
         }
      }
   }
   while (bad_zip);
}

void Mail::add_to_file(Mail *item)
{
   ofstream file;

   file.open(FILENAME, ios::app);    // Open file in append mode.
   if (!file)
   {
      err_msg("*** Disk error - please check disk drive ***");
      return;
   }
   file.write((const unsigned char *)(item), sizeof(Mail));
                                    // Add structure to file.

}

void Mail::enter_na(Mail *item)
{
   char ans;
```

```
   do
   {
      cout << "\n\n\n\n\nWhat is the name? ";
      cin.getline((*item).name, NAME_SIZE);
      cout << "What is the address? ";
      cin.getline((*item).address, ADDRESS_SIZE);
      cout << "What is the city? ";
      cin.getline((*item).city, CITY_SIZE);
      cout << "What is the state? (2 letter abbreviation only)";
      cin.getline((*item).state, STATE_SIZE);
      getzip(item); // Ensure that ZIP code is all digits.
      strcpy((*item).code, " ");   // Null out the code member.
      add_to_file(item); // Write new information to disk file.
      cout << "\n\nDo you want to enter another name " <<
              "and address? (Y/N) ";
      ans = get_answer();
   }
   while (toupper(ans) == 'Y');
}


//*************************************************************


// Defined constants
// MAX is total number of names allowed in memory for
// reading mailing list.

const int MAX = 250;
const char BELL = '\x07';


//*************************************************************


int main(void)
{
   char ans;
   Mail item;

   do
   {
      disp_menu();  // Display the menu for the user.
      ans = get_answer();
      switch (ans)
      {
        case '1':
```

```cpp
                item.enter_na(&item);
                break;
            case '2':
                item.change_na();
                break;
            case '3':
                print_na();
                break;
            case '4':
                break;
            default:
                err_msg("*** You have to enter 1 through 4 ***");
                break;
        }
    }
    while (ans != '4');
    return 0;
}


//***************************************************************

void disp_menu(void) // Display the main menu of program.
{
    clear_sc(); // Clear the screen.
    cout << "\t\t*** Mailing List Manager ***\n";
    cout << "\t\t     --------------------\n\n\n\n";
    cout << "Do you want to:\n\n\n";
    cout << "\t1. Add names and addresses to the list\n\n\n";
    cout << "\t2. Change names and addresses in the list\n\n\n";
    cout << "\t3. Print names and addresses in the list\n\n\n";
    cout << "\t4. Exit this program\n\n\n";
    cout << "What is your choice? ";
}


//***************************************************************

void clear_sc() // Clear the screen by sending 25 blank
                // lines to it.
{
    int ctr; // Counter for the 25 blank lines.

    for (ctr = 0; ctr < 25; ctr++)
```

```
      { cout << "\n"; }
}


//*************************************************************

void print_na(void)
{
   Mail item;
   ifstream file;
   int s;
   int linectr = 0;

   s = sizeof(Mail); // To ensure fread() reads properly.
   file.open(FILENAME);
   if (!file)
   {
      err_msg("*** Error - Ensure file exists before"
              "reading it ***");
      return;
   }
   do
   {
      file.read((signed char *)&item, s);
      if (file.gcount() != s)
      {
         if (file.eof()) // If EOF, quit reading.
         { break; }
      }
      if (linectr > 20) // Screen is full.
      {
         pause_sc();
         linectr = 0;
      }
      item.pr_data(&item); // Print the name and address.
      linectr += 4;
   }
   while (!file.eof());
   cout << "\n- End of list -";
   pause_sc(); // Give user a chance to see names
               // remaining on-screen.
}
```

```
//***************************************************************

void err_msg(char err_msg[ ])
{
   cout << "\n\n" << err_msg << BELL << "\n";
}

//***************************************************************

void pause_sc()
{
   cout << "\nPress the Enter key to continue...";
   while (getch() != '\r')
   { ; }  // Wait for Enter key.
}

//***************************************************************

char get_answer(void)
{
   char ans;

   ans = getch();
   while (kbhit())
   { getch(); }
   putch(ans);
   return ans;
}
```

Glossary

Address.   Each memory (RAM) location (each byte) has a unique address. The first address in memory is 0, the second RAM location's address is 1, and so on until the last RAM location (thousands of bytes later).

ANSI.   *American National Standards Institute*, the committee that approves computer standards.

Argument.   The value sent to a function or procedure. This can be a constant or a variable and is enclosed inside parentheses.

Array.   A list of variables, sometimes called a table of variables.

Array of Structures.   A table of one or more structure variables.

ASCII.   Acronym for *American Standard Code for Information Interchange*.

ASCII File.   A file containing characters that can be used by any program on most computers. Sometimes called a text file or an ASCII text file.

AUTOEXEC.BAT.   A batch file in PCs that executes a series of commands whenever you start or reset the computer.

Automatic Variables.   Local variables that lose their values when their block (the one in which they are defined) ends.

Backup File. A duplicate copy of a file that preserves your work in case you damage the original file. Files on a hard disk are commonly backed up on floppy disks or tapes.

Binary. A numbering system based on only two digits. The only valid digits in a binary system are 0 and 1. See also *Bit*.

Binary zero. Another name for null zero.

Bit. Binary digit, the smallest unit of storage on a computer. Each bit can have a value of 0 or 1, indicating the absence or presence of an electrical signal. See also *Binary*.

Bit Mask. A pattern of bits that changes other bits on and off to meet a certain logical condition.

Bitwise Operators. C++ operators that manipulate the binary representation of values.

Block. One or more statements treated as though they are a single statement. A block is always enclosed in braces, { and }.

Boot. To start a computer with the operating system software in place. You must boot your computer before using it.

Bubble Sort. A method of sorting data into ascending or descending order. See also *Quicksort, Shell Sort*.

Bug. An error in a program that prevents the program from running correctly. The term originated when a moth short-circuited a connection in one of the first computers, preventing the computer from working!

Byte. A basic unit of data storage and manipulation. A byte is equivalent to eight bits and can contain a value ranging from 0 to 255.

Cathode Ray Tube (CRT). The television-like screen, also called the *monitor*. It is one place to which the output of the computer can be sent.

Central Processing Unit (CPU). The controlling circuit responsible for operations in the computer. These operations generally include system timing, logical processing, and logical operations. It controls every operation of the computer system. On PCs, the central processing unit is called a microprocessor; it is stored on a single integrated circuit chip.

Code. A set of instructions written in a programming language. See *Source Code.*

Comment. A message in a program, ignored by the computer, that tells users what the program does.

Compile. Process of translating a program written in a programming language such as C++ into machine code that your computer understands.

Class. A C++ user-defined data type that consists of data members and member functions. Its members are private by default.

Concatenation. The process of attaching one string to the end of another or combining two or more strings into a longer string.

Conditional Loop. A series of C++ instructions that occurs a fixed number of times.

Constant. Data defined with the const keyword that do not change during a program run.

Constructor Function. The function executed when the program declares an instance of a class.

CPU. Central Processing Unit.

CRT. Cathode Ray Tube.

Data. Information stored in the computer as numbers, letters, and special symbols such as punctuation marks. This also refers to the characters you input into your program so the program can produce meaningful information.

Data Member. A data component of a class or structure.

Data Processing. What computers really do. They take data and manipulate it into meaningful output. The meaningful output is called information.

Data Validation. The process of testing the values entered in a program. Checking whether a number is negative or positive or simply ensuring that a number is in a certain range are two examples of data validation.

Debug. Process of locating an error (bug) in a program and removing it.

Declaration.   A statement that declares the existence of a data object or function. A declaration reserves memory.

Default.   A predefined action or command that the computer chooses unless you specify otherwise.

Default Argument List.   A list of argument values, specified in a function's prototypes, that determine initial values of the arguments if no values are passed for those arguments.

Definition.   A statement that defines the format of a data object or function. A definition reserves no memory.

Demodulate.   To convert an analog signal into a digital signal for use by a computer. See also *Modulate.*

Dereference.   The process of finding a value to which a pointer variable is pointing.

Destructor.   The function called when a class instance goes out of scope.

Determinate Loop.   A `for` loop that executes a fixed number of times.

Digital Computer.   A term that comes from the fact that your computer operates on binary (*on* and *off*) digital impulses of electricity.

Directory.   A list of files stored on a disk. Directories within existing directories are called *subdirectories.*

Disk.   A round, flat magnetic storage medium. Floppy disks are made of flexible material and enclosed in 5 1/4-inch or 3 1/2-inch protective cases. Hard disks consist of a stack of rigid disks housed in a single unit. A disk is sometimes called *external memory.* Disk storage is nonvolatile. When you turn off your computer, the disk's contents do not go away.

Disk Drive.   A device that reads and writes data to a floppy or hard disk.

Diskettes.   Another name for the removable floppy disks.

Display.   A screen or monitor.

Display Adapter.   Located in the system unit, the display adapter determines the amount of *resolution* and the possible number of colors on-screen.

DOS.   Disk Operating System.

Dot-Matrix Printer.   One of the two most common PC printers. The *laser* printer is the other. A dot-matrix printer is inexpensive and fast; it uses a series of small dots to represent printed text and graphics.

Element.   An individual variable in an array.

Execute.   To run a program.

Expanded Memory.   A tricky way of expanding your computer's memory capacity beyond the 640K barrier using a technique called bank switching. See also *Extended Memory*.

Extended Memory.   RAM above 640K, usually installed directly on the motherboard of your PC. You cannot access this extra RAM without special programs. See also *Expanded Memory*.

External Modem.   A modem that sits in a box outside your computer. See also *Internal Modem*.

Field.   A member in a data record.

File.   A collection of data stored as a single unit on a floppy or hard disk. Files always have a filename that identifies them.

File Extension.   Used by PCs and consists of a period followed by up to three characters. The file extension follows the filename.

Filename.   A unique name that identifies a file. Filenames can be up to eight characters long, and can have a period followed by an extension (normally three characters long).

Fixed Disk.   See *Hard Disk*.

Fixed-Length Records.   A record where each field takes the same amount of disk space, even if that field's data value does not fill the field.

Floppy Disk.   See *Disk*.

Format.   Process of creating a "map" on the disk that tells the operating system how the disk is structured. This process is how the operating system keeps track of where files are stored.

Function.   A self-contained coding segment designed to do a specific task. All C++ programs must have at least one function called `main()`. Some functions are library routines that manipulate numbers, strings, and output.

Function Keys.   The keys labeled F1 through F12 (some keyboards only have up to F10).

Global Variables.   A variable that can be seen from (and used by) every statement in the program.

Hard Copy.   The printout of a program (or its output). Also a safe backup copy for a program in case the disk is erased.

Hard Disk.   Sometimes called *fixed disks.* These hold much more data and are many times faster than floppy disks. See *Disk.*

Hardware.   The physical parts of the machine. Hardware has been defined as "anything you can kick."

Header Files.   Files that contain prototypes of C++'s built-in functions.

Hexadecimal.   A numbering system based on 16 elements. Digits are numbered 0 through F, as follows: 0, 1, 2, 3, 4, 5, 6, 7, 8, 9, A, B, C, D, E, F.

Hierarchy of Operators.   See *Order of Operators.*

Indeterminate Loop.   A loop that continues an indeterminate amount of times (unlike the `for` loop, which continues a known amount of times).

Infinite Loop.   The never-ending repetition of a block of C++ statements.

Information.   The meaningful product from a program. Data go into a program to produce meaningful output (information).

Inline Function.   A function that compiles as inline code each time the function is called.

Input.   The entry of data into a computer through a device such as the keyboard.

Input-Process-Output.   This model is the foundation of everything that happens in your computer. Data are input, then processed by your program in the computer, and finally information is output.

I/O.   Acronym for Input/Output.

Integer Variable.   Variables that can hold integers.

Internal Modem.   A modem that resides inside the system unit. See also *External Modem.*

Kilobyte (K).   A unit of measurement that refers to 1,024 bytes.

Laser Printer.   A type of printer that is faster, in general, than dot-matrix printers. Laser printer output is much sharper than that of a dot-matrix printer, because a laser beam actually burns toner ink into the paper. Laser printers are more expensive than dot-matrix printers.

Least Significant Bit.   The rightmost bit of a byte. For example, a binary 00000111 would have a 1 as the least significant bit.

Line Printer.   Another name for your printer.

Link Editing.   The last step the C++ compiler performs when preparing your program for execution.

Literal.   Data that remains the same during program execution.

Local Variable.   A variable that can be seen from (and used by) only the block in which it is defined.

Loop.   The repeated execution of one or more statements.

Machine Language.   The series of binary digits that a microprocessor executes to perform individual tasks. People seldom (if ever) program in machine language. Instead, they program in assembly language, and an assembler translates their instructions into machine language.

Main Module.   The first function of a modular program called `main()` that controls the execution of the other functions.

Maintainability.   The computer industry's word for the ability to change and update programs written in a simple style.

Manipulator.   A value used by a program to inform the stream to modify one of its modes.

Math Operator.   A symbol used for addition, subtraction, multiplication, division, or other calculations.

Megabyte (M).   In computer terminology, approximately a million bytes (1,048,576 bytes).

Member.   A piece of a structure variable that holds a specific type of data, or a class variable that holds a specific type of data or a function acting on that data.

Member Function.   A function defined inside a class.

Memory.   Storage area inside the computer, used to temporarily store data. The computer's memory is erased when the power is off.

Menu.   A list of commands or instructions displayed on-screen. These lists organize commands and make a program easier to use.

Menu-Driven.   Describes a program that provides menus for choosing commands.

Microchip.   A small wafer of silicon that holds computer components and occupies less space than a postage stamp.

Microcomputer.   A small computer that can fit on a desktop, such as a PC. The microchip is the heart of the microcomputer. Microcomputers are much less expensive than their larger counterparts.

Microprocessor.   The chip that does the calculations for PCs. Sometimes it is called the Central Processing Unit (CPU).

Modem.   A piece of hardware that modulates and demodulates signals so your computer can communicate with other computers over telephone lines. See also *External Modems, Internal Modems*.

Modular Programming.   The process of writing your programs in several modules rather than as one long program. By breaking a program into several smaller program-line routines, you can isolate problems better, write correct programs faster, and produce programs that are much easier to maintain.

Modulate.   Before your computer can transmit data over a telephone line, the information to be sent must be converted (modulated) into analog signals. See also *Demodulate*.

Modulus.   The integer remainder of division.

Monitor.   The television-like screen that enables the computer to display information. It is an output device.

Mouse.   A hand-held device that you move across the desktop to move an indicator, called a mouse pointer, across the screen. Used instead of the keyboard to select and move items (such as text or graphics), execute commands, and perform other tasks.

MS-DOS.   An operating system for IBM and compatible PCs.

Multidimensional Arrays.   Arrays with more than one dimension. As two-dimensional arrays, they are sometimes called tables or matrices, which have rows and columns.

Nested Loop.   A loop within a loop.

Null String.   An empty string with an initial character of null zero and with a length of 0.

Null Zero.   The string-terminating character. All C++ string constants and strings stored in character arrays end in null zero. The ASCII value for the null zero is 0.

Numeric Functions.   Library routines that work with numbers.

Object.   C++ class members consisting of both data and member functions.

Object Code.   A "halfway step" between source code and executable machine language. Object code consists mostly of machine language but is not directly executable by the computer. It must first be linked in order to resolve external references and address references. See also *Source Code, Machine Language*.

Object-Oriented Programming.   A programming approach that treats data as objects capable of manipulating themselves.

Operator.   An operator works on data and performs math calculations or changes data to other data types. Examples include the +, -, and `sizeof()` operators.

Order of Operators.   Sometimes called the *hierarchy of operators* or the *precedence of operators*. It determines exactly how C++ computes formulas.

Output Device.   Where the results of a program are output, such as the screen, the printer, or a disk file.

Overloading.   The process of writing more than one function with the same name. The functions must differ in their argument lists so C++ can identify which one to call.

Parallel Arrays.   Two arrays working side by side. Each element in each array corresponds to one in the other array.

Parallel Port.   A connector used to plug a device such as a printer into the computer. Transferring data through a parallel port is much faster than transferring data through a serial port.

Parameter.   A list of variables enclosed in parentheses that follow the name of a function or procedure. Parameters indicate the number and type of arguments that are sent to the function or procedure.

Passing by Address.   Also called *passing by reference*. When an argument (a local variable) is passed by address, the variable's address in memory is sent to, and is assigned to, the receiving function's parameter list. (If more than one variable is passed by address, each of their addresses is sent to and assigned to the receiving function's parameters.) A change made to the parameter in the function also changes the value of the argument variable.

Passing by Copy.   Another name for *passing by value*.

Passing by Reference.   Another name for *passing by address*.

Passing by Value.   By default, all C++ variable arguments are passed *by value*. When the value contained in a variable is passed to the parameter list of a receiving function, changes made to the parameter in the routine do not change the value of the argument variable. Also called *passing by copy*.

Path.   The route the computer travels from the root directory to any subdirectories when locating a file. The path also refers to the subdirectories that MS-DOS examines when you type a command that requires it to find and access a file.

Peripheral.   A device attached to the computer, such as a modem, disk drive, mouse, or printer.

Personal Computer.   A microcomputer, also called a PC, which stands for *p*ersonal *c*omputer.

Pointer.   A variable that holds the address of another variable.

Precedence of Operators.   See *Order of Operators.*

Preprocessor Directive.   A command, preceded by a #, that you place in your source code that directs the compiler to modify the source code in some fashion. The two most common preprocessor directives are #define and #include.

Printer.   A device that prints data from the computer to paper.

Private Class Member.   A class member inaccessible except to the class's member functions.

Program.   A group of instructions that tells the computer what to do.

Programming Language.   A set of rules for writing instructions for the computer. Popular programming languages include BASIC, C, Visual Basic, C++, and Pascal.

Prototype.   The definition of a function; includes its name, return type, and parameter list.

Public Class Member.   A class member accessible to any function.

Quicksort.   A method of sorting data values into ascending or descending order (faster than a Bubble Sort.) See also *Bubble Sort, Shell Sort.*

RAM.   Random-Access Memory.

Random-Access File.   Records in a file that can be accessed in any order you want.

Random-Access Memory.   Memory that your computer uses to temporarily store data and programs. RAM is measured in kilobytes and megabytes. Generally, the more RAM a computer has, the more powerful programs it can run.

Read-Only Memory. A permanent type of computer memory. It contains the BIOS (*Basic Input/Output System*), a special chip used to provide instructions to the computer when you turn the computer on.

Real Numbers. Numbers that have decimal points and a fractional part to the right of the decimal.

Record. Individual rows in files.

Relational Operators. Operators that compare data; they tell how two variables or constants relate to each other. They tell you whether two variables are equal or not equal, or which one is less than or more than the other.

ROM. Read-Only Memory.

Scientific Notation. A shortcut method of representing numbers of extreme values.

Sectors. A pattern of pie-shaped wedges on a disk. Formatting creates a pattern of *tracks* and sectors where your data and programs are stored.

Sequence Point/Comma Operator. This operator ensures that statements are performed in a left-to-right sequence.

Sequential File. A file that has to be accessed one record at a time beginning with the first record.

Serial Port. A connector used to plug in serial devices, such as a modem or a mouse.

Shell Sort. A method of sorting values into ascending or descending order. Named after the inventor of this method. See also *Bubble Sort, Quicksort.*

Single-Dimensional Arrays. Arrays that have only one subscript. Single-dimensional arrays represent a list of values.

Software. The data and programs that interact with your hardware. The C++ language is an example of software.

Sorting. A method of putting data in a specific order (such as alphabetical or numerical order), even if that order is not the same order in which the elements were entered.

Source Code.   The C++ language instructions, written by programmers, that the C++ compiler translates into object code. See also *Object Code.*

Spaghetti Code.   Term used when there are too many gotos in a program. If a program branches all over the place, it is difficult to follow and trying to follow the logic resembles a "bowl of spaghetti."

Static Variables.   Variables that do not lose their values when the block in which they are defined ends. See also *Automatic Variables.*

Standard Input Device.   The target of each cout and output function. Normally the screen unless rerouted to another device at the operating system's prompt.

Standard Output Device.   The target of each cin and input function. Normally the keyboard unless rerouted to another device at the operating system's prompt.

Stream.   Literally, a stream of characters, one following another, flowing among devices in your computer.

String.   One or more characters terminated with a null zero.

String Constant.   One or more groups of characters that end in a null zero.

String Delimiter.   See *Null Zero.*

String Literal.   Another name for a *String Constant.*

Structure.   A unit of related information containing one or more members, such as an employee number, employee name, employee address, employee pay rate, and so on.

Subscript.   A number inside brackets that differentiates one *element* of an array from another.

Syntax Error.   The most common error a programmer makes. Often a misspelled word.

System Unit.   The large box component of the computer. The system unit houses the PC's microchip (the *CPU*).

Timing Loop.   A loop used to delay the computer for a specific amount of time.

Tracks.   A pattern of paths on a disk. Formatting creates a pattern of tracks and *sectors* where your data and programs go.

Truncation.   The fractional part of a number (the part of the number to the right of the decimal point) is taken off the number. No rounding is done.

Two's Complement.   A method your computer uses to take the negative of a number. This method, plus addition, allows the computer to simulate subtraction.

Unary Operator.   The addition or subtraction operator used before a single variable or constant.

User-Friendliness.   A program is user-friendly if it makes the user comfortable and simulates an atmosphere that the user is already familiar with.

Variable.   Data that can change as the program runs.

Variable-Length Records.   A record that takes up no wasted space on the disk. As soon as a field's data value is saved to the file, the next field's data value is stored after it. There is usually a special separating character between the fields so your programs know where the fields begin and end.

Variable Scope.   Sometimes called the *visibility of variables*, this describes how variables are "seen" by your program. See also *Global Variables* and *Local Variables*.

Volatile.   Temporary state of memory. For example, when you turn the computer off, all the RAM is erased.

Word.   In PC usage, two consecutive bytes (16 bits) of data.

Index

I

Computer Books from Que Mean PC Performance!

Spreadsheets

1-2-3 Beyond the Basics	$24.95
1-2-3 for DOS Release 2.3 Quick Reference	$ 9.95
1-2-3 for DOS Release 2.3 QuickStart	$19.95
1-2-3 for DOS Release 3.1+ Quick Reference	$ 9.95
1-2-3 for DOS Release 3.1+ QuickStart	$19.95
1-2-3 for Windows Quick Reference	$ 9.95
1-2-3 for Windows QuickStart	$19.95
1-2-3 Personal Money Manager	$29.95
1-2-3 Power Macros	$39.95
1-2-3 Release 2.2 QueCards	$19.95
Easy 1-2-3	$19.95
Easy Excel	$19.95
Easy Quattro Pro	$19.95
Excel 3 for Windows QuickStart	$19.95
Excel for Windows Quick Reference	$ 9.95
Look Your Best with 1-2-3	$24.95
Quattro Pro 3 QuickStart	$19.95
Quattro Pro Quick Reference	$ 9.95
Using 1-2-3 for DOS Release 2.3, Special Edition	$29.95
Using 1-2-3 for Windows	$29.95
Using 1-2-3 for DOS Release 3.1, Special Edition	$29.95
Using Excel 4 for Windows, Special Edition	$29.95
Using Quattro Pro 4, Special Edition	$27.95
Using Quattro Pro for Windows	$24.95
Using SuperCalc5, 2nd Edition	$29.95

Databases

dBASE III Plus Handbook, 2nd Edition	$24.95
dBASE IV 1.1 Quick Reference	$ 9.95
dBASE IV 1.1 QuickStart	$19.95
Introduction to Databases	$19.95
Paradox 3.5 Quick Reference	$ 9.95
Paradox Quick Reference, 2nd Edition	$ 9.95
Using AlphaFOUR	$24.95
Using Clipper, 3rd Edition	$29.95
Using DataEase	$24.95
Using dBASE IV	$29.95
Using FoxPro 2	$29.95
Using ORACLE	$29.95
Using Paradox 3.5, Special Edition	$29.95
Using Paradox for Windows	$26.95
Using Paradox, Special Edition	$29.95
Using PC-File	$24.95
Using R:BASE	$29.95

Business Applications

CheckFree Quick Reference	$ 9.95
Easy Quicken	$19.95
Microsoft Works Quick Reference	$ 9.95
Norton Utilities 6 Quick Reference	$ 9.95
PC Tools 7 Quick Reference	$ 9.95
Q&A 4 Database Techniques	$29.95
Q&A 4 Quick Reference	$ 9.95
Q&A 4 QuickStart	$19.95
Q&A 4 Que Cards	$19.95
Que's Computer User's Dictionary, 2nd Edition	$10.95
Que's Using Enable	$29.95
Quicken 5 Quick Reference	$ 9.95
SmartWare Tips, Tricks, and Traps, 2nd Edition	$26.95
Using DacEasy, 2nd Edition	$24.95
Using Microsoft Money	$19.95
Using Microsoft Works: IBM Version	$22.95
Using Microsoft Works for Windows, Special Edition	$24.95
Using MoneyCounts	$19.95
Using Pacioli 2000	$19.95
Using Norton Utilities 6	$24.95
Using PC Tools Deluxe 7	$24.95
Using PFS: First Choice	$22.95
Using PFS: WindowWorks	$24.95
Using Q&A 4	$27.95
Using Quicken 5	$19.95
Using Quicken for Windows	$19.95
Using Smart	$29.95
Using TimeLine	$24.95
Using TurboTax: 1992 Edition	$19.95

CAD

AutoCAD Quick Reference, 2nd Edition	$ 8.95
Using AutoCAD, 3rd Edition	$29.95

Word Processing

Easy WordPerfect	$19.95
Easy WordPerfect for Windows	$19.95

Look Your Best with WordPerfect 5.1	$24.95
Look Your Best with WordPerfect for Windows	$24.95
Microsoft Word Quick Reference	$ 9.95
Using Ami Pro	$24.95
Using LetterPerfect	$22.95
Using Microsoft Word 5.5: IBM Version, 2nd Edition	$24.95
Using MultiMate	$24.95
Using PC-Write	$22.95
Using Professional Write	$22.95
Using Professional Write Plus for Windows	$24.95
Using Word for Windows 2, Special Edition	$27.95
Using WordPerfect 5	$27.95
Using WordPerfect 5.1, Special Edition	$27.95
Using WordPerfect for Windows, Special Edition	$29.95
Using WordStar 7	$19.95
Using WordStar, 3rd Edition	$27.95
WordPerfect 5.1 Power Macros	$39.95
WordPerfect 5.1 QueCards	$19.95
WordPerfect 5.1 Quick Reference	$ 9.95
WordPerfect 5.1 QuickStart	$19.95
WordPerfect 5.1 Tips, Tricks, and Traps	$24.95
WordPerfect for Windows Power Pack	$39.95
WordPerfect for Windows Quick Reference	$ 9.95
WordPerfect for Windows Quick Start	$19.95
WordPerfect Power Pack	$39.95
WordPerfect Quick Reference	$ 9.95

Hardware/Systems

Batch File and Macros Quick Reference	$ 9.95
Computerizing Your Small Business	$19.95
DR DOS 6 Quick Reference	$ 9.95
Easy DOS	$19.95
Easy Windows	$19.95
Fastback Quick Reference	$ 0.95
Hard Disk Quick Reference	$ 8.95
Hard Disk Quick Reference, 1992 Edition	$ 9.95
Introduction to Hard Disk Management	$24.95
Introduction to Networking	$24.95
Introduction to PC Communications	$24.95
Introduction to Personal Computers, 2nd Edition	$19.95
Introduction to UNIX	$24.95
Laplink Quick Reference	$ 9.95
MS-DOS 5 Que Cards	$19.95
MS-DOS 5 Quick Reference	$ 9.95
MS-DOS 5 QuickStart	$19.95
MS-DOS Quick Reference	$ 8.95
MS-DOS QuickStart, 2nd Edition	$19.95
Networking Personal Computers, 3rd Edition	$24.95
Que's Computer Buyer's Guide, 1992 Edition	$14.95
Que's Guide to CompuServe	$12.95
Que's Guide to DataRecovery	$29.95
Que's Guide to XTree	$12.95
Que's MS-DOS User's Guide, Special Edition	$29.95
Que's PS/1 Book	$22.95
TurboCharging MS-DOS	$24.95
Upgrading and Repairing PCs	$29.95
Upgrading and Repairing PCs, 2nd Edition	$29.95
Upgrading to MS-DOS 5	$14.95
Using GeoWorks Pro	$24.95
Using Microsoft Windows 3, Special Edition	$24.95
Using MS-DOS 5	$24.95
Using Novell NetWare, 2nd Edition	$29.95
Using OS/2 2.0	$24.95
Using PC DOS, 3rd Edition	$27.95
Using Prodigy	$19.95
Using UNIX	$29.95
Using Windows 3.1	$26.95
Using Your Hard Disk	$29.95
Windows 3 Quick Reference	$ 8.95
Windows 3 QuickStart	$19.95
Windows 3.1 Quick Reference	$ 9.95
Windows 3.1 QuickStart	$19.95

Desktop Publishing/Graphics

CorelDRAW! Quick Reference	$ 8.95
Harvard Graphics 3 Quick Reference	$ 9.95
Harvard Graphics Quick Reference	$ 9.95
Que's Using Ventura Publisher	$29.95
Using DrawPerfect	$24.95
Using Freelance Plus	$24.95
Using Harvard Graphics 3	$29.95
Using Harvard Graphics for Windows	$24.95
Using Harvard Graphics, 2nd Edition	$24.95
Using Microsoft Publisher	$22.95
Using PageMaker 4 for Windows	$29.95
Using PFS: First Publisher, 2nd Edition	$24.95
Using PowerPoint	$24.95
Using Publish It!	$24.95

Macintosh/Apple II

Easy Macintosh	$19.95
HyperCard 2 QuickStart	$19.95
PageMaker 4 for the Mac Quick Reference	$ 9.95
The Big Mac Book, 2nd Edition	$29.95
The Little Mac Book	$12.95
QuarkXPress 3.1 Quick Reference	$ 9.95
Que's Big Mac Book, 3rd Edition	$29.95
Que's Little Mac Book, 2nd Edition	$12.95
Que's Mac Classic Book	$24.95
Que's Macintosh Multimedia Handbook	$24.95
System 7 Quick Reference	$ 9.95
Using 1-2-3 for the Mac	$24.95
Using AppleWorks, 3rd Edition	$24.95
Using Excel 3 for the Macintosh	$24.95
Using FileMaker Pro	$24.95
Using MacDraw Pro	$24.95
Using MacroMind Director	$29.95
Using MacWrite Pro	$24.95
Using Microsoft Word 5 for the Mac	$27.95
Using Microsoft Works: Macintosh Version, 2nd Edition	$24.95
Using Microsoft Works for the Mac	$24.95
Using PageMaker 4 for the Macintosh	$24.95
Using Quicken 3 for the Mac	$19.95
Using the Macintosh with System 7	$24.95
Using Word for the Mac, Special Edition	$24.95
Using WordPerfect 2 for the Mac	$24.95
Word for the Mac Quick Reference	$ 9.95

Programming/Technical

Borland C++ 3 By Example	$21.95
Borland C++ Programmer's Reference	$29.95
C By Example	$21.95
C Programmer's Toolkit, 2nd Edition	$39.95
Clipper Programmer's Reference	$29.95
DOS Programmer's Reference, 3rd Edition	$29.95
FoxPro Programmer's Reference	$29.95
Network Programming in C	$49.95
Paradox Programmer's Reference	$29.95
Programming in Windows 3.1	$39.95
QBasic By Example	$21.95
Turbo Pascal 6 By Example	$21.95
Turbo Pascal 6 Programmer's Reference	$29.95
UNIX Programmer's Reference	$29.95
UNIX Shell Commands Quick Reference	$ 8.95
Using Assembly Language, 2nd Edition	$29.95
Using Assembly Language, 3rd Edition	$29.95
Using BASIC	$24.95
Using Borland C++	$29.95
Using Borland C++ 3, 2nd Edition	$29.95
Using C	$29.95
Using Microsoft C	$29.95
Using QBasic	$24.95
Using QuickBASIC 4	$24.95
Using QuickC for Windows	$29.95
Using Turbo Pascal 6, 2nd Edition	$29.95
Using Turbo Pascal for Windows	$29.95
Using Visual Basic	$29.95
Visual Basic by Example	$21.95
Visual Basic Programmer's Reference	$29.95
Windows 3.1 Programmer's Reference	$39.95

For More Information,
Call Toll Free!
1-800-428-5331

All prices and titles subject to change without notice.
Non-U.S. prices may be higher. Printed in the U.S.A.

Order Your Disk Program Today!

You can save yourself hours of tedious, error-prone typing by ordering the companion disk to *C++ By Example.* The disk contains the source code for all the complete programs and many of the shorter samples in the book. Appendix F's complete mailing-list application is also included on the disk, as well as the answers to many of the review exercises.

You will get code that shows you how to use most the features of C++. Samples include code for keyboard control, screen control, file I/O, control statements, structures, pointers, and more.

Disks are available in 3 1/2-inch format (high density). The cost is $10 per disk. (When ordering outside the US, please add $5 for shipping and handling.)

Just make a copy of this page, fill in the blanks, and mail it with your check or money order to:

C++ Disk
Greg Perry
P.O. Box 35752
Tulsa, OK 74135-0752

Please **print** the following information:

Payment method: *Check*_____ *Money Order*_____

Number of Disks:_____@ $10.00 =_____

Name: _____

Street Address:_____

City:_____State:_____

ZIP:_____

(On foreign orders, please use a separate page to give your mailing address in the format required by your post office.)

Checks and money orders should be made payable to:

Greg Perry

(This offer is made by Greg Perry, not by Que Corporation.)